Modigliani and His Models

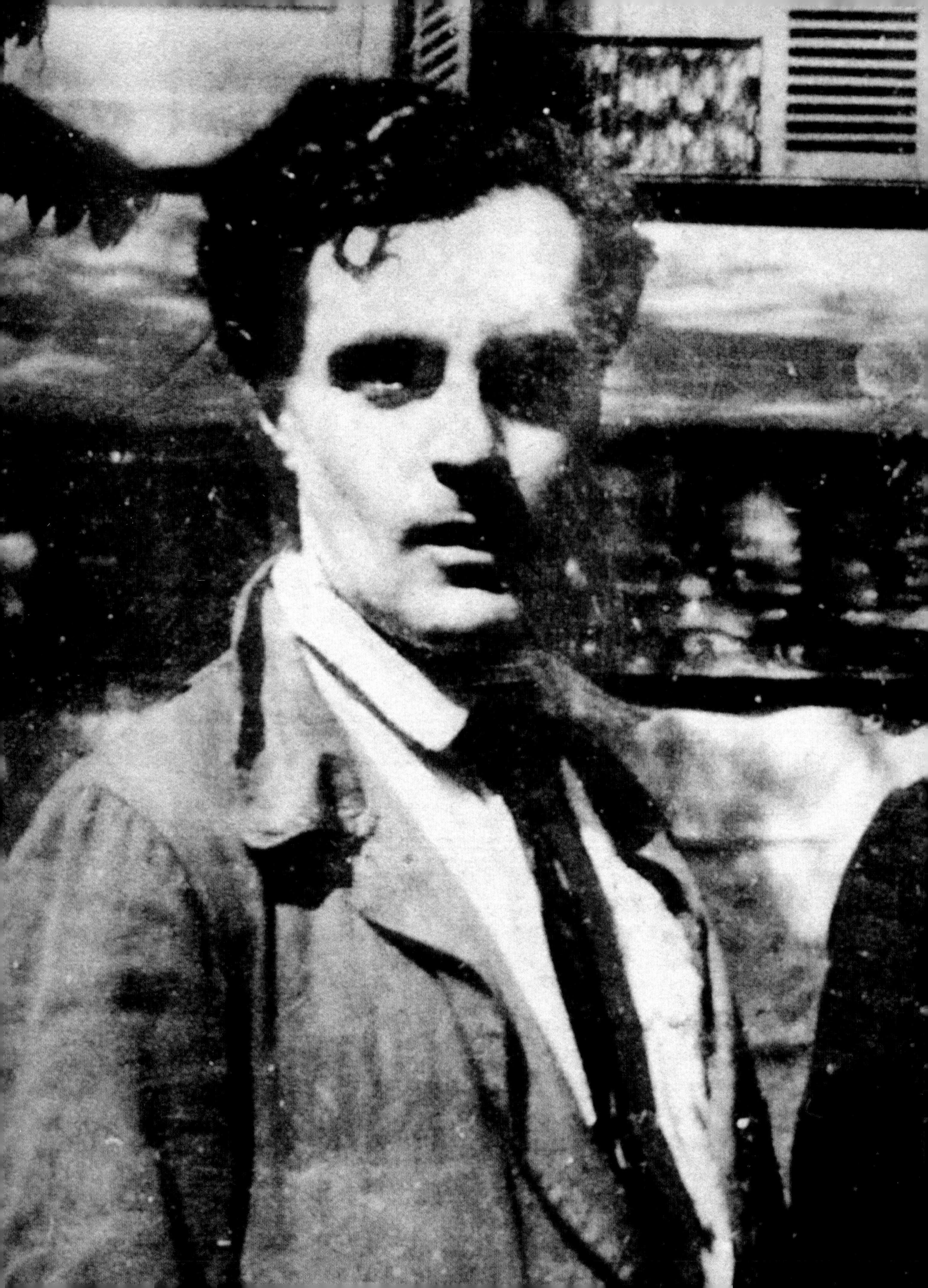

Modigliani
and His Models

Royal Academy of Arts

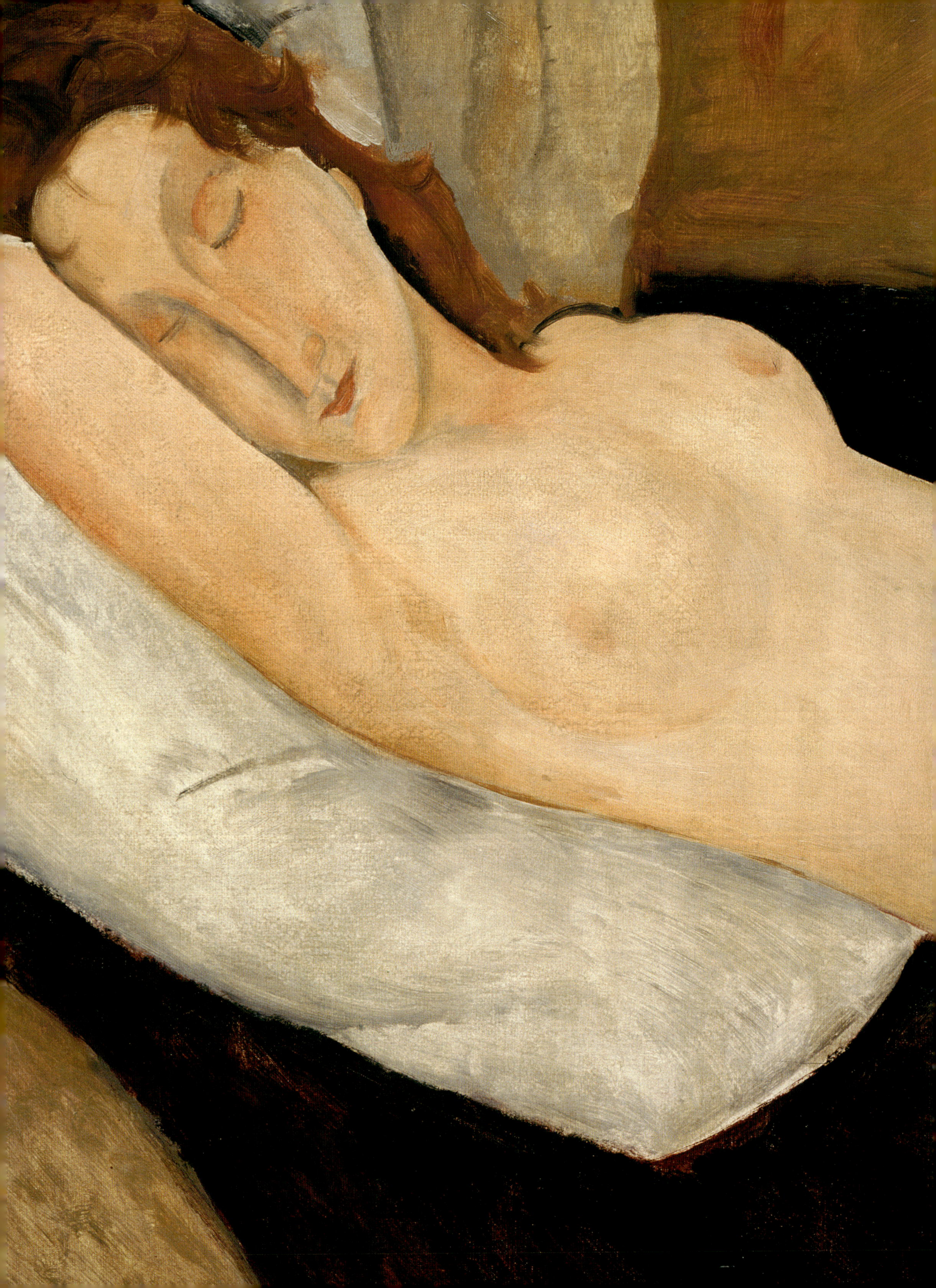

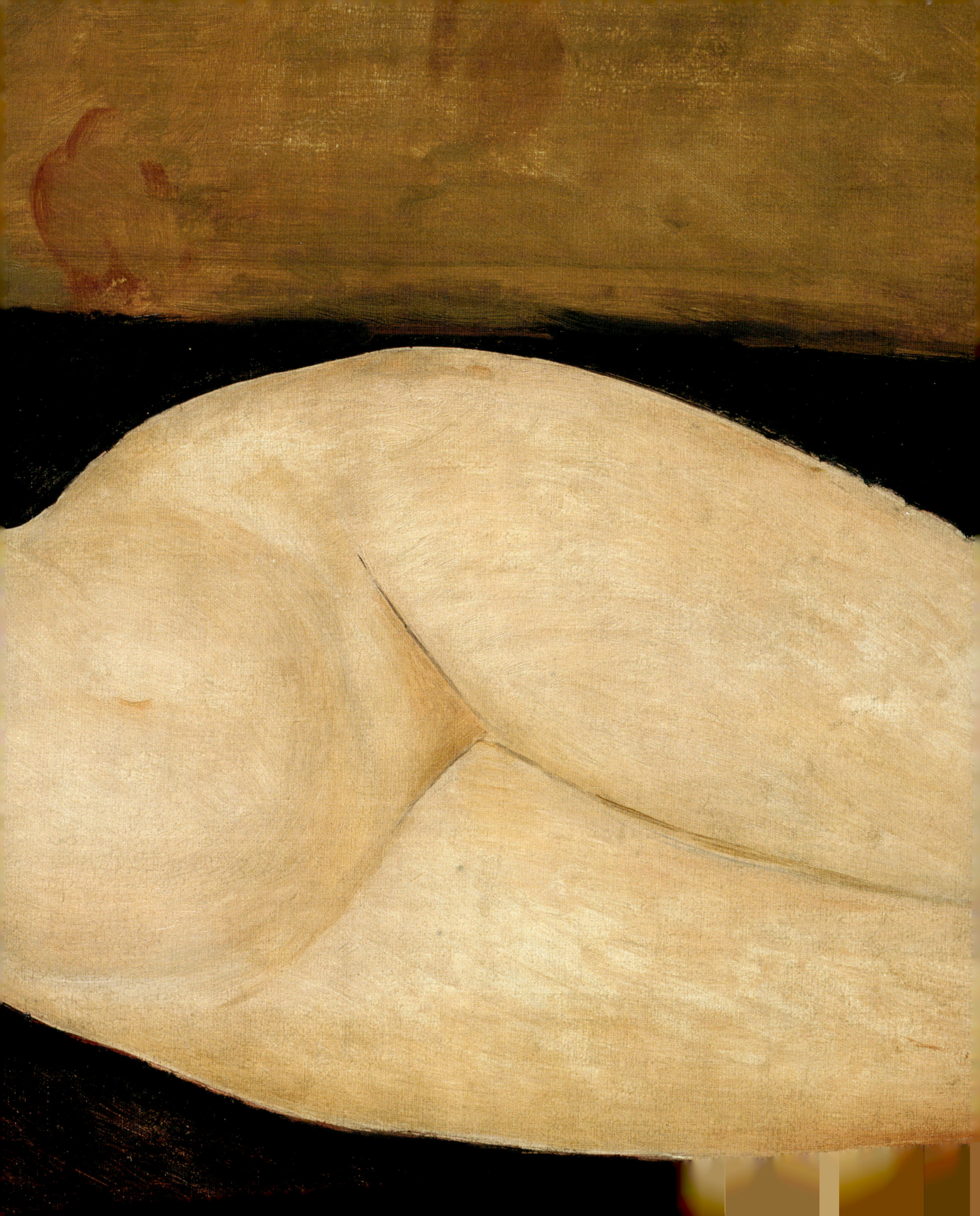

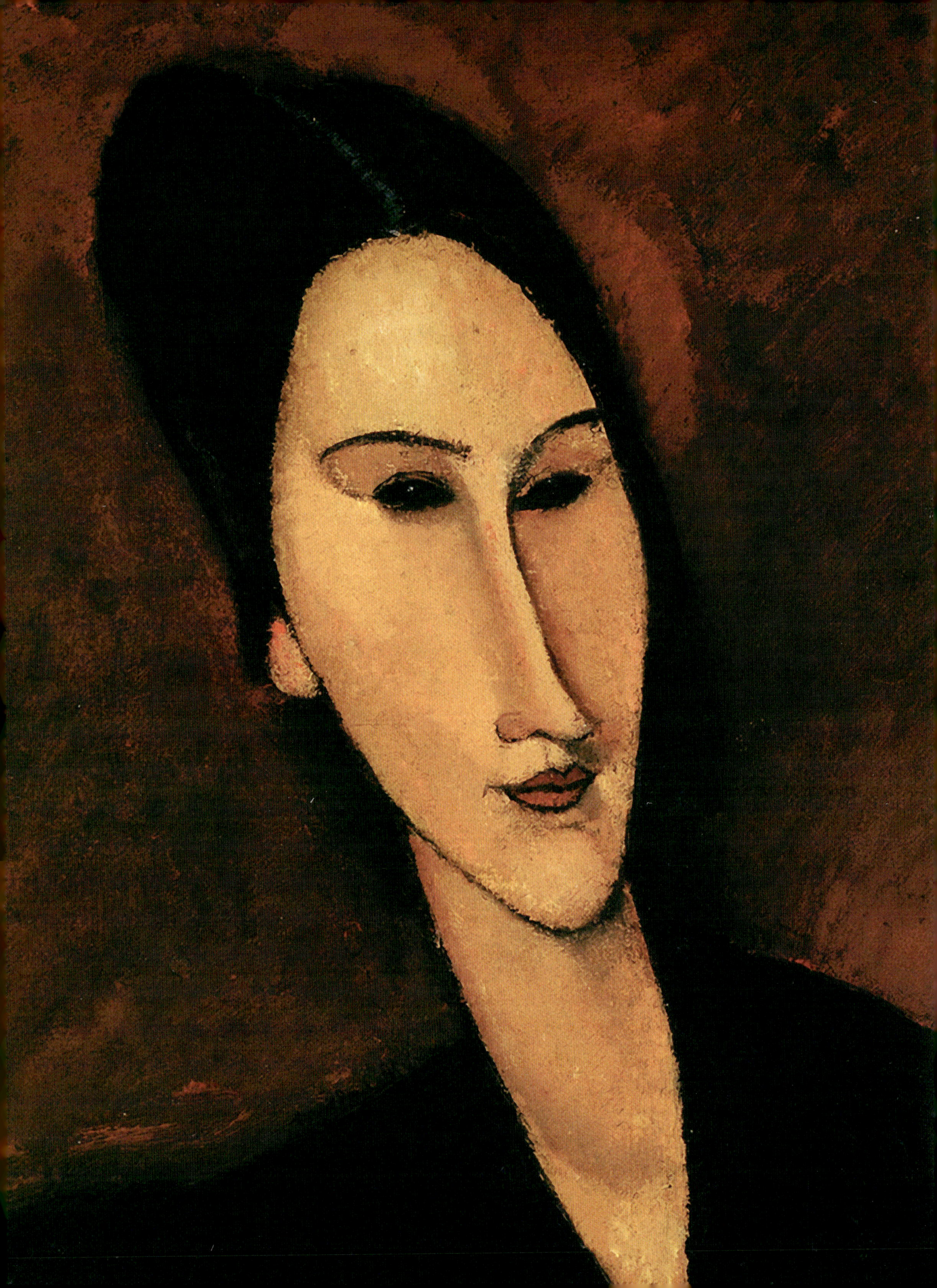

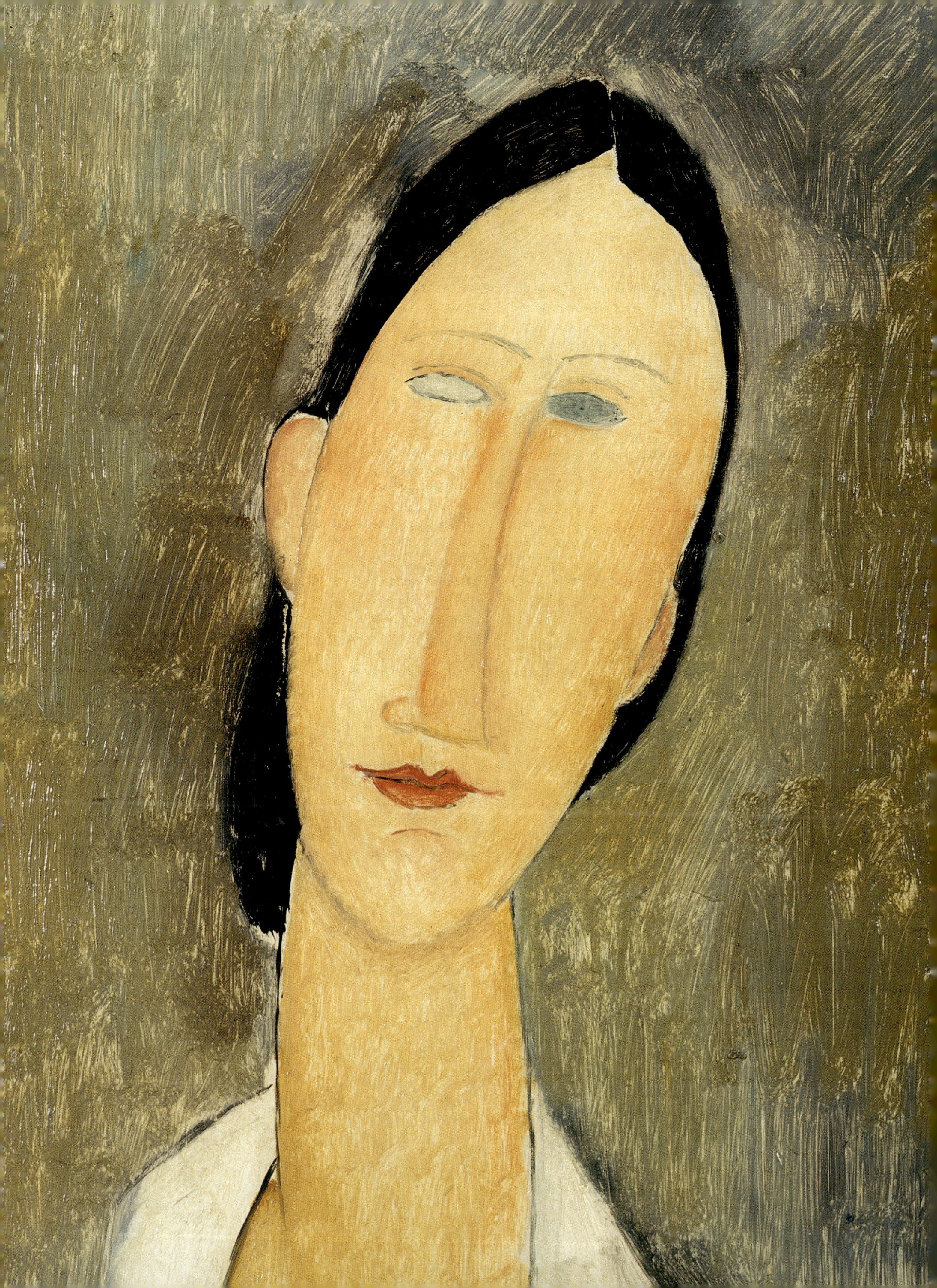

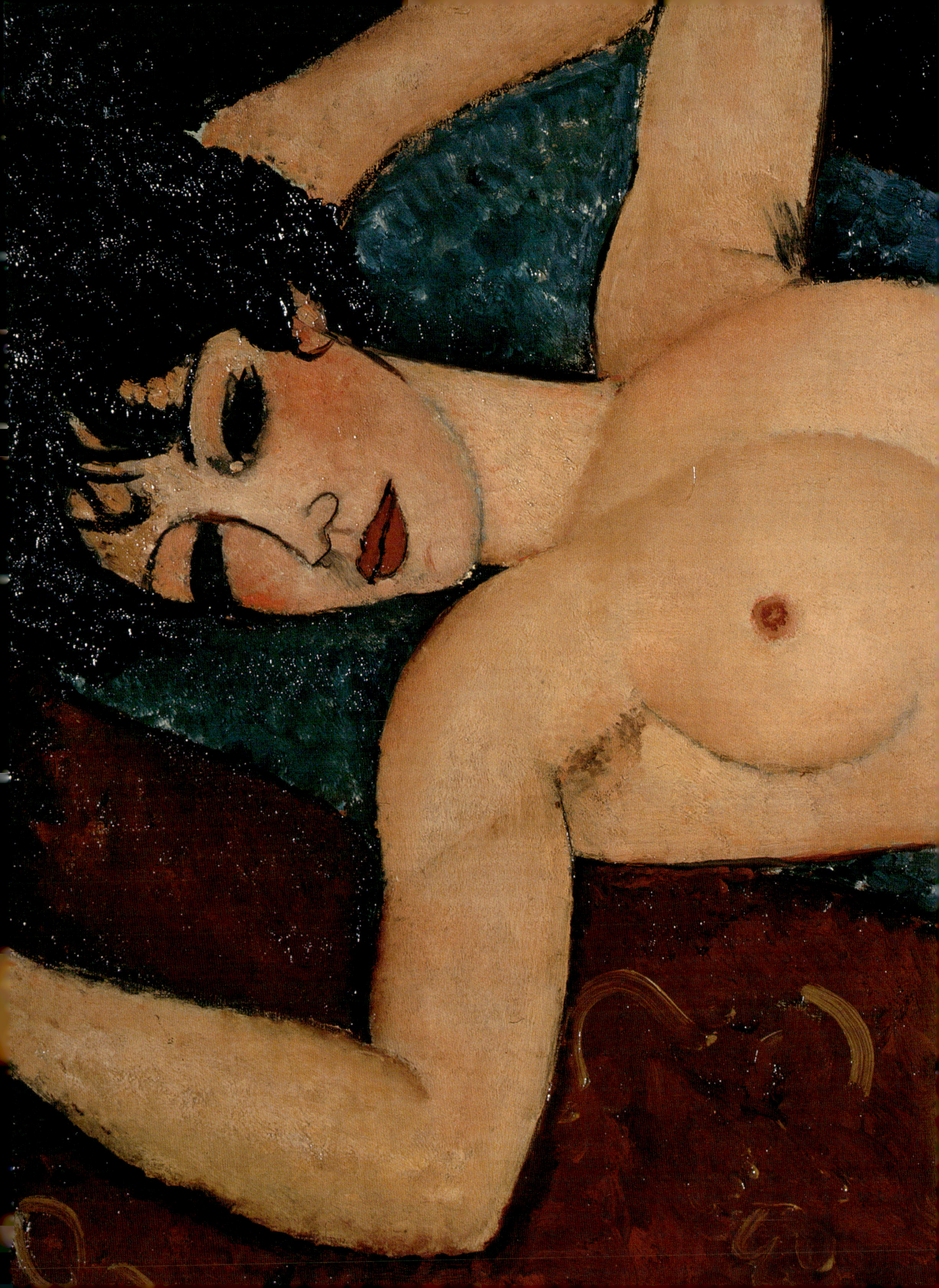

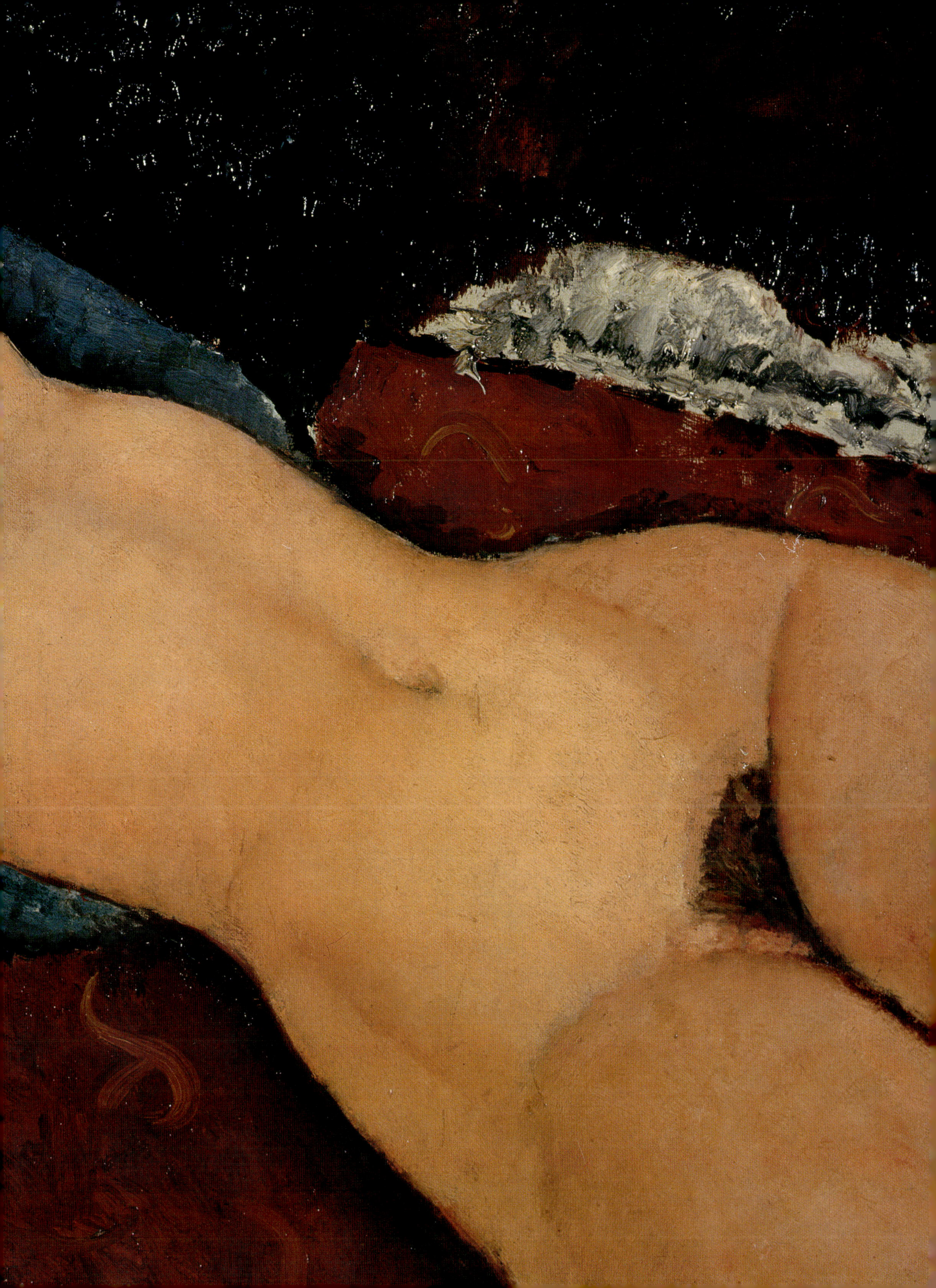

First published on the occasion of the exhibition 'Modigliani and His Models'

Royal Academy of Arts, London
8 July – 15 October 2006

The Royal Academy of Arts is grateful to Her Majesty's Government for agreeing to indemnify this exhibition under the National Heritage Act 1980, and to Resource, The Council for Museums, Archives and Libraries, for its help in arranging the indemnity.

Exhibition curators
Simonetta Fraquelli
Norman Rosenthal

Exhibition organisation
Idoya Beitia

Photographic and copyright co-ordination
Roberta Stansfield

Catalogue
Royal Academy Publications
David Breuer
Harry Burden
Claire Callow
Carola Krueger
Peter Sawbridge
Nick Tite

Copy-editing and proofreading: Rosalind Neely
Design: 01.02
Picture research: Sara Ayad
Colour origination: DawkinsColour

Printed in Italy by Graphicom

British Library Cataloguing-in-Publication Data

A catalogue record for this book is available from the British Library

Hardback
ISBN 10: 1-903973-81-3
ISBN 13: 978-1-903973-81-3

Paperback
ISBN 10: 1-903973-82-1
ISBN 13: 978-1-903973-82-0

Distributed outside the United States and Canada by Thames & Hudson Ltd, London

Distributed in the United States and Canada by Harry N. Abrams, Inc., New York

Editorial note
All works are by Amedeo Modigliani unless otherwise stated.

All measurements are given in centimetres, height before width (before depth).

Cross-references in the Biographies of Modigliani's Models are indicated by an asterisk (*).

Illustrations
Page 2: detail of photograph reproduced on p. 146
Pages 4–5: detail of cat. 40
Page 6: detail of cat. 43
Page 7: detail of cat. 27
Pages 8–9: detail of cat. 21
Page 12: detail of cat. 47
Pages 14–15: detail of cat. 37
Page 17: detail of cat. 46

Contents

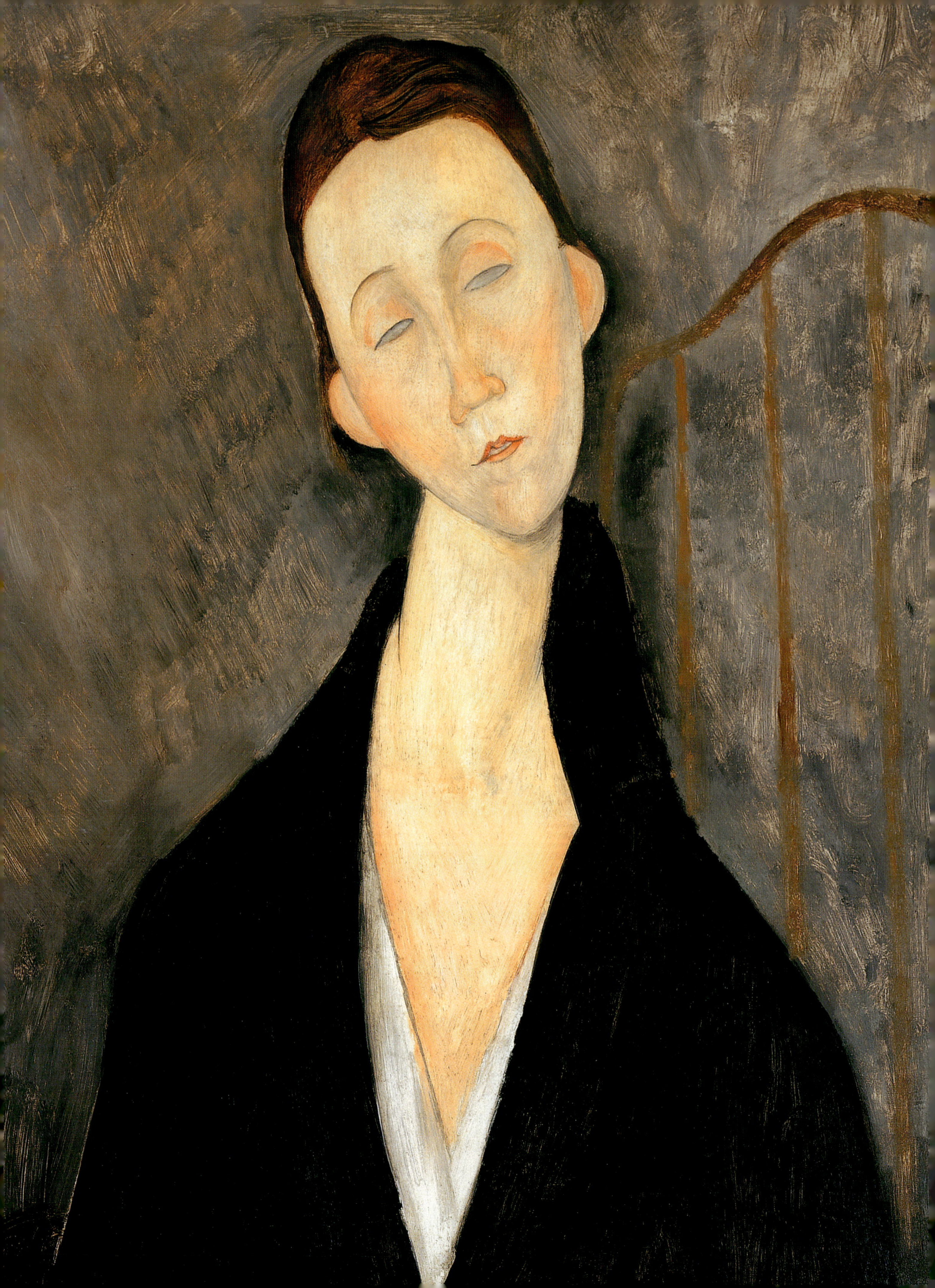

Foreword

During the last two decades, the Royal Academy has been privileged to show a number of masterpieces by Amedeo Modigliani. In 1989, several key works by the artist were included in our landmark exhibition 'Italian Art in the Twentieth Century', and in 1994 we were delighted to be able to show the then newly discovered collection of Modigliani drawings belonging to the artist's first patron and collector, Dr Paul Alexandre. It is now a great honour and pleasure for the Royal Academy to present the first major show dedicated to Modigliani's paintings to be held in Great Britain for over forty years.

Modigliani's celebrity status is unquestioned; however, his role as a modernist artist is rarely acknowledged. By bringing together over fifty of his most extraordinary paintings, this exhibition aims to demonstrate how Modigliani's art, which draws on many different styles and cultures, European and non-European, past and present, is both highly individual and thoroughly modern. An exceptional portraitist and painter of nudes, Modigliani created some of the most memorable and popular images of the twentieth century.

We are indebted to the show's two curators, Simonetta Fraquelli, a specialist in twentieth-century Italian art, and Norman Rosenthal, our Exhibitions Secretary. They have succeeded in bringing together some of Modigliani's most striking works that do full justice to his genius. We thank also Idoya Beitia, Exhibition Organiser, and Roberta Stansfield, Photographic and Copyright Co-ordinator, who have worked tirelessly on the project throughout.

We are particularly grateful to John and Gail Coombe, Simon and Virginia Robertson, Dame Jillian Sackler, Richard and Victoria Sharp, and David Tang, all Trustees of the Royal Academy Trust. Their generous donations have helped to make this exhibition possible. Further valuable support has been provided by the Royal Academy Exhibition Patrons Group.

Every exhibition depends ultimately on the goodwill and generosity of its lenders, and in this case these qualities have been particularly evident. We are indebted to all our lenders, public and private, on both sides of the Atlantic, and thank them for allowing us to enjoy their masterpieces for the duration of this show.

Sir Nicholas Grimshaw
President, Royal Academy of Arts

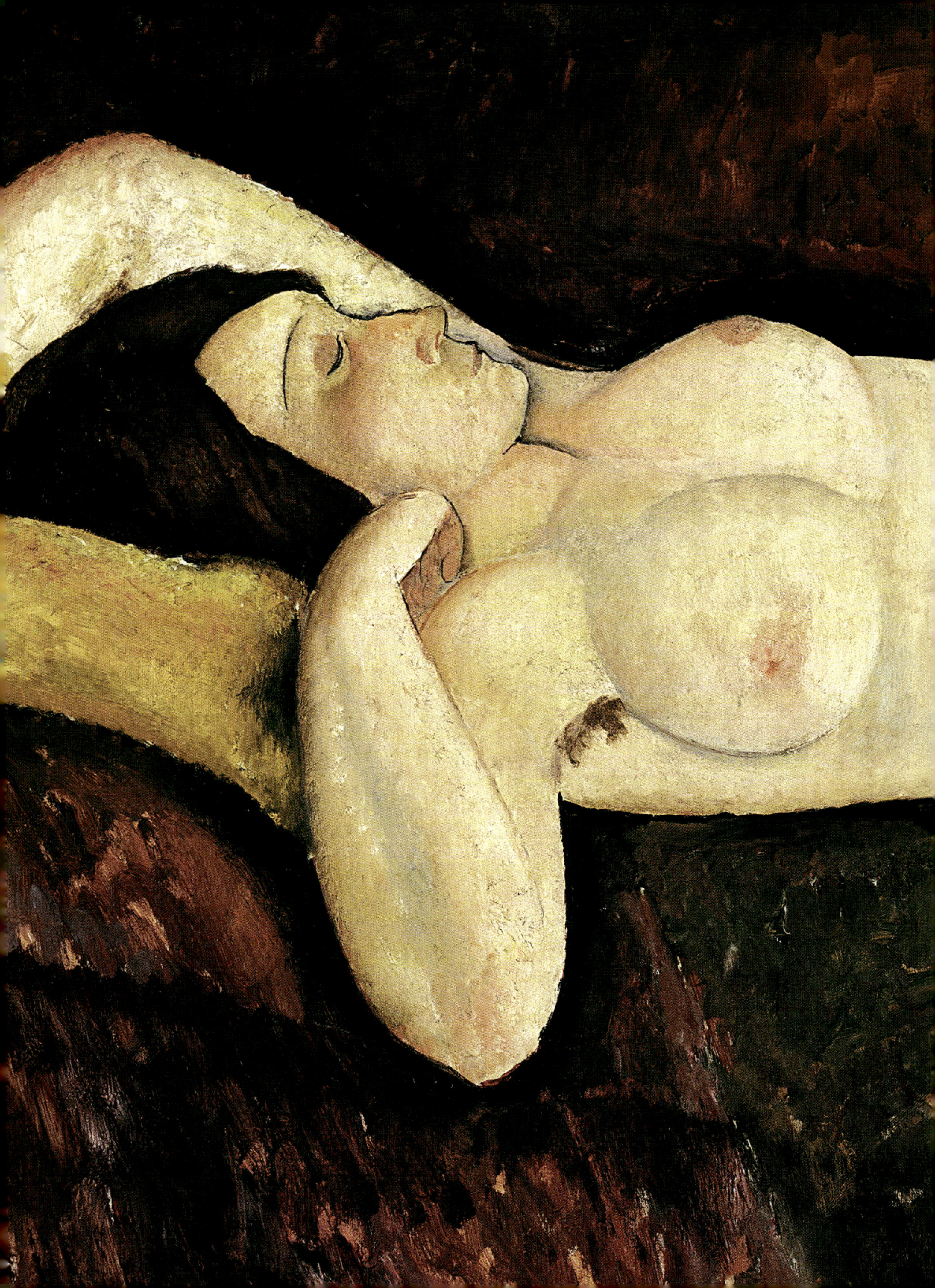

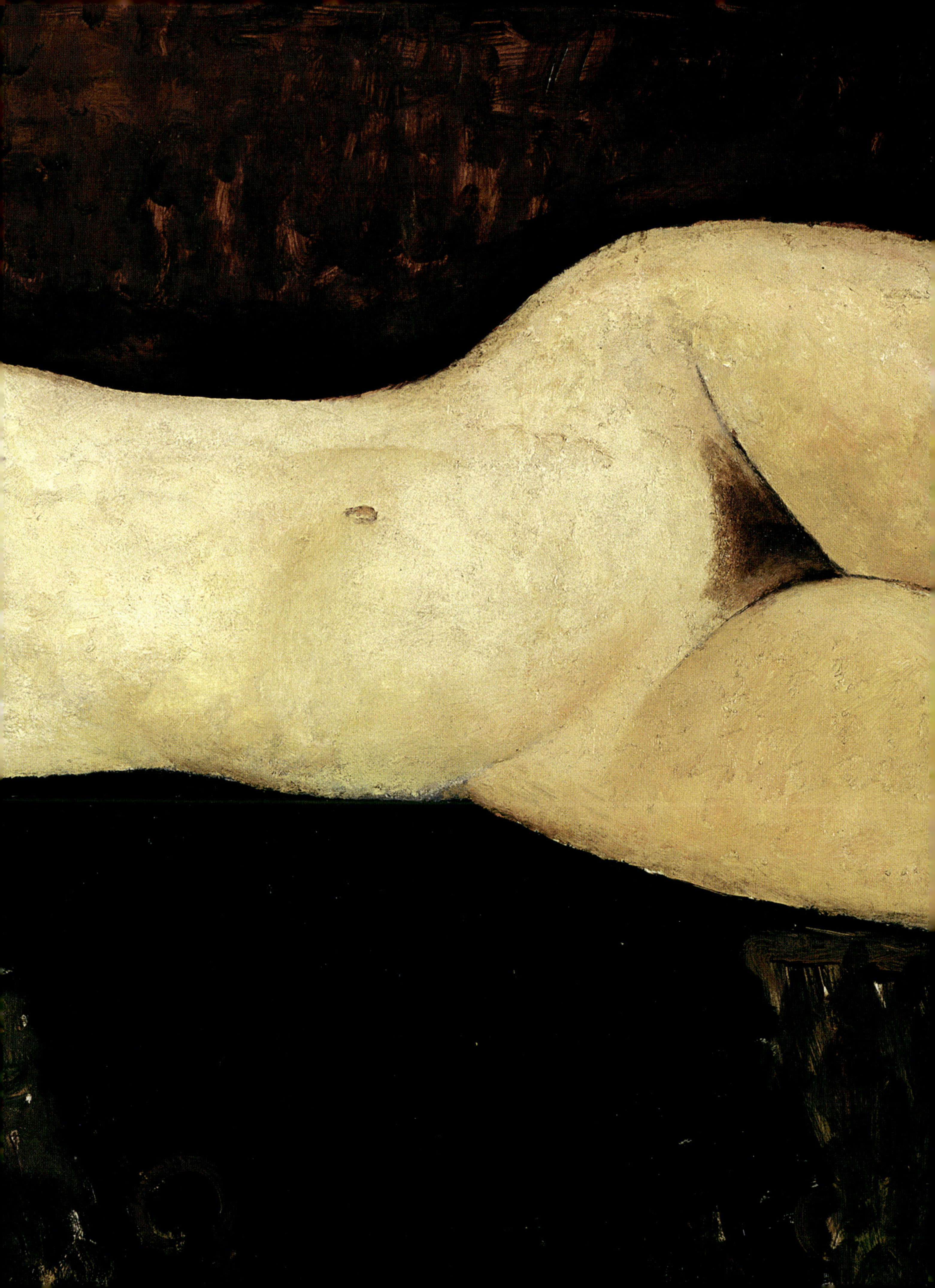

Acknowledgements

The organisation of this exhibition and the creation of its catalogue have engaged the energies of many colleagues and individuals both inside and outside the Royal Academy; without their help and commitment none of this would have been possible. We owe a particular debt of gratitude to Daniel Marchesseau and Kenneth Wayne, both of whom have organised major Modigliani exhibitions in the past, and to Helly Nahmad for their invaluable advice and encouragement. Special acknowledgement is also due to the following, whose crucial support and generosity have enabled us to bring the project to fruition:

Charles Allsopp, Maria Alonso, Dany Ardouin, Sara Ayad, Don Bacigalupi, Ida Balboul, Anne Baldassari, Alain Bouret, Ivor Braka, Emily Braun, Adam Brown, Olivier Camu, Rudy Chiappini, Maria Vittoria Clarelli, Melanie Clore, Susan Davidson, Lisa Dennison, Florence Ducharne, Alice Dugdale, Ann Dumas, John Elderfield, Maria Teresa Fiorio, Michael Foster, Matthew Gale, Anthony Hirschel, Philip Hook, Ellen Josefowitz, Ulrike Köberl, Isabella Kullman, Steve Little, Marilyn McCully, Duncan MacGuigan, Nicholas Maclean, Daniel Malingue, Rebekah Marshall, Marzina Marzotto, David Mason, Laura Mattioli, Werner Merzbacher, Lucy Mitchell Innes, Charles Moffett, Alessandra Mottola Molfino, Richard Nagy, Edward Tyler Nahem, Helly Nahmad, David Nash, Rosalind Neely, Angela Nevill, Helena Newman, Sarah Noreika, Suzanne Pagé, Katia Pisvin, Jussi Pylkkanen, Michael Raeburn, Eliza Rathbone, Joe Rishel, Cora Rosevear, James Roundell, Jennifer Saville, George Shackelford, Caroline Schmidt, Manuel Schmit, Kenneth Silver, Calum Storrie, Martin Summers, Gary Tinterow, Vicente Todolí, Vladimir Tsarenkov, Patricia J. Whitesides, Ully Wille, Anne Winton, Robin Woodhead and Massimo Vitta Zelman.

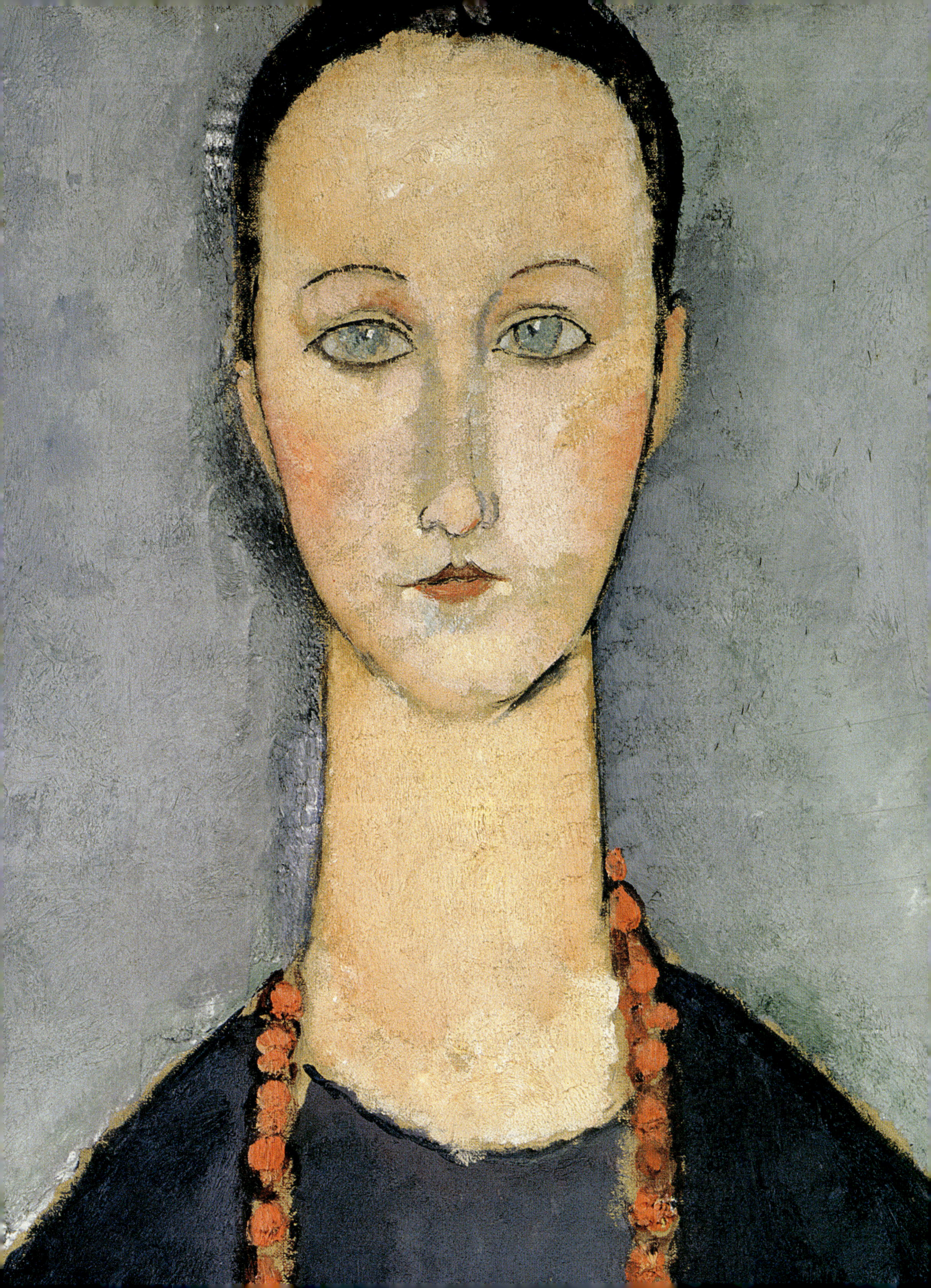

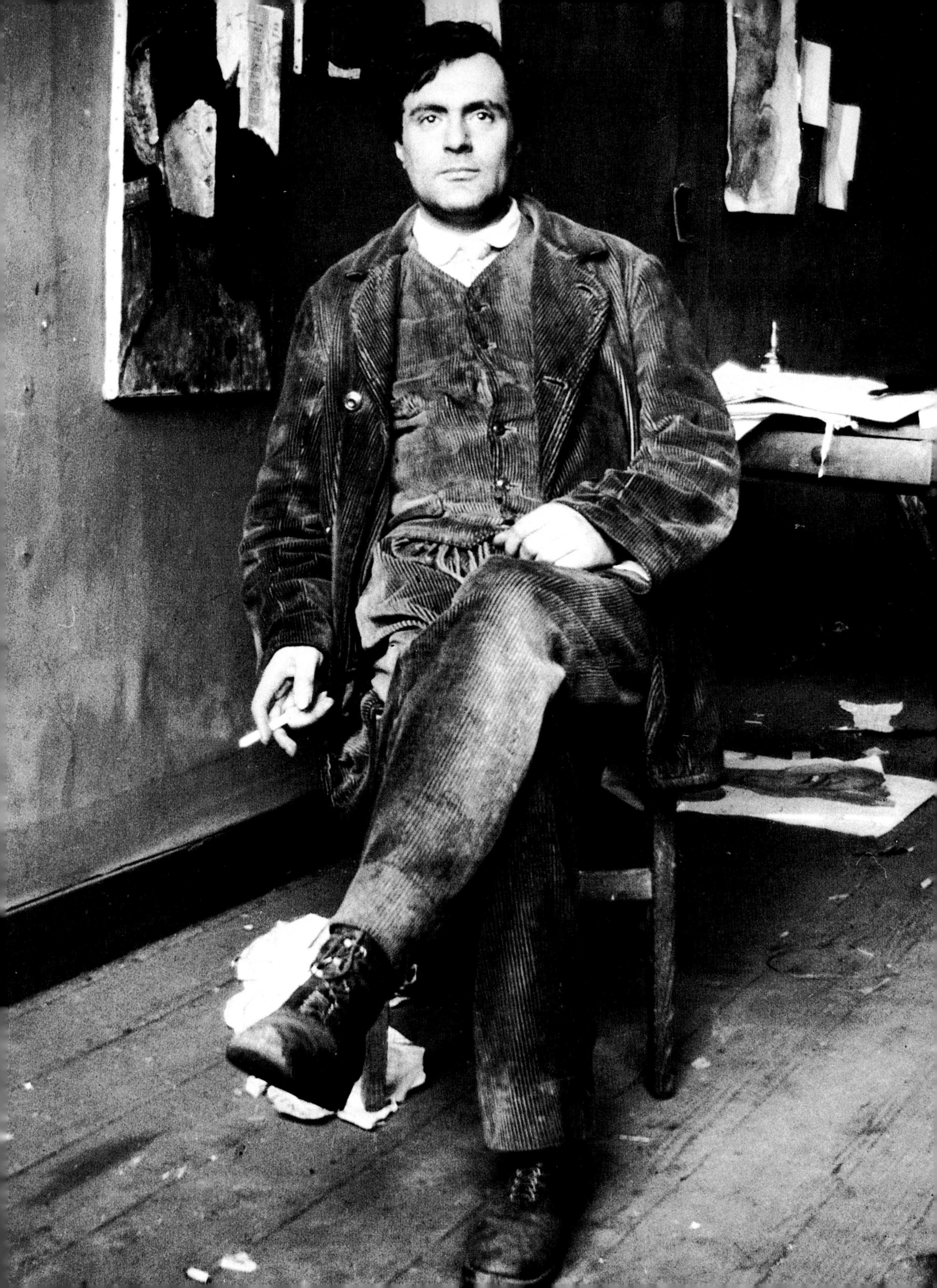

'Too many last words!': The Myth of Modigliani

Kenneth E. Silver

Amedeo Modigliani's canny daughter, Jeanne Modigliani, wrote about her father on his deathbed in the following way – as she was only fourteen months old when he died, she had reconstructed the scene from the standard sources:

> Legend says that as he was dying he recommended Soutine to Zborowski, asked his wife to follow him to the grave, 'so that I can have my favourite model in Paradise and with her enjoy eternal happiness', and confessed to Ortiz that only a fragment of his brain remained to him. While he was being taken to the hospital, the legend adds, he murmured 'Cara Italia!' Too many last words! [1]

In French her scepticism is even more explicit: 'Un peu trop de "dernières paroles" pour un seul homme!' (a few too many 'last words' for just one man!). She was understandably fed up with the surfeit of anecdotes, quotations and epigrams that, since his death in 1920, had been written about, or attributed to, a man she hardly knew. 'The life of Modigliani [fig. 1], wandering artist, so often resembles a legend that it is difficult to determine clearly fact from fiction' is the way one of his first chroniclers put it.[2] In order to set the record straight, Jeanne Modigliani (fig. 2) published a carefully researched account of her father's life, *Modigliani: Man and Myth,* first in English, in 1958, and three years later, in French, as *Modigliani sans légende.*

Trying to see Modigliani unencumbered by his legend was extremely difficult, partly because his illegitimate daughter had perhaps invested a bit too much in the pursuit. If we believe the great actress Sarah Bernhardt, the confusion of fact and fiction is built into the artist's relationship to the public:

> On occasion I have tried, along with the dramatist, to force the audience to return to the truth and to destroy the legendary aspect of certain characters whose true nature modern historians have revealed, but the audience has not followed me. I soon came to the realisation that legend always triumphs over historical fact ... Jesus, Joan of Arc, Shakespeare, the Virgin Mary, Mohammed and Napoleon have all entered into legend.[3]

So, of course, has Amedeo Modigliani, probably the most mythologised modern artist after Van Gogh. The focus of myriad art-historical texts, he has often served as the subject of biography, both historical and fictionalised, with titles that tell us a good deal about their orientation, including: André Salmon, *La Vie passionnée de Modigliani* (1957); the 'fictional biography' by Frederick Wight, *Verge of Glory* (1957); June Rose, *Modigliani: The Pure Bohemian* (1990); and, a variation on the theme, Patrice Chaplin, *Into the Darkness Laughing: The Story of Modigliani's Last Mistress, Jeanne Hébuterne* (1990).

Fig. 1
Detail of Modigliani sitting in his studio, 1915–16
Photograph by Paul Guillaume
Archives Jean Bouret, Paris

Fig. 2
Jeanne Modigliani,
Modigliani's daughter, 1924
Photograph. Unknown
photographer
Archives Roger-Viollet, Paris

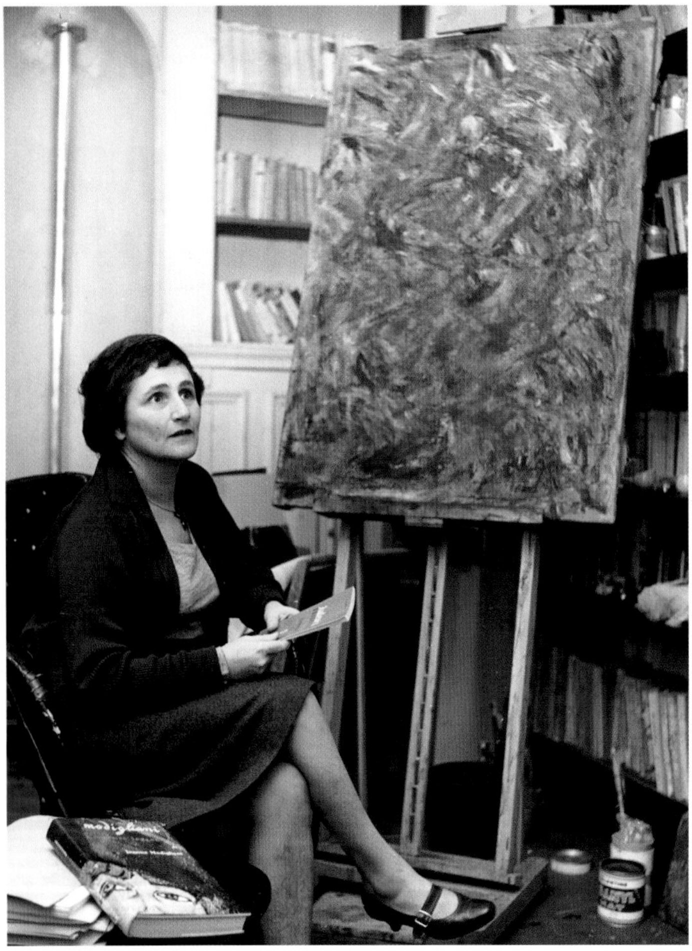

The romantic myth of the artist, firmly in place since at least the end of the eighteenth century, is a hyperbolic version of a rather dreary truth – artists' careers are difficult and likely to be unrewarding (at least in comparison with other kinds of bourgeois, professional pursuits). Gambling on one's talent, without the aid of a secure system of compensation, is treacherous, leaving those who seek fulfilment in the arts exposed to ridicule and probably doomed to failure. The image of the suffering artist is a form of communal sympathy for a group that is usually ignored, left to its own devices, irrespective of talent. A moral high ground is carved out for those among us who risk all in the unregulated market of modern art. What is more, the romantic myth provides a window onto the often spectacularly intense life of artists and, at the same time, functions as a moralising tale (of the toll it can take) for those outside the art world. Modigliani's loquacious passing, in 1920, demonstrates how this myth works – each of his (supposed) last utterances has both a narrative function and a moral dimension, as we shall see. In order to understand the Modigliani legend, let us work backwards in Jeanne Modigliani's account of her father's deathbed scene, from his beloved Italy to his devoted Parisian dealer, Léopold Zborowski.

'Cara Italia!'

Modigliani may well have invoked his dear homeland in his last hours, as he never lost contact with his family in Livorno (or Leghorn) during the fifteen years he spent in France. The legend of Modigliani began to develop in Paris in the decade after the artist's death. Many writers placed great significance on his Italian origins. In his initial study of the artist, of 1926, Salmon wrote that '[He] loved to declaim the verses of Dante Alighieri.... He knew them by heart, as they say,'[4] something that the sculptor Jacques Lipchitz also recalled many years later, 'when I think of him now, I always associate him with poetry... is it because when Max [Jacob] introduced us – it was in the Luxembourg Gardens in Paris, in 1913 – Modigliani suddenly began to recite by heart *The Divine Comedy* at the top of his voice?'[5] Arthur Pfannstiel, author of a major biographical and analytical monograph of 1929, called him, 'this young Tuscan, this great lyricist, at once draughtsman, sculptor, painter',[6] suggesting a link to those other multi-talented Tuscans, Leonardo da Vinci and Michelangelo Buonarroti. Likewise, Gustave Coquiot, in *Des Peintres maudits*, of 1924 – a key text in the creation of the new romantic myth of Montmartre and Montparnasse – insisted on the Italian aspect of Modigliani's

Fig. 3
Modigliani's studio, 6th floor, 8 rue de la Grande Chaumière, Montparnasse
Photograph. Unknown photographer
Archives Legales Modigliani, Paris

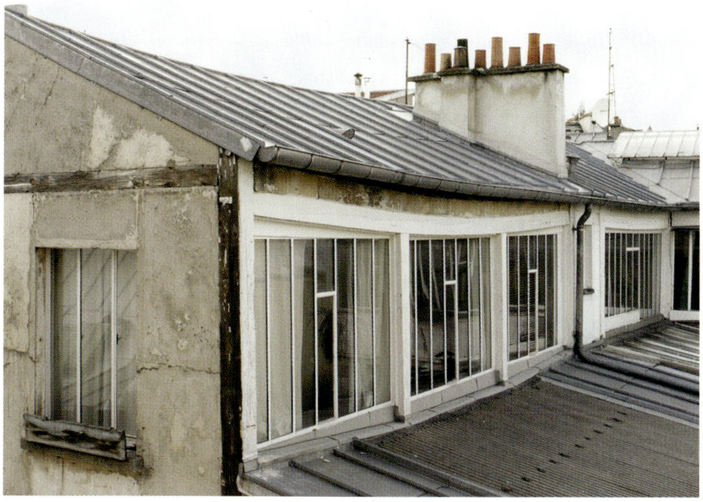

aesthetics, claiming that his studio wall was filled with photographs of works by Carpaccio, Lotto, Orcagna, Veronese, Lippi, Titian, Correggio, Andrea del Sarto and Botticelli,[7] just as, in reference to the artist's interest in African sculpture, Adolphe Basler and Charles Kunstler went so far as to say that 'Modigliani is a species of negro Botticelli'.[8]

Italian verse, Italian painting, the Renaissance – the allure of Modigliani-the-Italian was especially appealing in the polyglot world of artistic Paris, where so many of the other foreigners were from places much further away and far less familiar. Indeed, Modigliani's mother's family was from Marseilles, which helped account for his perfect French. Basler and Kunstler said Modigliani was 'the most picturesque figure in the Babel of Montparnasse',[9] which was probably a polite way of referring to Jews, among others (in the years following the end of the Dreyfus affair, the number of Jews in the Parisian art world was much discussed).[10]

As Modigliani was Italian, French *and* Jewish, he could function as a kind of discursive fulcrum, providing a midway point between the different types of immigrants in Paris and the familiarity of home-grown artists. In 1920, Coquiot said that Modigliani possessed 'all the qualities of his nervous, refined, exalted Italy',[11] and four years later wrote: 'Once upon a time at Livorno, in Italy, there was a little Jew cherished by his parents.'[12] In the same sentence in which he invoked Benvenuto Cellini and Catherine de' Medici at Fontainebleau, André Salmon also referred to Modigliani as 'the little Jew from Livorno'.[13] Pfannstiel said Modigliani's physical beauty was 'at one and the same time Semitic and Venetian'.[14]

Modigliani's allure is obvious in many of the photographs that have come down to us, and it rarely escaped comment by his contemporaries. 'How beautiful he was, my God, how beautiful!,'[15] exclaimed the artist's model, Aicha. 'Modigliani was handsome, virile, with his wavy locks, his large forehead and his diamond-black eyes,'[16] writes André Warnod, and then refers to the brown corduroy suit that we see in so many images of the artist (fig. 1), which 'he wore like a prince'.[17] 'Was he handsome?' asked the great connoisseur of male pulchritude, Jean Cocteau: 'I have been wondering since I saw Gérard Philipe portray him in a film [*Montparnasse 19* of 1957]. No. He was something better.'[18] The theme of Modigliani's *je ne sais quoi* – his beauty, his manners and his generous behaviour – runs throughout the literature and reappears in almost every anecdotal account as a form of nobility: 'well-bred, elegant in every sense' (André Salmon);[19] 'I was fascinated by his ... handsome appearance....

Fig. 4
Modigliani, shortly after his arrival in Paris, *c.* 1906
Photograph from *The Jewish Chronicle*.
Unknown photographer
Private collection

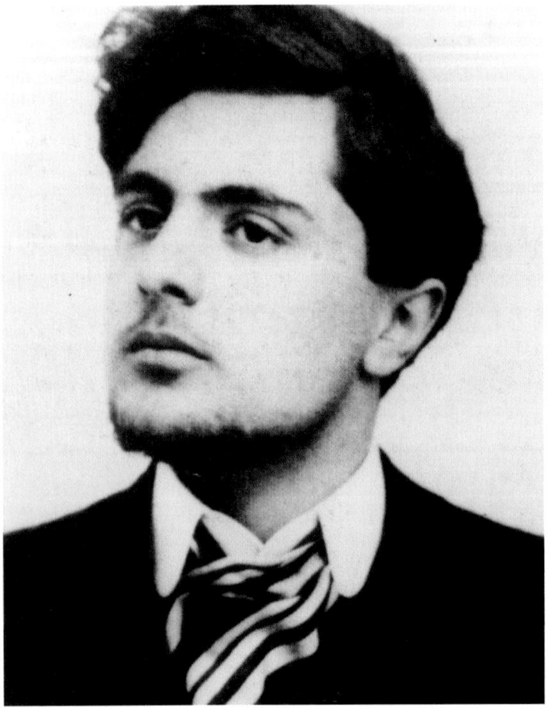

He looked aristocratic even in his worn-out corduroys' (Jacques Lipchitz);[20] 'Modigliani was an aristocrat. His entire oeuvre is the most powerful proof of it. His paintings are all marked by great distinction. Crudity, banality, vulgarity are completely excluded' (Maurice de Vlaminck).[21] He proceeds to recount two examples of Modigliani's princely generosity, from which he benefited:

> One winter morning in 1917, on a median of the Boulevard Raspail, proud, aloof, he watched the taxis pass with the look of a general in the midst of manoeuvres. A freezing-cold wind bit at the skin. The minute he saw me he approached, and, as if he had absolutely no need of it, he said, 'I offer you my overcoat, it's too big for me and will fit you perfectly.'[22]

Vlaminck's other example of Modigliani's largesse – a story that has been recounted in most biographies of the artist – involved his dropping a twenty-franc note on the floor of a café so that a hungry fellow artist, who was presumably too embarrassed to accept charity, would find it (moral: discretion is the better part of valour).

'Dear wounded prince'

Upon learning of his brother's death Emanuele Modigliani is reported to have telegraphed to Moïse Kisling: 'Bury him like a prince!',[23] which set the stage for Salmon's description of the artist, several years later, as a 'dear *wounded* prince'.[24] In the only article devoted to Modigliani during his lifetime, Francis Carco said that the artist was already being 'talked about by some with this outmoded, romantic idea of misfortune'.[25] Like Mimi in *La Bohème*, this sensitive denizen of the Parisian art world was doomed to die of consumption – 'Amedeo Modigliani, suffering from tuberculosis, was a genuine aristocrat, pale and handsome'.[26] Of course, he had not only done nothing to improve his congenitally weak lungs, but he had also made a point of exacerbating his condition. When he said to his friend, the Chilean artist Ortiz de Zárate (see fig. 5), 'I have only a little piece of brain left ... I know this is the end,'[27] he was doing no more than fulfilling his destiny (which is essential to all tragic tales).

During the decade following his death, Modigliani's demise was gradually written into his legend as only the last act in an inexorable decline that began a few years after his arrival in the French capital. One version of this moralising tale is that of the provincial who comes to the big city and is corrupted: 'The little Jew from Livorno becomes a good-for-nothing. Formerly he was stylish, now he's dirty, unkempt. He starts to drink, a lot. The war begins. He has trouble with the police.'[28]

Fig. 5
Group at the Café de La Rotonde, Montparnasse, 12 August 1916. From left: Manuel Ortiz de Zárate, Max Jacob, Moïse Kisling, Pâquerette (fashion model for Paul Poiret and Picasso's mistress at the time) and Picasso

Photograph by Jean Cocteau from a series interleaved in a book by Max Jacob, *Le Cornet à dés*, 1917 Musée Picasso, Paris MP2003-15; fol.74

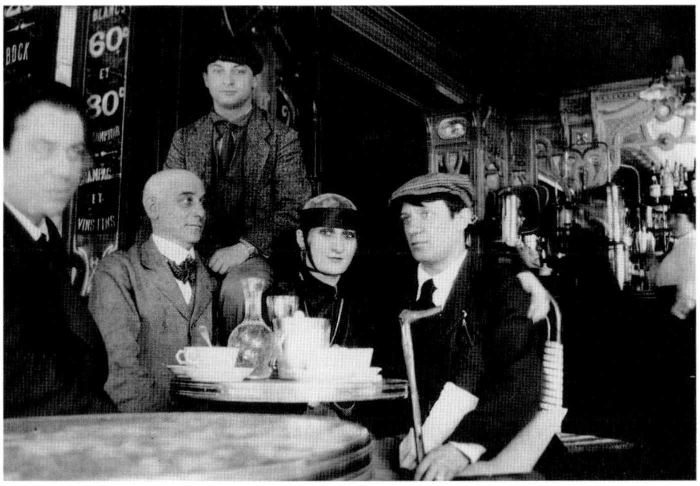

Describing the artist's dissolute life, as he wandered from one borrowed lodging to the next, Pfannstiel writes:

> This regime undermined his health, which had never been good. Alcohol also began to take its toll. To avoid painful reality, to escape from the tormenting worries of art-making, the poor boy developed a taste for absinthe and cognac. He looked for occasions to drink. Le Lapin [Agile] and A l'Ami Emile, rue Ravignan, were familiar with the disorderly conduct caused by his intoxicated state.[29]

Opium, cocaine and ether were eventually added to the alcohol;[30] Coquiot mentions hashish as well.[31] His daughter says that the respectably abstemious Modigiliani family back in Livorno insisted that her father was *not* an alcoholic – but allowed that he might have been addicted to drugs, as they snobbishly admired the work of Baudelaire and de Quincey![32]

Handsome and aristocratic, Modigliani becomes a martyr in the drama of Parisian bohemia. 'I met Modigliani at the Café [de la] Rotonde in October 1919,' a young Swedish woman, Thora Klinckowström, wrote, 'He was very handsome and romantic. Nils [Dardel] told me that before the war Modigliani had magnificent beauty, but that now he had lost it through debauchery and alcohol.'[33] Or he is among the beautiful and the damned: 'There was something like a curse on this very noble boy. He was beautiful; alcohol and misfortune took their toll on him.'[34] Yet, even as Modigliani's rapid fall from grace added to his bad-boy image, with its voluptuous loss of self-control as its centrepiece, his mythologists were careful to insist that he never worked while intoxicated nor found inspiration in his drug-induced ecstasies: 'Modigliani, who drank out of desperation, owed none of his genius to alcohol. Nor to the diabolical concoctions of the Asian pharmacy.'[35] The point, of course, was not to throw the baby out with the bathwater – he may have been tragically flawed, but Modigliani's talent, and his oeuvre, are not to be tarnished with the brush of his degeneracy. As art historian Maurice Berger has recently written:

> Modigliani has come to exemplify a decidedly unengaged and isolated modernist character type: the bohemian.... He refuses to engage in the routine, repetitive tasks of the labourer or serve the greedy bosses of industry and commerce ... he looks to pleasure, passion and self-expression ... [he is] a person who suffers for art and pays a steep price for a life of debauchery, poverty and neglect.[36]

Don Juan in Hell, Don Juan Redeemed

Francis Carco helped build the case for Modigliani as a Lothario: 'Women, struck by his great beauty, pined with love for him. Foreigners, simple girls. But Modi dropped them before they could get attached.'[37] Both his early sexual escapades and the romantic attachment of his last years became key elements in his legend. Louis Latourrettes, a poet and financial reporter, who was a close friend of the artist from his first days in Montmartre, commented, 'at the time, he drank only wine, Vouvray or Asti, with a sobriety that he soon lost. By contrast, he was strongly inclined to abuse the success that his attractiveness assured him in the circles of the Montmartre girls.'[38] Warnod – without crediting his source, which he practically paraphrases – raised the artist's sexuality to mythic proportions and, like his predecessor, pictured his libidinous exploits as a form of addiction: 'It is worth pointing out that at first he did not drink alcohol; he liked wine, but did not abuse it. Still, if he scorned Bacchus – who would eventually take his revenge – he adored Venus. He wasn't a pretty boy for nothing, using and abusing the success that his handsome face assured him with the Montmartre girls, not prudish by nature.'[39]

Even more than alcohol and drugs, sex is the touchstone of the Modigliani myth, which may help explain its enduring appeal. Two of the key scandals of his legend relate to sexuality and transform it from biographical anecdote into artistic folklore. The first is Modigliani's infamous exhibition, in 1917, at Berthe Weill's gallery in the rue Taitbout – the only solo show, as far as we know, that he ever had (fig. 6). As the dealer explained:

> [Léopold] Zborowoski asked me to do a Modigliani exhibition of painting and drawing; I accepted, of course ... Sunday we hung and Monday, 3 October, was the opening. Sumptuous nudes, angular faces, tasty portraits.... A passer-by, curious at how many people were in the gallery, stopped in his tracks. Two passers-by ... three passers-by ... a crowd gathered. My neighbour, the police chief, exclaimed: 'What's this? A nude!' (A nude was displayed in the window....) 'I order you to take all this filth down....' 'What's wrong with these nudes?...' 'These nudes! ... these nudes have p-p-p-pubic hair!... And if my orders are not followed immediately, I will have them all seized by my agents....'
>
> I closed the gallery soon after, and the guests who were thus imprisoned helped in taking down the paintings....
>
> After all the paintings had been taken down,[40] the exhibition continued: only two drawings were sold ... 30 francs each.[41]

Although the ostensible moral of this tale is that the public (here in the guise of the civil authorities) does not understand serious art, its centrality in the Modigliani legend is, I think, due to its salaciousness. Not only are the exhibition and removal of Modigliani's nudes a kind of transference of the exhibition and removal of the (offending) body hair, but, just as he was helpless

Fig. 6
Catalogue cover for Modigliani's exhibition at Berthe Weill's gallery, 3 to 30 December 1917
Modigliani Institut, Archives Legales, Paris

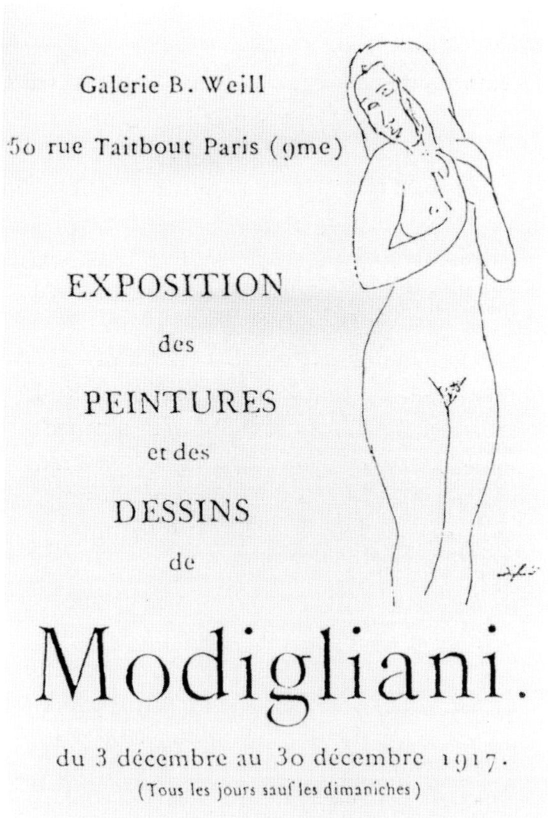

to ignore the entreaties of languishing women (according to Carco, Latourrettes and Warnod), so he is incapable of making safe and inoffensive art. Another way of putting it is that Modigliani's sexuality is of such magnitude that it overcomes all obstacles, even if it is to his disadvantage. That there is no clear distinction made between Modigliani's sex life and his artistic life is obvious.

The other scandal that betrays its connection to the myth of Modigliani's sexuality involves Pierre-Auguste Renoir. In 1918, when Jeanne Hébuterne (fig. 7) was pregnant with Modigliani's daughter, she and Modigliani went to live in Nice and Cagnes, the town to which the Impressionist had retired.

> The story goes that his friends persuaded [Modigliani] to visit Renoir, then a very old man and half paralysed, but who went on painting with his brush strapped to his hand.[42]

Renoir told Modigliani that he should:

> 'Paint with joy, with the same joy with which you make love....'
> 'Do you caress your canvases a long time?...'
> 'I stroke the buttocks for days before finishing a painting.'...
> Modigliani got up brusquely and, his hand on the doorknob, said brutally, 'I don't like buttocks, sir.'[43]

Jeanne Modigliani reports the phrase that her father used to one of the grand old men of French art, severely crippled with arthritis, in French as: 'Je n'aime pas les belles fesses.'[44] Hadn't Modigliani painted enough attractive posteriors to make this statement seem peculiar? Had the rue Taitbout affair made him feel that he had no choice but to counteract his reputation for prurience? Or is this the assertion of a younger generation's idea of sexuality in contrast to the previous one – so that Renoir's sexual arousals become no more than the unseemly manifestations of a dirty old man's dirty mind, whereas Modigliani's (disdainful) refusal of sexual titillation becomes a sign of his real, active, potency?

In narrative terms, there is yet another significance to the artist's rude response to Renoir: it comes at the point in the Modigliani legend at which the libertine becomes the devoted mate to his true love, the mother of his daughter. 'Jeanne Hébuterne? Ah! This wouldn't be a woman like the others. So many others! The Gabys, the Lolas, the Loulous from Montmartre ... the girls from Montparnasse ... Jeanne Hébuterne? This wouldn't be a Mrs [Beatrice] Hastings [a former lover], virtuoso of pleasure; this wasn't a poor Thérèse or Suzanne or Germaine ... [This was] Jeanne Hébuterne, whose

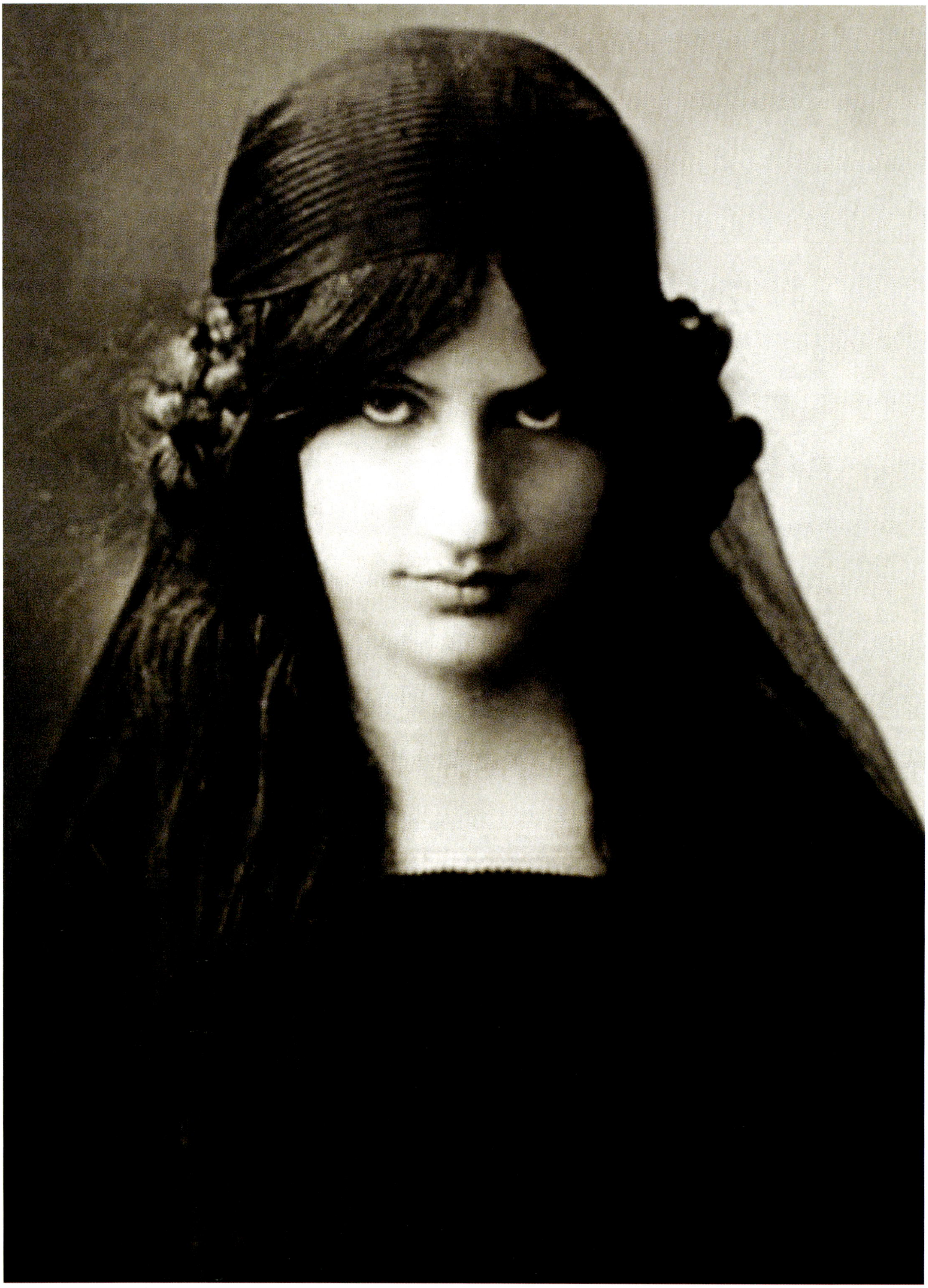

Fig. 7
Jeanne Hébuterne, *c.* 1919
Photograph. Unknown photographer
Archives Roger-Viollet, Paris

angelic sweetness had nothing to fear from her lover's rages.'[45] As a discursive ploy, Modigliani's early promiscuity now functions in the opposite way, just as his beauty, innocence and innate nobility had. If those characteristics had established the lofty heights from which he would fall to a drunken and drugged damnation, Modigliani's youthful sexual adventurism now establishes the debased beginning from which he may climb to fidelity and redemption. As we know, Jeanne Modigliani says that her father, on his deathbed, 'asked his wife' – her mother, Jeanne Hébuterne – 'to follow him to the grave'. According to Pfannstiel, Modigliani's mourners had no idea what awaited them after the artist's burial at Père-Lachaise, Paris:

> Their return was marked by a tragic surprise. Modigliani's [common-law] wife, having learned of the death of her beloved – despite efforts to keep the news from her – in a moment of despair threw herself from the fifth-floor window of her parents' house. It's almost unbelievable that [her parents] refused to gather up the body of this noble Catholic girl to bury her next to this Jew. It was only several years later that her parents relented and that, in 1928, their bodies were reunited.[46]

Hébuterne's suicide when she was pregnant was the shocking conclusion to a love story that, in the years to come, the artist's mythologists would exploit for everything it was worth.

Enduring Value

'An hour after [his death] dealers and collectors, wallets in hand, desperately grabbed every painting and drawing by Modigliani they could find,'[47] reported Gustave Coquiot. With no grieving widow to muddy the waters of the artist's myth nor reap the rewards of his posthumous fame, the work itself was suddenly worth a great deal. A frustrated dealer who came away empty-handed begged André Salmon to alert him to the next time a brilliant young artist came along: 'I'm really annoyed to have missed the boat on Modigliani,' he told the critic.[48] Another critic, Francis Carco, was keenly aware of the time lag that often separated artists from their just rewards; he was proud that, on the basis of the article he had published on Modigliani, in 1917, several Swiss collectors had bought some nudes for 'almost nothing'.[49] Indeed, the vast prices that Modigliani's work brought during the 1920s after his death were noted by fellow artists as well. Writing about his old friend almost three decades later, Jacques Lipchitz commented on the fact that a Modigliani nude had recently sold for one million francs (a great deal of money in 1952).[50] Surely part of the piquancy of Modigliani's ever-escalating popularity came from his mythic *lack* of

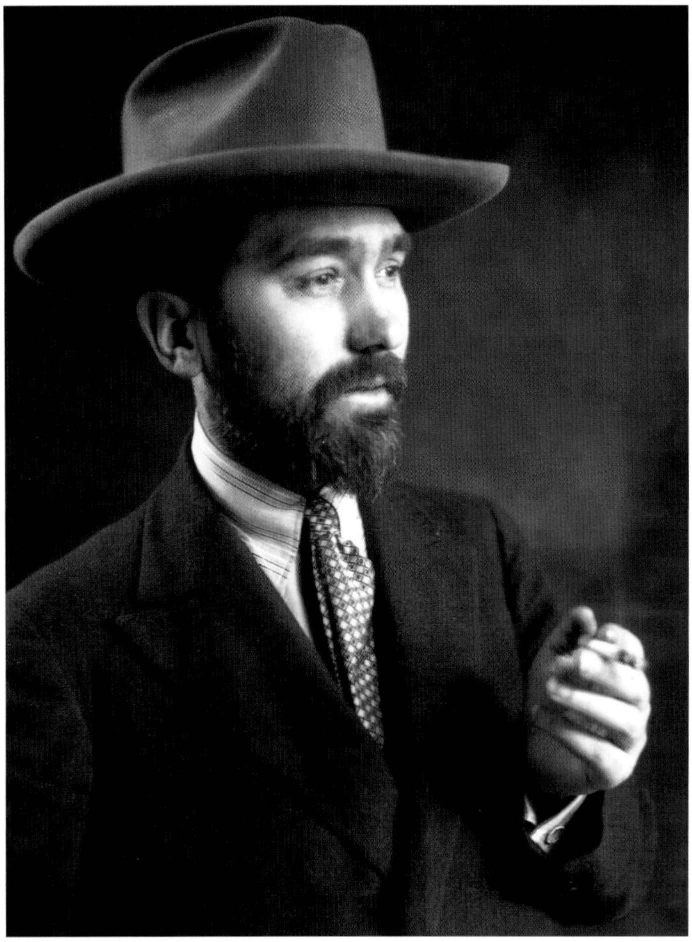

Fig. 8
Léopold Zborowski,
probably early 1920s
Photograph. Unknown
photographer
Archives Roger-Viollet, Paris

materialism. Maurice de Vlaminck, who had told the story of being offered the artist's topcoat on the Boulevard Raspail, recounted another scene that took place nearby, at the Café de la Rotonde: an 'American woman' (read: materialistic *arriviste*) desperately wanted Modigliani's signature on one of his drawings, but she annoyed the artist so much by her insistence that he defaced the drawing by writing his name across it.[51]

His mythologists realised how much more effective his story would be if, rather than emphasising his not inconsequential lifetime reputation,[52] they presented an artist whose ability had gone unrecognised. In 1926 Warnod wrote: 'There are glories for which one must wait. Modigliani's began the day he died.'[53] Carco said that after Modigliani's death 'he came to occupy, in time, the role he should have played for his generation'.[54] We might restate this cliché of the eventual *gloire* of the romantic artist in strictly economic terms: in any investment, the greatest gain comes to those who can see value where others cannot. According to Pfannstiel, Modigliani's dealer Léopold Zborowski (fig. 8), 'never doubted for a minute the glorious future reserved for the unknown artist',[55] which explains why, on his deathbed, Modigliani took care to tell him: 'No matter what happens, you have nothing to worry about. In [Chaïm] Soutine I'm leaving you a great artist,'[56] a reference to the Lithuanian Expressionist whose work was later snapped up in Paris. In the Modigliani legend – like everything else in this moralising tale – there are not only bad, opportunistic art dealers but also a supremely good one: 'What love Zborowski had for his painter!' Carco wrote in *De Montmartre au Quartier Latin*, 'What great and total admiration! He deprived himself of everything for him.'[57]

Homesickness, beauty, nobility, drugs, alcohol, sex, love, money and great art – Modigliani had it all. 'Is there anything more moving than the spectacle of a life made up of misery and struggle ... being snuffed out at just the moment when success was at hand?'[58] asked Pfannstiel in the opening sentence of his monograph of 1929. Apparently there is not, because in the battle between the man portrayed by his daughter and the artistic hero of his highly developed myth, the latter wins, hands down.

Notes

All translations are my own unless otherwise specified.

1 Modigliani 1958, pp. 97–8.
2 Pfannstiel 1929, p. 20.
3 Bernhardt 1999, p. 59. See my discussion of this issue in 'Sarah Bernhardt and the Theatrics of French Nationalism: From Roland's Daughter to Napoleon's Son' in *Sarah Bernhardt: The Art of High Drama*, Carol Ockman and Kenneth E. Silver, exh. cat., The Jewish Museum, New York, 2005.
4 Salmon 1926, p. 9.
5 Lipchitz 1952, p. 3.
6 Pfannstiel 1929, p. 2.
7 Gustave Coquiot, *Des Peintres maudits*, Paris, 1924, p. 102.
8 Adolphe Basler and Charles Kunstler, *Modern French Painting – The Modernists: From Matisse to de Segonzac*, London and New York, 1931, p. 72.
9 Adolphe Basler and Charles Kunstler, *Modern French Painting – The Modernists: From Matisse to de Segonzac*, London and New York, 1931, p. 71.
10 See Romy Golan, 'The Ecole Française vs. the Ecole de Paris: The Debate about the Status of Jewish Artists in Paris between the Wars' in *The Circle of Montparnasse: Jewish Artists in Paris*, 1905–1945, Kenneth E. Silver and Romy Golan, exh. cat., The Jewish Museum, New York, 1985, pp. 80–7. For foreigners in Paris, see also *L'Ecole de Paris: la part de l'Autre*, Jean-Louis Andral and Sophie Krebs (eds), exh. cat., Musée d'Art Moderne de la Ville de Paris, 2000.
11 Gustave Coquiot, *Des Peintres maudits*, Paris, 1924, p. 108. In fact, Coquiot quotes from this section in his own, earlier book, *Les Indépendants*, of 1920.
12 Gustave Coquiot, *Des Peintres maudits*, Paris, 1924, p. 101.
13 Salmon 1926, p. 20.
14 Pfannstiel 1929, p. II. For Modigliani's reputation in Italy following his death, see Emily Braun's excellent 'The Faces of Modigliani: Identity Politics under Fascism' in New York 2004, pp. 24–41. Among other things, Braun discusses issues of Modigliani's Italian identity in the context of Fascist culture.
15 Aicha (Goblet), *Paris-Montparnasse*, no. 13 (February 1930), p. 16, cited in Sichel 1967, p. 232.
16 André Warnod, *Ceux de la Butte*, Paris, 1947, p. 172.
17 André Warnod, *Ceux de la Butte*, Paris, 1947, p. 172.
18 Cited in Sichel 1967, p. 377.
19 Salmon 1926, p. 11.
20 Lipchitz 1952, p. 3.
21 Vlaminck 1925, p. 1.
22 Vlaminck 1925, p. 1.
23 Salmon 1926, p. 8.
24 Salmon 1926, p. 11.
25 Carco 1919, p. 202.
26 Cocteau 1950, n.p.
27 Aicha (Goblet), *Paris-Montparnasse*, no. 13 (February 1930), cited in Rose 1990, p. 211.
28 Gustave Coquiot, *Des Peintres maudits*, Paris, 1924, p. 107.
29 Pfannstiel 1929, p. viii.
30 Pfannstiel 1929, p. xi.
31 Gustave Coquiot, *Des Peintres maudits*, Paris, 1924, p. 104.
32 Jeanne Modigliani in Modigliani 1961 in Paris 1981, p. 58.
33 Thora Klinckowström (from a letter dated 1974, Stockholm) in Fifield 1976, pp. 247–8. Klinckowström is the subject of a portrait by Modigliani (cat. 49).
34 Francis Carco, *De Montmartre au Quartier Latin*, Paris, 1927, p. 193.
35 Salmon 1926, p. 10.
36 Maurice Berger, 'Epilogue: The Modigliani Myth' in New York 2004, p. 77.
37 Francis Carco, *De Montmartre au Quartier Latin*, Paris, 1927, p. 194.
38 Louis Latourrettes, 'Preface' in Pfannstiel 1929, p. iii.
39 André Warnod, *Ceux de la Butte*, Paris, 1947, p. 172.
40 Presumably Weill meant 'all' of the nudes rather than all of the paintings.
41 Weill 1933, pp. 227–9.
42 As recounted in Roy 1958, p. 104.
43 Sichel 1967, p. 413.
44 Jeanne Modigliani in Modigliani 1961 in Paris 1981, p. 93.
45 Salmon 1957, p. 285.
46 Pfannstiel 1929, pp. 31–2.
47 Gustave Coquiot, *Des Peintres maudits*, Paris, 1924, p. 112.
48 Salmon 1926, p. 8.
49 Francis Carco, *De Montmartre au Quartier Latin*, Paris, 1927, p. 192.
50 Lipchitz 1952, p. 22.
51 Vlaminck 1925, p. 1.
52 For Modigliani's lifetime recognition, see Buffalo 2002.
53 André Warnod, *Les Berceaux de la jeune peinture (Montmartre/Montparnasse)*, Paris, 1926, p. 233.
54 Francis Carco, *De Montmartre au Quartier Latin*, Paris, 1927, p. 192.
55 Pfannstiel 1929, p. 23.
56 Modigliani to Zborowski, cited in Sichel 1967, p. 298. For the 'myths' of Soutine, see my 'Where Soutine Belongs: His Art and Critical Reception in Paris between the Wars' in *An Expressionist in Paris: The Paintings of Chaïm Soutine*, Norman Kleeblatt and Kenneth E. Silver, exh. cat., The Jewish Museum, New York, 1998.
57 Francis Carco, *De Montmartre au Quartier Latin*, Paris, 1927, p. 196.
58 Pfannstiel 1929, p. 1.

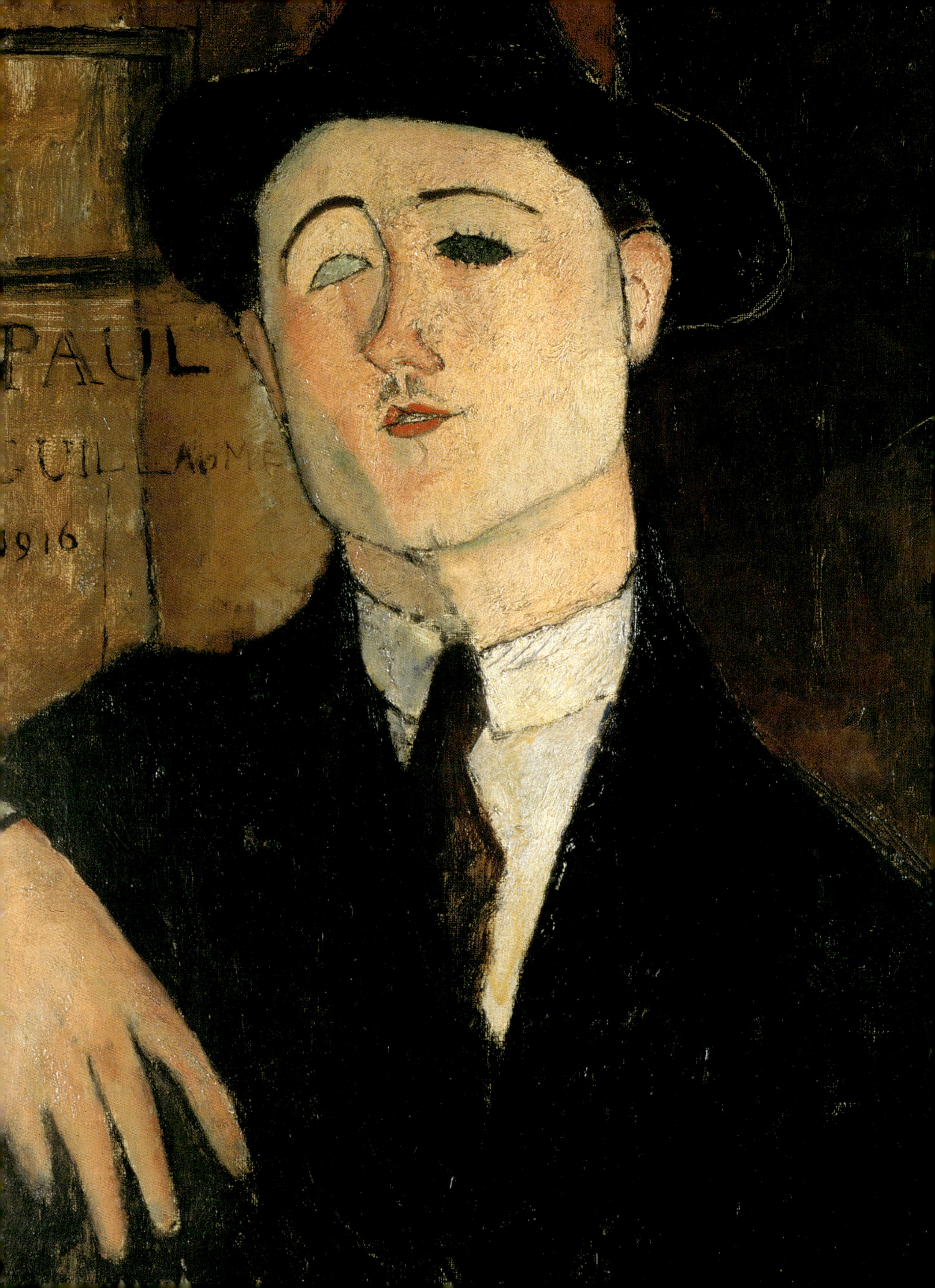
PAUL
GUILLAUME
1916

A Personal Universe: Modigliani's Portraits and Figure Paintings

Simonetta Fraquelli

'To do any work, I must have a living person ... I must be able to see him opposite me.'[1]

Modigliani's portraits and single-figure paintings are among the most memorable and popular images of the early twentieth century. Accounting for some 90% of his total output, they possess an archetypal quality that sets them apart from the art of his contemporaries in Paris in the first two decades of the last century. Like the artist's nudes, they testify to an enduring fascination with the human form and physiognomy. Modigliani's mastery lies in his ability to retain the essential likeness of his sitters while couching that likeness in his own circumscribed vocabulary of forms.

Modigliani's life story, as told by contemporaries and biographers since his premature death at the age of 35 in 1920, has overshadowed his achievements as an artist. The enthralling narrative of the handsome and dissolute young bohemian, killed by a combination of ill health, alcohol consumption and drug abuse, has acquired legendary status. Interpretation of his work primarily in biographical terms has been encouraged by the fact that, apart from a handful of youthful letters, it seems that Modigliani never commented in writing on his artistic practices. His portraits, almost exclusively of people in his immediate circle, have been used to underpin the biographical approach. Moreover, Modigliani's relationship with the art of the past has often been misconstrued as reactionary. Unlike his contemporaries the Futurists, he did not abandon his cultural heritage; on the contrary, it provided him with a continual source of inspiration and guidance. Subtly combining elements derived from his native Italy and his Jewish background with current artistic developments in Paris, Modigliani created a portrait style that was modern and original.

Born in 1884 into a cultivated Sephardic Jewish family in Livorno (also known previously as Leghorn), Modigliani studied there and in Florence and Venice, before moving to Paris in 1906.[2] During his first years in the French capital, he lived in Montmartre, but his early portraits and figure paintings have little in common with the avant-garde art of his neighbours at the Bateau-Lavoir, who included Pablo Picasso. Modigliani's early Parisian works recall the flattened, graphic style of Henri de Toulouse-Lautrec and the anguished Expressionism of Edvard Munch.[3] The more cerebral art of Paul Cézanne, especially its depiction of volumes, proved to be another lasting influence on the Italian artist's portrait style, one that is clearly visible in the two versions of *The Cellist* (1909).[4]

Fig. 9
Detail of cat. 13

Fig. 10
Jean Cocteau, 1916
Oil on canvas,
100 × 81 cm
The Henry and Rose Pearlman Foundation, Inc.; on long-term loan to Princeton University Art Museum L.1988.62.18

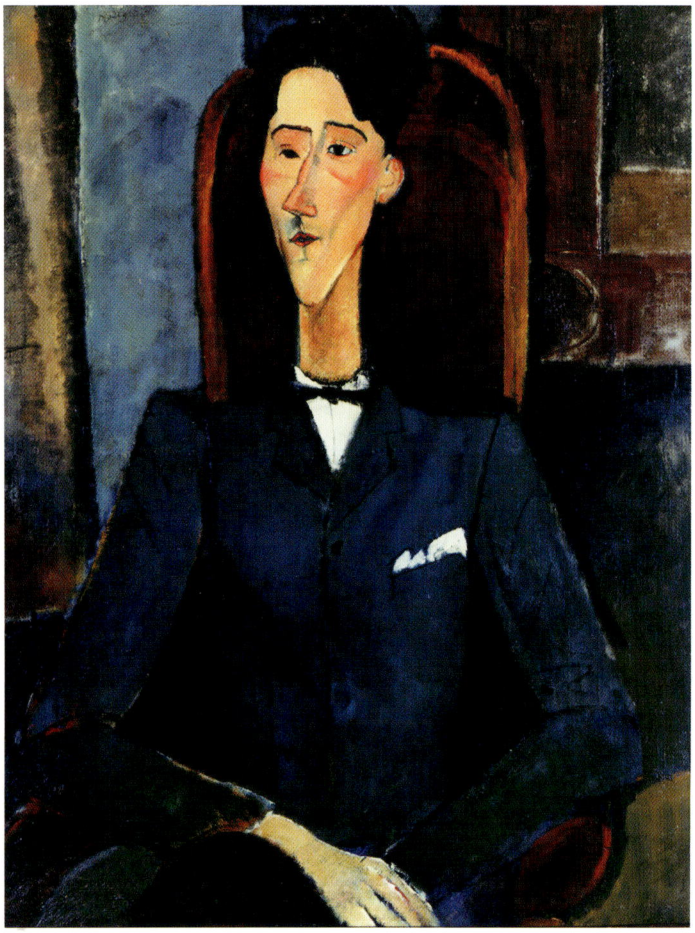

Wishing to become a sculptor, Modigliani had experimented with stone carving at Carrara in the summer of 1902. The ill health that had plagued him from childhood initially prevented him from pursuing this aim, but in 1909 the physician Paul Alexandre, his friend and first faithful patron, introduced him to Constantin Brancusi. This encounter encouraged Modigliani to return to sculpture and for almost three years (1910–13) he virtually abandoned painting. Some 25 sculptures survive from this crucial period in the artist's career. Most are limestone heads, some rough-hewn, others highly finished (cat. 1; *c.* 1911–12), the majority elongated, but some squatter and more block-like. Modigliani produced a considerable number of sculpture-related drawings of heads and caryatids at this time. With their simple, elegant outlines and broken rhythms, they were inspired – as were the three-dimensional works – by medieval Italian sculpture and, more importantly, by non-European art, including African and Asian sculpture, much in vogue in Paris at the time and accessible to Modigliani at the Musée Guimet and the ethnographic galleries of the Trocadéro. The attenuated forms and stylised features of the stone pieces and the flat, linear style of the drawings were to form the basis of the artist's mature pictorial language, their hieratic simplicity and serene equilibrium resurfacing in his later paintings.

Modigliani's portraits both draw on tradition and contest it. Though accepting the premise that a portrait should resemble the sitter, he makes the model conform to his personal formal vocabulary, so that the painting is recognisable in the first instance as 'a Modigliani'. The principal aim is neither to aggrandise the sitter nor to record him or her for posterity, but rather to capture the image of an individual at a specific moment in the artist's life. Those closest to him – his friend and protégé the painter Chaïm Soutine (1917; see p. 146), for example – are rendered sympathetically and women are generally flattered more than men, who are sometimes almost caricatured or satirised, as in *Jean Cocteau* (1916; 10) and *Juan Gris* (1915; cat. 7)[5] Like the Italian Renaissance works he admired so much, Modigliani's portraits have the kind of distancing effect that invites the viewer to penetrate beyond the surface of the image in order to unlock its secrets. This effect is achieved primarily through expressive eyes, which, when blank or painted in a single colour, often make the sitter appear absorbed in his or her thoughts. Only rarely does Modigliani avail himself of a centuries-old convention and incorporate clues as to the status of the sitter. Objects are generally absent from the settings, with their notably even, shadowless light, and, if any

Fig. 11
Diego Rivera, 1914
Oil on canvas
100 × 81 cm
Kunstsammlung Nordrhein
Westfalen, Düsseldorf

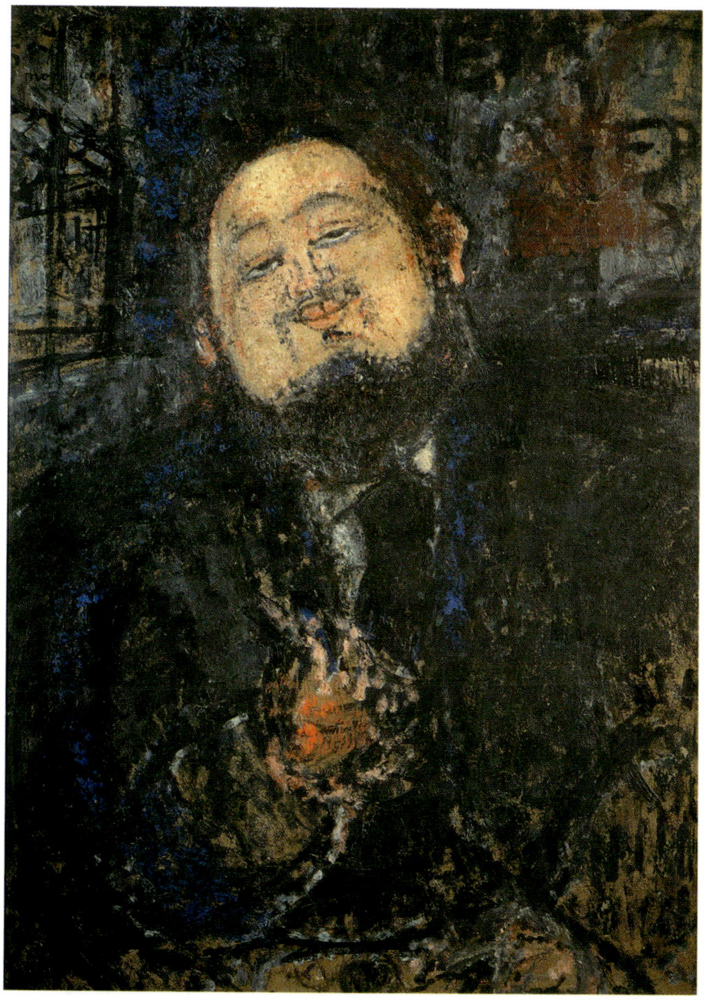

are included, their function is purely compositional, as with the chairs in the portraits of Jeanne Hébuterne or the door in the image of the melancholy Madame Eyraud-Vaillant (1919; cat. 48), who, like the artist's caryatids, seems to carry the weight of the world on her shoulders.

From 1913 to early 1920 Modigliani produced over 250 oils – the majority of his extant paintings. This output is especially remarkable given that this period included the four years of the First World War, when materials and portrait commissions were scarce.[6] The portraits and figure paintings from these years, which vary in technique and degree of finish, fall into three main groups.

The first, dating from 1913 to 1916, consists primarily of images of people from the artist's milieu in Montparnasse. By the time he moved there in 1909, Montparnasse had become the leading artistic quarter in Paris, a melting pot of French and foreign artists, writers, musicians and critics who worked side by side to create what we now call modern art. Each brought with them their own history and culture and each was influenced by what they saw around them. Kenneth Wayne has suggested that Modigliani's paintings evince a wider range of sources than any other work produced in Paris at this time, encompassing ancient Egyptian and classical Greek art, Cambodian and African art, Renaissance painting and the jungle fantasies of Henri Rousseau, Jewish mysticism and Catholicism, not to mention recent or contemporary local trends in art and literature.[7] This capacity to embrace new cultural influences may have been seen as evidence of Modigliani's sophisticated origins, along with his elegant manners and attire, but this view of him must have squared oddly with his often outlandish and quarrelsome behaviour. Perhaps this very combination explains why he became an iconic figure among his peers in Montparnasse.[8]

Although Modigliani disliked theoretical statements and never joined an artistic group, his art clearly reveals knowledge of recent pictorial trends.[9] The 1914 portraits of the Mexican painter Diego Rivera (fig. 11) and the artist-collector Frank Burty Haviland (cat. 5), for example, share a coarse, Fauve-inspired Pointillism, their essentially linear conception rendered more painterly by stippled and irregularly stroked areas of unmodulated colour. Such innovations of Analytical Cubism and Futurism as faceted forms, rigorously structured compositions and the incorporation of lettering also occur in Modigliani's paintings and drawings of these years. Inscriptions in his portraits usually consist of the sitter's name, but occasionally he would add something. The word *savoir*

Fig. 12
The Young Apprentice, c. 1918
Oil on canvas
100 × 65 cm
Collection Jean Walter
and Paul Guillaume
Musée de l'Orangerie, Paris

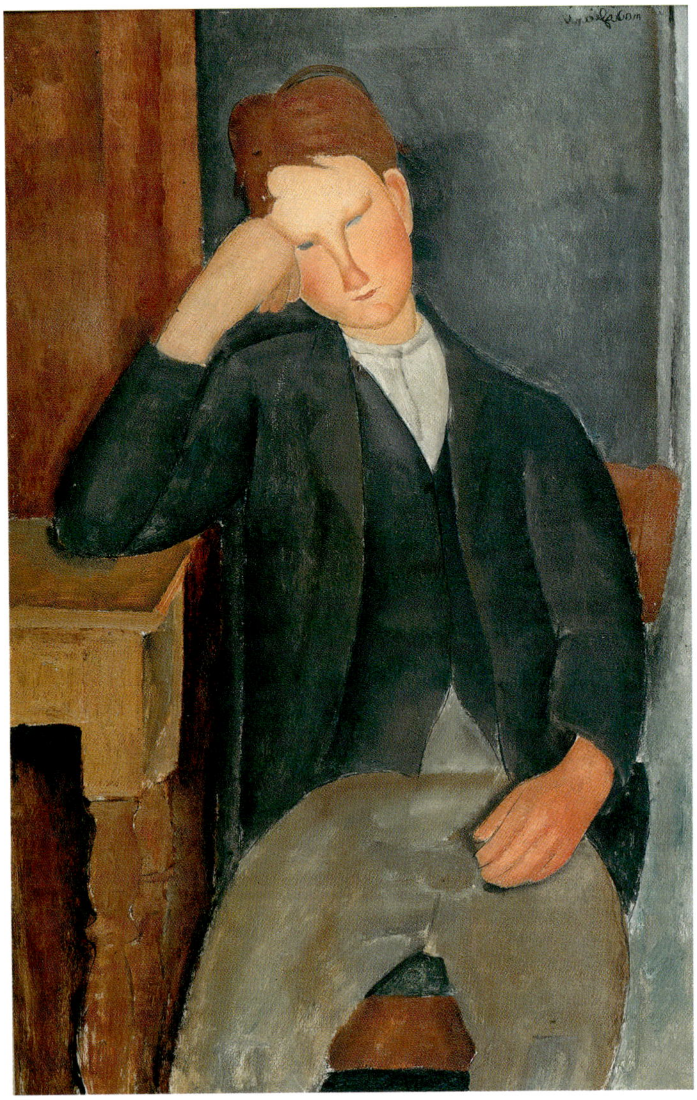

('knowledge', 'understanding') appears at the lower left in Picasso's portrait (1915; cat. 6), for instance, and may reflect his admiration for the Spanish artist, whom he probably envied.[10] Modigliani annotated drawings with quotes from his favourite poets: Dante, Gabriele D'Annunzio, Le Comte de Lautréamont and Nostradamus. This practice may have been stimulated by the paintings of Paul Gauguin, which he studied at the major exhibition of that artist's work mounted at the Salon d'Automne in 1906.[11]

Modigliani's muse from 1914 to 1916 was the British-born South African writer and poet Beatrice Hastings.[12] His fourteen portraits of her convey the delicacy of her features and her sophistication, but give no indication of her irascible personality or of the stormy nature of their relationship, which she and others acknowledged.[13] The paintings suggest something of the artist's changing attitudes towards Hastings. In the 1914 portraits she appears serene and inscrutable, with a rounded face, small nose and narrow, piercing eyes. The following year, in *Madam Pompadour* (Art Institute of Chicago), Modigliani's view is playful and mocking, the title referring to her both as Louis XV's famous mistress and as an English 'madam'. By contrast, another painting from 1915, *Beatrice Hastings in front of a Door* (cat. 9), communicates a previously unexpressed empathy, through the graceful neck, the flushed cheeks and the asymmetrical treatment of the eyes. By 1916 the portraits have become more angular, the eyes are blank and Hastings appears haughty and detached – an indication, perhaps, of the imminent end of their liaison. Most of the portraits are bust-length, with an emphasis on the sitter's long neck (see cats 9 and 10); only two show her hands (see cat. 8). This format contrasts with that used by Modigliani for portraits of his other great love, Jeanne Hébuterne, which generally show a half-length serpentine form, with the arms and hands in a variety of suggestive and sometimes submissive poses (cats 39 and 44).

The paintings in the second group of works by Modigliani discussed here – single-figure images of peasants and young working girls and boys – are among his most sublime (cats 32 and 33). Painted from 1918 to 1919 in the South of France, they overlap chronologically with the third group, which is examined below. In 1918 Modigliani's health was deteriorating and his dealer, Léopold Zborowski, arranged for him to move with Hébuterne to the Côte d'Azur. Lacking professional models and the desire to paint his familiar circle of friends, Modigliani chose to paint the local people for human, not social, reasons.[14]

The subjects are not named, and this practice is a further indication that the artist was primarily concerned in his portraits and figure paintings with the variety of the human form as such, rather than with the specifics of a given sitter.[15] The monumentality of these paintings, and their feeling for mass, testify to the underlying influence of Cézanne and distinguish them from the grandiose linear eloquence of Modigliani's later Paris portraits (see cat. 50). More naturalistic and extremely restrained emotionally, the single-figure pieces have been called 'visions of humanity'.[16] The surfaces are thinly painted and smooth, and the palette is cooler than that of the sometimes almost garish Parisian works. The figure paintings coincide with a brief excursion into landscape painting, again in emulation of Cézanne, to whom Modigliani undoubtedly felt particularly close in the South of France.

The final group of works investigated here comprises the portraits Modigliani painted in Paris from 1917 onwards. With their long, curved necks, their flat, elongated, oval faces, almond-shaped eyes and small, pursed lips, these images conform most obviously to what is now perceived as the artist's signature style. The monochromatic tones and structural concerns of his earlier portraits have become less important than the inherently expressive, harmonious, curvilinear compositions, closer to the sinuous lines of the caryatid drawings of 1913. Despite subtle allusions to location – a dado rail, a door frame, a fireplace – the backgrounds generally consist of painterly areas of pure, abstract colour, reminiscent of paintings by Henri Matisse.

In contrast to the nervous energy characteristic of much early twentieth-century portraiture – that of Oskar Kokoschka and Egon Schiele, for example – these late works by Modigliani radiate controlled emotional intensity. They are suffused with melancholy, and it has often been remarked that their calm contrasts with the artist's chaotic personal life. Although Modigliani was evidently more interested in physiognomy *per se* than in psychology or character analysis, he does hint at his own feelings towards his sitters by the way in which he uses facial expressions or the position of the hands to capture something of their personality.[17] While he regularly distorts certain elements – extending necks, for instance, or emphasising long or bulbous noses and other imperfections – he never offends traditional notions of beauty completely. His pronounced 'Mannerist' style lent itself most successfully to the portrayal of characteristics generally perceived as typically feminine; hence it can scarcely be coincidental that he painted women more often than men in this last period.

From 1917 to 1920 three women in Modigliani's immediate circle became his principal models: Hanka (or Anna) Zborowska, the partner of his dealer (cats 15, 27, 28 and 43); Lunia Czechowska (cats 47 and 51), a friend and house guest of the Zborowskis; and Jeanne Hébuterne, a young art student who became Modigliani's companion and the mother of his child (for example, cats 25, 26, 38, 39, 41, 42 and 44).[18] These women's appearance (especially Czechowska's and Hebuterne's) accorded well with his pictorial aspirations, and their ready availability allowed him to paint them repeatedly (at least 25 times in Jeanne's case). Their portraits share abstracted facial features, flowing lines and compositions dominated by S-shapes; figure and background are bound together by a series of interlocking forms or areas of colour, transforming the sitters into essentially aesthetic phenomena.

Despite these points in common, the portraits reveal the artist's different feelings towards each of the three women. Hanka Zborowska, with her elongated, oval face and long, slender neck, seems aloof, almost haughty. In this way Modigliani expresses a cool respect for his dealer's wife (1917; cat. 28), whom he portrays unsmiling and with hands firmly clasped, but possessing the elegance of an eighteenth-century portrait. The portraits of Czechowska are more sympathetic. With pointed chin, high cheekbones and slanting eyes, she is depicted in a variety of poses – holding a fan, resting her chin on her hand, leaning on her elbows. With an understanding and inquisitive air, she appears more at one with herself than the other women and Modigliani would seem to be implying that she is his equal. The countless portraits of Hébuterne evince a more consistent approach. She appears loving, submissive and doe-eyed, a poignant figure depicted in all manner of poses – in profile, seated, with 'attenuated' arms and so forth. The images convey both Modigliani's affection for his young lover and his impatience with her for apparently offering no resistance to his intolerable behaviour.[19]

The emancipation of the Jews in Italy after the Risorgimento, and the libertarian ideals it encouraged, fostered the emergence of independent Jewish artists. Modigliani followed in the footsteps of other Italian-Jewish artists who had made portraiture a major theme of their work.[20] It has recently been suggested that his penchant for painting those around him sprang from a desire to document 'otherness'[21] and it has also been convincingly argued that he was schooled in the philosophy of Spinoza and other Jewish thinkers who embraced humanism.[22] Modigliani would certainly have been made

Fig. 13
Max Jacob, 1915–16
Pencil on paper
34.5 × 26.5 cm
Fonds Joseph Altounian.
Musée des beaux-arts,
Quimper

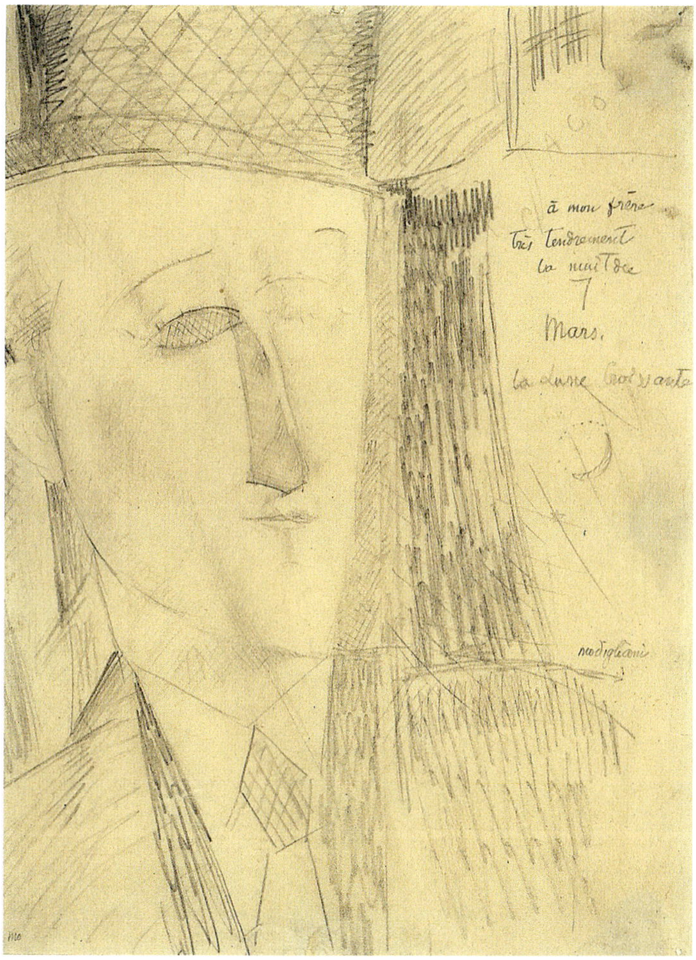

acutely aware of his Jewishness in Paris and he may well have adopted the role of outsider as a way of coping with an anti-Semitism far greater than any he might have encountered in Italy.

As an outsider, he was better positioned to absorb other cultures and, significantly, despite such French sitters as Henri Laurens, Raymond Radiguet and Roger Dutilleul, many of his portrait subjects were foreign – American, English, Greek, Italian, Lithuanian, Mexican, Polish, Russian, Spanish and so on. Mason Klein suggests that by extracting 'from the various ethnographic models a mysterious, and enduring, elemental quality, and [bracketing] a universal language against the individual conceits of portraiture', Modigliani expresses something of the essence of human existence, and that, by retaining his sitters' likeness while imposing his individual style on their physiognomy, he makes them his own, shaping them into part of his personal universe.[23] This desire to produce a 'pantheon' of those around him is perhaps comparable to the vast compilation of images of all prominent residents of Paris planned by the famous nineteenth-century photographer Nadar, although Modigliani's sitters were less well known than Nadar's at the time he painted them. It is surprising that the artist's restrained portrait style even bears a certain resemblance to Nadar's photographs of the 1870s.[24]

Contemporary accounts of Modigliani sitting in cafés in Montparnasse, sketching incessantly and then handing out drawings in exchange for a drink or a few francs have diverted attention from the importance of drawings as an essential stage in the genesis of the artist's portraits.[25] Modigliani would make several drawings, as if to familiarise himself with his sitters before fixing them in paint.[26] Sometimes the drawings relate directly to the final image, as with the sketch for a portrait of Max Jacob (1915–16; fig. 13), but more often they do not, showing the sitter from various angles or in a number of poses. Their variety contrasts with the finished portraits, which are generally frontal images of a bust- or half-length figure. Modigliani painted few profile views or three-quarter-length portraits and, with the notable exceptions of *The Little Girl in Blue* (1918) and *The Servant Girl* (*c.* 1918; cat. 31), no full-length examples.[27]

In her biography of her father Jeanne Modigliani writes, 'we know little about his working methods; he preferred a closely woven canvas and sometimes he spread a sheet of paper over the fresh paint in order to obtain a better blending of his colours.... Occasionally he finished a picture alone but in order to begin

Fig. 14 (below)
Paul Alexandre in his surgery, 1909
Photograph. Unknown photographer
Reproduced in *The Unknown Modigliani*, Paris, 1993, p. 18

Fig. 15 (opposite)
Paul Alexandre in front of a Window, 1913
Oil on canvas
81 × 45.6 cm
Musée d'Art, Rouen

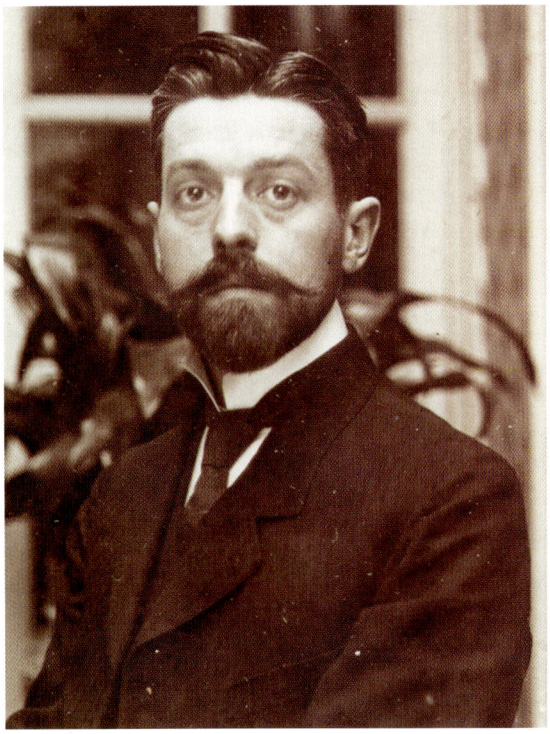

one, he always had to have a model. "To do any work, I must have a living person," he explained to [the painter Léopold] Survage, "I must be able to see him opposite me".'[28] This was not always the case, however, and Modigliani may have used photographs as aides-memoires or as tools for constructing compositions. This aspect of his creative process has yet to be explored in depth.[29]

Many artists in the early twentieth century, most notably Picasso,[30] employed photography in various ways, and Modigliani must have been aware of its potential.[31] He seems not to have owned a camera. Yet this would not have prevented him from obtaining photographs of his sitters or from being aware of the conventions and innovations of contemporary photography. The 'instantaneous' quality of his repeated images of certain sitters recalls a succession of photographic exposures.[32] Moreover, he may occasionally have recorded his work in photographs[33] and he certainly affixed reproductions and photographs of Old Master paintings to the walls of his various studios.[34]

The influence of photography may be detected in a practice that recurs regularly in Modigliani's portraits. The sitter is painted twice in a similar pose. In one image he or she appears as a half-length or almost three-quarter-length figure; omitting the feet, the artist directs the viewer's attention to the head, and often the hands, in a way familiar from traditional portraiture. In the other image Modigliani focuses solely on the head and shoulders, with particular emphasis on the eyes.[35] It is not always clear which portrait came first, but the 'cropped' version certainly recalls an image made by a photographer who has moved in to take a close-up.

Modigliani's four portraits of Paul Alexandre (three painted in 1909 and one in 1913) betray the influence of a photograph. The doctor is known to have sat for the three earlier images,[36] but not for the fourth (1913; fig. 15). The shading of the forehead and the emphasis on the eyes in the first three portraits bear a strong resemblance to a photograph of Alexandre taken in his surgery in Montmartre in 1909 (fig. 14), whereas in the later painting it is the composition that recalls the photograph, in which the windowpanes indicate a cross behind the sitter's head. In the latter instance Modigliani may have had recourse to the photograph as a means of re-familiarising himself with Alexandre at a later date, even though the stylisation of the features – reminiscent of the artist's contemporary carvings – has become more extreme and the likeness less clear than in the 1909 images.

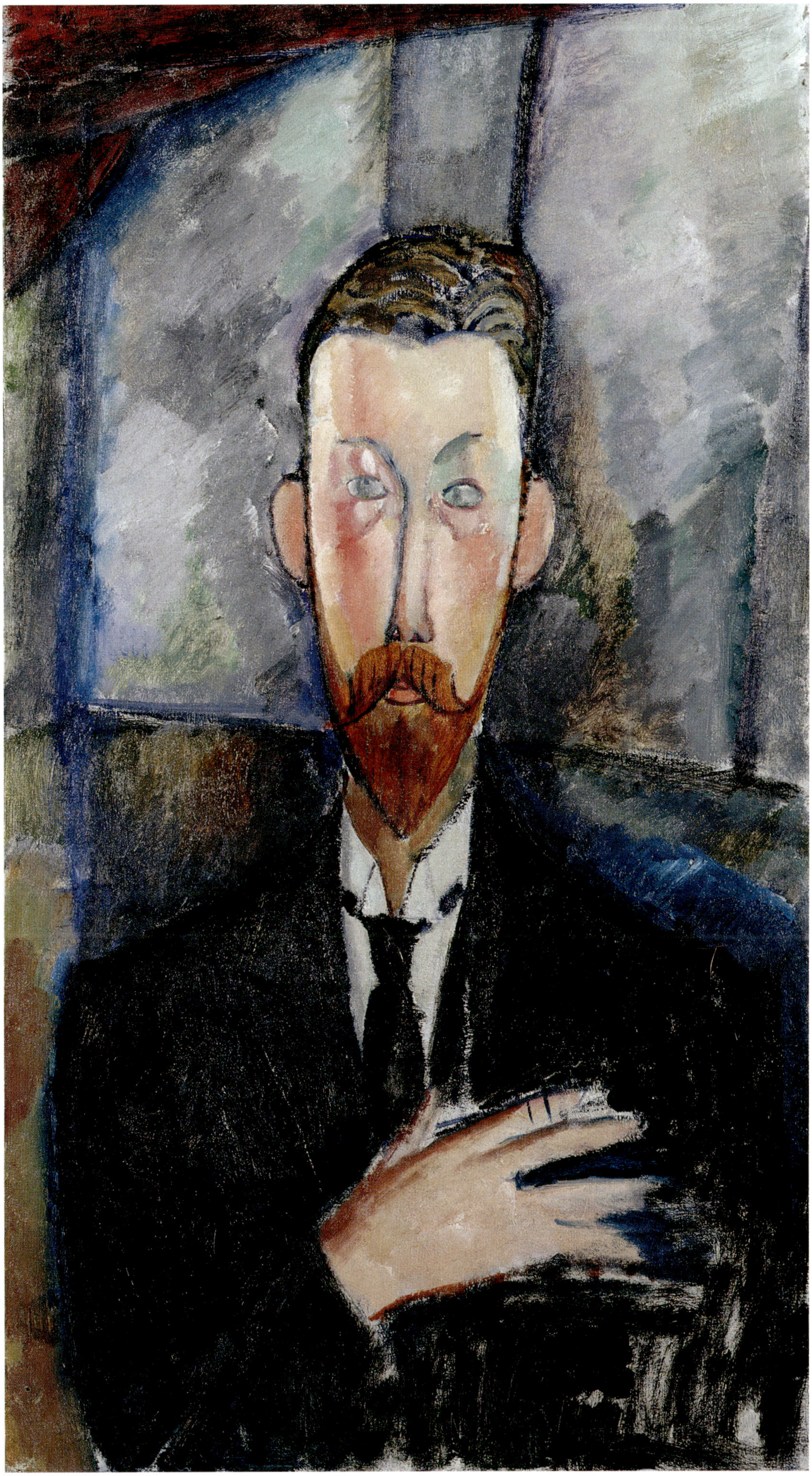

Fig. 16
Modigliani standing in his studio at the Bateau-Lavoir, Montparnasse, 1915–16
Photograph by Paul Guillaume
Archives Jean Bouret, Paris

Fig. 17
Modigliani sitting in his studio at the Bateau-Lavoir, Montparnasse, 1915–16.
(His portrait of Beatrice Hastings is behind him.)
Photograph by Paul Guillaume
Archives Jean Bouret, Paris

Fig. 18
Paul Guillaume in Modigliani's studio at the Bateau-Lavoir, Montparnasse, 1915–16
Photograph. Unknown photographer
Archives Jean Bouret, Paris

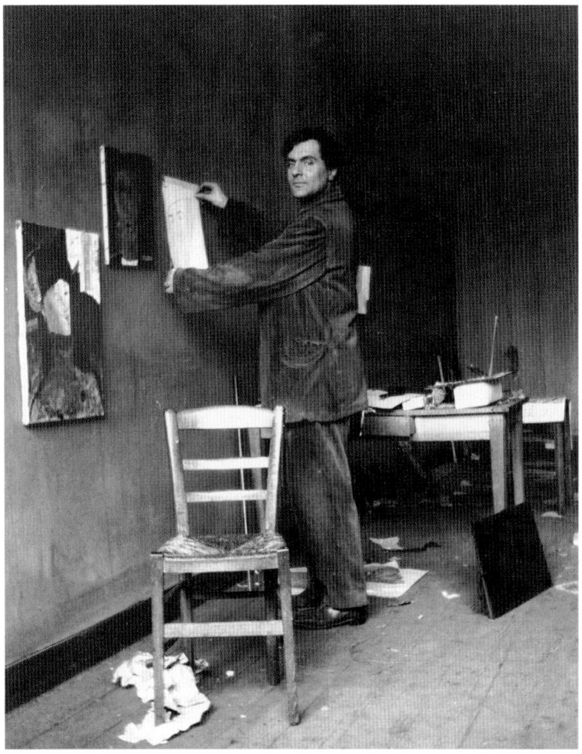

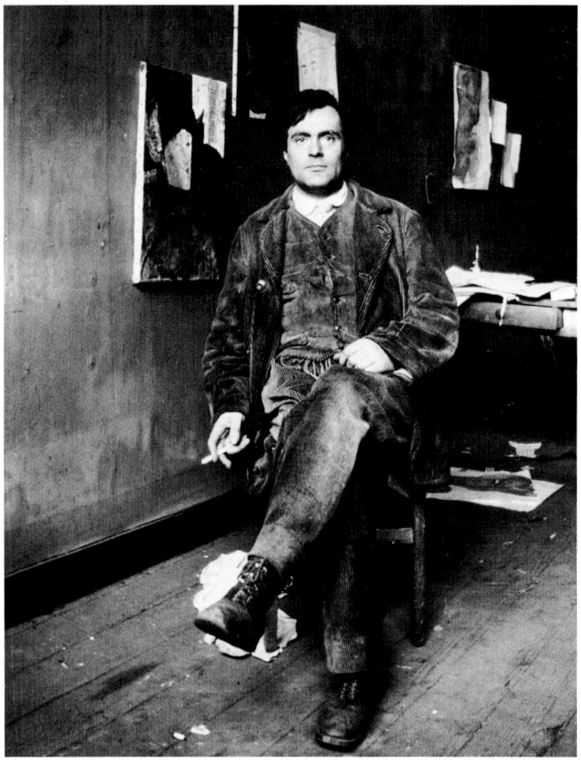

Photographs may also have played a part in one of the four portraits that Modigliani painted of Paul Guillaume, a dealer and collector of African art to whom Max Jacob introduced the artist in 1914.[37] The Milan portrait (cat. 13), painted in 1916, resembles more closely than the others a sequence of photographs taken in 1915 or 1916 in the studio in the rue Ravignan that Guillaume had rented for Modigliani (figs 16, 17 and 18). The identical position of the objects in all the photographs – the paintings and drawings on the wall, the items on the desk, even the discarded paper on the floor under the chair in the foreground – suggests that they were taken in a single session, probably in quick succession.

The first photograph (fig. 16) shows Modigliani establishing the setting for the portrait: he is tacking a drawing of a man with a hat (Guillaume?) to the wall next to his portraits of Raymond Radiguet and Beatrice Hastings; behind him are other drawings, one of a caryatid; and the chair is positioned so that the sitter's head will be flanked by the portraits. In the next two photographs Modigliani is demonstrating the desired pose, seated in front of the works on the wall (fig. 17), and in the final image (fig. 18) his place is taken by Guillaume.[38] The resemblances between this last photograph and the finished portrait are manifest: Guillaume is seated on a similar wooden chair; the fingers of his right hand are splayed; next to his head is an empty picture frame (the paintings are unframed in the photograph) with his name and the date inscribed in it at the bottom; his trilby is tilted backwards very slightly; and his head is lifted just enough to indicate that he is looking down at the artist with an almost condescending air. The painting reveals a greater degree of abstraction than the 'constructed' reality of the photographic image, but Guillaume's affectation, already apparent in the photograph, has been reinforced to suggest the artist's mistrust of his young dealer. When the urbane Guillaume took him on, Modigliani may have hoped for an improvement in his fortunes, but the dealer's motivation was primarily financial and this eventually caused a clash with the artist. By 1916 Guillaume had persuaded the more bohemian and tolerant Zborowski to take his place.[39]

A further case of Modigliani using a photograph concerns the wedding portrait of Jacques Lipchitz and Berthe Kitrosser that the Cubist sculptor commissioned from him in 1916 (fig. 20). This is one of only three double portraits that Modigliani painted – the others are *The Bride and Groom* (1915) and *Two Little Girls* (1918) – and it was one of the few paid commissions he received.[40] Lipchitz describes the genesis of the portrait:

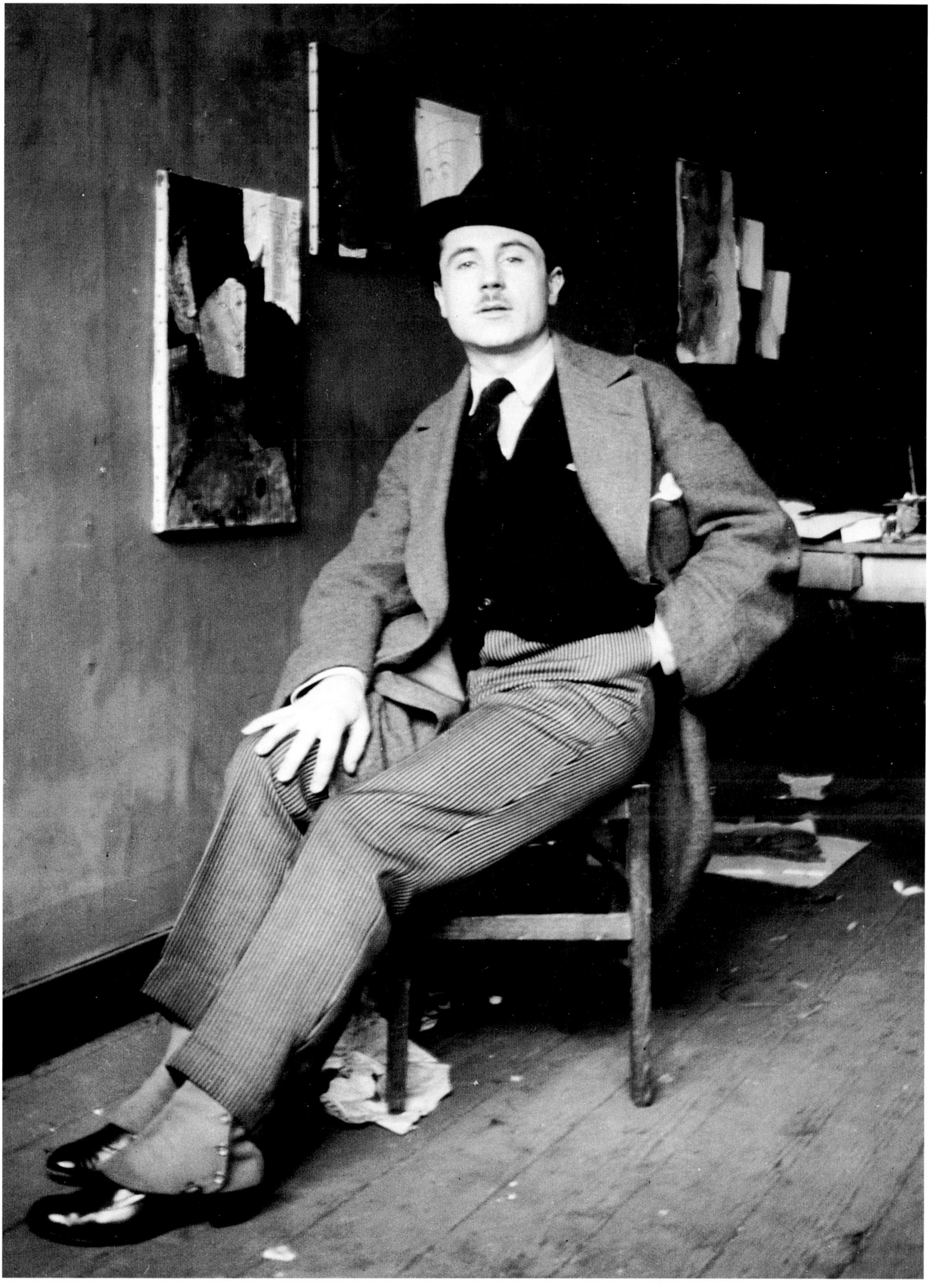

Fig. 19 (below right)
Wedding photograph of Jacques and Berthe Lipchitz, 1916
Photograph by Marc Vaux (1895–1971)
Bibliothèque Kandinsky, Centre Georges Pompidou, Musée National d'Art Moderne, Paris

Fig. 20 (bottom)
Jacques and Berthe Lipchitz, 1917
Oil on canvas
80.7 × 54 cm
The Art Institute of Chicago, Helen Birch Barlett Memorial Collection 1926.221

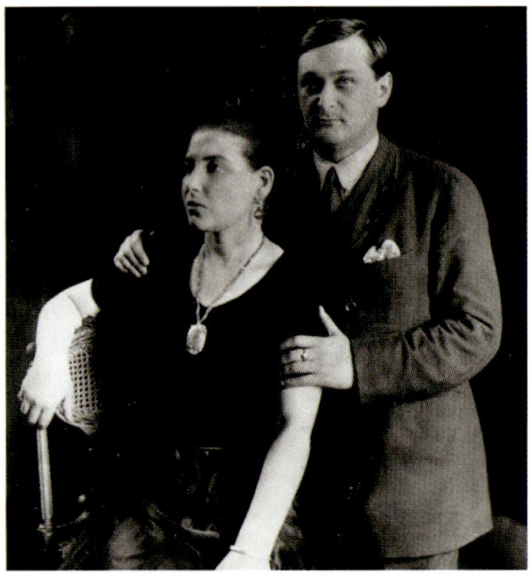

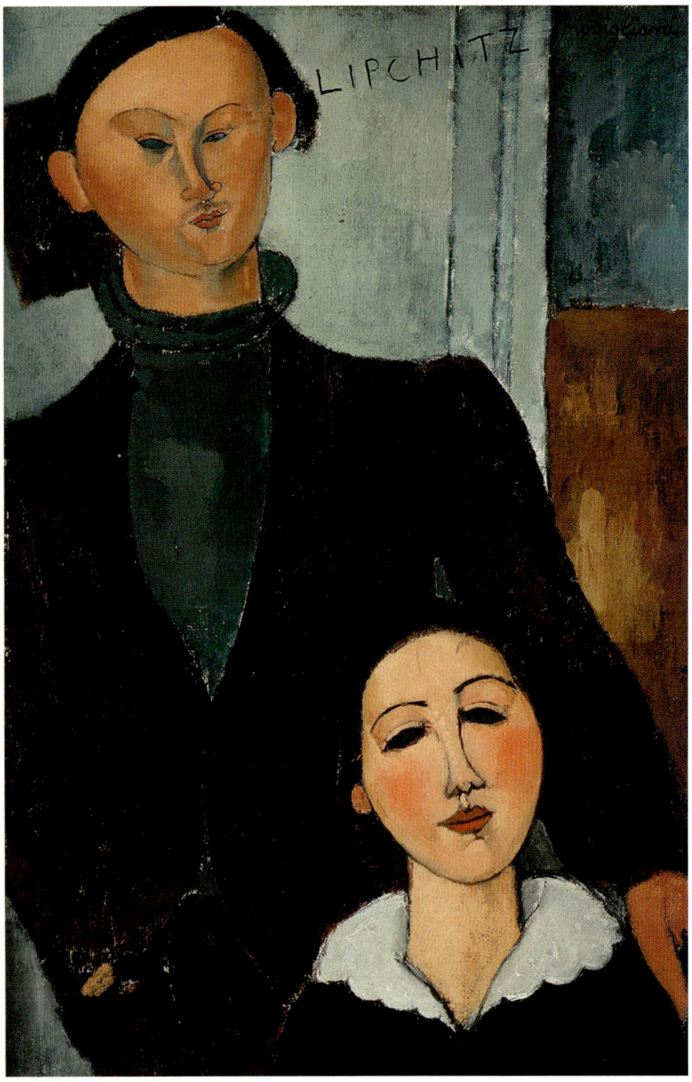

'He came the next day and made perhaps twenty preparatory drawings, very quickly, beginning with the eyes and then continuing without any hesitation. I had a photograph made by a well-known photographer [Marc Vaux] which I intended to send my parents, so he used the pose of this. The next day he came with an old canvas and began to paint at one o'clock. From time to time he would take a drink and stand back and look at it: then around five o'clock he said that it was ready.'[41]

Although Modigliani reversed the pose as shown in the photograph, he retained the relationship between the sitters: the photograph (fig. 19) shows them looking in different directions and in the painting (fig. 20), too, they appear psychologically separated. This impression evinces a lack of sympathy that is rare in Modigliani's work and may be related to the formal nature of the photograph. It also provides further evidence that the artist, though aware that an image could never reproduce fully the reality of a living person, strove to record some essential truth about the people he portrayed. Photography, which likewise produces an alternative reality, may have helped him to accomplish this aim.

At the most, two painted self-portraits by Modigliani have survived: *Pierrot* of 1915, which several historians do not accept as a self-portrait,[42] and *Self-portrait* of 1919 (cat. 52), probably the artist's last work, in which his face resembles an effigy, as though in anticipation of his imminent death.[43] This paucity of self-portraits is unusual. Many contemporaries used the genre as a vehicle of self-reflection and/or stylistic experimentation, but Modigliani preferred to scrutinise the faces of others. In a sense, however, his persistent recording of those around him constituted a voyage of self-discovery. Certainly, the resulting body of work reveals more about the artist than about his sitters. As Werner Schmalenbach has written: 'Modigliani was never tempted to tamper with the physical and physiognomic integrity of the human individual. The look of the individual was the stimulus that prompted him to draw or to paint, though all his sitters had then to be brought in line with his own idiosyncratic pictorial concerns.'[44] In making his sitters conform in this way he created a world of his own, a world filled with his vision of humanity.

Notes

1 Quoted in Modigliani 1958, p. 81.
2 Since the Risorgimento, which granted Italian Jews full legal and civil emancipation, Livorno had been notably open-minded in religious and cultural matters. Several important Italian-Jewish artists of the late nineteenth century, including Serafino De Tivoli and Vittorio Matteo Corcos, came from Livorno, which had never had a ghetto. See Emily Braun, 'From the Risorgimento to the Resistance: One Hundred Years of Jewish Artists in Italy' in New York 1989.
3 Modigliani had become acquainted with Munch's work in Venice and he will also have seen paintings by the Norwegian artist at the Salon des Indépendants in Paris in 1908, at which he himself exhibited *The Jewess* (1908) and other works.
4 Modigliani saw paintings by Cézanne at the Salon d'Automne and the Galerie Bernheim Jeune in 1907 and thenceforth always carried in his pocket a reproduction of Cézanne's *Boy in a Red Waistcoat* (1888–90; National Gallery of Art, Washington DC).
5 For a full discussion of the relationship between Modigliani's portraits and caricature, see Harrison 2000.
6 Ceroni 1970, p. 87.
7 See Buffalo 2002, p. 17.
8 For an account of Modigliani's connections to the avant-garde in Montparnasse, see Buffalo 2002, pp. 30–47.
9 Modigliani painted the portraits of no less than eight Cubists and associated with many more, but he remained independent of *la bande à Picasso*. He was thus not a representative of a notable tendency among modernist painters to depict fellow artists as a way of gaining acceptance or declaring allegiance. Shearer West, 'Masks or Identities?' in Christos Joachimides and Norman Rosenthal (eds), *The Age of Modernism: Art in the 20th Century*, Stuttgart, 1997, pp. 65–71.
10 For an account of the friendship between Modigliani and Picasso, see John Richardson, *A Life of Picasso, 1907–1917: The Painter of Modern Life*, London and New York, 1996, pp. 265 and 368–9. See also Tamar Garb, 'Making and Masking: Modigliani and the Problematic of Portraiture' in New York 2004, p. 52.
11 See Ludwig Meidner, 'The Young Modigliani: Some Memories', *The Burlington Magazine* (April 1943), pp. 87–91: 'Among more recent artists Toulouse-Lautrec and Gauguin fascinated him above all. Of the latter we had just seen the wonderful retrospective in the *salon d'automne* (1906) which intoxicated us with excitement.'
12 For an account of Hastings's life (including her relationship with Modigliani) and her writings, see John Carswell, *Lives and Letters*, London, 1978.
13 From 1914 Hastings was Paris correspondent for the English periodical *New Age*, to which she contributed a column entitled 'Impressions de Paris' until 1916. She often referred to her relationship with the artist in it.
14 Although other artists, such as Léopold Survage, Chaïm Soutine and Tsuguharu Foujita were also in the South at the time, Modigliani chose not to paint them.
15 As Shearer West has argued in 'Masks or Identities?' in Christos Joachimides and Norman Rosenthal (eds), *The Age of Modernism: Art in the 20th Century*, Stuttgart, 1997: 'The valorisation of the twentieth-century artist has also extended the meaning of portraiture, which no longer only involves producing a likeness of a named sitter.'
16 Düsseldorf 2005, p. 44.
17 Düsseldorf 2005. p. 33.
18 Léopold Zborowski was paying for Modigliani's nude models at this time and was probably unable to afford the additional cost of portrait sitters, which may account for the artist's reliance on the three women. See the essay 'Carnal Knowledge' by Emily Braun in this catalogue.
19 Mann 1980, pp. 172–3.
20 Emily Braun has noted that a high percentage of Italian-Jewish artists devoted themselves to portraiture. See Braun, 'From the Risorgimento to the Resistance: One Hundred Years of Jewish Artists in Italy' in New York 1989, p. 138.
21 Mason Klein, 'Modigliani against the Grain', and Emily Braun, 'The Faces of Modigliani: Identity Politics Under Fascism', both in New York 2004, pp. 1–24 and 25–41.
22 Mason Klein in New York 2004, p. 9. In his own mythological family history Modigliani claimed that his mother's family, the Garsins, were descended from Spinoza.
23 Mason Klein in New York 2004, p. 9.
24 Modigliani may also have been familiar with a more recent 'photographic pantheon', the official project begun in 1908 by the Italian-Jewish photographer Mario Nunes Vais of Tuscany to document the famous men and women of Italy. See Emily Braun, 'From the Risorgimento to the Resistance: One Hundred Years of Jewish Artists in Italy' in New York 1989, p. 150.
25 Modigliani 1958.
26 Neal Benezra, 'A Study in Irony: Modigliani's *Jacques and Berthe Lipchitz*', *Museum Studies*, vol. 12, no. 2 (1986), pp. 188–99.
27 It is perhaps not entirely coincidental that these full-length images are of young people, for this format was commonly used for children in contemporary studio photography. Although studio portrait photographs of adults had customarily been full-length in the nineteenth century, by the early twentieth century this convention had been abandoned in favour of three-quarter-length or, more often, half-length images, following the conventions of traditional portraiture. See Audrey Linkman, *The Victorian Photographic Portrait*, London, 1993, p. 111.
28 See Modigliani 1958 and Cocteau 1950, p. 5.
29 Those who have alluded to, but not investigated, Modigliani's use of photography are Werner Schmalenbach in Düsseldorf 2005, p. 28, and Krystof 2000, p. 19.
30 Anne Baldassari, *Picasso and Photography: The Dark Mirror*, Paris, 1997.
31 *The Artist and the Camera: Degas to Picasso*, Dorothy Kosinski, exh. cat., San Francisco Museum of Modern Art and Dallas Museum of Art, 2000.
32 See Maurizio Fagiolo dell'Arco, 'Modigliani e il ritratto. Il volto della bohème, lo specchio della cultura, l'autoindentificazione' in Lugano 1999, pp. 87–112.
33 He mentions a photograph of his sculptures in a postcard to his friend, the painter Gino Romiti. See Hall 1998, p. 10.
34 Gustave Coquiot, *Des Peintres maudits*, Paris, 1924, pp. 102–3.
35 For some examples of this, see *Frank Burty Haviland* (Ceroni 1970, 43 and 44), *Beatrice Hastings* (Ceroni 1970, 79 and 80), *Manuel Humbert* (Ceroni 1970, 135 and 136) and *Léopold Zborowski* (Ceroni 1970, 309 and 310).
36 Alexandre 1993, p. 414.
37 For an overview of Paul Guillaume and his activities as dealer and collector, see Michel Hoog, *Catalogue de la Collection Jean Walter et Paul Guillaume*, Paris, 1984.
38 The photographs have been reproduced several times and dated variously. Since the two paintings seen in them were created in 1915 and 1916 at the earliest, the photographs are probably more or less contemporary with the Milan portrait. Whether they were taken by Modigliani and Guillaume or by a third person is unknown, but the former possibility seems more likely. I thank Alain Bouret for making these photographs available to me.
39 It was not uncommon among avant-garde artists of the day to paint their dealers and patrons, and Modigliani produced portraits of Paul Alexandre, Roger Dutilleul, Léopold Zborowski (cats 16 and 29), Paul Guillaume (cats 12 and 13) and Paul Chéron.
40 Others included works ordered by Jean Alexandre, Léon Bakst and Roger Dutilleul. Modigliani's single foray into society portraiture, *L'Amazone* (1909), backfired when the sitter, a baroness, refused the work, which was then bought by Alexandre.
41 Neal Benezra, 'A Study in Irony: Modigliani's *Jacques and Berthe Lipchitz*', *Museum Studies*, vol. 12, no. 2 (1986), pp. 188–9.
42 Düsseldorf 2005, p. 31.
43 Sara Harrison in Harrison 2000 and Tamar Garb in 'Making and Masking: Modigliani and the Problematic of Portraiture' in New York 2004 liken it to a mask.
44 Düsseldorf 2005, p. 31.

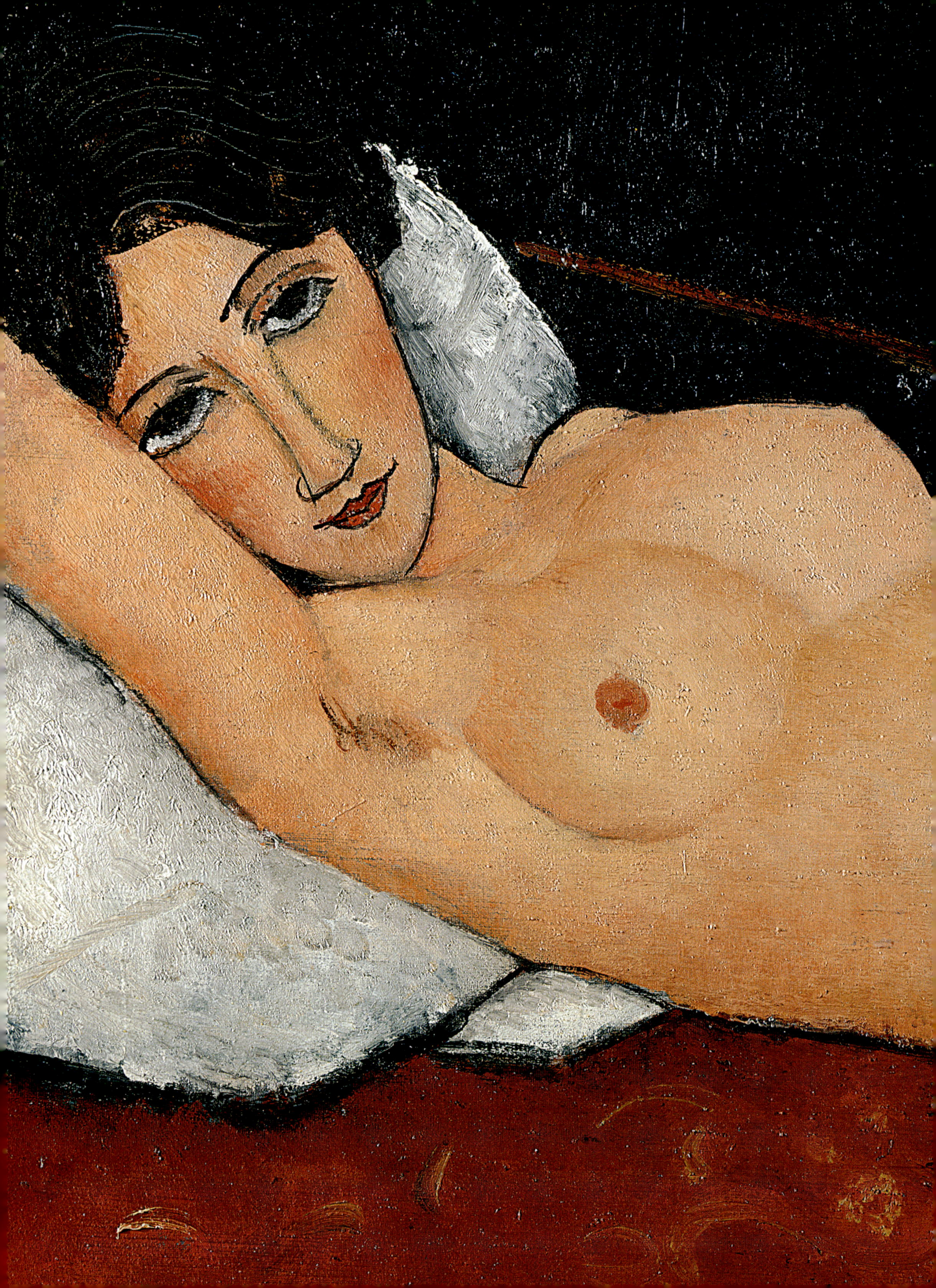

Carnal Knowledge

Emily Braun

> This only – of that moment – can I tell:
> that even as I gazed at her, my soul
> was free from any other need as long
> as the Eternal Loveliness that shone
> on Beatrice directly, from her eyes,
> contented me with the reflected light,
> But, conquering my will with her smile's splendour,
> she told me: 'Turn to him and listen – for
> not only in my eyes is Paradise.'[1]

The most startling aspect of a Modigliani nude, what makes it immediately identifiable, is the way in which the female body is literally in your face. A more delicate way of putting it is not possible, nor would it do justice to the manner in which the bodies languish parallel to the picture plane and then sprawl into the foreground (cats 18, 21 and 23 and fig. 31). The torso rotates so that the pelvis twists up, tilts back and pushes the hips and thighs into the viewer's proximity, disarmingly so, since the perspectival distortion makes the pubic area loom overly large by comparison with the rest of the body. The models lie with their shoulders back and arms raised, their round abundant breasts echoing the undulations upward and out. The women's bodies flow expansively beyond the edge, as if to emphasise that the bounded plane of the canvas cannot adequately encompass the swell and stretch of line and muscle. Modigliani's compositional strategies draw attention to the physicality of the human form and to a female sexuality that exceeds the 'normal' confinements of the nude in painting. Although his canvases are only average size, these images often take up the entire room. Long before Helmut Newton, Amedeo Modigliani did *big* nudes, big in presence, sexuality and historical ambition.

The seductive quality of Modigliani's nudes presents a problem: are they compelling experiments in modernist form, or kitschy images of women putting on the look of sexual desire? Are they art, or are they soft pornography? The aesthetics of high art tease out the perceptual capacities with the aim of transcending the material everyday. Vulgar and demeaning by definition, soft pornography plays on our 'base' instincts. But perhaps the two are not such strange bedfellows here. What may begin as disinterested formal analysis or salacious curiosity turns into an engagement of the senses and the mind, not only with the female as sex object, but also with the pictorial embodiment of carnality, with the unadulterated truth of the body. Canonically beautiful bodies, true, but here and there an ungainly limb or wayward breast, a sag or protuberance aggresses in visceral plenitude, distant antecedents of Jenny

Fig. 21
Reclining Nude (La réveuse),
1917
Oil on canvas
23.5 ×36.5 cm
Collection of William I. Koch

Fig. 22
Erotic postcard, late nineteenth century
Hand-coloured photograph
Unknown photographer
Private collection

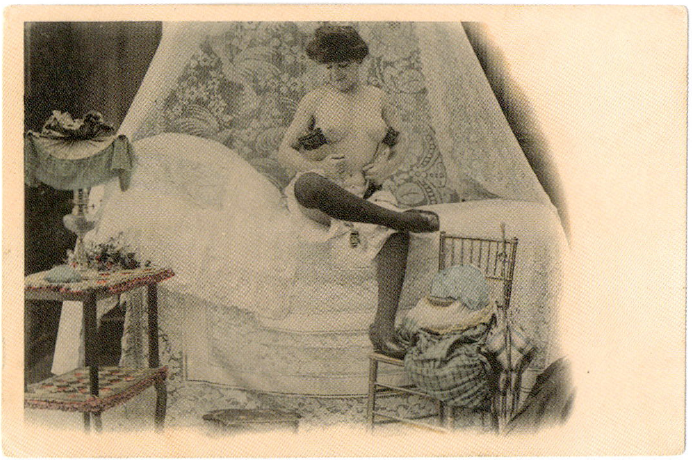

Saville's gorgeously painted grotesques. Modigliani unites the flesh of the model and the pictorial surface into something sentient and alive.

It is often observed that a Modigliani nude resembles a *Playboy* centrefold, but it is really the other way around:[2] Modigliani initiated the compressed view and rectangular format whereby nudity unfolds before the eye. He was the first to represent a female (or any) body in this manner and, in doing so, upset the conventional relationship between the viewer and the flesh and genitalia on display. As with Giorgione's *Sleeping Venus* (*c.* 1510) or Edouard Manet's *Olympia* (1863), the unclothed woman normally reclines in the middle ground; a distance of decorum protects the viewer from a potentially unsettling confrontation with nakedness, or, alternatively, bestows a more commanding vantage point. Though the bare body is 'natural', its natural condition is not one of public display. Distance also brings with it the space necessary to fill the scene with other information, such as the allegorical realms and attributes that situate the nude as a figure both of nature and of culture, a symbol of biological destiny and creative inspiration. Modigliani's nudes, by contrast, lie in a restricted visual field that allows for minimum allusion. The broad areas of colour and shape designate the background wall, the surface of a couch, a blanket and a pillow, but their identities are almost unimportant, as the luxuriant hues serve only to accentuate the bodies' curves and highlight the glow of skin, to force the viewer into close encounters of an overly familiar kind.

The frankness of Modigliani's bodies collapses the distinction between naked and nude, and follows from the invasive and liberating 'honesty' of the camera. By the late nineteenth century, naked bodies were being seen aplenty in snapshots and postcards in the pornographic image trade. Despite the harsh realism of photography, conventions still distanced the figure by placing it in the middle ground or seeing it from behind, with the face hidden.[3] Pornography as a genre of visual representation originated with reproductive print technologies, but it exploded with the invention of photography and its promiscuous traffic of images: what was once reserved for a select few in private became vulgar through public dissemination.[4] Through the ubiquity of the postcard, collectors could even own a series of striptease images with the same model in a series of progressive undress (fig. 22).[5] These aptly named 'nudie shots', diminutive and diminished in their attempt to mimic high art, copied the poses of famous paintings, or included 'classy' accoutrements in the attempt to give respectability to the prurient. Those who

Fig. 23
Paul Outerbridge, Jr (1896–1958)
Reclining Nude, *c.* 1937
Carbro colour print
31.1 × 46 cm
Phillips de Pury and Co, New York

Fig. 24
Lee Friedlander (b. 1934)
Nude, 1980
Photograph
Courtesy of Fraenkel Gallery, San Francisco, and Lee Friedlander

– then and now – deem Modigliani's nudes trashy use the same reasoning: the tradition of the nude and the designation of 'high art' are merely covers for ogling the female body.

Yet photographic images of naked female bodies before Modigliani do not come close to his compositional daring. Instead it is in 'art' photography after Modigliani (photography of the nude) that we see his singular influence. In the anatomical twists or exaggerated close-ups by Paul Strand, Alfred Stieglitz and Edward Weston, the subtle stylisations of Modigliani's forms become exercises in sculptural rhythm and riveting defamiliarisation. Other photographers, such as Paul Outerbridge, mimicked the effects of Modigliani's carnal verisimilitude in the use of painterly colour, light and texture (fig. 23). Lee Friedlander's series of nudes from the 1980s represent a direct homage to Modigliani's modernist legacy of formal innovation, right down to specific poses. The body presses up against the plane and occupies the entire spatial field. Friedlander indulges in the same elongations and linear sweeps of the torso, the same compressions of the bent leg or elbow that result in weird, abstracted shapes of what remains recognisably the body (fig. 24). For these images, like those of Strand, Stieglitz and Weston, distinguish themselves from the violent distortions and fragmentations of Surrealist trick photography. This is the body whole and photography straight, as Friedlander seizes precisely on the visual edge between naturalism and formalism first articulated by the Modigliani nude.

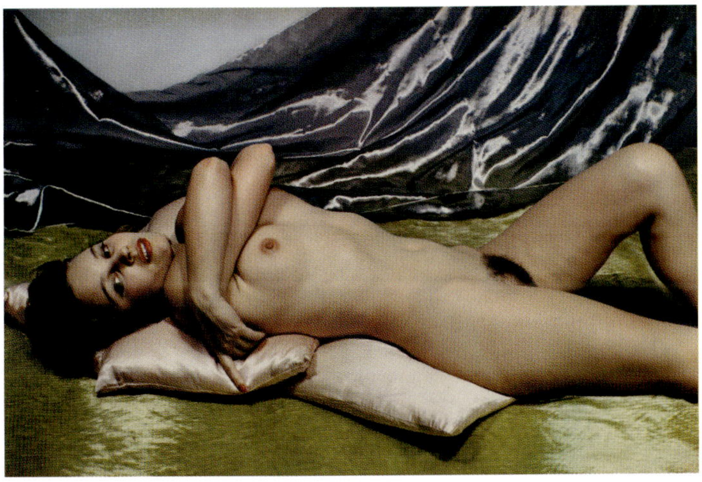

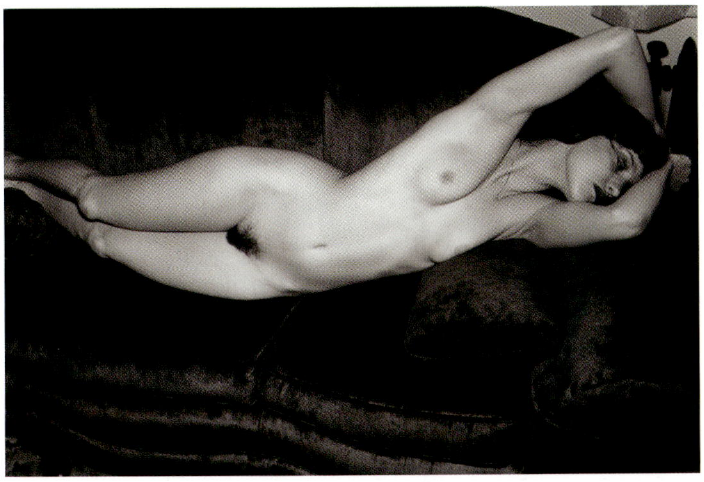

When photography usurps Modigliani's viewing position, it trumps him in raw explicitness. Photography cannot compete, however, with the actual sensuality of the painterly medium, no matter what pose the model strikes. The disembodied transparency of the photograph is sensorily deprived, as the eye comes into contact with a reflected or imprinted surface, not actual texture, with light, not material substance. By contrast, Modigliani's brushwork acts like touch: it dabs, with the pressure of a finger against the epidermis, or strokes with the motion and feel of a caress. (Although all the clichés of the male artist's possession of the female form in creative delectation come to the fore in this description, here the pleasured viewer is a woman.) Colour does not work alone. Line, for its part, grabs the edges of skin pulled over bones, or feels the weight of fatty tissue. The senses are intensified as sight couples with tactility.

Modigliani's ability to create a visual and textural analogue to the plumpness, softness and sheen of real skin deliberately rivals that of Titian, but from his pearlescent hues of pink and gold, Modigliani visually raises the temperature of the body with

Fig. 25
Lisa Yuskavage (b. 1962)
Beads, 1999
Oil on linen
50.8 × 35.6 cm
Courtesy of the artist and
David Zwirner, New York

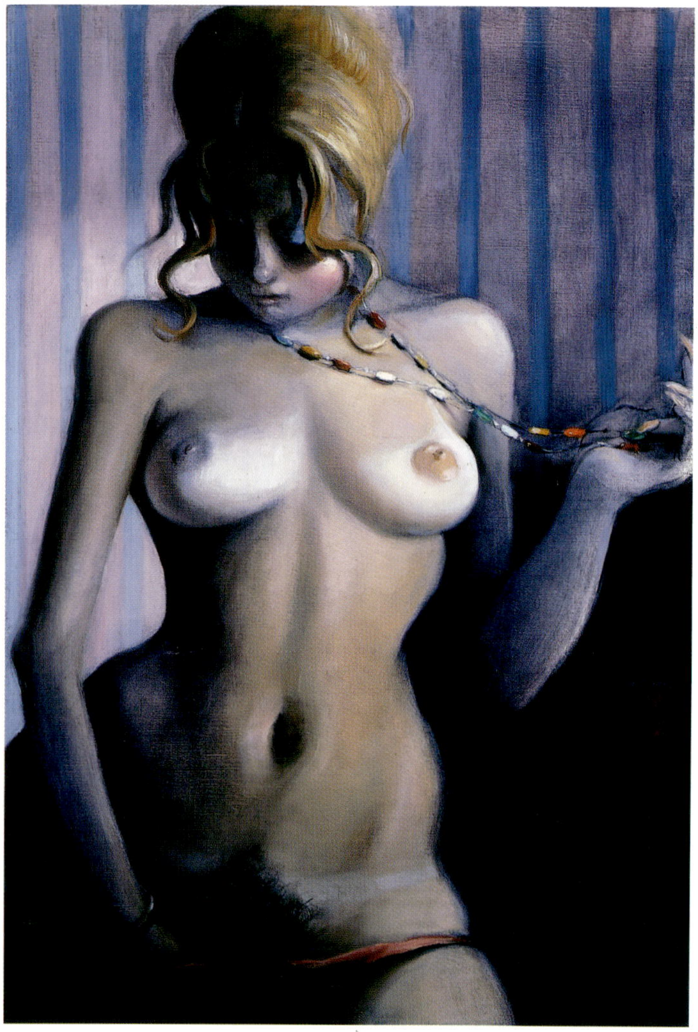

post-Fauve red, apricot and deep rose (see cats 18 and 21). He often applies a red aura at the contours of the figures to force the association of a body flush with desire. The viscous medium of oil adds to the affinity between paint and skin that goes beyond mere cultural convention. Varnish can further the visual effect of sheen after the paint has dried. Modigliani applies the layers to the surface so one perceives the oily shine of the hair, the slightest perspiration of a moist and breathing skin. The surface appears more translucent where flesh merely covers bone, becomes thicker over areas of corpulence and the occasional scabrous patch at knee or elbow acknowledges that skin has a life of its own.

As David Rosand has observed, the perception of sensual beauty 'traps the gaze', channels the other senses through the eyes – 'touch above all' – and 'enlivens' it.[6] The 'danger' this power of arousal may create, the crossing of the line between the erotic and the pornographic, depends on who is viewing what, and where. Obscenity is defined by what certain groups deem offensive to common decency (and not only in the realm of sexuality). In his 1927 monograph on Modigliani, Giovanni Scheiwiller admitted that he chose not to reproduce some of the artist's nudes, so 'as not to run the risk of being fined according to the statute in Article 339 of the Penal Code'.[7] Modigliani's 'sumptuous' images had already caused a minor scandal in late 1917 when exhibited at Berthe Weill's gallery in Paris, in his first and only one-man show. One nude, visible through the gallery window, drew a crowd that gathered to leer at, or be shocked by, the glorious expanse of unrepentant flesh. The local police chief (whose offices were located across the street) sent an officer to order that the nudes be removed, and the exhibition was temporarily disrupted.

Modigliani's painting of a nude, displayed to every passer-by on the pavement, threatened civic order and affronted public morality. It had the power to draw a crowd, incite a fracas, but, according to Weill, the grounds for censorship were specifically the 'indecent' depiction of pubic hair.[8] The conventions of visual representation in early twentieth-century art had not yet admitted this degree of explicitness, especially in public, and even in a house of art. Despite the standard association of woman with nature, this depiction was evidently much too natural, down to Modigliani's ability to evoke the assortment of lifelike textures – furry, bristly and wiry – with the hair of the paintbrush.

By today's standards, of course, Modigliani nudes seem tame. Compare them with Lisa Yuskavage's *Beads* (1999; fig. 25), with its lurid colours and blatantly smutty scenario. The spectator is inextricably put in the position of the voyeur, that is, the model is supposedly unaware that she is arousing the male viewer. But because the image is photographically derived – in source material and airbrush effect – we know that she knows that we know she is posing for the viewfinder, while pretending to unselfconsciously fondle herself. The nudes of Yuskavage, a woman artist, can be taken as ironic riffs on the degrading conventions of media representations of women.[9] Some of her images exaggerate the breasts and buttocks to the point of absurdity and evoke discomfort or pain. Like most pornography, the blatant realism, the ugliness, repels. It actually fails to arouse, unlike a Modigliani. Yuskavage, like Jeff Koons before her, challenges the distinction between art and pornography – traditionally held to be aesthetic and moral opposites – by simply applying Marcel Duchamp's principle of the readymade: can you make a work of art out of something that is not a work of art? If *Beads* had been painted by a man instead of a woman, the argument for its being a critique of humiliating representations of female sexuality would have fallen by the wayside. In the same way that the nude in high art can be a cover for nakedness, gender fallacy can accommodate – and intellectualise – bad taste and bad painting.

Are Modigliani's nudes guilty of what Yuskavage critiques, of being party to an exploitative viewpoint by fiat, gendered male and inherently lascivious? Theorists of the male gaze collapse Kenneth Clark's original distinction between the naked and the nude into a series of binary opposites that expose the unequal power relations between nature and culture, passive object and active creator, female and male.[10] But perhaps the ladies and gentlemen do protest too much. The presumption of a typecast, prejudicial beholder forecloses contextual interpretation, denies the role of a female viewer (as well as the allure of images of men), while ignoring crucial distinctions in the construction of subjectivity, such as class, education, sexual orientation and religion. Emphasising the literalness of looking blinds one to the complexity of metaphor; it also ignores the potential for mediating gender difference, as the beautiful thing perceived returns the gaze with the 'aliveness of the person's own consciousness'.[11]

That blatant desire is projected onto the nude is now a given; more critical is whether that desire is inspiring or repressive, and how it relates to an understanding of human sexuality, gender and aesthetic discourse in a specific historical culture. Modigliani's nudes are uniquely poised to take centre stage in the debate on looking because they are both 'sexy babes' and an exegesis on the equivalence of female and artistic beauty. In the context of the modernist avant-garde, where the aesthetic notion of the beautiful is vanquished by the sublime, Modigliani's nudes bravely, or naively, proffer seductive beauty. They self-consciously refer to the idealist tradition of the Renaissance, while being painted in the historical moment of 'love for sale'. A connoisseur of Dante as well as of women, Modigliani understood the subtleties and variations of Beatrice's gaze after the glare of Zola's Nana.

The link between his nudes and those of the Italian Renaissance was paramount to Modigliani, as a proudly Italian artist and émigré in Paris, where he moved in 1906 from his native Tuscany. Immersed in the art of Florence and Venice, he would have been well aware of the age-old *paragone*, the rivalry between sculpture and painting and the primacy of sight over the other senses in the perception of beauty and creation of desire. His peers in Montparnasse always perceived the literate Modigliani as the sophisticate *à part* in bohemia, 'a pig and a pearl', as his former lover Beatrice Hastings confirmed.[12] Artists and critics in Montparnasse testified to his affection for early Renaissance art and his deep familiarity with the poetic conventions of chivalric love in *The Divine Comedy* and Petrarch's sonnets.[13] He had reproductions of the Old Masters in his studio, in particular, works by Botticelli, Titian and the consummate painter of sensuality, Correggio. Modigliani aimed at revitalising the Italian humanist tradition of the nude, in which ideal female beauty, and hence art itself, embody 'all sensuous pleasure, including sexual pleasures of the flesh'.[14]

Several of Modigliani's compositions emulate the archetypal poses of the Renaissance nude: the raised arm of the sleeping Venus or abandoned Ariadne; the at-ease demeanour of the reclining, open-eyed Venus propped up triumphantly on her pillows. His *Reclining Nude with Loose Hair* (1917) quotes Titian's *Venus of Urbino* (1538; fig. 29) – and in turn, Giorgione's *Sleeping Venus* – with the left arm emerging narrowly from under the left breast, widening slightly as it rises alongside the abdomen to end with the hand falling over the pubic area in the gesture of the Venus Pudica (fig. 29). Yet Modigliani's women are hardly modest – how could they pretend to be or want to be? Bashfulness runs contrary to all the libidinous associations evoked by Modigliani's enlivening touch and to the images of women depicted by his artistic forebears. Certain gestures betray his implicit understanding of venerable iconographic devices: fingers curled at the pudenda denote the self-pleasure allowed

Fig. 26
Ivan Meštrović (1883–1962)
Caryatids
Plate V from *Ivan Meštrović: A Monograph*, London, 1919
The British Library

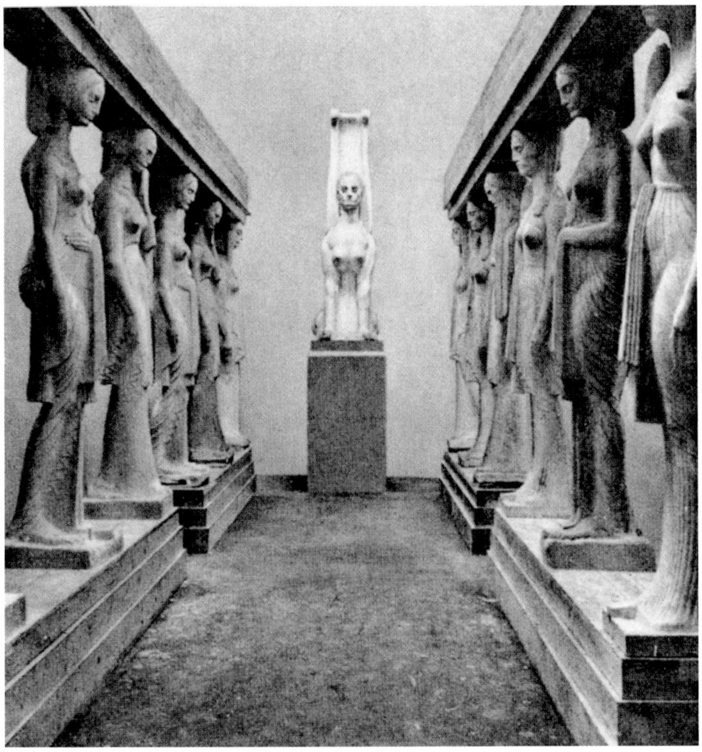

to the female sex, by sixteenth-century theology and medical science, for procreative purposes.[15] Moreover, in his beloved Renaissance prototypes the artist found many examples of visual pulchritude stimulated by a female gaze, where women gloat over their conquests, punish illicit looking with merciless regard, or are bestirred by male beauty. To perceive the sexual confidence of Modigliani's women as exclusively modern is to misunderstand the power afforded them in Renaissance images. Titian's nudes, or works such as Botticelli's *Venus and Mars* (*c.* 1485), embodied a powerful female sexuality, one established in mythology and theology and keenly attuned to the lively gazes of goddesses and brides – proud, retributive, tender, confident or attentive – anything but passive.

Modigliani's first concerted efforts at the nude were conducted in sculptural form. Between 1909 and 1914 he experimented in direct carving, tutored by his neighbour Constantin Brancusi and under the influence of Cycladic art and African sculpture. His series of limestone heads, hieratic and totemic, reduce the facial features into a graceful and contemplative symmetry. Yet with one exception, a carved caryatid, Modigliani drew his sculptures of the female body. His numerous watercolours, pencil drawings and gouaches of load-bearing caryatids articulate the body in rhythmic volumes, abstracting the swells of breast, thighs and abdomens in formal unison. Though they would ostensibly have been carved out of limestone, Modigliani coloured them for the most part in red and rose. Occasionally one finds a voluptuously open mouth, thrown-back head, or surreptitiously brazen pose; otherwise sexuality is sublimated by the ornamental fringes of hair and almond-shaped eyes, notably orientalist in flavour.

Modigliani intended his standing and kneeling figures to be architectural elements, 'columns of tenderness' in a 'Temple to Beauty'.[16] He exhibited the carved heads as a 'decorative ensemble' in the 1912 Salon d'Automne. Scholars cite Brancusi as a major influence on his sculpture, but Modigliani's idea to create an edifice of worship undoubtedly owed much to a widely exhibited project by the sculptor Ivan Meštrović for his *Temple of Kosovo* (fig. 27). A Croatian and Yugoslavian nationalist, Meštrović conceived his memorial to the fourteenth-century defeat of the Eastern Orthodox Serbian kingdom by the Ottoman Turks as an overt call for independence from Austria-Hungary in the years before the First World War. Meštrović maintained a studio in Montparnasse in the impasse du Maine from 1907 to 1909, and exhibited numerous works in the Salon of 1908, including figures of kneeling and crouching women carved in stone and wood. Encouraged by Auguste Rodin, he showed eighteen sculptures in the 1909 Salon d'Automne, among them 'fragments' and caryatids from the Kosovo series. Modigliani's caryatids – otherwise an aberration in contemporary Parisian sculpture – can be explained by Meštrović's functional use of such figures in the loggia and tower of his monument.[17] Not only the temple idea came from Meštrović: Modigliani found an affinity also with the Croatian artist's stylised figures and surface patterning, full of references to Egyptian art and Assyrian reliefs.

More thematic fantasy than architectural reality, Modigliani's 'Temple to Beauty' nonetheless revealed his desire to worship on the altar of visual pleasure, to revive a humanist theme in a secular age and still keep it sacred. The idea of a profane temple was a contradiction in terms; better to treat the live and present body as something to revere in itself. He could not revive the Renaissance tradition of the sensual nude without turning to the carnal verisimilitude of paint. In the *paragone* of the arts, painting triumphs over sculpture because it simulates the perception of touch, despite the actual three-dimensionality of the carved or modelled form. At a time when lifelikeness in art determined artistic greatness, Renaissance artists engaged in a debate over colour versus line, the feminine versus the masculine art of representing nature. In this contest Modigliani sided with Titian over Michelangelo. Moreover, the modernist distillation of pure form, the process of abstraction epitomised by Brancusi, ran counter to Modigliani's interest in the human comedy, as manifested in his lasting fame as a portraitist. Yet his work with sculpture inevitably left its mark on his painted depiction of the body, in the incised quality of the outlines, the internal arabesques and inscribed volumes. The visual tension between painting and sculpture, flatness and rotundity, the eye and the hand, only adds to the efficacy of perception in Modigliani's work.

Like the caryatids, the nudes were the result of a concerted effort. He completed 35 between 1916 and 1919 (the majority in 1917) on commission from the Polish expatriate and dealer, Léopold Zborowski. Modigliani painted the live models in a makeshift studio, a room in Zborowski's own apartment at 3 rue Joseph Bara. He continued in his new dwellings at 8 rue de la Grande Chaumière – also found for him by Zborowksi and his wife, Hanka. Zborowski supplied the materials as well as the models, and paid Modigliani fifteen francs a day against his cumulative production. Apparently the models received five francs per sitting.[18] The artist demanded isolation and was

Fig. 27
Ivan Meštrović
Temple of Kosovo
Plate II from *Ivan Meštrović: A Monograph*, London, 1919
The British Library

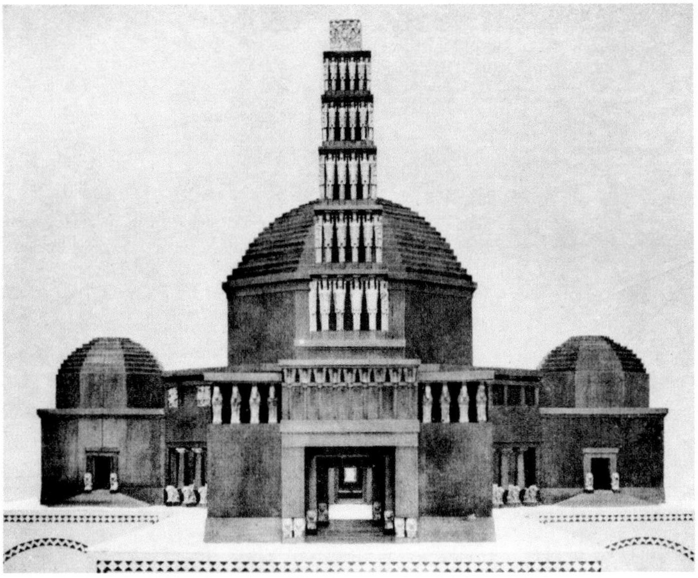

furious when Zborowski once interrupted him to steal a glance at a particularly attractive blonde model.[19]

Modernist artists work in series to reduce and extrapolate an overriding abstract principle, yet Modigliani's nudes reveal as much about the idiosyncrasies of individual anatomies as they do about the constancy of pure form. Knowing them to be a group obliges us to consider the individual in relation to the larger whole, and the minor variations from one to another are as telling as any one painting. Of the 35 nudes, some two-thirds feature models reclining along the horizontal axis, while the remaining stand or sit in a vertical format. The artist's fully nude 'grand horizontals' are far more successful than the upright figures, whose bodies appear stiffer in pose and pictorial handling, and are often semi-draped, their facial demeanours less at ease (cats 17 and 36).[20] Dark-haired, naturally voluptuous, with sun-imbued skin, most of Modigliani's models conform to the ethnicities of many professional, paid models in turn-of-the-century Paris: Italians and Jews.[21] Their specific type and their stereotyped carnality are borne out by comparison with the thirteen paintings in which Modigliani depicts the thinner, pale-skinned Parisian grisette. Distinctly less sensual, the fair-haired models consistently appear in the less satisfactory, vertical paintings. That Modigliani painted for the most part *la belle italienne* or *la belle juive*, and made her all the more appealing, begs the question of his identification with them as others, like himself, in a foreign land. Sexual difference may well be mitigated here by commonality of other kinds, which partially explains the pointed lack of misogyny in his images.

Modigliani had to revive the sensual nude after its artistic decline in the late nineteenth century, for under the aegis of an outworn neoclassicism, it had become little more than a genre of trite dishabille in mythological or biblical guise. Works such as Alexandre Cabanel's *The Birth of Venus* (1863; fig. 28), the archetypal example, relied on slick props and surfaces to offset the scurrilous pretext of leering at a passive or coy femininity. Typically, the female deflects her own gaze or bats a *faux-modeste* eye in a staging of the voyeuristic act introduced by photographic theatricality: the *pretence* that the model is unaware of being seen – though she may or may not be. The instantaneous image, unlike the painted one, can be taken furtively. (That an image is 'taken', and not rendered, is instructive here.) Because the eye behind the lens is hidden from others' sight (the observed cannot judge exactly where the gaze rests) and, as the camera can be wholly concealed, photography reproduces the conditions of the peephole, the

Fig. 28
Alexandre Cabanel (1823–89)
The Birth of Venus, 1863
Oil on canvas
130 × 225 cm
Musee d'Orsay, Paris

pornographic view. Whether the model was actually aware of being photographed or not, the ontology of the photograph also tells us that the image is a real person, not a potential figure of the imagination. The realism of being 'caught' (feigned or actual) constructs a new, unequal power relation of viewer and subject, and sets in motion the dehumanising process of routine appraisal. Like the provisional gaze of the *flaneur*, with which it is often conflated, the camera eye roves; it shuns mutuality and empathy. Aware that everyone is looking, the model now performs for an audience: she is no longer the *femme honnête* but a *fille publique*. What was once intended for a single viewer as the beloved's gaze becomes a come-on available to all.

The debasement of the Salon nude in the later nineteenth century results from the absorption of the voyeuristic theatricality of photography and, with it, the performative role of the model (as opposed to the rhetorical role of the earlier nude in painting). *Olympia* could have been conceived only post-photography. The confrontational comportment of Olympia – the stunning force of her ocular retort – was a realignment of what had recently become a parsimonious and exploitative

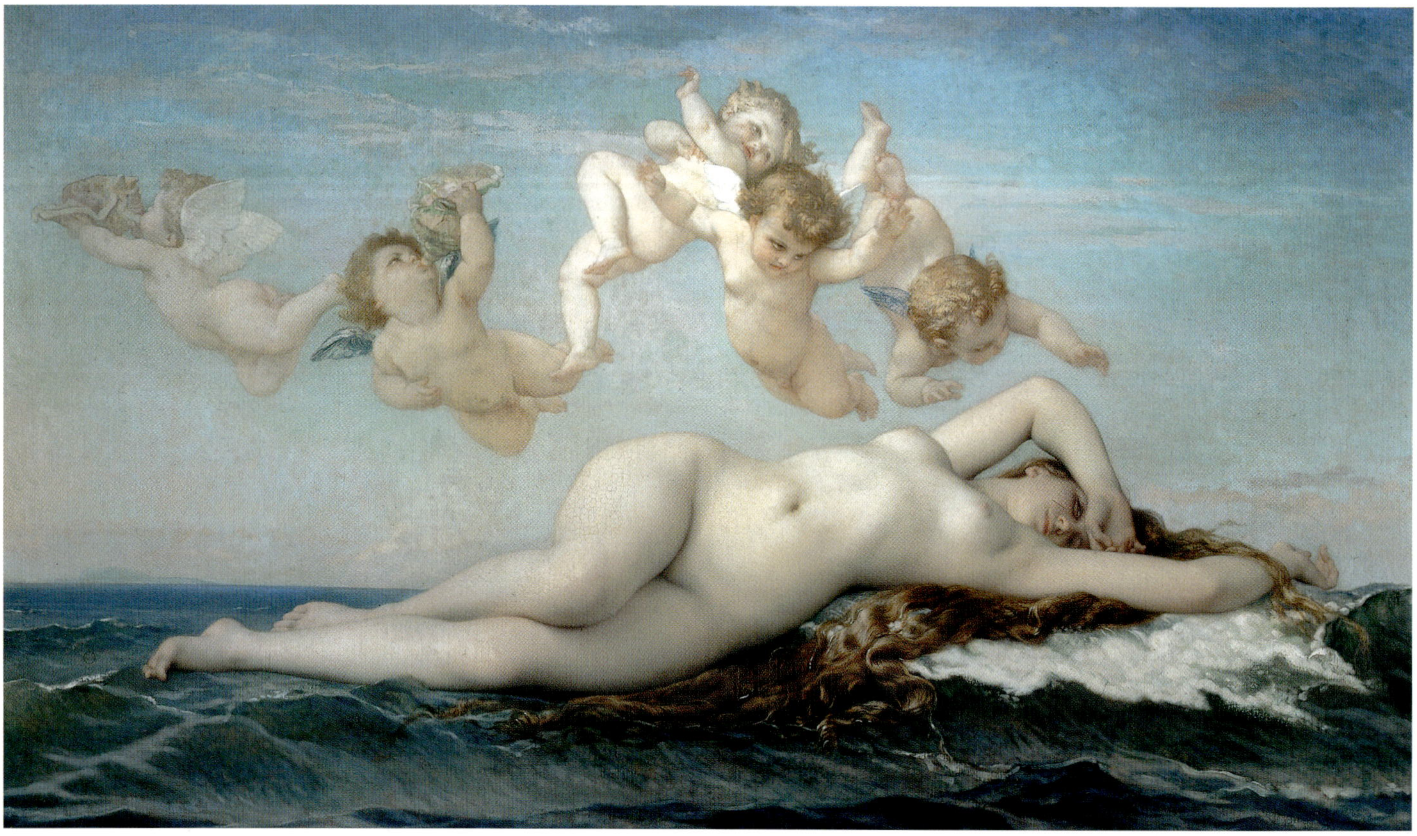

Fig. 29
Titian (*c.* 1487–1576)
Venus of Urbino, 1538
Oil on canvas
119 × 165 cm
Galleria degli Uffizi, Florence

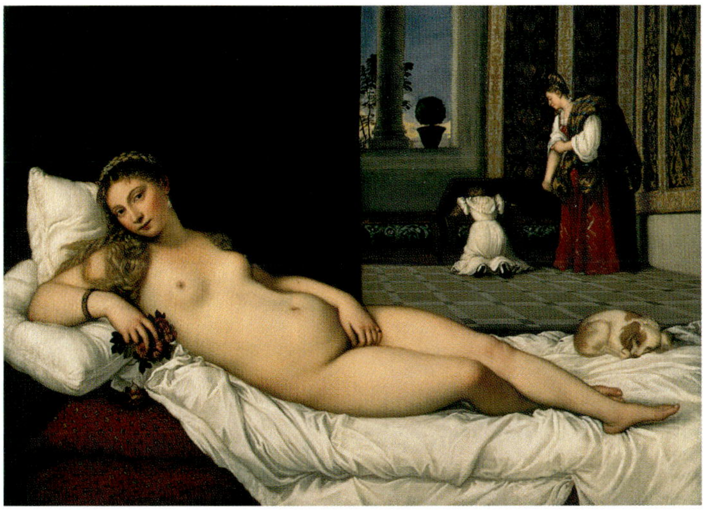

beholder's share. Not by chance, the theory of the objectifying male gaze that took hold in art-historical studies as a universal condition of viewing (paradoxically, given its critique of Kant's universalising aesthetic of beauty) originated in the domain of cinema and photography studies in the mid-1970s.[22] As an interpretative tool, it has had valuable currency for late nineteenth-century art, where 'the relations and disjunctions of the terms "woman"/ "nude"/ "prostitute" were obsessively rehearsed'.[23] The view from *Olympia*, however, must not prejudice our eyes to an understanding of the gaze in earlier centuries. Made for private beholding and often for the purposes of symbolising the conjugal compact, paintings of the nude were proprietary but not improper. The little dog, symbol of fidelity in Titian's *Venus of Urbino* (1538; fig. 29), the painting on which Manet's exposé turns, reveals all: unlike the startled cat belonging to the prostitute Olympia, the dog sleeps, because the one who has just entered the room to admire and be admired is the husband and master of the household.[24]

Damaged goods, the nude could never be looked at again in the same way after Manet's candid irony, and as if to underline this fact, he rendered the female figure in a distinctly uncorpulent, unsensual way. Nor could modelling be easily distinguished from whoredom. It would take decades, until Modigliani, for the woman-goddess to be made beautiful again, and then merely as human flesh, not divine substance, formal experiment or diseased body. After Manet, the next step in decontextualising the nude was to paint the model at work, the sociological reality of ordinary, money-earning women, as in Georges Seurat's *Poseuses* (1886–8).[25] Here is the raw material of art – mundane, bored, and mute – Seurat seems to say, as he even debunks the potential erotic frisson of undress in the studio by having the models perfunctorily place their clothes, rather than strew them with zest. In these same years Edgar Degas observed the female model with unprecedented proximity and intimacy. He avoids depicting their faces, as if to protect their privacy as he scrutinises the body as specimen, in all of its awkward physiognomy.[26] As close as he is, Degas allows enough space for the viewer to understand that these women are going about the daily ritual of the bath, lest the strange contortions of their bodies suggest that he is up to something deviant. In Degas, we have the beauty of the body as line, form and colour, beauty uncoupled from carnality of sexual desire.

The erotic nude fought back, though, with new strategies to recuperate it from the realist assault. Artists once again removed woman from everyday life and immersed her in the unspoiled

Fig. 30
Paul Gauguin (1848–1903)
Manao tupapau (Spirit of the Dead Watching), 1892
Oil on canvas
72.4 × 92.4 cm
Albright-Knox Art Gallery, Buffalo, New York

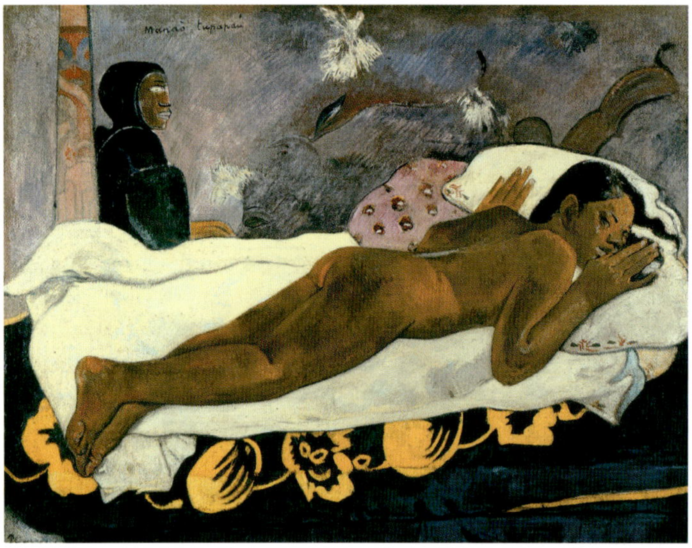

Fig. 31
Nude with Coral Necklace, 1917
Oil on canvas
66.5 × 101.1 cm
Gift of Joseph and Enid Bissett, 1955. Allen Memorial Art Museum, Oberlin College, Ohio 1955.59

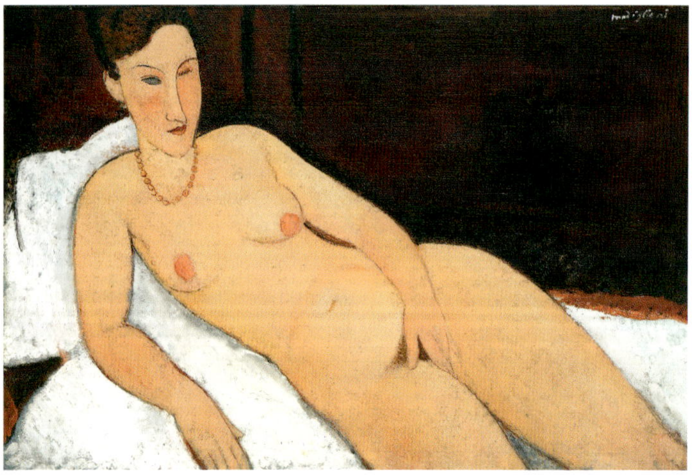

nature of field and jungle. Though painters such as Paul Gauguin and Pierre-Auguste Renoir rebelled against the academic tradition in their depiction of the female body, they subscribed to the official view of female sexuality (imparted by evolutionary theory and medical anthropology) as atavistic and animalistic. Lounging and preening in the woodland glades, Renoir's nudes play the role of fecund nymphs bathed in the mythic glow of lubricious ease. The posturing of an unfettered sexuality for the male viewer meets its match in the dreamy (read: vacant) looks of the women. Modigliani's reputed disgust over a conversation with Renoir about painting 'buttocks' warrants belief.[27] For Gauguin, an artist whose work Modigliani did admire, the nude is naked savage draped in otherness and superstition. In *Manao tupapau (Spirit of the Dead Watching)* (1892; fig. 30) the nubile young woman cowers provocatively from the gaze of the menacing eye of the idol behind her, embodying Gauguin's fantasy, as he put it, that women 'long to be "taken", violently'.[28]

What is immediately apparent by comparison with these predecessors is how naked Modigliani's models, and the paintings, really are. He dispenses with the tease of partially clothed bodies, and even the realist trope of depicting the model's unworn street apparel. In four images the models wear jewellery: in *Nude with Coral Necklace* (1917; fig. 31), it functions equally as a formal device and an erotic enticement, the loop and coral colour echoing the curves and palette of the body. Red lips abound, but the faces are not heavily made up in a masquerade of femininity or in allusion to the meretricious profession, nor are there mirrors or other articles of the feminine toilette to impugn the narcissism of the female. There is, notably, a pointed lack of rhetorical gestures of feigned modesty (a few do look dubious), mock terror or self-adoration. Distanced from exotic or Arcadian locales, the images are likewise denuded of any narrative – anecdotal, erotic, melodramatic, or moralising – and this bareness allows the eye to concentrate on the senses. There are no episodic events save painterly ones: corpulent strokes that burst through the inscribed volumes of a limb, areas of impacted brushwork, the stain of pigment in the aureole of a breast.

Yet the mannered visages and honed undulations of Modigliani's nudes point to a new development in the Parisian avant-garde. By the first decade of the twentieth century, the relatively benign South Sea idylls of Gauguin were replaced by a ferocity and fetishism directly inspired by African sculpture. The competition for artistic greatness again took place over the

Fig. 32
Henri Matisse (1869–1954)
Blue Nude (Memory of Biskra), 1907
Oil on canvas
92.1 × 140.4 cm
Museum of Art, Baltimore. The Cone Collection, formed by Dr Claribel Cone and Miss Etta Cone of Baltimore, Maryland, BMA 1950.228

body of women, but this time in daring pursuit of pure form and wanton experimentation.[29] Henri Matisse's *Blue Nude: Memory of Biskra* (1907; fig. 32), like Ernst Ludwig Kirchner's *Girl Under a Japanese Umbrella* (*c.* 1909), aggressively presses the nude into the foreground plane like a Modigliani, but intimacy is, paradoxically, withheld by the dehumanising mask and pictorial violence. What Wendy Steiner has termed the 'prostitutional sublime' – the estrangement of beauty in favour of the monstrous pleasure of otherness – culminates in Pablo Picasso's *Les Demoiselles d'Avignon* (1907).[30] By affixing tribal masks onto the faces of his whores, Picasso made explicit the prevalent association of the atavistic female with promiscuity, savagery and black skin. Marriage to Venus now implied cursory, adversarial and sadistic coupling, filled with mortal danger and sexual deviance.

Modigliani's style reflects the linear schematisations and formal reductions of the masks and carvings he saw in the collection of Frank Burty Haviland or filtered through the work of Picasso, Brancusi and others. However, in his case, modernist devices compete with the influence of Trecento and Quattrocento Italian primitives, with the rudimentary features and asymmetrical eyes of Simone Martini's Madonnas and the elongated bodies and unquiet torsions of Botticelli. Italian critics between the First and Second World War were quick to point out the 'spirituality' and 'chasteness' of his nudes as a result of these sources.[31] To be sure, elements of the non-Western primitive add to the heightened sense of eroticism in Modigliani's work, for it connotes a sexuality free of Christian Puritanism and guilt (in contrast to his Jewish heritage, which had a less fraught attitude toward carnality).[32] Most important, unlike his avant-garde contemporaries, Modigliani does no harm to the female person: he shuns the representation of disjointed body parts, lacerations or scarification of the flesh or the projection of pain. Ultimately, his stylisations, the formalist curves, bends, protrusions and cavities, are the means to an end of an intense tactile sensation, a more naturalistic sensuous experience. Precisely because his gentle modernism (too elegant for some) is much less 'advanced' than the radical deformations of his Parisian peers, it relinquishes the expression of misogyny. Likewise, his evocation of lifelike flesh poignantly reminds one of the carnality of any body, female or male, and eliminates the distance between self and other.

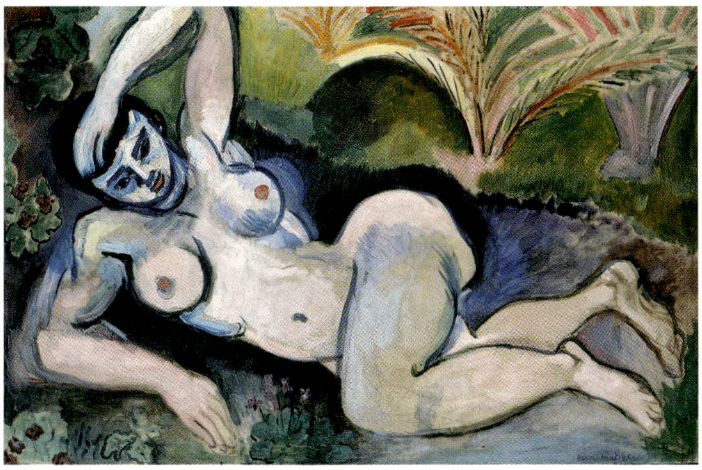

Instead of degradation and fear, Modigliani's nudes display a comfort with the female body – on the part of the artist and the model – a comfort that comes forth in the here and now of the practical, protected environment of the studio. While other modernist nudes did not need a real person for their abstracted, corporeal fantasies, Modigliani's subjects, as the viewer has no doubt, were live and lively. We presume them to be neither goddesses nor whores, but simply women; and the artist does not intimate that their work entailed sexual favours. Modigliani apparently did not mix work and romance; the women with whom he conducted long-term affairs do not feature as painted nudes.[33] A viewer can fantasise about Modigliani's relationship with his models: a vision of fleeting consummation perhaps, or, given the long hours of posing and painting, a fantasy of conversation between them – dialogues about Italy with the Italian models, or about being Jewish with the Jewish, or gossip about personalities in Montparnasse. In the workaday tedium and concentration of their tasks, one can imagine them breaking for a cup of tea or coffee or, as was Modigliani's wont, a smoke of hashish. Amid this conjecture, the fact of their equal status is clear. Some of the models may or may not have worked as prostitutes, as the professions often crossed over, but Modigliani's position was just as ambiguous and commercially driven. Destitute and desperate, hardly the master of his own genius, he worked for hire, obliged by Zborowski to paint nudes because they were easy to sell and to use his seductive artistry for predetermined financial gain. Under the circumstances, these women 'sold' themselves no more or less than he did.

All told, the demeanour of the nudes reverses the usual power relations of domineering artist and passive model, accentuated under modernist primitivism, to one of reciprocity. The faces of Modigliani's nudes are not portraits, but neither are they standardised. The mask works both ways: it can intensify desire by suggesting the illicitness of the unknown, or protect the individual from full exposure. Modigliani's reliance on a masklike visage exempts him from a descriptive realism, as the face becomes congruent with the overall seductive schema of the tactile body. Even then, individuals emerge, and we can thus ascertain that some of the women posed for the artist more than once, and that some were quite plain, their homely features breaking through the stylised mould. Nor do the masklike inflections prevent the variety of countenances one would expect from the comings and goings of different personalities, the initial awkwardness, subsequent indifference and fatigue of endless looking. Most have direct contact with the artist and the viewer: some faces are a little bored, a few look querulous, and others throw off a come-hither invitation. Several of the images do attend to the slumbering female, yet even here Modigliani

Fig. 33
Lucian Freud (b. 1922),
Nude With Leg Up (Leigh Bowery), 1992.
Oil on linen
182.9 × 229 cm
Joseph H. Hirshhorn Purchase Fund, 1993 (93.7). Hirshhorn Museum and Sculpture Garden, Smithsonian Institution, Washington DC

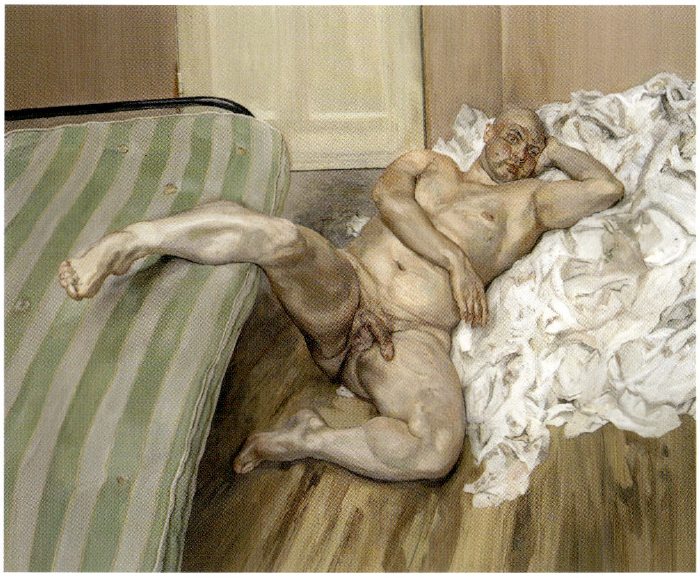

makes the body tensile, not supine, in its languor. Confidence, ease and self-possession rule. The women of Modigliani's nudes are actively and pleasurably looking too, and why not? Modigliani was a famously beautiful man, the constant object of covetous gazes, a man as deeply aware of observing as of being observed.

No wonder André Salmon declared Modigliani 'our only painter of nudes', the sole 'painter of women from life'.[34] The naturalism of the models' nakedness and their comfort with it, as evidenced by their gazes, distinguished them from the kickers and screamers of Kees van Dongen, the sentimental, domestic nudes of Pierre Bonnard (namely, his pictorially concealed wife) and the later sloe-eyed odalisques of Matisse. The fact of the matter is that Modigliani was a loner, because the nude had reached a dead end by the beginning of the First World War. With Cubism, the nude became a ghost of its former self or a series of non-sentient body parts geared to mechanistic dynamism and simultaneity. Carnality was at furthest remove from the high-modernist project. In their 1910 manifesto of painting, the Italian Futurists, Modigliani's compatriots, banished the female nude, declaring it a symbol of all that was abject and enervating. Filippo Tommaso Marinetti produced his fantasy of a non-organic, self-procreative male out of his frustration with the sexual allure of women and the inevitable decrepitude of the body. According to the sublimated desire of his machine aesthetics, the invincibility of a speeding car proved more seductive than the delicacy of the Winged Victory of Samothrace. Modigliani must have realised that the sensual nude was taking its last breaths, and his was the last attempt to revive it.

The lack of conviction in the modern nude becomes immediately apparent in the work of his followers, in the school of the wooden dolls (André Derain) or vacuous Barbies (Moïse Kisling). Women artists did not yet have the opportunities, social permission or sexual confidence to paint the nude in this sensual way, the exception being the bisexual Emilie Charmy, whose paintings of the pleasured female body from the 1920s have clear affinities with Modigliani's style.[35] Only with Lucian Freud several decades later does the carnal nude show its skin again, with men seen in the same close-ups and angled views that Modigliani had reserved for women (fig. 33). If Degas had uncoupled beauty from carnality, Freud now unleashed carnality from beauty. In this unforeseen mating of Venus and Marsyas, flesh appears flayed and overly bountiful, at times hideously alive.

Fig. 34
Egon Schiele (1890–1918)
Girl with Black Hair, 1911
Watercolour and
pencil on paper
56.2 × 36.7 cm
Gift of the Galerie St Etienne,
New York, in memory of Dr
Otto Kallir; promised gift of
Jo Carole and Ronald S. Lauder;
and purchase. Museum of
Modern Art (MOMA), New
York. Drawing 626

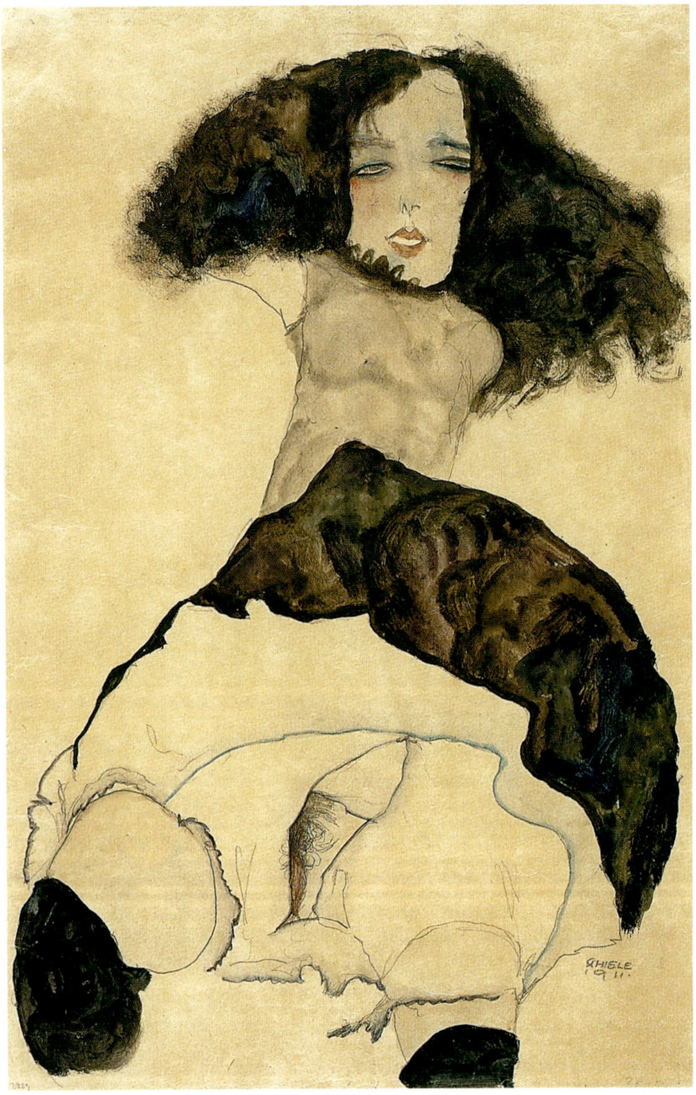

In the midst of the First World War, Modigliani was the last practitioner of the sensual nude; but this is not to say that the nude was not concurrently being pursued in other ways – primarily two. With Egon Schiele, the models open their legs to the unconscious and a probing exploration of human sexuality, to the eyes of the clinic and psychoanalysis (fig. 34). Schiele's images of men and women, with their lacerating line and cool pallor, frequently sick-coloured or decaying with green and black wash, flirt with the strange beauty of abjectness. Schiele's naked self-portraits announce a new genre – body art, no longer the nude – with its attendant sadistic motions and narcissistic self-regard. The modern psyche's traffic with perturbation and titillating disgust in these still, patently, carnal bodies rendered Modigliani's vision anachronistic.

Yet Duchamp made both their approaches to the nude simultaneously irrelevant, when, in *The Large Glass* (also known as *The Bride Stripped Bare by her Bachelors, Even*; 1915–23) he stripped the bride of art bare altogether. The nude in modern times had become mere fetish, he opined, reducing the heights of aesthetic pleasure to the depths of sexual gratification. In the logic of his neo-Kantian project to return art to the pureness of the mind and divorce it from the senses, Duchamp extirpated the nude by refuting painting. He devoted his intellectual energies to *Etant donnés* (1946–66), which enshrines the painted mise-en-scène of illicit looking presented in Manet's *Olympia*. Peering through two holes in a wooden door, we are taken aback by the shocking sight of a three-dimensional cast of a naked, hairless, lifeless female body (fig. 35). Duchamp ritualises the dehumanising experience of the onanistic disembodied eye, by arresting our gaze and projecting it violently back at us.[36]

Duchamp's apotheosis of the desensitised male gaze, child of the camera, is woefully inadequate for the viewing experience of a Modigliani nude, which demands a long and deep engagement of the eye and the other senses: these were the conditions of their making, and their present-day beholding substantiates the reciprocity of the original exchange between artist and model. In a daily professional relationship with a flesh-and-blood woman about the representation of carnality, the gaze is anything but voyeuristic, because there is no pretending or hiding of sight. Nakedness, defined by Kenneth Clark as the body 'huddled and defenceless',[37] reveals itself to be a body unashamed, filled with the humility, pride and sensual delights of carnal

Fig. 35
Marcel Duchamp (1887–1968)
The peephole view of *Etant donnés. (1. The Waterfall 2. The Illuminating Gas)*, 1946–66.
Mixed media assemblage
Approx. 242.5 × 177.5 cm
Philadelphia Museum of Art

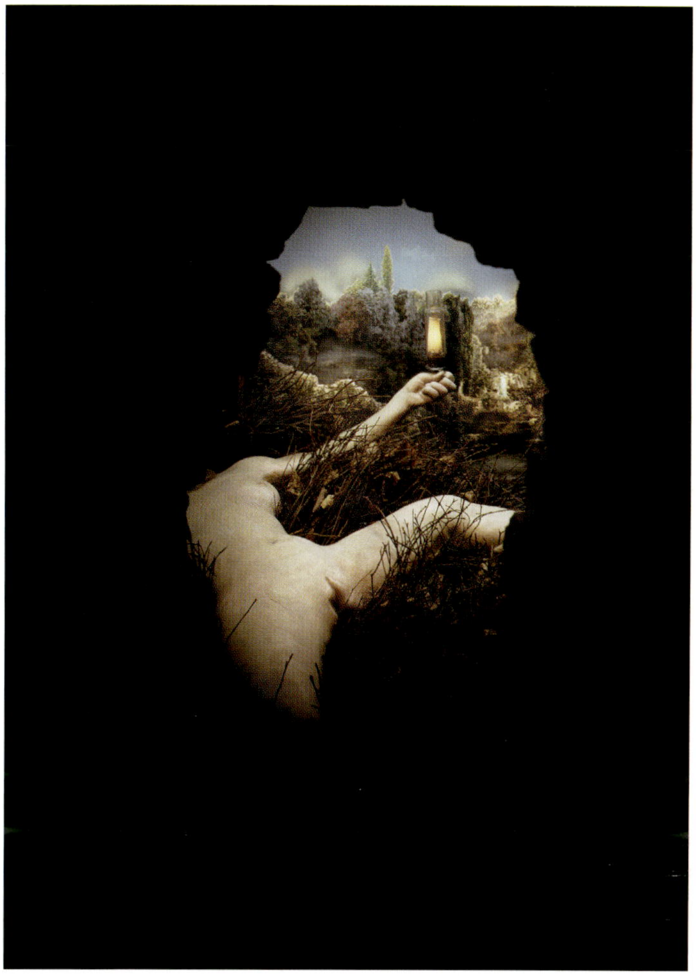

knowledge. That Modigliani's nudes are visibly pleasurable is undeniable, but since when is the perception of loveliness harmful to the thing perceived? More often than not, the confrontation with beauty can decentre, disarm and overpower, making the viewer vulnerable. As Elaine Scarry has written, beauty can move one to empathy and insight, and it creates the desire to protect, not destroy, to please the other, not degrade. Far from being injurious, the gaze here instils a longing for social equality through the aesthetics of fairness – fair play and fair countenance – that animates the beholder's senses *and* the sense of being just.[38]

Finally, we should ask, just who is gazing at these pictures from 1916 to 1918? Where are the men supposedly enjoying the female sex of Modigliani's big nudes? Most young men of procreative age were away fighting in the war. While he painted in relative comfort in his studio, drugging his already tubercular

Fig. 36
Blinded gas casualties of the 11th Brigade, Australian Imperial Force, lying out on the Casualty Clearing near Bois l'Abbée, 27 May 1918.
Photograph. Unknown photographer
Imperial War Museum, London, E (Aus)4852

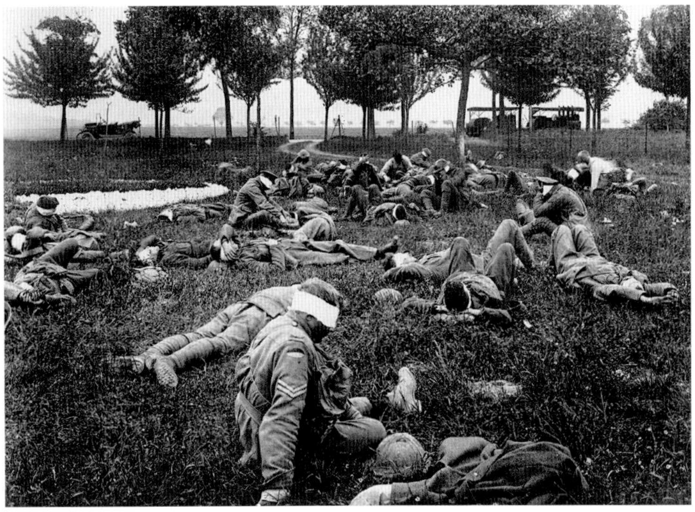

self to death, one and a half million Frenchmen lost their lives in the trenches, and three times as many were brutally and for ever injured. The male gaze in these years is bandaged, face down in the mud or obstructed by mustard and tear-gas (fig. 36). Loss of sight – actual or as a metaphor for the total darkness of death – fills the literature of the war years: in the fragmentary sensations of *Notturno* by Gabriele D'Annunzio (1921), written on thousands of strips of paper to guide his fingertips during a temporary loss of vision; or in the British poetry of the trenches, 'blind with blood', in the words of Siegfried Sassoon.[39] Many soldiers lived to hear, but not see, the women teaching them Braille. Men cannot gaze when they have no sight.

Herein lies the offence of Modigliani's nudes, their affront to common decency. What is truly obscene is that Modigliani painted such gorgeous female bodies, whole and sensual, flushed rose by the vitality of a beating heart and pumping arteries, while several miles away the limbs of men were being blown to bits. That marks their gender difference in 1917.

Notes

I am grateful to Simonetta Fraquelli for inviting me to write about Modigliani's nudes, to my sisters Marta Braun and Anita Agar for their comments on the manuscript and to my editor, Anna Jardine.

1 *The Divine Comedy of Dante Alighieri. Paradiso*, trans. by Allen Mandelbaum, New York, 2004, p. 159, lines 13–21

2 Kruszynski 1996, p. 96, compares some of the artist's nudes to Playmates.

3 As James Elkins writes in *Picturing the Body: Pain and Metamorphosis*, Stanford, California, 1999, p. 195, pornographic images without faces block the 'possibility of human discourse' and allow 'nothing further to be deduced about relationships'.

4 Lynn Hunt, 'Introduction: Obscenity and the Origins of Modernity 1500–1800' in Hunt (ed.), *The Invention of Pornography: Obscenity and the Origins of Modernity*, 1500–1800, New York, 1993, p. 13.

5 See Lynda Klich, 'The Female Nude in the Golden Age of the Picture Postcard', *Visual Resources* 17 (2001), pp. 435–48.

6 David Rosand, *The Power of Images: Studies in the History and Theory of Response*, Chicago and London, 1989, pp. 349–61, and, especially, p. 354.

7 Scheiwiller 1927, p. 10.

8 Weill 1933, pp. 224–9. When she asked what was wrong with the nudes, the officer stuttered: 'These nudes! ... they have hhhair [sic]!'

9 *Lisa Yuskavage*, Claudia Gould (ed.), exh. cat., Institute of Contemporary Art, Philadelphia, 2000.

10 Sir Kenneth Clark, *The Nude: A Study in Ideal Form*, London and Princeton, New Jersey, 1956. For an excellent summary of the discourse on the nude and nudity and its relationship to the male gaze, see Lynda Nead, *The Female Nude: Art, Obscenity and Sexuality*, London and New York, 1993, especially Part 1, 'Theorizing the Female Nude', pp. 5–33. An early critique of the overuse of the male gaze by the art-history academy is made by Marcia Pointon in Chapter 1, 'Reading the Body: Historiography and the Case of the Female Nude' of *Naked Authority: The Body in Western Painting 1830–1908*, Cambridge, England, and New York, 1990, pp. 11–34.

11 Elaine Scarry, *On Beauty and Being Just*, Princeton, New Jersey, 1999, and London, 2000, p. 89. A similar argument for 'the meeting of self and Other in a "beautiful we"' is proposed by Wendy Steiner, *Venus in Exile: The Rejection of Beauty in Twentieth-Century Art*, New York, 2001, p. 93.

12 Hastings quoted in Düsseldorf 1990, p. 194. Hastings and Modigliani, by all accounts, had an abusive relationship, exacerbated by excessive drinking on both their parts.

13 As Jacques Lipchitz wrote in Lipchitz 1952, n.p., 'Even after I had known him a long time, Modigliani would surprise us often with his love and knowledge of poetry – sometimes at the most awkward moments.' Like Lipchitz and other biographers who knew him, Adolphe Basler in Basler 1931, p. 8, recalls that Modigliani specifically recited from Petrarch's sonnets and from Dante's *Divine Comedy* and *Vita nuova*, and was also enamoured of the French Symbolists, the Comte de Lautréamont, Baudelaire, Verlaine, Rimbaud and Mallarmé. See also Salmon 1926, p. 9, and Ilya Ehrenberg (cited in Düsseldorf 1990, p. 191): 'I don't think I have ever met another painter who loved poetry so deeply. He could recite by heart verses from Dante, Villon, Leopardi, Baudelaire and Rimbaud.'

14 Rona Goffen, *Titian's Women*, London and New Haven, Connecticut, 1997, p. 169. The Italian artist Osvaldo Licini recounted Modigliani's awareness of the long-standing aesthetic principle that the mastery of art meant the mastery of women: 'To draw is to possess', he cried 'an act of knowledge and possessing that is more real than sexual intercourse,' (cited in Düsseldorf 1990, p. 196).

15 See Rona Goffen, *Titian's Women*, London and New Haven, Connecticut, 1997, pp. 152–3. In the sixteenth century, the woman's 'emission' (orgasm) was considered essential for conception, and thus masturbation was tolerated under these circumstances and implicit allusions were made to it in certain representations of the female nude. On a different view of the 'pudicated' nude as a device of male mastery and power hierarchies, see Nanette Salomon, 'The Venus Pudica: Uncovering Art History's "Hidden Agendas" and Pernicious Pedigrees' in Griselda Pollock (ed.), *Generations and Geographies in the Visual Arts: Feminist Readings*, London, 1996, pp. 69–87.

16 Modigliani described his caryatids in this way, according to Ossip Zadkine and Paul Guillaume, cited in Düsseldorf 1990, p. 20. See also Werner 1962, pp. XXII and XXVI. Zadkine also reported that Modigliani painted some of his sculptures.

17 *Exposition Ivan Meštrović*, exh. cat., Jeu de Paume, Paris, 1933, p. 6; *Ivan Meštrović: A Monograph*, London, 1919, pp. 32–3 and 60–2; and *Société du Salon d'Automne. Exposition de 1909*, Paris, 1909, pp. 149–50. Modigliani would have known also that the *Temple of Kosovo* was first presented in full in Rome, in the Serbian pavilion of the 1911 Esposizione Internazionale in Rome, where it achieved widespread attention for its political message; see Emily Braun, 'Klimtomania/Klimtophobia' in *Gustav Klimt: Modernism in the Making*, Colin Bailey (ed.), exh. cat., National Gallery of Canada, Ottawa, 2001, pp. 49–50.

18 In 'Les Souvenirs de Lunia Czechowska' in Ceroni 1958, p. 20, the author states that Zborowski began his role as Modigliani's dealer with the commitment to earn an extra fifteen francs a day to put towards the artist's production and to supply him with materials. She does not state that this was only for the nudes. On p. 26, Czechowska recalls that, while Modigliani's friends posed for free when he did their portraits, the models charged 'five francs per sitting'. Francis Carco opined that the nudes were 'flung so thoughtlessly into the marketplace'; in 'Modigliani', *L'Eventail* (15 July 1919), cited in Düsseldorf 1990, p. 187.

19 The episode is recounted in 'Les Souvenirs de Lunia Czechowska' in Ceroni 1958, p. 30.

20 Ceroni 1970. The horizontal nudes are nos 131, 144–8, 184–6, 194–203, 323–5; the vertical, nos 187–93, 264–7, 271–2. The same model, Elvira, posed for nos 271 and 272, while Almaisa, the 'Algerian woman', posed for no. 131 and two portraits (nos 132 and 133). A reference is made to the nude no. 192 in a related sketch as 'La Belle romaine'. Other models appear more than once, as in the women posing for nos 188 and 190; nos 185 and 186; and the unfinished series of three, nos 323–5.

21 Marie Lathers, *Bodies of Art: French Literary Realism and the Artist's Model*, Lincoln, Nebraska, 2001, especially pp. 21–59.

22 John Berger, *Ways of Seeing*, Harmondsworth, 1972. As Pointon notes in *Naked Authority: The Body in Western Painting 1830–1908*, Cambridge, England, and New York, 1990, p. 4, Berger's proposition that 'women watch themselves being looked at' and 'the surveyor of woman in herself is male', insinuated itself into the art-historical academy (assisted by psychoanalytic theory). In his survey, Berger includes one image by Modigliani of a nude with eyes closed (p. 38), superimposed over a larger 'men's magazine' photograph of a naked woman, drenched in water and in the staged throes of erotic ecstasy. Besides Berger's work, which can be defined in the categories of visual culture and photography studies, the other key text in establishing the tyranny of the male gaze was Laura Mulvey, 'Visual Pleasure and Narrative Cinema', originally published in *Screen* (1975), reprinted in Mulvey, *Visual and Other Pleasures*, Basingstoke and Bloomington and Indianapolis, Indiana, 1989, pp. 14–26. Subsequently, one of the most influential art-historical texts implicating the voyeuristic beholder, T. J. Clark's 'Preliminaries to a Possible Treatment of Olympia in 1865', was also published in *Screen*, 21 (spring 1980), pp. 18–41.

23 T. J. Clark, 'Preliminaries to a Possible Treatment of Olympia in 1865', reprinted in *Modern Art and Modernism*, Francis Frascina and Charles Harrison (eds), London and New York, 1982, p. 261. See also Tamar Garb, *Bodies of Modernity: Figure and Flesh in Fin-de-Siècle France*, London, 1998, and Linda Nochlin, *Representing Women*, London, 1999. For a critique of feminist perspectives that focus more on the male gaze than on class differences, see Gen Doy, *Seeing and Class Consciousness: Women, Class and Representation*, Oxford and Washington DC, 1995.

24 Rona Goffen's superb study of the *Venus of Urbino*, and of its misinterpretation as 'pornography for the elite', is found in *Titian's Women*, London and New Haven, Connecticut, 1997, pp. 146–59.

25 Linda Nochlin, 'Body Politics: Seurat's *Poseuses*' in *Representing Women*, London, 1999, pp. 217–37.

26 The ambiguity of Degas's bathers in relation to his sexuality and alleged misogyny is analysed in a measured way by Wendy Lesser, 'Degas's Nudes' in Lesser, *His Other Half: Men Looking at Women Through Art*, Cambridge, Massachusetts, 1991, pp. 53–80: and by Carol Armstrong, *Odd Man Out: Readings of the Work and Reputation of Edgar Degas*, Chicago, 1991.

27 E. Brummer, 'Modigliani chez Renoir', *Paris-Montparnasse* (February 1930), cited in Sichel 1967, p. 413. Modigliani met Renoir in 1918, while staying with the painter Anders Osterlind and his wife Rachel in Cagnes. As Anders Osterlind recounted, Renoir had some of his works taken off the wall so that he and Modigliani could view them together more closely, and the following conversation ensued: '"So you're a painter too then, eh, young man?" he said to Modigliani, who was looking at the paintings.... "Paint with joy, with the same joy with which you make love...." "Do you caress your canvases a long time?..." "I stroke the buttocks for days before finishing a painting." It seemed to me Modigliani was suffering and that a catastrophe was imminent. It happened. Modigliani got up brusquely and, his hand on the doorknob, said brutally, "I don't like buttocks, sir."' (Sichel 1967, p. 413.)

28 Stephen Eisenman, *Gauguin's Skirt*, New York, 1997, p. 330.

29 Carol Duncan, 'Virility and Domination in Early Twentieth-Century Vanguard Painting' (1973), reprinted in Norma Broude and Mary D. Garrard (eds), *Feminism and Art History*, New York, 1982, pp. 293–313; Modigliani's nudes are absent from Duncan's discussion. A similar argument is made by Wendy Steiner in *Venus in Exile: The Rejection of Beauty in Twentieth-Century Art*, New York, 2001, where the modernist treatment of the female body is seen as a misguided triumph of the Kantian sublime over the beautiful.

30 Wendy Steiner, *Venus in Exile: The Rejection of Beauty in Twentieth-Century Art*, New York, 2001, p. 75.

31 Scheiwiller 1927, pp. 10–12; Lamberto Vitali, *Disegni di Modigliani*, Milan, 1929, pp. 5–11; and Raffaello Franchi, *Modigliani*, Florence, 1946, p. 9. For an elaboration of the perceived religiosity of his work by Italian critics, see Emily Braun, 'The Faces of Modigliani: Identity Politics Under Fascism' in New York 2004, pp. 25–39.

32 David Biale, *Eros and the Jews: From Biblical Israel to Contemporary America*, New York, 1992, and Daniel Boyarin, *Carnal Israel: Reading Sex in Talmudic Culture*, Berkeley, California, 1993.

33 Griselda Pollock, 'Modigliani and the Bodies of Art: Carnality, Attentiveness and the Modernist Struggle' in New York 2004, p. 64, and see p. 222, note 25.

34 André Salmon, *L'art vivant*, Paris, 1920, cited in Ceroni 1970, p. 11. For a contemporary survey of the nude, see Francis Carco, *Le Nu dans la peinture moderne (1863–1920)*, Paris, 1924, where a Modigliani nude – *Standing Nude (Nu blonde)* of 1917, owned by Carco – is reproduced as the frontispiece.

35 Gill Perry, *Women Artists and the Parisian Avant-Garde*, Oxford, 1995, in particular the section 'The Female Nude: (De)Constructing a Feminine Body', pp. 118–36.

36 Amelia Jones, *Postmodern and the En-Gendering of Marcel Duchamp*, Cambridge, England, 1994, pp. 191–204. See also Thierry de Duve, *Kant After Duchamp*, London and Cambridge, Massachusetts, 1996.

37 Sir Kenneth Clark, *The Nude: A Study in Ideal Form*, London and Princeton, New Jersey, 1956, p. 3.

38 Elaine Scarry, *On Beauty and Being Just*, Princeton, New Jersey, 1999.

39 Siegfried Sassoon, 'Glory of Women' (1917) in *The Penguin Book of First World War Poetry*, Jon Silkin (ed.), 2nd ed., London, 1996.

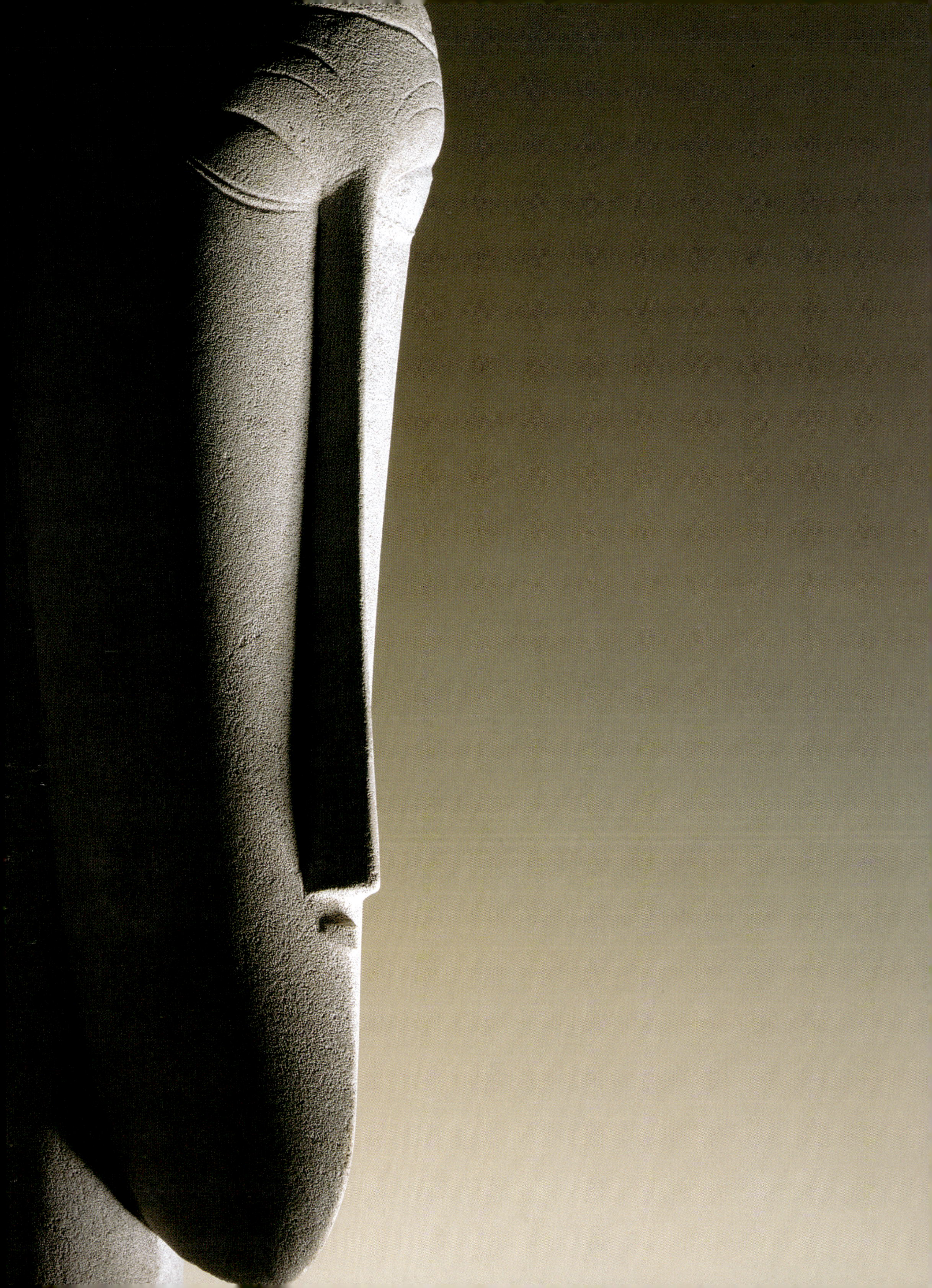

Modigliani and England

Kenneth Wayne

By background and nature, Amedeo Modigliani was very cosmopolitan and sophisticated. Born to an Italian father and a French mother (née Garsin), both with Sephardic Jewish/Spanish roots, Modigliani looked to art from many cultures and periods for inspiration: Cycladic sculpture; African sculpture; Cambodian sculpture; Oceanic art; Gothic art; Michelangelo; the Italian Primitives; Jewish mysticism and the cabbala; French Impressionism; Paul Cézanne; Paul Gauguin; Henri Rousseau; Symbolism; Cubism; and Fauvism, among others. However, one aspect of Modigliani's cosmopolitanism has not yet received significant attention or mention: his extensive ties to Englishmen, England and English art.

Modigliani had many close friends and acquaintances from England who were artists and writers, as well as strong family ties to the country, through both his immediate and extended family. Modigliani was fascinated by the Pre-Raphaelites,[1] an interest that his works of art certainly support with their many elongated, ethereal figures. He is even reported to have visited London, where he said that he had had an exhibition with the Pre-Raphaelites.[2] There could have been other visits as well.

The interest was mutual, as England had eyes for Modigliani from early on. He exhibited in England in several group shows during his lifetime – more than in any other country except for France – and was featured in the English press on many occasions. Indeed, it appears that more was written about Modigliani in England during his lifetime than in any other country, even in France. The first full biography of the artist was published in 1941 by two Englishmen, Douglas Goldring and Charles Beadle, who used the pen-name Charles Douglas.[3]

The first Modigliani work to enter a public collection did so in England, in 1922: the sculpture *Head* (*c.* 1911–12; figs 37 and 38) was accepted as a gift by the Victoria and Albert Museum, London; it has since been transferred to Tate Liverpool. In 1925, the Manchester City Art Gallery obtained a Modigliani drawing, *The Violin Player* (*c.* 1918), that had been exhibited at the Eldar Gallery in London from March to May 1919. In 1931, the Victoria and Albert Museum acquired Modigliani's *Study for 'Head'* (*c.* 1911), a blue, green and black chalk study for the stone *Head* then in its collection. Samuel Courtauld donated the famous *Female Nude* (*c.* 1916) by Modigliani to the newly established Courtauld Institute of Art Gallery in 1932. In 1933, the Tate Gallery, London, received Modigliani's *Portrait of a Girl* (*c.* 1917; now on display at Tate Liverpool) from the Dutch businessman and art collector Frank Stoop.

Fig. 37
Detail of cat. 1

Fig. 38
Study for 'Head', *c.* 1911
Blue, green and black
chalk study
63.5 × 12.5 cm
Victoria and Albert
Museum, London

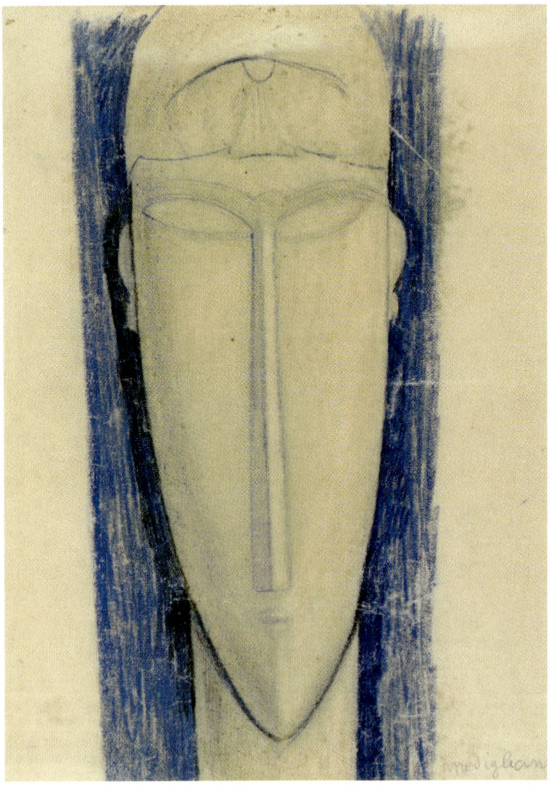

As an interesting side note, it was apparently not until 1933 that a Picasso painting or sculpture entered an English public collection (several works were acquired then by the Tate by purchase or donation). Picasso's etching *Le Repas frugal* (1904) had gone into the collection of the Victoria and Albert Museum in 1930. Modigliani's work went into a public collection in England even before his native Italy: two Modigliani drawings were acquired by the Uffizi Gallery, Florence, in 1932.[4]

Modigliani grew up in a very Anglo-oriented environment. Cosmopolitan Livorno, a trading port on the Mediterranean, had a substantial expatriate English community, as its large English cemetery attests. Amedeo's maternal grandfather Isaac lived with the family and was very close to Amedeo; he had had a business with a branch in London during his working life.[5] The business partner of Amedeo's father and uncles in the exploration of zinc mines from 1874 to 1884 was an Englishman, William Gerard Gibson of London, of the Crown Spelter Company.[6] Amedeo's mother Eugenia was raised in Marseilles by an English governess named Miss Whitfield,[7] and had a school in Livorno where she reportedly taught English (and French) to make money for her financially stretched family.[8] It is likely that the Modigliani household was involved with the English community of Livorno. It is also probable that Amedeo knew English through his mother. Modigliani later gave a book in English on Whistler to the collector Dr Paul Alexandre.[9]

It was Eugenia's older brother Joseph Evariste Garsin, Amedeo's maternal uncle, who moved to London in 1877.[10] He married an Englishwoman from Plymouth, Devon, named Jessie and they had three children together, all very close in age to Amedeo: Nellie, Minnie and Henry.[11] It is likely that Amedeo saw this family when he reportedly visited London. Indeed, their presence in London would have made it even more likely that Amedeo visited. The Garsin family was very close, according to Modigliani's daughter Jeanne in her biography of her father.

There is another Modigliani family member, one with whom Amedeo was known to be in contact, who had very strong ties to England: Ettore Modigliani, Amedeo's second cousin (their fathers were first cousins). Ettore was a famous art historian who was Director of the Pinacoteca di Brera in Milan off and on from 1909 to the end of his life, specialising in Old Master and ancient art. He was married to an Englishwoman.[12] He was a frequent contributor of scholarly articles to *The Burlington Magazine*. In addition, he co-organised an important exhibition on Italian art with Kenneth Clark for the Royal Academy of Arts in 1930, for which he was given an honorary knighthood by His Majesty the

Fig. 39 (below)
Portrait of a Poet (Arthur Cravan), *c.* 1916
Pencil on tracing paper
42.3 × 25.7 cm
Thaw Collection, The Pierpont Morgan Library EVT 121

Fig. 40 (bottom)
Caryatid, *c.* 1912–14
Pencil and blue crayon on paper
55 × 41.4 cm
The Garman Ryan Collection, The New Art Gallery, Walsall (previously collection of Jacob Epstein)

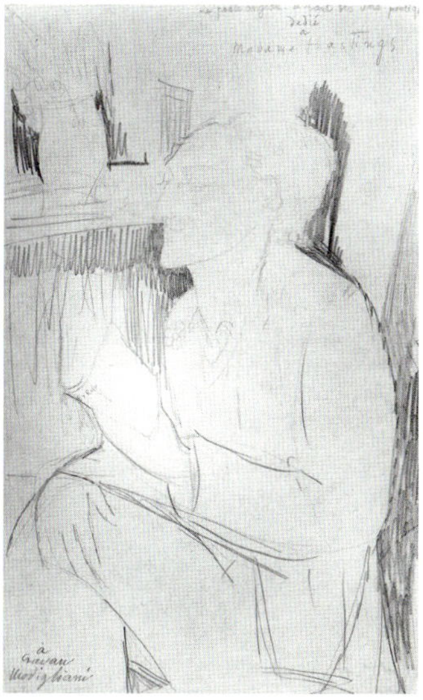

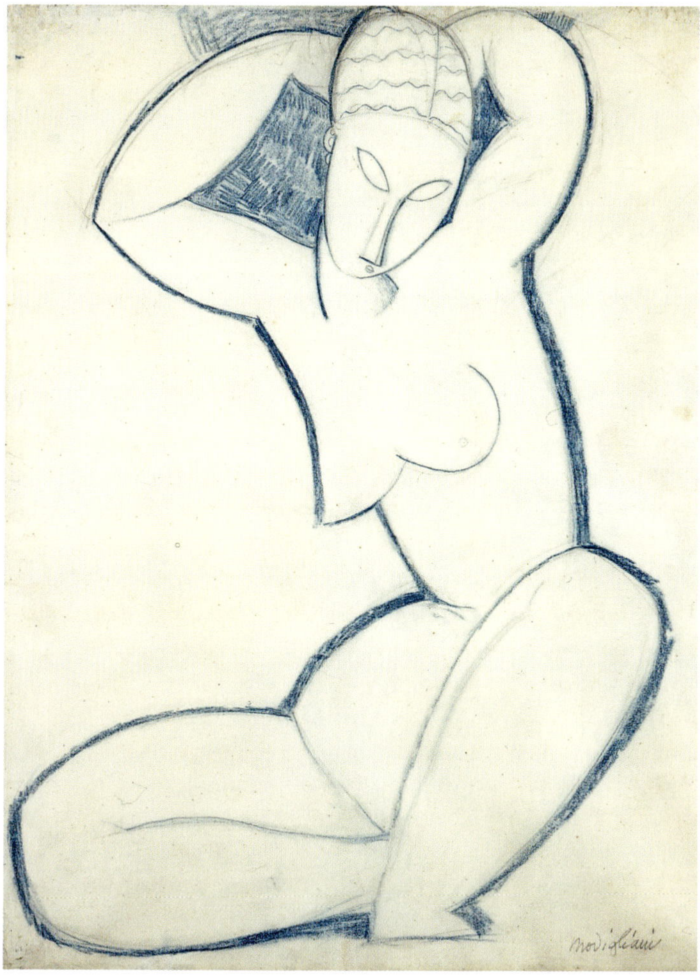

King. Ettore managed to put on such a successful exhibition despite a problem in transporting the works by boat when rough seas almost caused the art to be lost for ever. According to an amusing story passed down in the Modigliani family, Amedeo talked to his older cousin Ettore when he thought of becoming an artist and was strongly dissuaded from doing so.[13] Ettore counselled Amedeo that the life of an artist was too difficult. Yet Ettore could have facilitated Amedeo's trip to London.

Amedeo was a real Anglophile, having many friends, acquaintances and collectors in or from England: the painters David Bomberg, Edward Roworth, Augustus John and Christopher Nevinson, the painter and Bohemian free spirit Nina Hamnett, the sculptor Jacob Epstein and the aristocratic men-of-letters Osbert and Sacheverell Sitwell. Nevinson writes in his autobiography that he knew Modigliani from 1911 until Modigliani's death in 1920 and even shared a studio with him in Paris for a period. One of Modigliani's three main girlfriends, Beatrice Hastings was known in Paris as *la poétesse anglaise*. Born in London, she was raised in South Africa before returning to London.[14] As the Paris correspondent of the London periodical *The New Age*, she sent back to her English readers reports of her exploits, including details of her relationship with Modigliani. Epstein and Modigliani were closest, seeing each other 'daily', when Epstein was in Paris for six months in 1912 to install his *Tomb of Oscar Wilde* (1912). The following year Epstein stayed in Paris for an even longer period, eight months, and they continued their close friendship. Modigliani himself worked primarily on sculpture at this time. The blocky angular primitivism of the work of Epstein (fig. 45), Bomberg and French-born English sculptor Henri Gaudier-Brzeska (fig. 42) resonates with Modigliani's art, particularly his sculpture and caryatids on paper. Epstein owned one of these Modigliani drawings, *Caryatid* (*c.* 1912–14; fig. 40), now in the collection of the New Art Gallery, Walsall.

Modigliani knew, at least casually, the English poets Arthur Cravan (fig. 39) and his wife Mina Loy, whose pencil portraits he drew (Morgan Library, New York; Princeton University Art Museum, New Jersey, respectively) around 1916. As a poet himself, Modigliani would have been pleased to have become acquainted with Cravan and Loy. In addition, Cravan was a nephew of the writer Oscar Wilde and it is known that Modigliani was familiar with Wilde's writings; at the end of 1905, Modigliani's mother gave him a fine edition of Wilde's *The Ballad of Reading Gaol* (1898) and he spoke to Dr Paul Alexandre before the war about Wilde's writing.[15] Beatrice Hastings's name

Fig. 41
Head, 1911–13
Limestone
63.5 × 15.2 × 21 cm
Solomon R. Guggenheim Museum, New York (ex-collection Augustus John) 55.1421

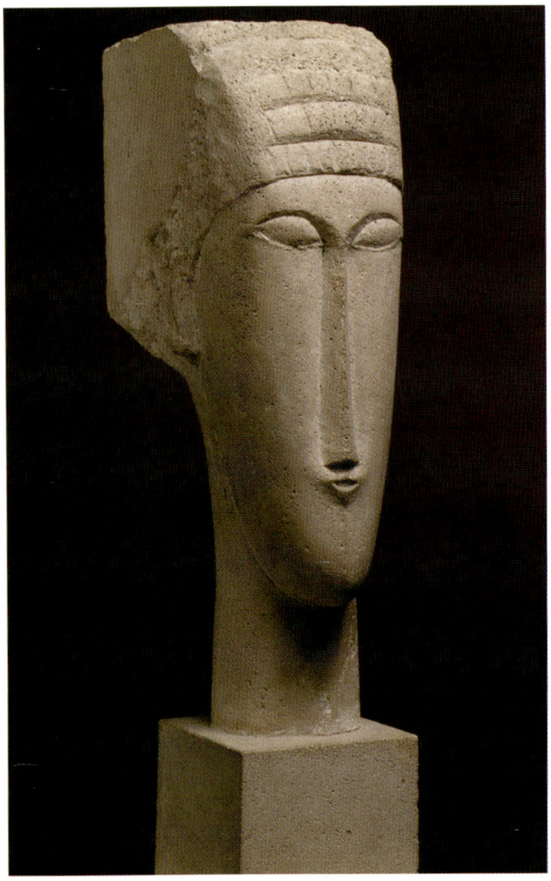

is mentioned on the drawing of Cravan. She undoubtedly met Cravan with Modigliani and it is highly likely that she would have bonded well with him given that she was, it appears, previously married to a boxer, while Cravan was himself a boxer.

David Bomberg was in Paris with Jacob Epstein in the spring of 1913 to put together the Jewish section of the exhibition entitled 'Twentieth-Century Art: A Review of Modern Movements' that took place at the Whitechapel Art Gallery, London, from 8 May to 20 June 1914.[16] According to the catalogue introduction, the point of the exhibition was to show the recent move away from Naturalism and imitation to something more profound. In his unpublished writings, Bomberg commented: 'Modigliani gave me a roll of his drawings ... to commemorate our meeting and my appreciation of his approach. I advised two of my friends visiting Paris with me at the time to acquire two of the negroid-style Egyptian-looking heads – these two sculptures came to England.'[17] It is not known what happened to these Modigliani drawings that had been given to Bomberg.

The two friends mentioned by Bomberg were undoubtedly the painters Edward Roworth, then studying in London at the Slade School of Art (from 1911 to 1914), and Augustus John.[18] Roworth bought around this time the Modigliani head (*c.* 1911–12) that is now at Tate Liverpool. John purchased two Modigliani sculptures: one now at the Solomon R. Guggenheim Museum in New York (fig. 41), while the other one appears to be the sculpture last known to be in a private collection in Brussels (Ceroni XXII). So neither of them has remained in England.

Roworth lent the Modigliani sculpture that he had recently purchased from the artist to the Whitechapel for its 1914 exhibition. This show was given extensive coverage in the London press, with many fascinating discussions appearing about modernism and its meaning. The reviews concentrated on the English artists, whose work was the focus of the show. Many of the reviews referred to the featured art as 'Cubist', while others labelled it 'Futurist'. Other adjectives used included 'humorous' and 'insane'.[19] Writing about Modigliani's sculpture in the Whitechapel show, a reviewer in the *Jewish Chronicle* asserted that: 'The piece of Futurist sculpture by Modigliani is beyond our comprehension.'[20]

Other artists featured in the exhibition included Wyndham Lewis, Gaudier-Brzeska, Paul Nash, Vanessa Bell, Duncan Grant, Walter Sickert and Roger Fry. Indeed, the Omega Workshops were particularly well represented. These artists would have become familiar with Modigliani's name and art through this exhibition, if they did not already know it.

Fig. 42
Henri Gaudier-Brzeska
(1891–1915)
Red Stone Dancer, *c.* 1913
Red Mansfield stone
43.2 × 22.9 × 22.9 cm
Presented by C. Frank Stoop
through the Contemporary
Art Society 1930.
Tate, London, N04515

It is evident that Gaudier-Brzeska was aware of Modigliani's art, for he refers to it in a text he wrote. On the day that the exhibition closed, Gaudier-Brzeska published an article called 'Vortex' in the first issue of Wyndham Lewis's Vorticist journal *Blast*, in which he mentioned Modigliani, citing him as one of the 'moderns': 'And WE the moderns: Epstein, [Constantin] Brancusi, [Alexander] Archipenko, [Xawery] Dunikowski, Modigliani, and myself, through the incessant struggle in the complex city, have likewise to spend much energy.'[21] It is surely no coincidence that this piece coincided with the Whitechapel exhibition: Gaudier-Brzeska would have seen the exhibition and confirmed in his own mind Modigliani's importance, especially as a sculptor, citing the artist with himself and other sculptors. Published in London (as well as New York and Toronto), the *Blast* article helped to secure Modigliani's place in the international avant-garde in 1914.

Modigliani's art was enthusiastically discussed and reproduced in a February 1919 article by Roger Fry on drawing in the pages of *The Burlington Magazine*. In it Fry attests to Britain's early and enthusiastic appreciation of the artist. Fry's statement was the first lengthy discussion of Modigliani's art in print and assumes, therefore, major importance. Accompanying the article were reproductions of two Modigliani works: a watercolour and pastel colour drawing of a caryatid (fig. 44) and a pencil drawing of 'Mlle. G.'. The whereabouts of these works are currently unknown.

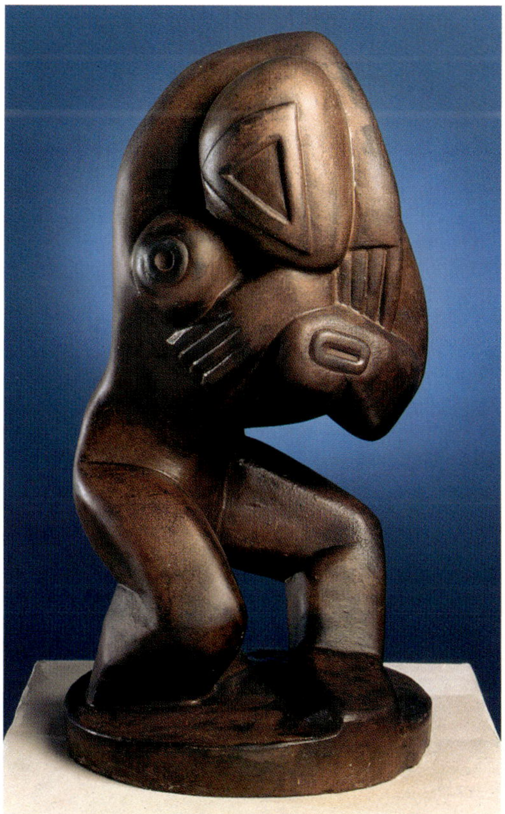

From August to early September 1919, Modigliani was featured in a very important show at Heal's Mansard Gallery on Tottenham Court Road, London, called an 'Exhibition of French Art, 1914–1919' (fig. 43). It was an enormous show with 338 works (177 paintings and sculptures, 141 drawings) by 39 artists. Among the artists featured with Modigliani were Picasso, Matisse and Léger. With 59 works (9 paintings and 50 drawings), Modigliani was the best-represented artist in the show. He received very high praise from the novelist and critic Arnold Bennett, who wrote in the catalogue: 'But I am determined to say that the four figure subjects of Modigliani seem to me to have a suspicious resemblance to masterpieces.'[22] According to Bennett, the exhibition was intended to give English artists and the public a taste of the 'younger pioneers' from the continent to keep his countrymen from being too insular.

The critical reaction was very favourable. English theorist, critic and painter Roger Fry wrote a long, thoughtful and enthusiastic two-part review in *The Athenaeum* saying: 'Nothing like such a representative show of modern French art has been

Fig. 43
The poster advertising 'The Exhibition of French Art 1914–1919' at the Mansard Gallery, Heal & Son, 1919 (possibly designed by Wyndham Lewis; 1882–1957). Poster
76 × 50.6 cm
Victoria and Albert Museum, London

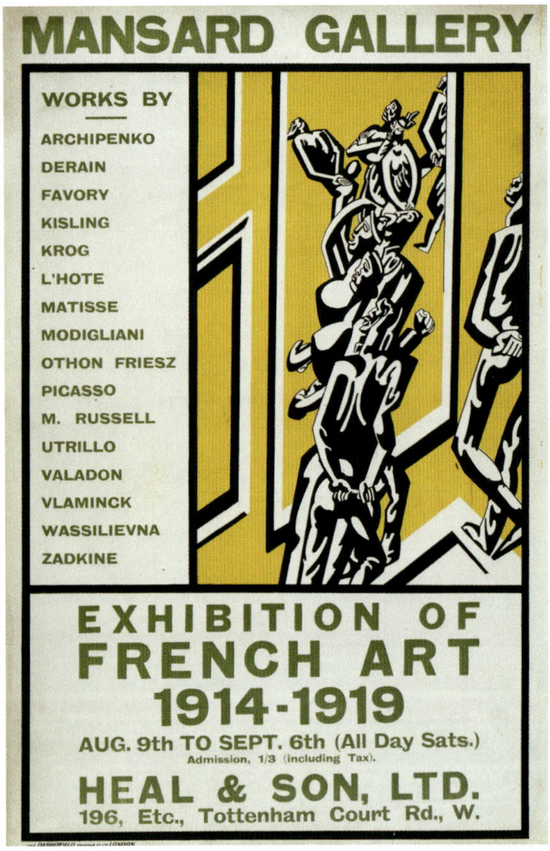

seen in London for many years.'[23] He proceeded to give his insights on modernism and the struggle between Naturalism and Cubism. While he mentioned Modigliani briefly at the end of the first part of the article – 'and such a show of de Vlaminck and Modigliani as has never before been seen in England' – he reserved the bulk of his comments on the artist for the second part, stressing the artist's brilliance as a draughtsman. He asserted that Modigliani had never been shown in England before, though his drawings had been for some years coveted by English collectors. The writer Clive Bell was generally positive about Modigliani and had almost identical views about the artist being above all a draughtsman.[24] The unsigned article in *The Times* also celebrated Modigliani's drawings.[25] The reviewer for *The Burlington Magazine*, 'M. S. P.', expressed great excitement about Modigliani's art: 'The two painters whose work will probably be the greatest surprises are Modigliani and Vlaminck. Modigliani's uncommon feeling for character finds expression through an extreme simplification of colour and contour and the most astonishing distortions.'[26] The article reproduced the painting *The Little Peasant*, which was featured in the exhibition and which now hangs in Tate Liverpool (*c.* 1918; cat. 33). Jan Gordon asserted in a review in *The Observer* that 'Modigliani stands in front ... and shows a strong alliance with the early Florentine painters'.[27] Gordon extols Modigliani's subtlety, intelligence, use of colour and technical skill.

The exhibition was organised by Osbert and Sacheverell Sitwell. It had been planned since the previous winter, as Osbert chronicled in his autobiography.[28] Osbert Sitwell said that he and his brother could claim the credit for being the first to introduce Modigliani's work to the English public.[29] The Sitwells were able to acquire a Modigliani painting at this time entitled *Peasant Girl*.[30] It has not so far been possible to identify the exact painting or its current whereabouts with any certainty.

The Sitwells were not the only Englishmen to acquire a Modigliani at this time, as Osbert noted: 'We were fortunate enough to sell a good many pictures on the opening day. Arnold Bennett bought on my advice a splendid nude by Modigliani, and to someone else who consulted me, I recommended another fine picture by the same master, and a Utrillo. For these two, he paid a sum of about seventy pounds.'[31] It appears that Bennett also acquired a portrait of Lunia Czechowska, probably the *Portrait de Madame C* listed in the catalogue. In her memoirs, Czechowska reported that: 'Zbo[orowski] sent the following telegram: "Lunia sold for 1,000 francs; bought by Arnold Bennett." Zbo told us upon his return that Bennet[t] already

Fig. 44
Caryatid, date unknown
Watercolour (or gouache?)
and pastel on paper
Original size unknown
Whereabouts unknown
Illustration from *The Burlington Magazine*, February 1919

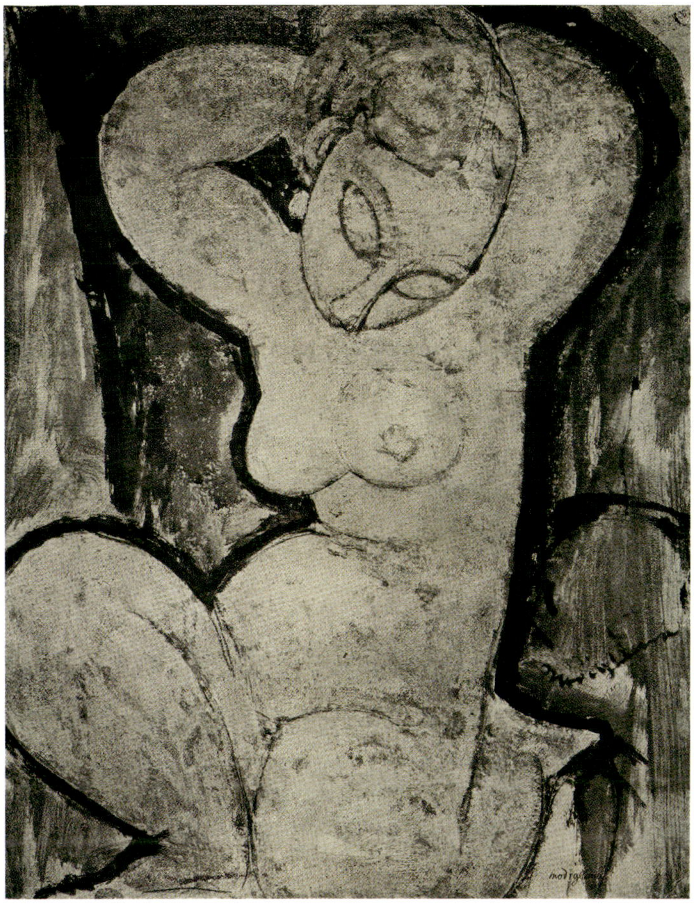

knew Modigliani's work and admired it enormously. He particularly liked the portraits, he said, because the sitter reminds him of the heroine in his novels.'[32] She added that this painting obtained the highest price and that Modigliani had the most success of all Zborowski's artists in the London exhibition. The Sitwells liked Modigliani's art so much that they were in negotiation to buy 100 or more of his paintings in the autumn of 1919, but that plan did not reach fruition because they could not arrange the necessary financing.[33]

That autumn interest in Modigliani's work continued in England as two British arts journals reproduced drawings by him. The autumn 1919 issue of *Art and Letters*, a journal edited by Osbert Sitwell, featured Modigliani's *Woman's Head.*[34] That issue also contained drawings by Wyndham Lewis, John Nash, Paul Nash and Gaudier-Brzeska, and poetry by Osbert Sitwell and their sister Edith Sitwell, as well as criticism by T. S. Eliot. The December 1919 issue of the journal *Coterie: Art, Prose and Poetry, A Quarterly* featured a Modigliani drawing of Paul Delay.

Fig. 45
Sir Jacob Epstein (1880–1959)
Torso in Metal from 'The Rock Drill', 1913–14
Bronze
70.5 × 58.4 × 44.5 cm
Purchased 1960.
Tate, London, T00340

It is highly likely that *Woman's Head* and *Paul Delay* were two of the fifty Modigliani drawings exhibited at the Mansard Gallery.

An exhibition of modern drawings was also held that autumn in a special gallery at *Cambridge Magazine* in Cambridge. It featured Modigliani, Picasso, Matisse, Gaudier-Brzeska, Mark Gertler and Augustus John, among others.[35] On 26 December 1919, less than a month before Modigliani's death, Wyndham Lewis referred to Modigliani in a London newspaper as being the best-respected painter in Paris.[36]

A discussion about Modigliani and England would not be complete without mentioning an extraordinary individual named Hugh Blaker, who was Curator of the Holbourne of Menstrie Museum, Bath, from 1906 to 1913. He bought four Modigliani paintings – including the spectacular work *The Little Peasant* (cat. 33) – from Modigliani's dealer, Léopold Zborowski, in 1919, when Zborowski was in town for the Mansard Gallery show.[37]

Modigliani's family ties, combined with his artistic interests, bonded him to England. His painting has much in common with the Pre-Raphaelites, whose work he admired so much, including elongation, a certain spiritual quality and an emphasis on the human figure. His predilection for portraiture was shared by not only the Omega Workshop artists, with whom he exhibited in 1914, but also Augustus John. The Vorticists, with whom he made friends and his art was discussed, shared a certain blocky primitivism, especially in sculpture. Modigliani's art appeared in two of the most important exhibitions of the 1910s in London (the Whitechapel and the Mansard Gallery shows). Moreover, his art was collected by numerous individuals in England (Augustus John, Edward Roworth, Arnold Bennett, the Sitwells and Hugh Blaker). English critics loved his art and wrote more about him than anyone else. In short, Modigliani had a remarkably strong and close relationship with England during his lifetime.

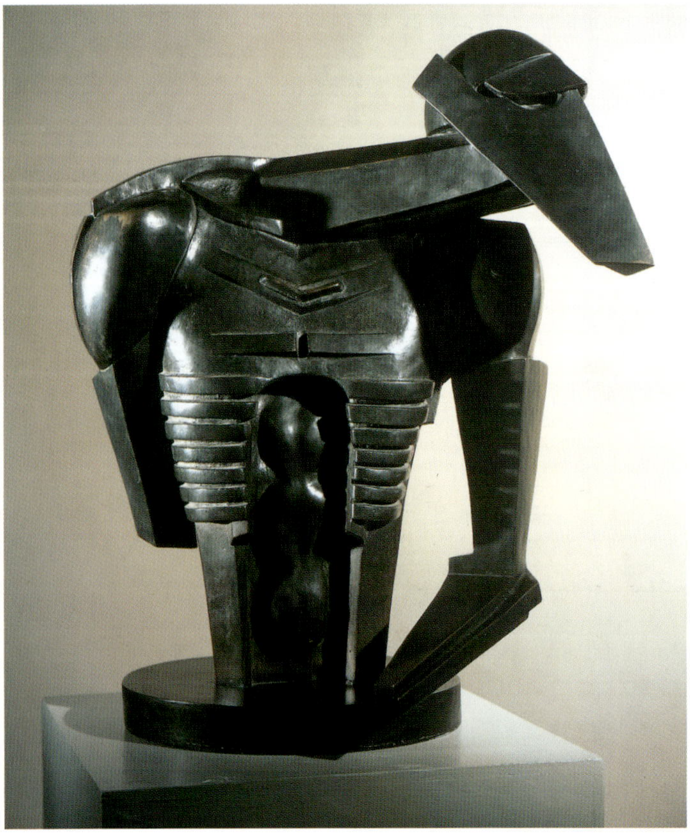

Notes

1 Per Silvano Filippelli, 'Testimonianze livornesi per Modi', *Rivista di Livorno* (July–August 1956), p. 225, in Modigliani 1958, p. 24. Reported elsewhere as well: 'When he was a little over twenty and lived in Florence, Amedeo Modigliani adored the English Pre-Raphaelites,' in Ugo Ojetti, 'Amedeo Modigliani', *Corriere della Sera* (28 January 1930) in Sichel 1967, p. 64, Chapter 4, note 4.
2 Per André Utter, Maurice Utrillo's stepfather, in Douglas 1941, p. 89. The London visit seems to have occurred during Amedeo's Montmartre period, which would mean some time between 1906 and 1909. Attempts to prove that Modigliani exhibited in a Pre-Raphaelite exhibition have not yet been successful.
3 Douglas 1941.
4 I am grateful to Alessandro de Stefani for this information. A fellow Modigliani researcher, he has been a valued colleague.
5 Modigliani 1958, p. 13.
6 Adrio Bocci, 'I Modigliani dalla legenda alla realta', *Notiziario del Gruppo Orobico Minerali*, no. 1 (2000). This article can be found on the Internet.
7 Modigliani 1958, p. 9.
8 Sichel 1967, p. 31.
9 Alexandre 1993, p. 63 (note reproduced indicating that the book is in English).
10 National Archives, London, ref. HO144/94/A13774 24377. He established his own business, E. Garsin & Company, Ltd, as a 'hider skin agent'.
11 National Archives, 1901 Census, RG number 13, piece 467, folio 117, p. 21, schedule number 153. Available on the Internet.
12 For biographical information on Ettore Modigliani (1873–1947), see the obituaries on him: F. Wittgens, 'Ettore Modigliani', *The Burlington Magazine*, no. 539, vol. 90 (February 1948), p. 59; 'Dr Ettore Modigliani', *The Times* (7 July 1947), p. 7.
13 Lazzaro Giuseppe Modigliani (known as Nick), in Massachusetts, USA, by telephone with the author, December 2005. Nick is the first cousin twice removed of Amedeo. His grandfather Umberto Modigliani (1875–1939) was a first cousin of Amedeo. Nick was born in 1932, so he was alive at the same time as Ettore.
14 For much more on this fascinating individual, see Gray 2004.
15 Modigliani 1958, p. 35. It is not known if the copy was in English. See Alexandre 1993, p. 62, regarding Paul Alexandre.
16 For an extended discussion of this exhibition, see my book, Buffalo 2002. For more on this important exhibition, see 'Twentieth-Century Art and the Whitechapel Exhibition of 1914' in Lisa Tickner, *Modern Life and Modern Subjects: British Art in the Early Twentieth Century*, New Haven and London, 2000, pp. 1–9; and 'Twentieth-Century Art: A Review of Modern Movements' in Anna Gruetzner Robins, *Modern Art in Britain 1910–1914*, London, 1997, pp. 139–58.
17 Bomberg's unpublished writings from the period 1953 to 1954, as quoted in Richard Cork, *David Bomberg*, London and New Haven, 1987, p. 48, and footnote 92. At the time, the unpublished writings were in the possession of the artist's family. They are now apparently in the Tate archive.
18 P. Mitford-Barberton, Edward Roworth entry in *Dictionary of South African Biography*, Pretoria, 1981, pp. 523–4. Roworth (1880–1964) was born in Lancashire, England, and settled in South Africa in 1902, becoming one of its most famous artists. See more about this purchase in my book, Buffalo 2002, p. 56. For more on the purchase of the stone heads by Augustus John, see Buffalo 2002, p. 176.
19 See the Appendix in my book, Buffalo 2002, p. 201, for a list of reviews of this and other exhibitions.
20 'Jewish Art at the Whitechapel: Twentieth-Century Exhibition', *The Jewish Chronicle* (15 May 1914) in *Modern Art in Britain*, 1910–1914, Anna Gruetzner Robins, exh. cat., Barbican Art Gallery, London, 1997, p. 140.
21 Henri Gaudier-Brzeska, 'Vortex', *Blast*, no. 1 (20 June 1914), pp. 155–8: 158.
22 Arnold Bennett preface in *Exhibition of French Art, 1914–1919*, exh. cat., Mansard Gallery, London, 1919, n.p.
23 Roger Fry, 'Modern French Art at the Mansard Gallery', *The Athenaeum* (8 August 1919), pp. 723–4, and Roger Fry, 'Modern French Painting at the Mansard Gallery II', *The Athenaeum* (15 August 1919), pp. 754–5.
24 Clive Bell, A Notice by, 'The French Pictures at Heal's', *The Nation* (16 August 1919), reprinted with many letters to the editor in response to this article in Osbert Sitwell, *Laughter in the Next Room, Being the Fourth Volume of Left Hand, Right Hand! An Autobiography by Osbert Sitwell*, London, 1949, Appendix A.
25 'Naked and Unashamed: French Pictures at the Mansard Gallery', *The Times* (4 September 1919), p. 13.
26 M. S. P., 'Monthly Chronicle and Notes: Modern French Art', *The Burlington Magazine* (September 1919), pp. 120–5.
27 Jan Gordon, 'Art and Artists: Modern Parisian Artists', *The Observer* (Sunday, 10 August 1919), p. 6.
28 Osbert Sitwell, *Laughter in the Next Room, Being the Fourth Volume of Left Hand, Right Hand! An Autobiography by Osbert Sitwell*, London, 1949.
29 Osbert Sitwell, *Laughter in the Next Room, Being the Fourth Volume of Left Hand, Right Hand! An Autobiography by Osbert Sitwell*, London, 1949, p. 150.
30 Osbert Sitwell, *Laughter in the Next Room, Being the Fourth Volume of Left Hand, Right Hand! An Autobiography by Osbert Sitwell*, London, 1949, p. 150.
31 Osbert Sitwell, *Laughter in the Next Room, Being the Fourth Volume of Left Hand, Right Hand! An Autobiography by Osbert Sitwell*, London, 1949, p. 154.
32 'Souvenirs de Lunia Czechowska' in Ceroni 1958, pp. 7–34: 29–30.
33 Osbert Sitwell, *Laughter in the Next Room, Being the Fourth Volume of Left Hand, Right Hand! An Autobiography by Osbert Sitwell*, London, 1949, pp. 160.
34 Modigliani drawing, *Woman's Head* in *Art and Letters*, vol. 2, no. 4 (new series, autumn 1919).
35 See J. W., 'Modern Drawings at Cambridge' in *The Cambridge Magazine* (29 November 1919).
36 Wyndham Lewis, 'Prevalent Design, Part II', *The Athenaeum* (26 December 1919) in Walter Michel and C. J. Fox (eds), *Wyndham Lewis on Art: Collected Writings*, 1913–1956, New York, 1969, p. 167.
37 On Blaker (1873–1936), see 'The Blaker Diary: Some Extracts with a Memoir by Murray Urquhart', *Apollo* (October 1963), pp. 293–8, and Robert Meyrick, 'Hugh Blaker: Doing his Bit for the Moderns', *Journal of the History of Collections*, vol. 16, no. 2 (2004), pp. 173–89.

Overleaf
Modigliani (centre) in a bar with unidentified friends, date unknown
Photograph.
Unknown photographer
Archives Paul Guillaume, Paris

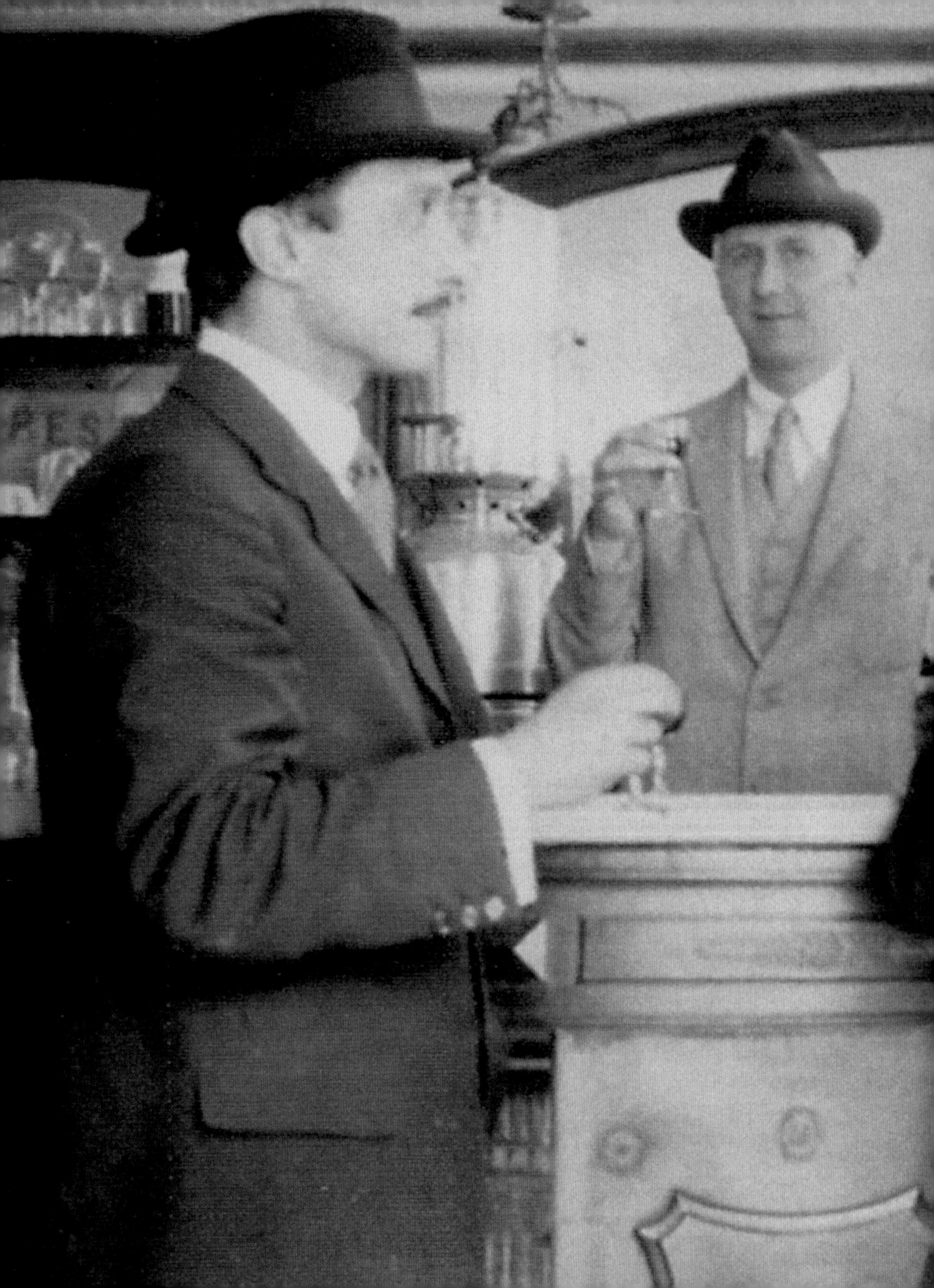

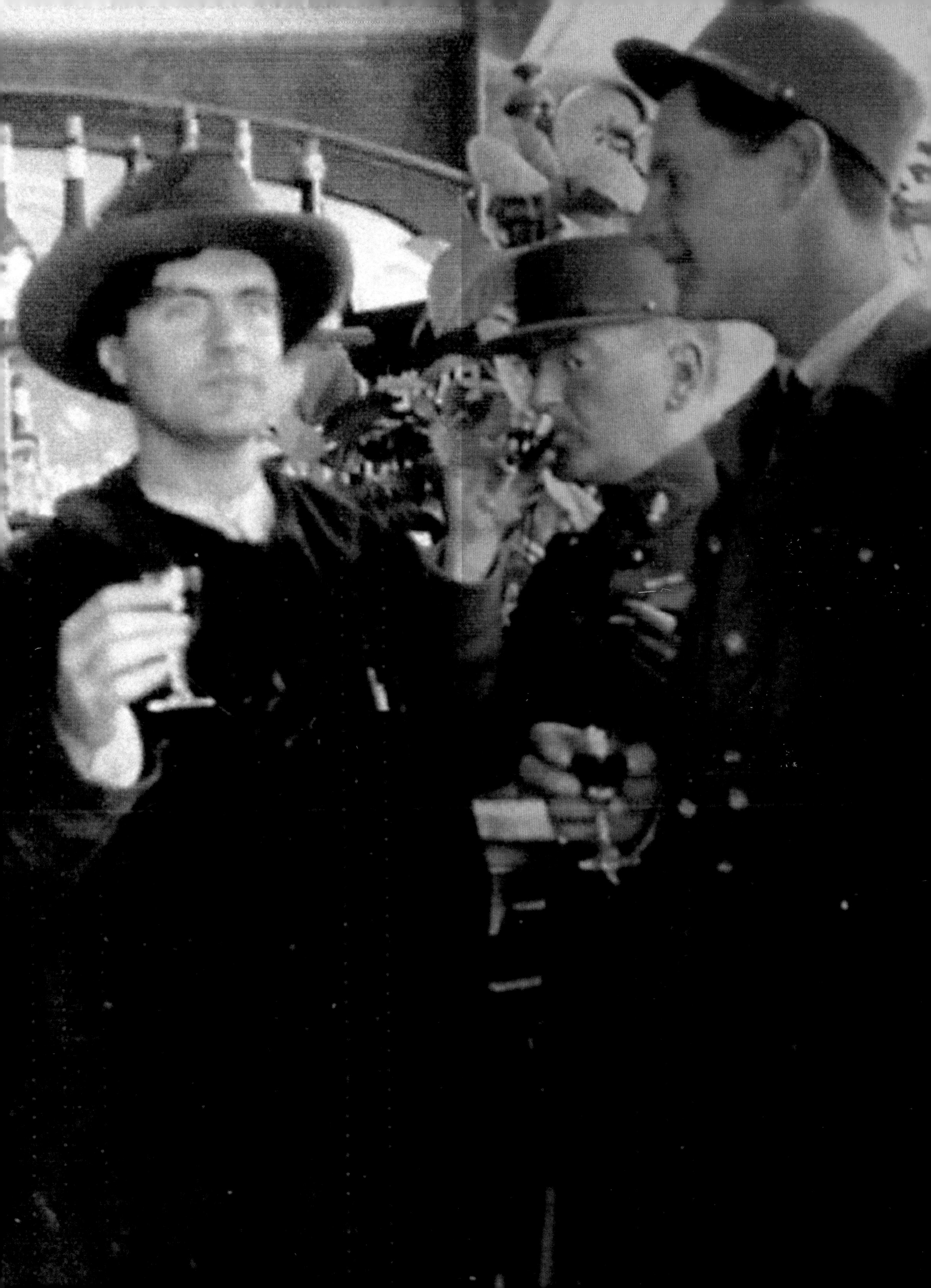

I Head, c. 1911–12
Limestone
89.2 × 14 × 35.2 cm
(including stand)
Tate, London.
Transferred from the
Victoria and Albert
Museum, London, 1983

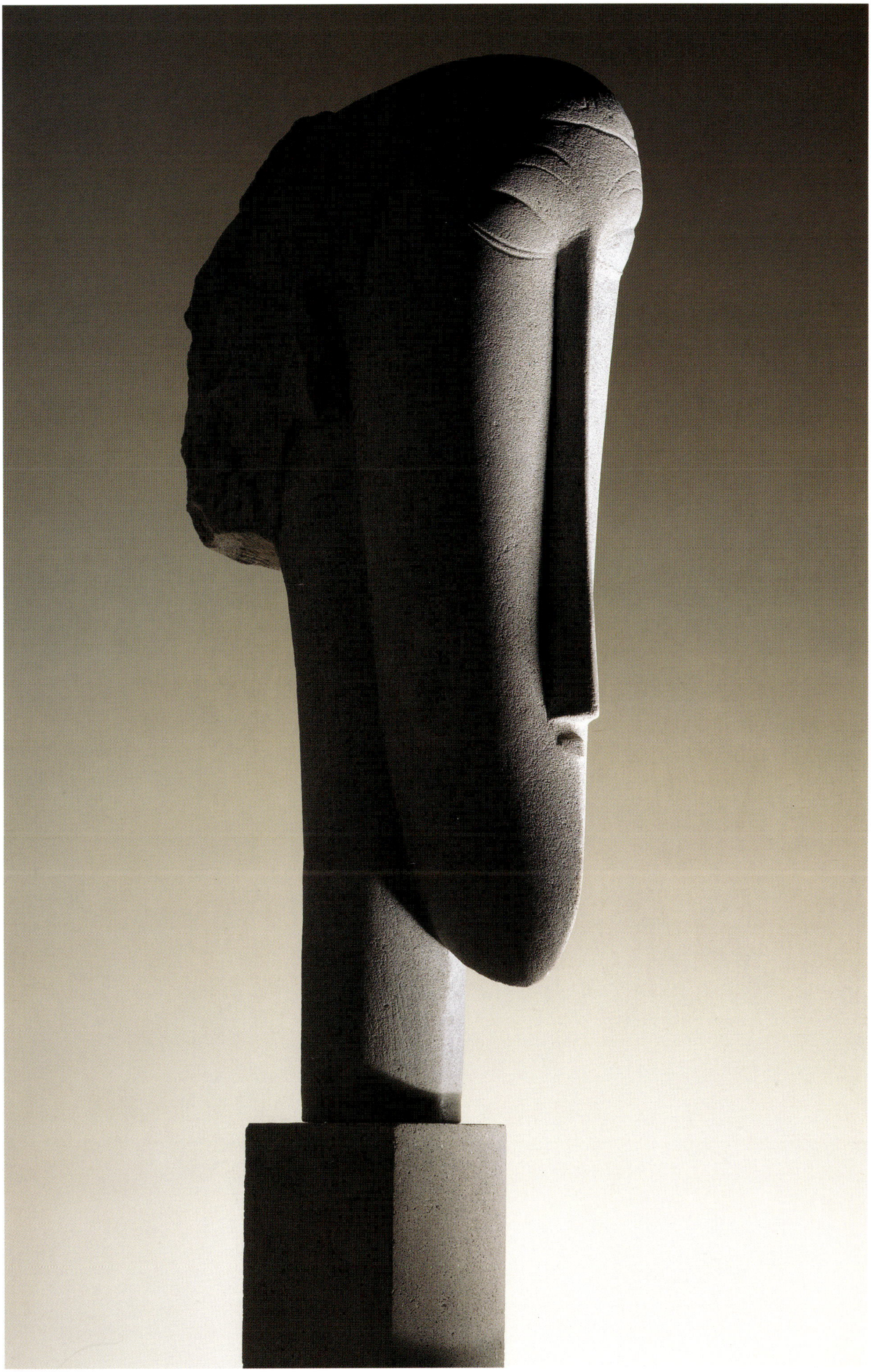

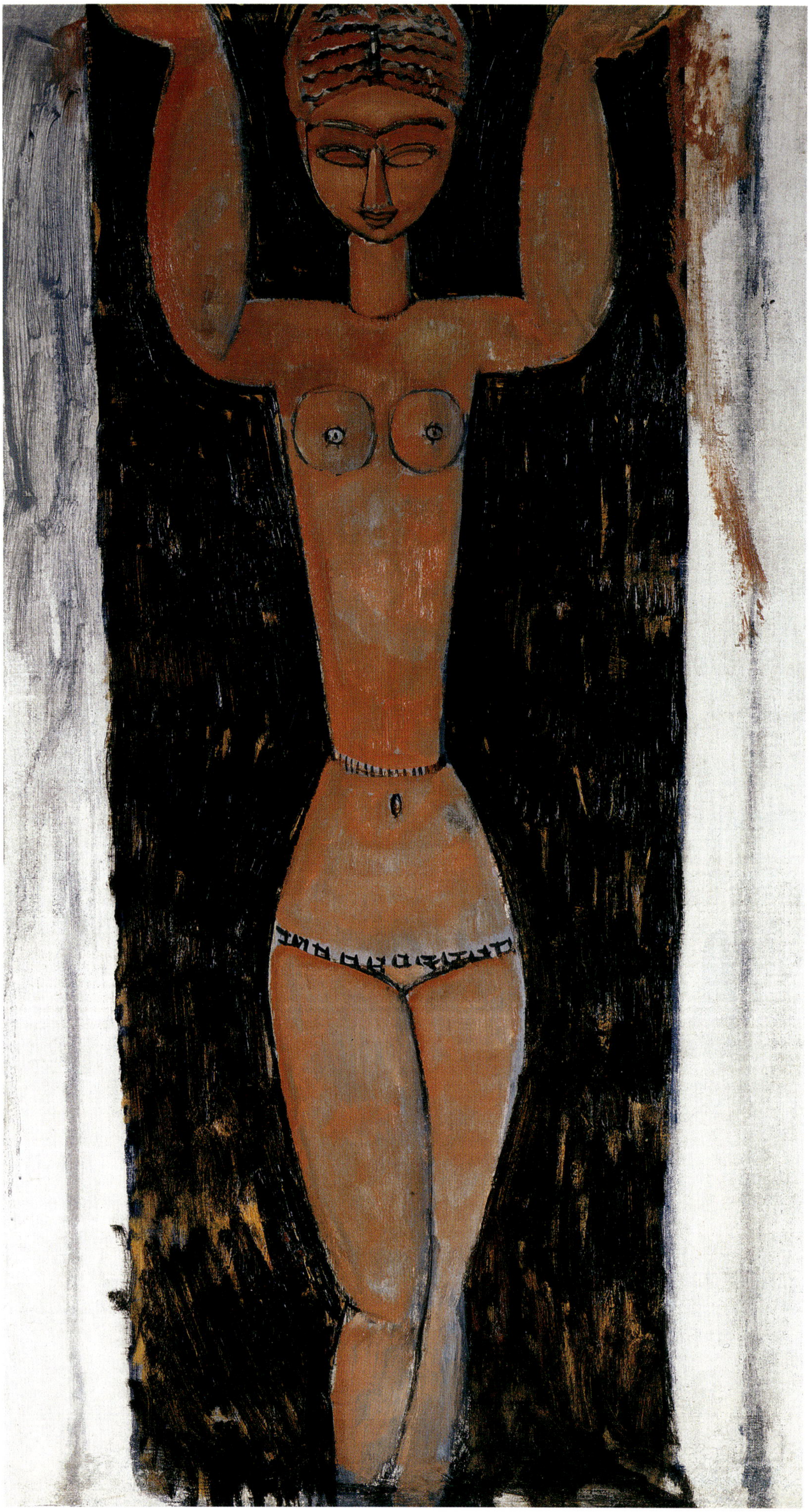

2 *Caryatid*, 1913
Oil on canvas
81 × 45 cm
Private collection

3 *Large Red Bust*, 1913
Oil on cardboard
81.5 × 51 cm
Courtesy of Gallery
Cazeau-Béraudière, Paris

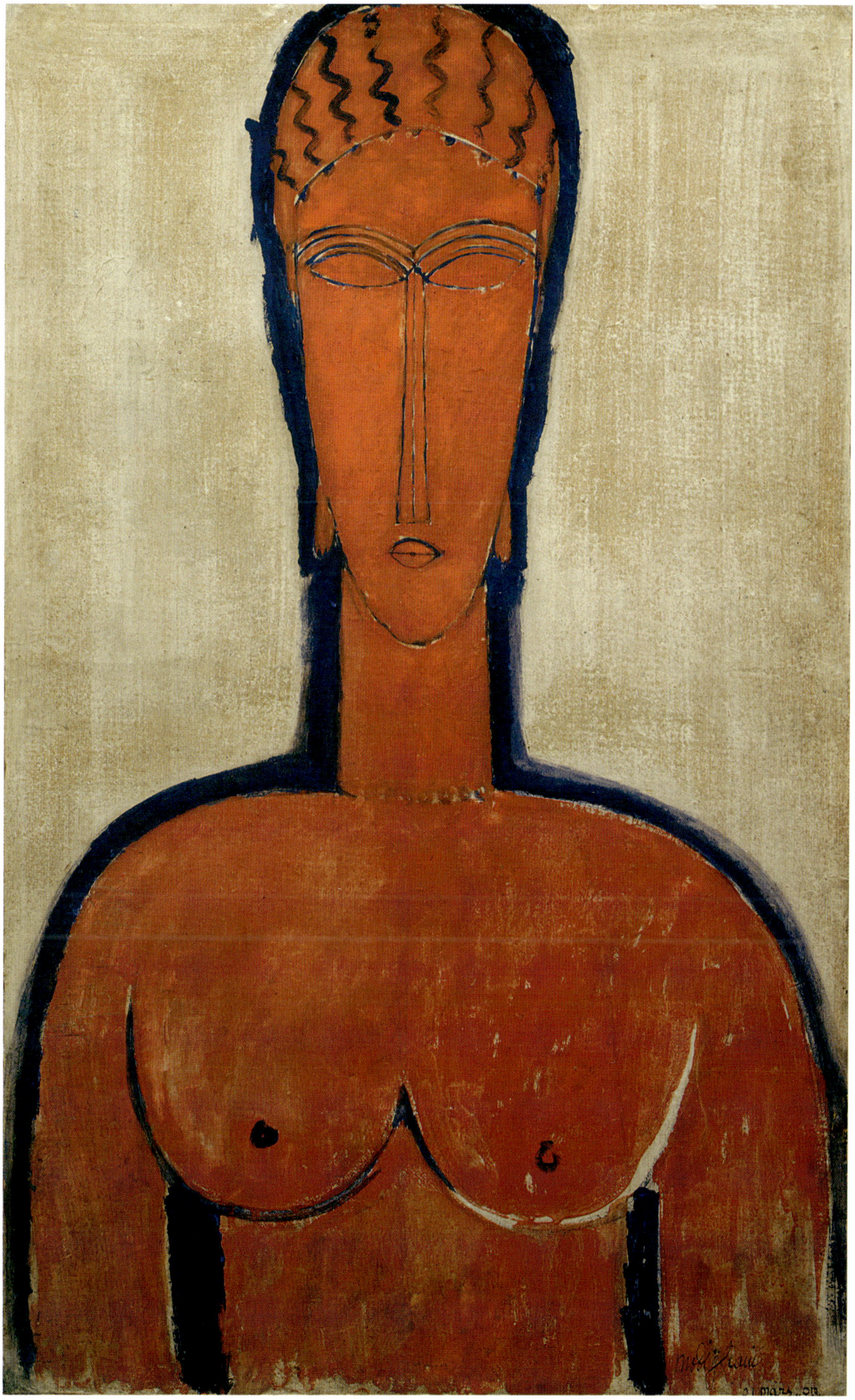

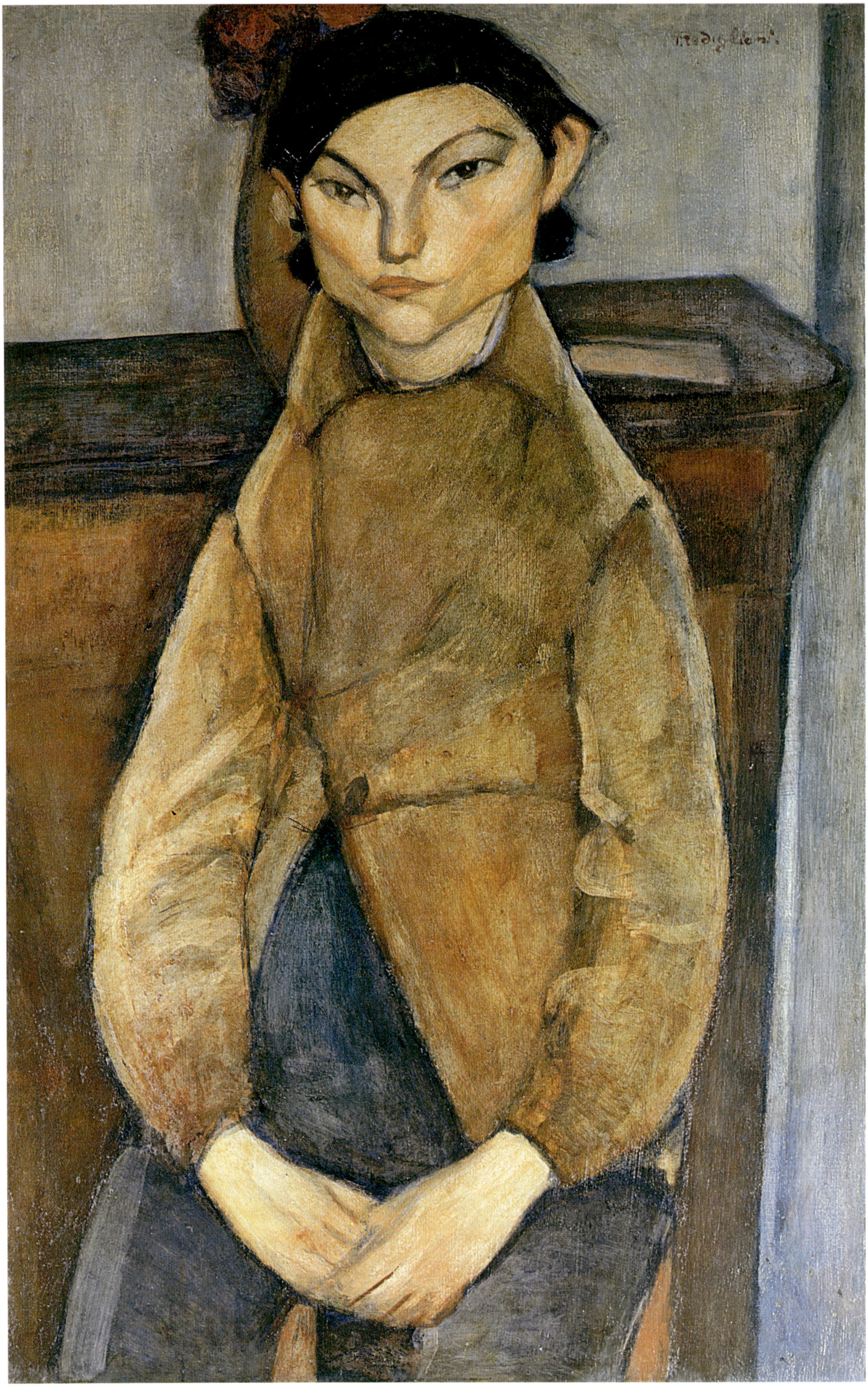

4 *Young Gypsy*, 1909
Oil on canvas
81 × 54 cm
Private collection

5 *Portrait of Frank Burty Haviland*, 1914
Oil on cardboard
73 × 60 cm
Gianni Mattioli Collection.
On long-term loan
to the Peggy Guggenheim
Collection, Venice

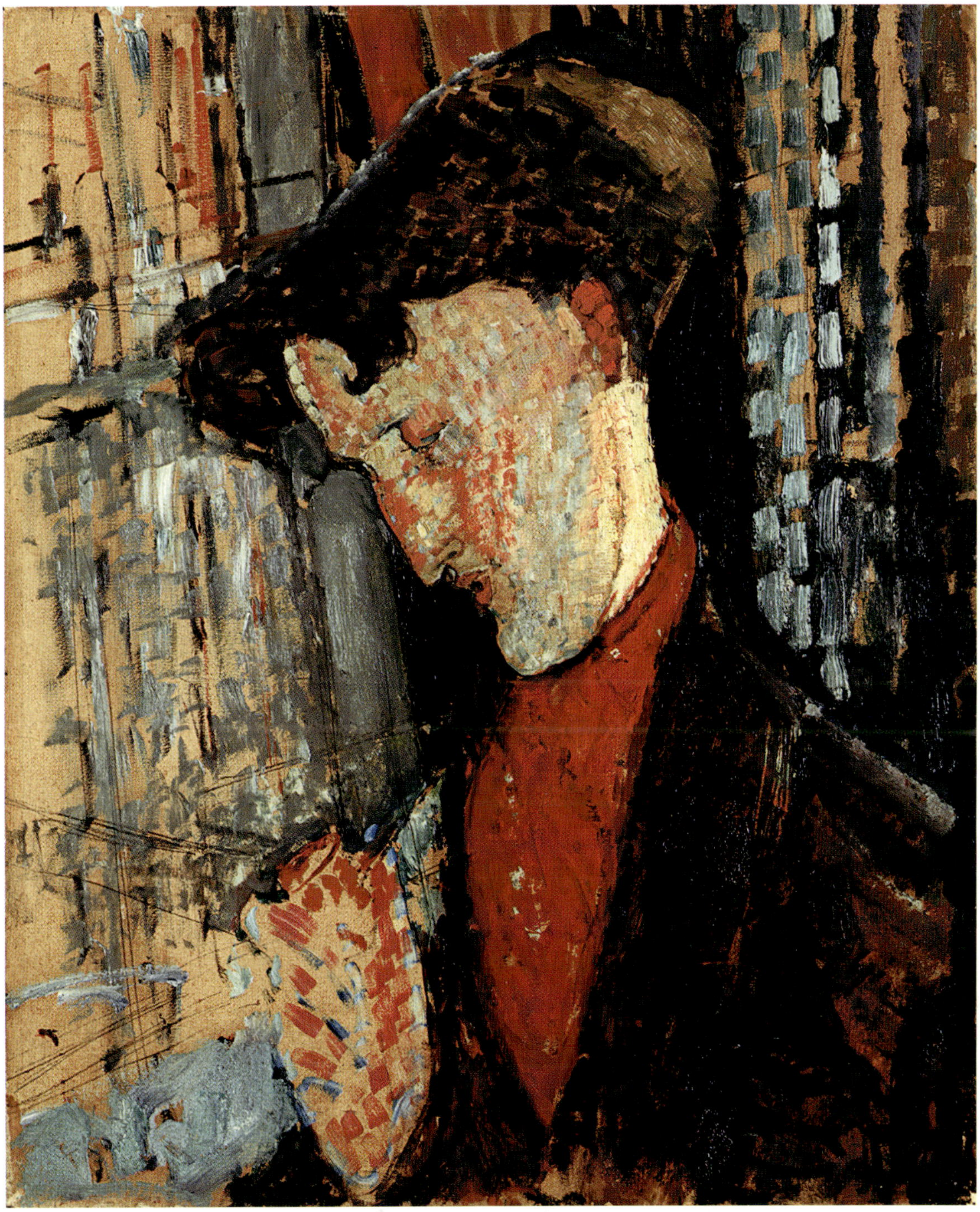

6 *Portrait of Picasso*, 1915
Oil on board
34.2 × 26.3 cm
Private collection,
Moscow

7 *Juan Gris*, 1915
Oil on canvas
54.9 × 38.1 cm
Lent by The Metropolitan
Museum of Art, New York.
Bequest of Miss Adelaide
Milton de Groot
(1876–1967), 1967
(67.187.85)

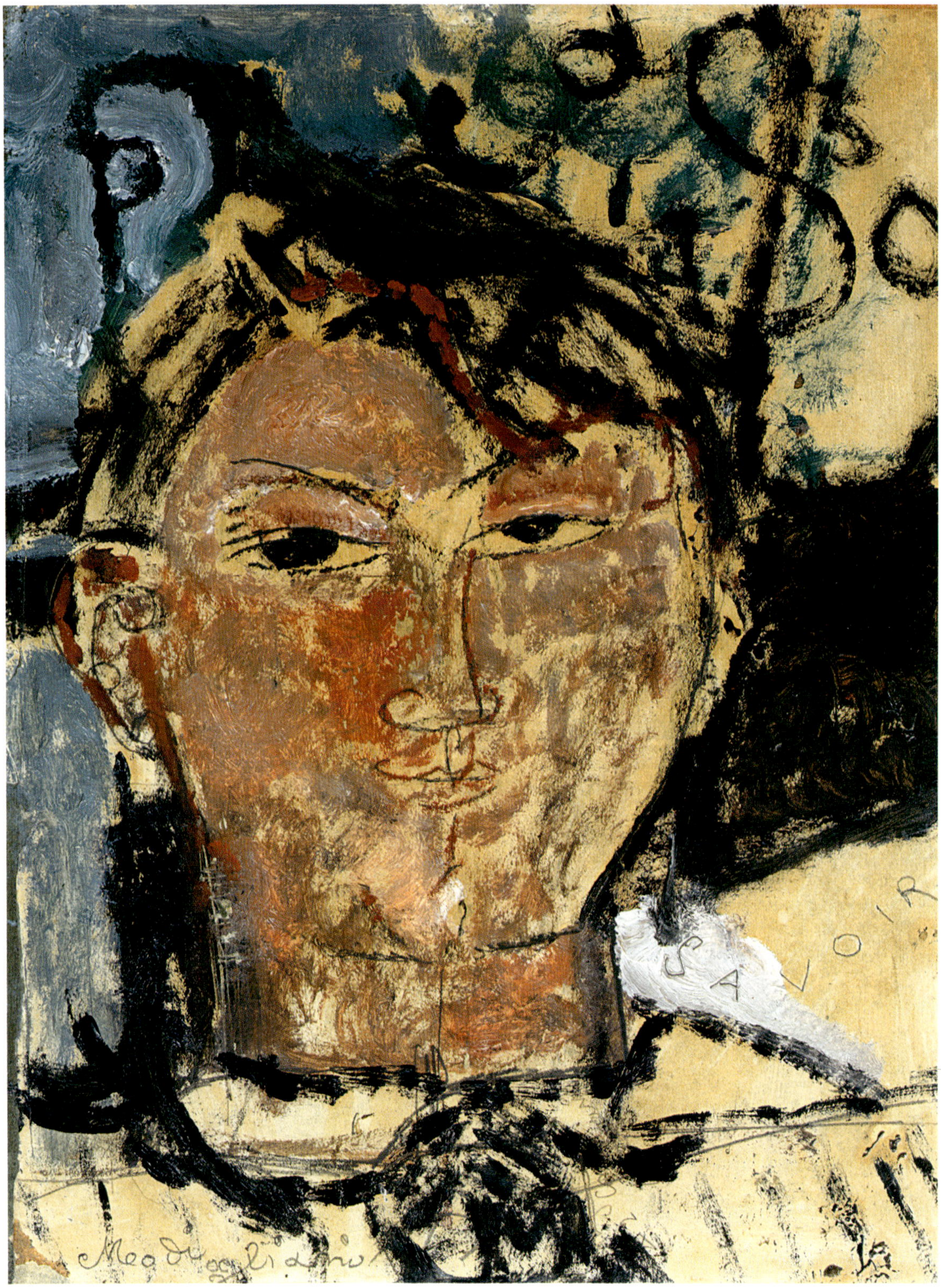

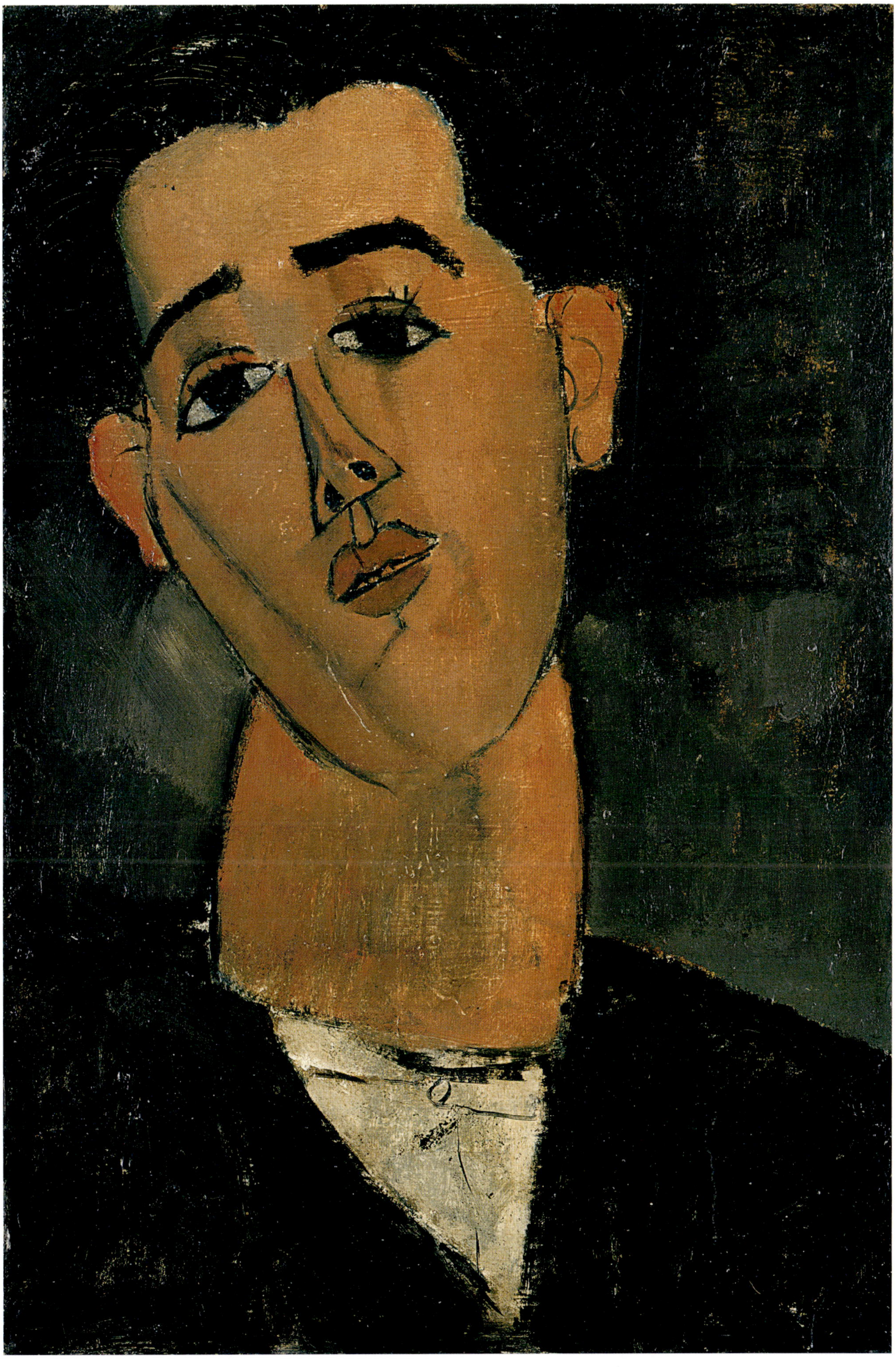

8 *Woman Seated in front of a Fireplace (Beatrice Hastings)*, 1915
Oil on canvas
81 × 65 cm
Private collection.
Courtesy of Helly Nahmad

9 *Beatrice Hastings in front of a Door*, 1915
Oil on canvas
81.3 × 46.4 cm
Private collection.
Courtesy of Ivor Braka Ltd

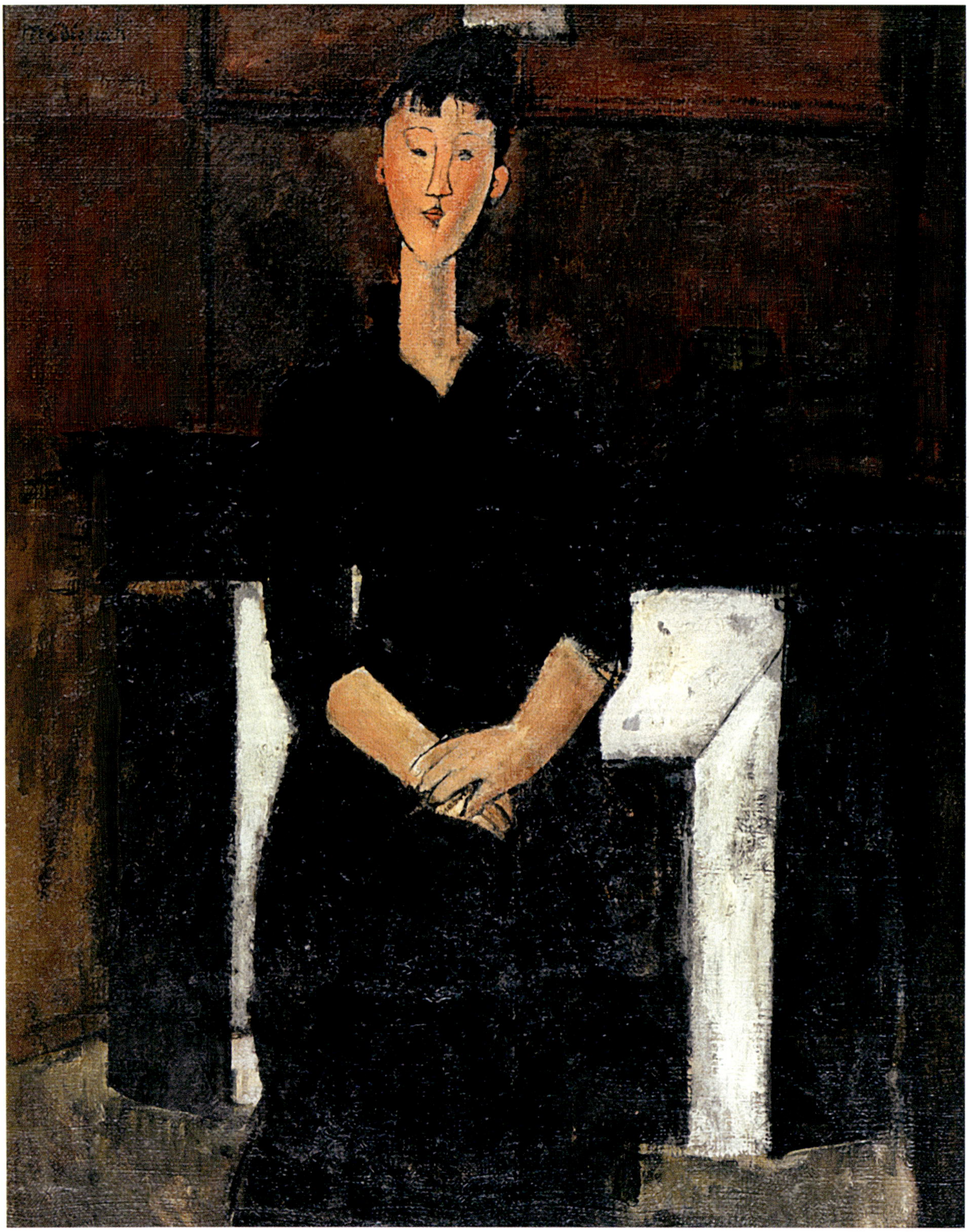

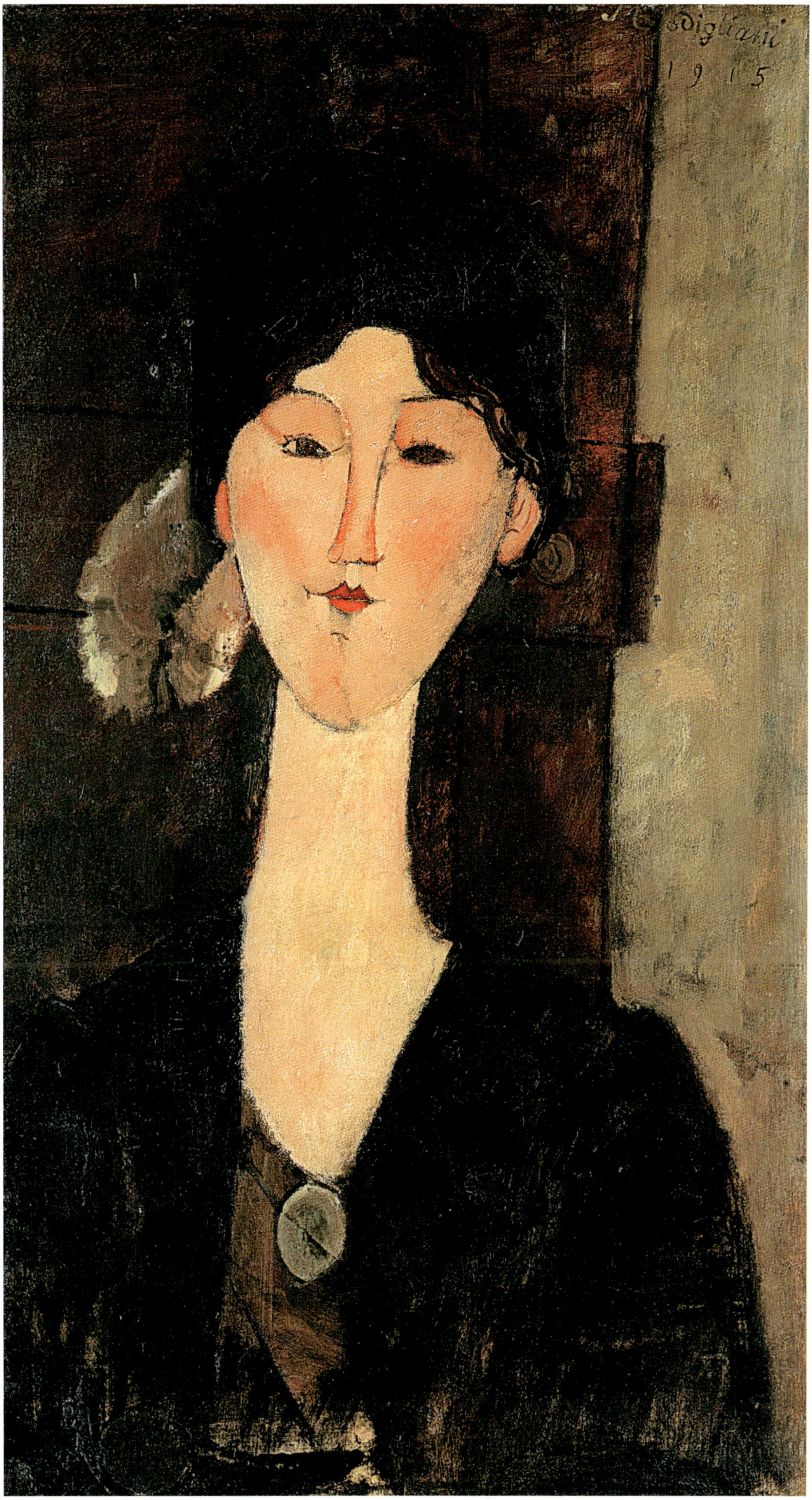

10 *Beatrice Hastings in Checkered Shirt*, 1916
Oil on canvas
65 × 46 cm
John C. Whitehead.
Courtesy of Achim Moeller, New York

11 *Young Woman in a Striped Blouse*, 1917
Oil on canvas
92 × 60 cm
Private collection.
Courtesy of Helly Nahmad

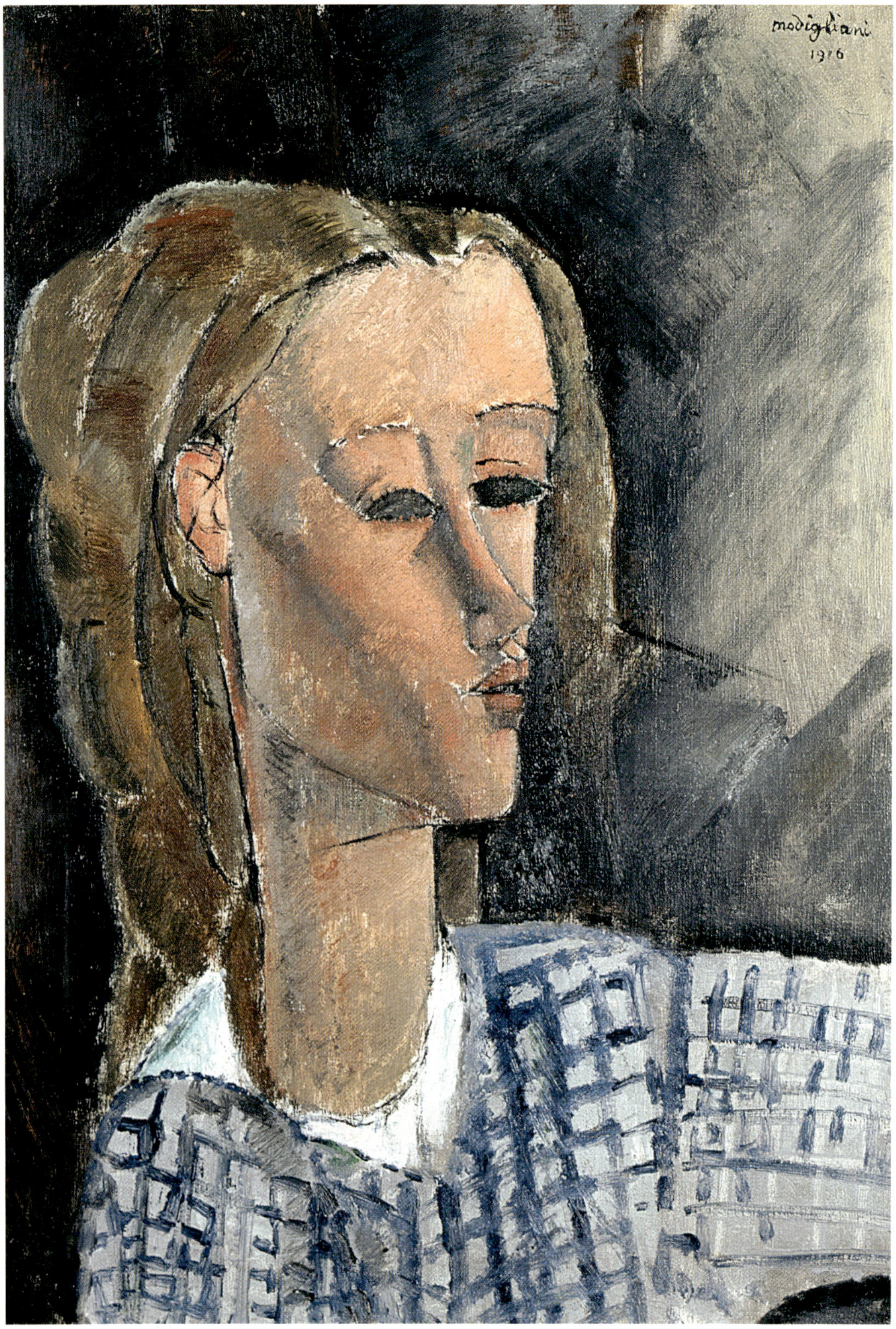

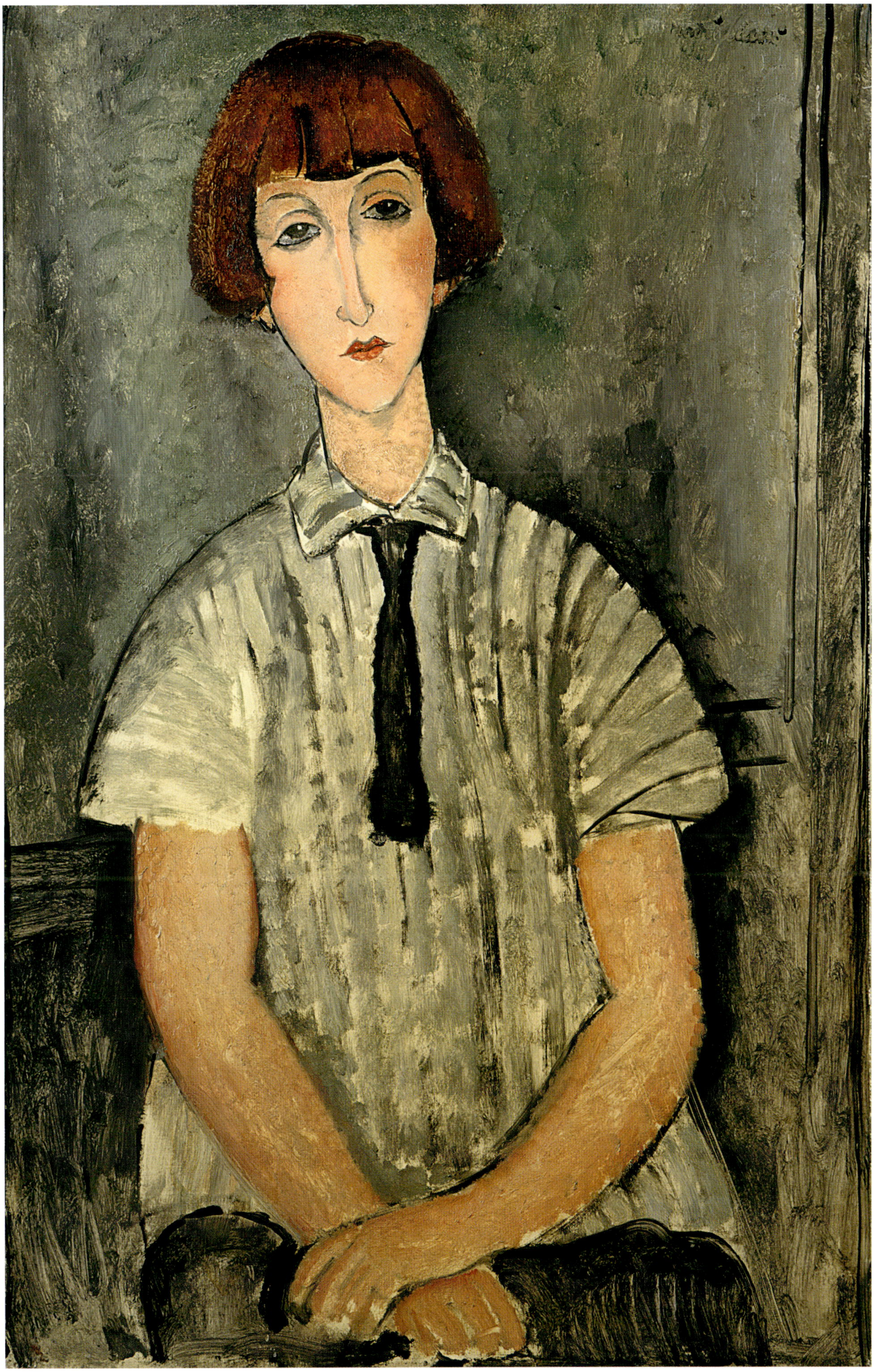

12 *Paul Guillaume*, 1915
Oil on board
74.9 × 52.1 cm
Lent by the Toledo Museum of Art.
Gift of Mrs C. Lockhart McKelvy

13 *Paul Guillaume Seated*, 1916
Oil on canvas
81 × 54 cm
Civico Museo d'Arte Contemporanea, Milan

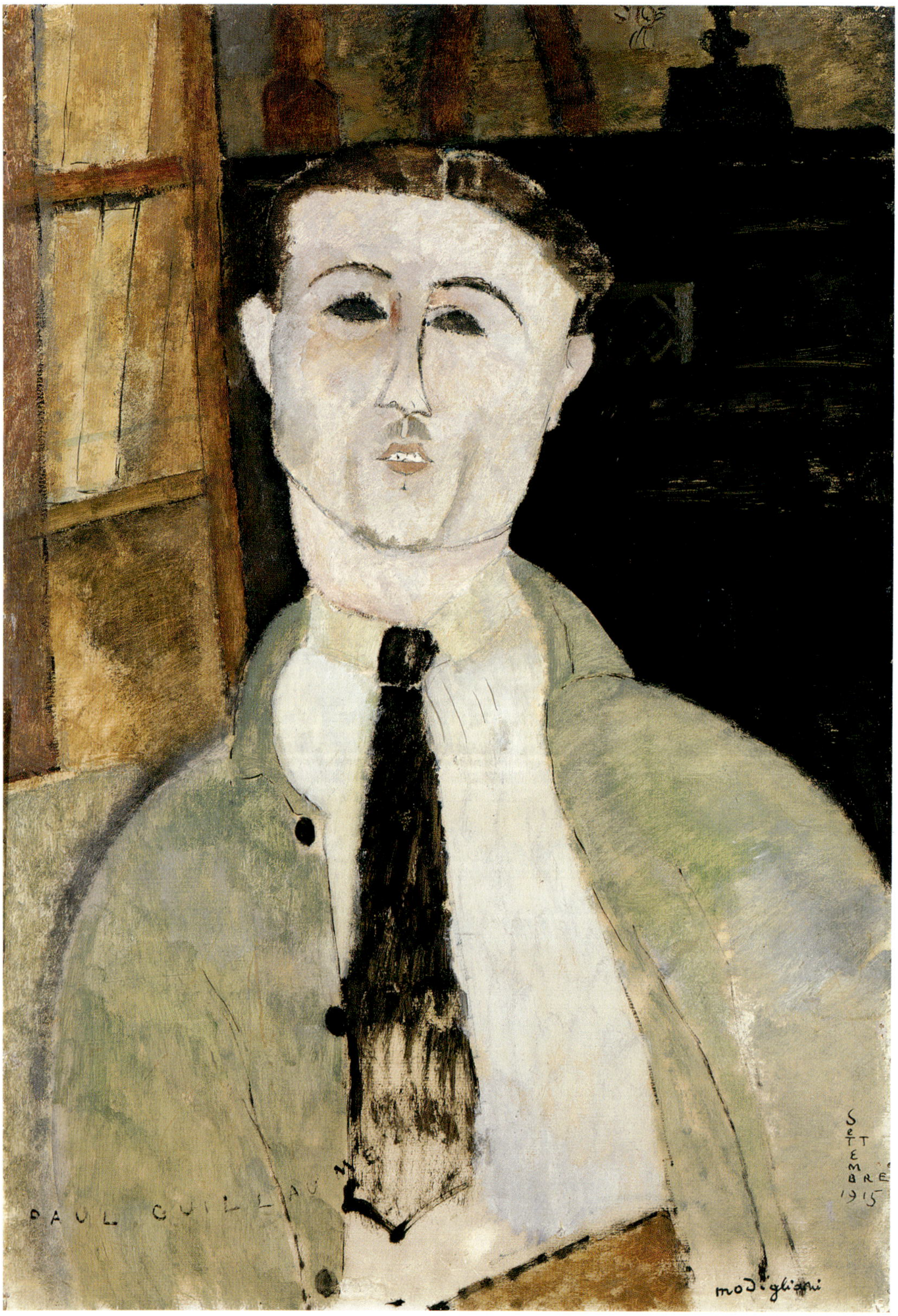

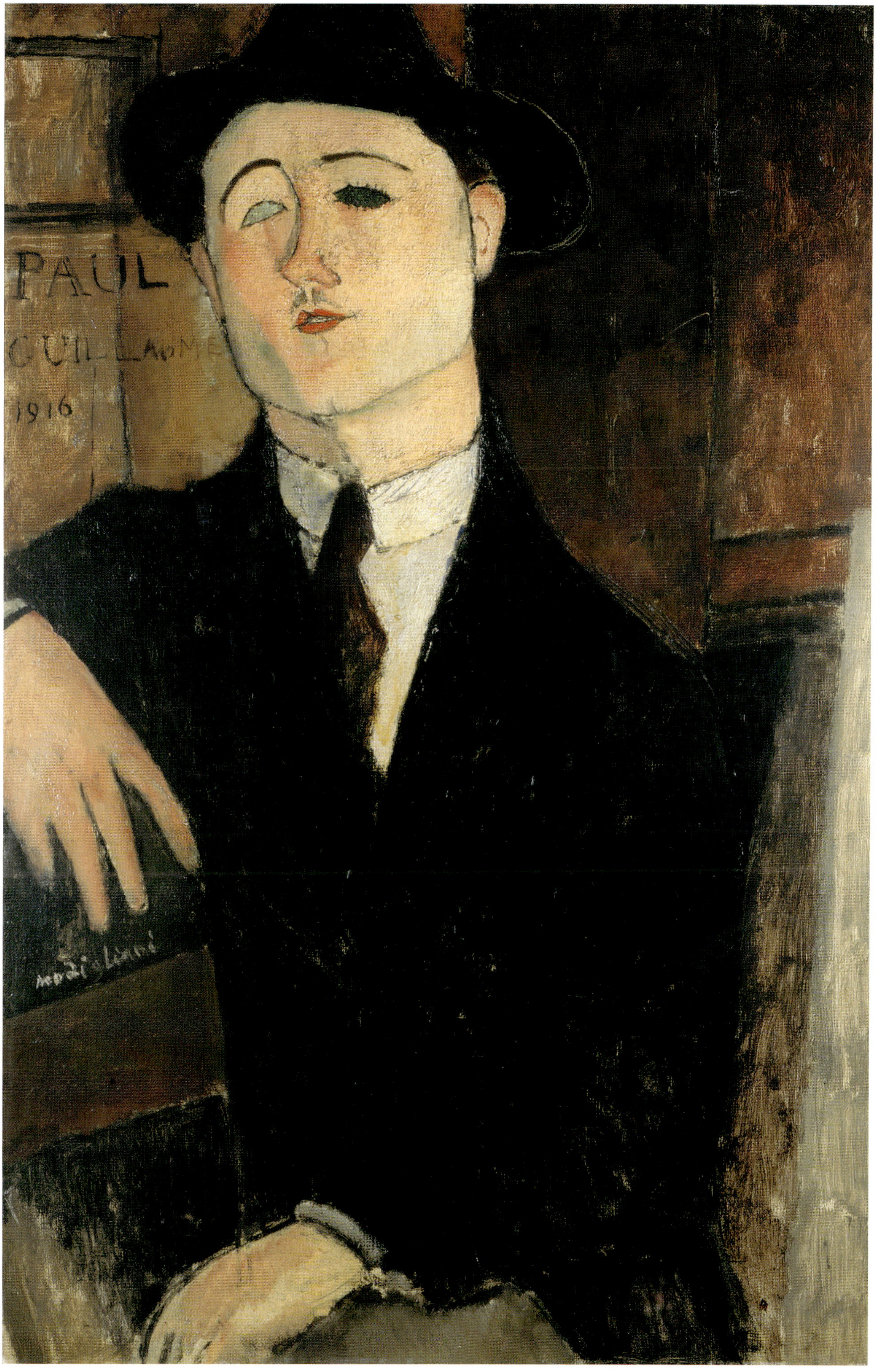
PAUL
GUILLAUME
1916
modigliani

14 *Female Nude*, *c.* 1916
Oil on canvas
92.4 × 59.8 cm
The Samuel Courtauld Trust, Courtauld Institute of Art Gallery, London

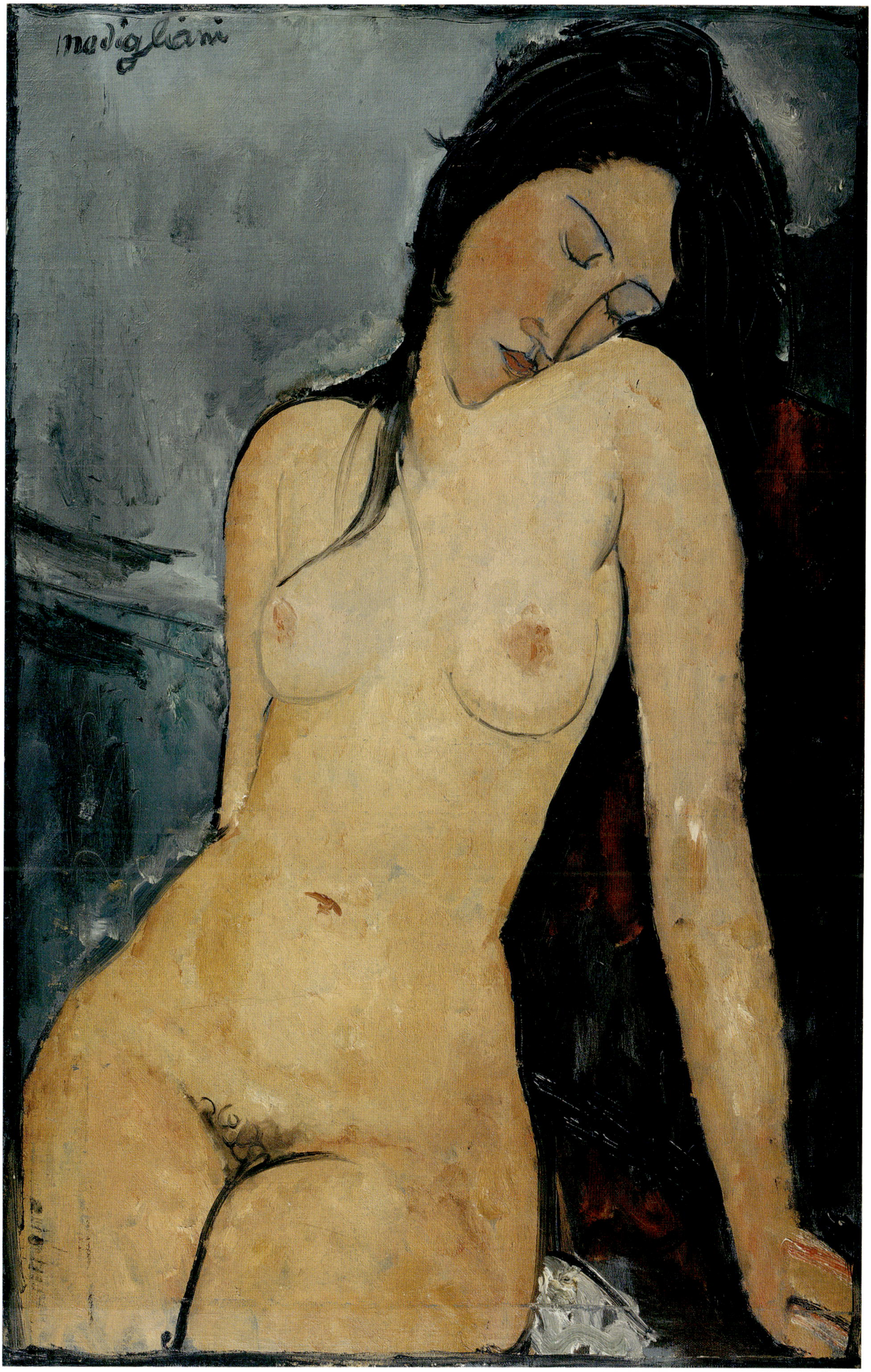
modigliani

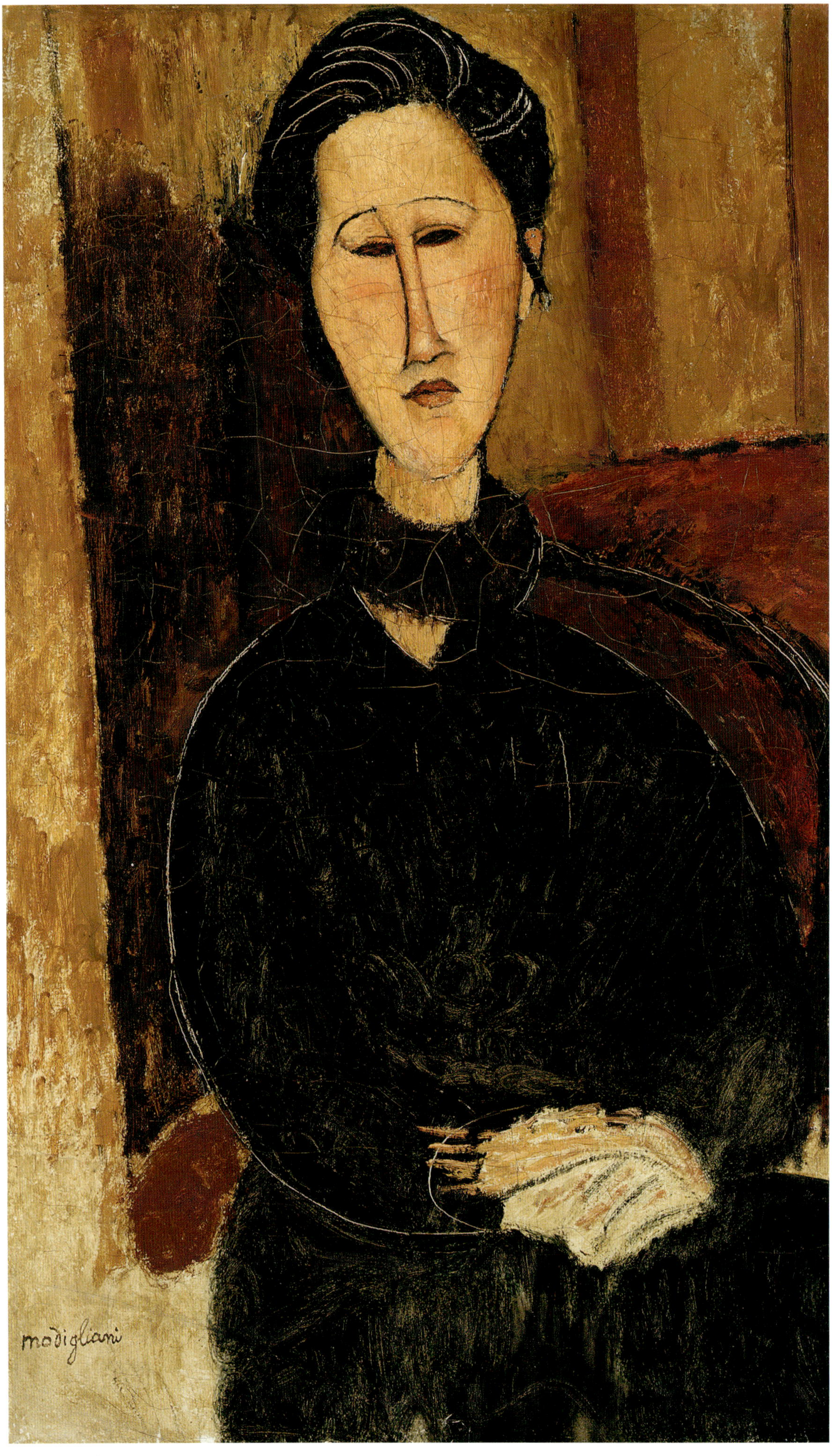

15 *Anna Zborowska*, 1916
Oil on canvas
76.2 × 45.1 cm
Courtesy of The Metropolitan Museum of Art, New York.
Lent by The Alex Hillman Family Foundation (L.1991.19.24)

16 *Léopold Zborowski*, 1916
Oil on canvas
65 × 43 cm
Collection of The Israel Museum, Jerusalem

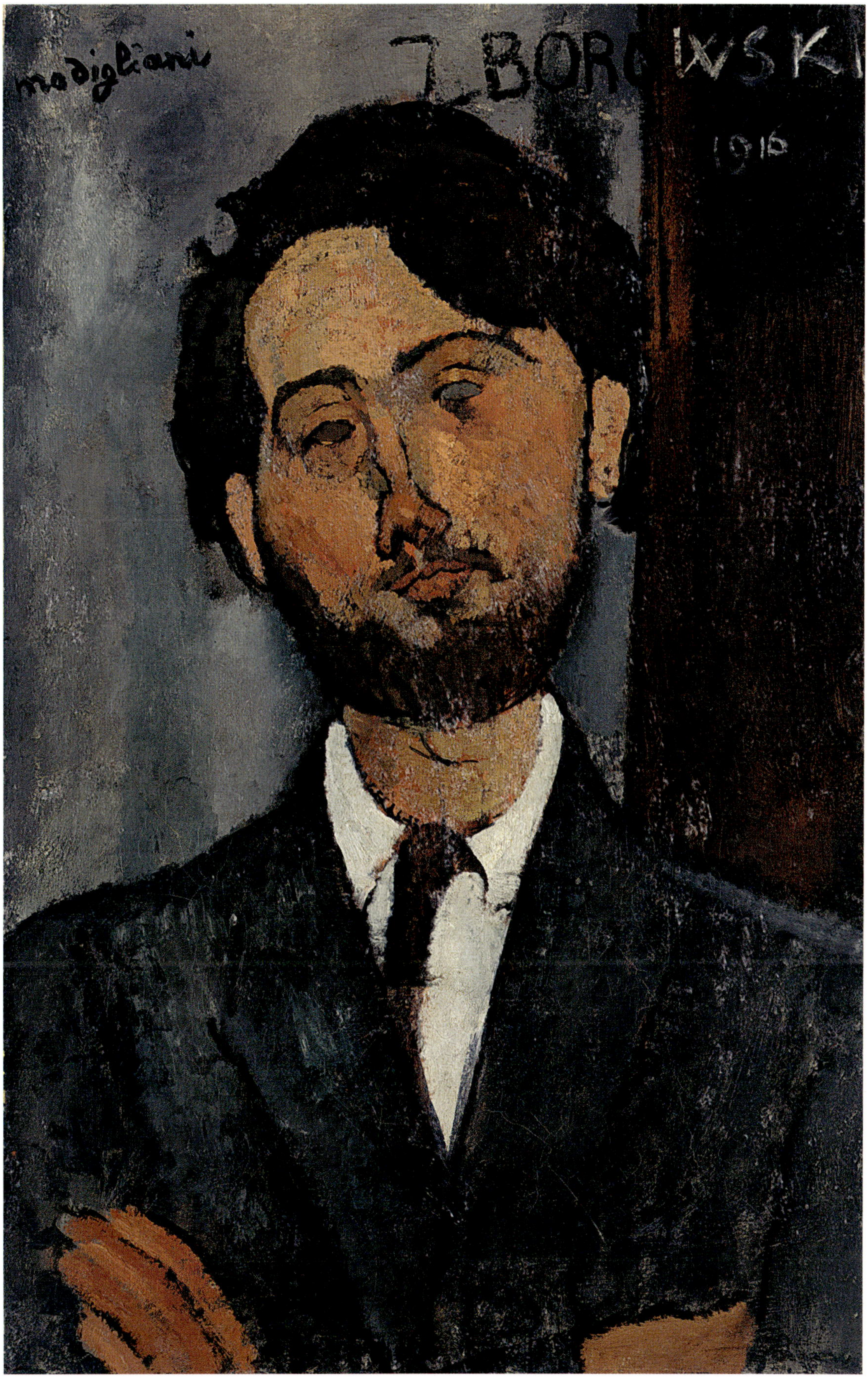

17 *Draped Nude*, 1917
Oil on canvas
114 × 74 cm
Koninklijk Museum
voor Schone
Kunsten, Antwerp

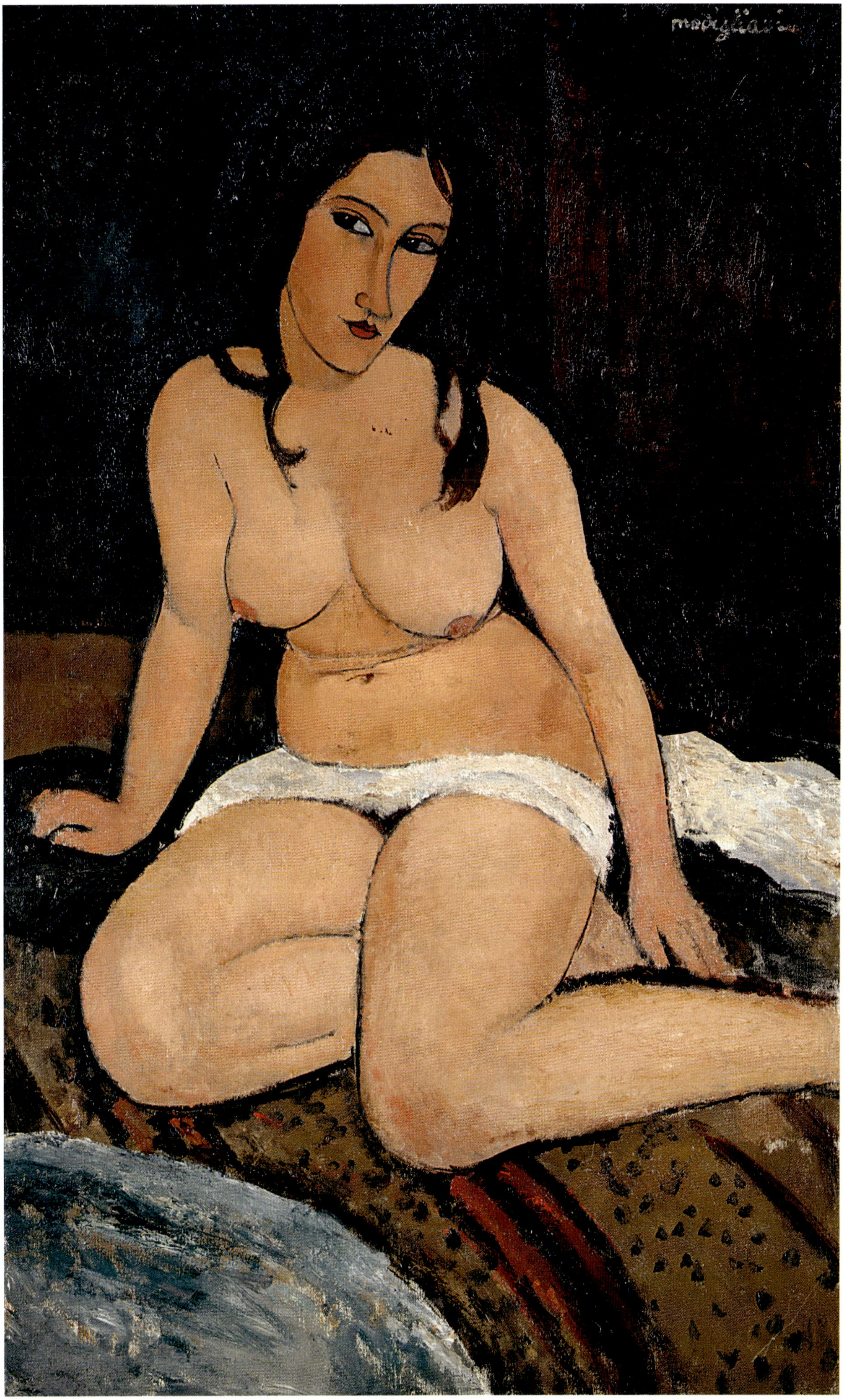
modigliani

18

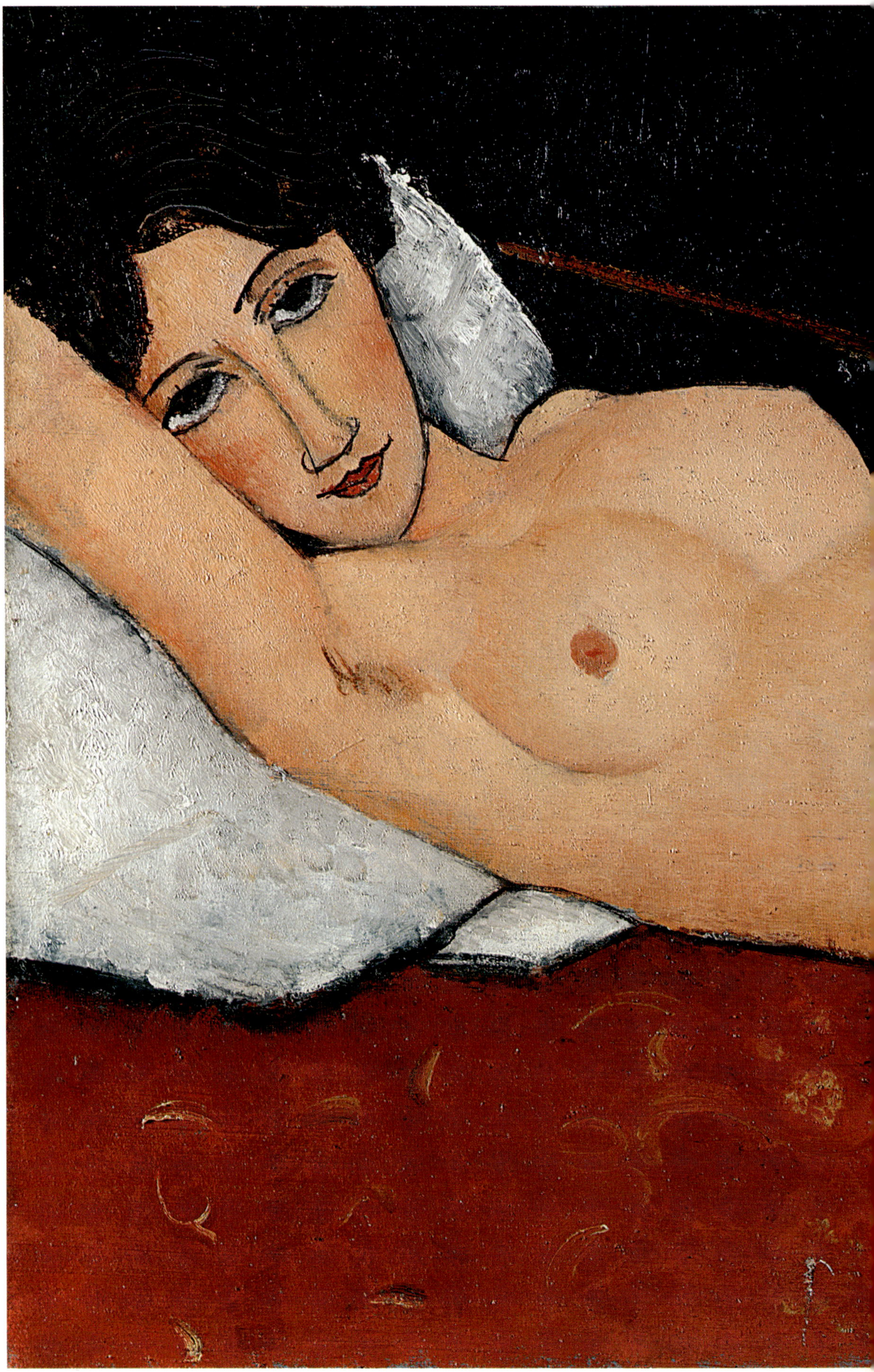

Reclining Nude on Red Couch, 1917
Oil on canvas
60 × 92 cm
Staatsgalerie Stuttgart

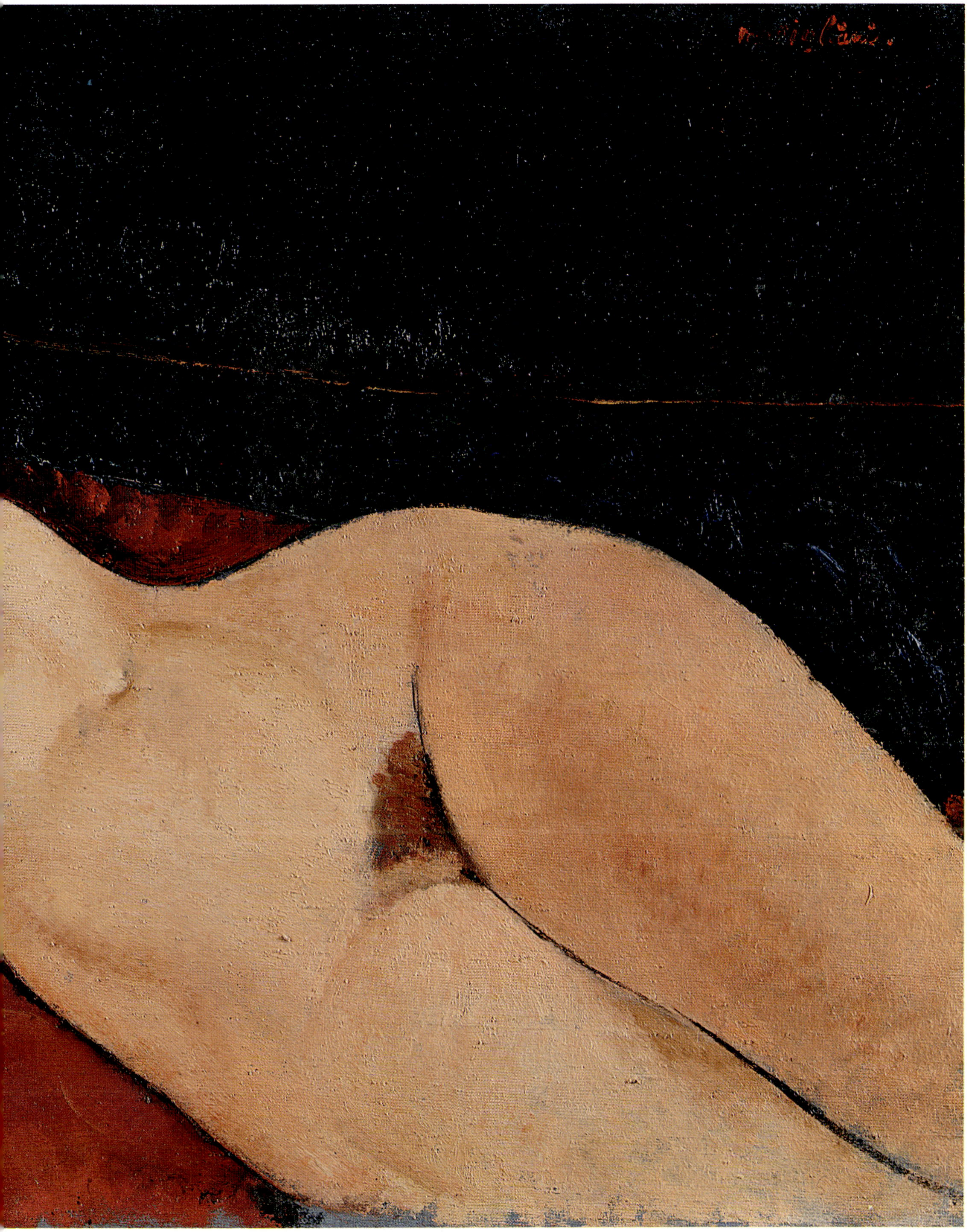

19 *Elena Povolozky*, 1917
Oil on canvas
45.8 × 33.1 cm
Private collection.
Courtesy of Helly Nahmad

20 *Oscar Miestchaninoff*, 1917
Oil on canvas
46 × 33 cm
Private collection.
Courtesy of Helly Nahmad

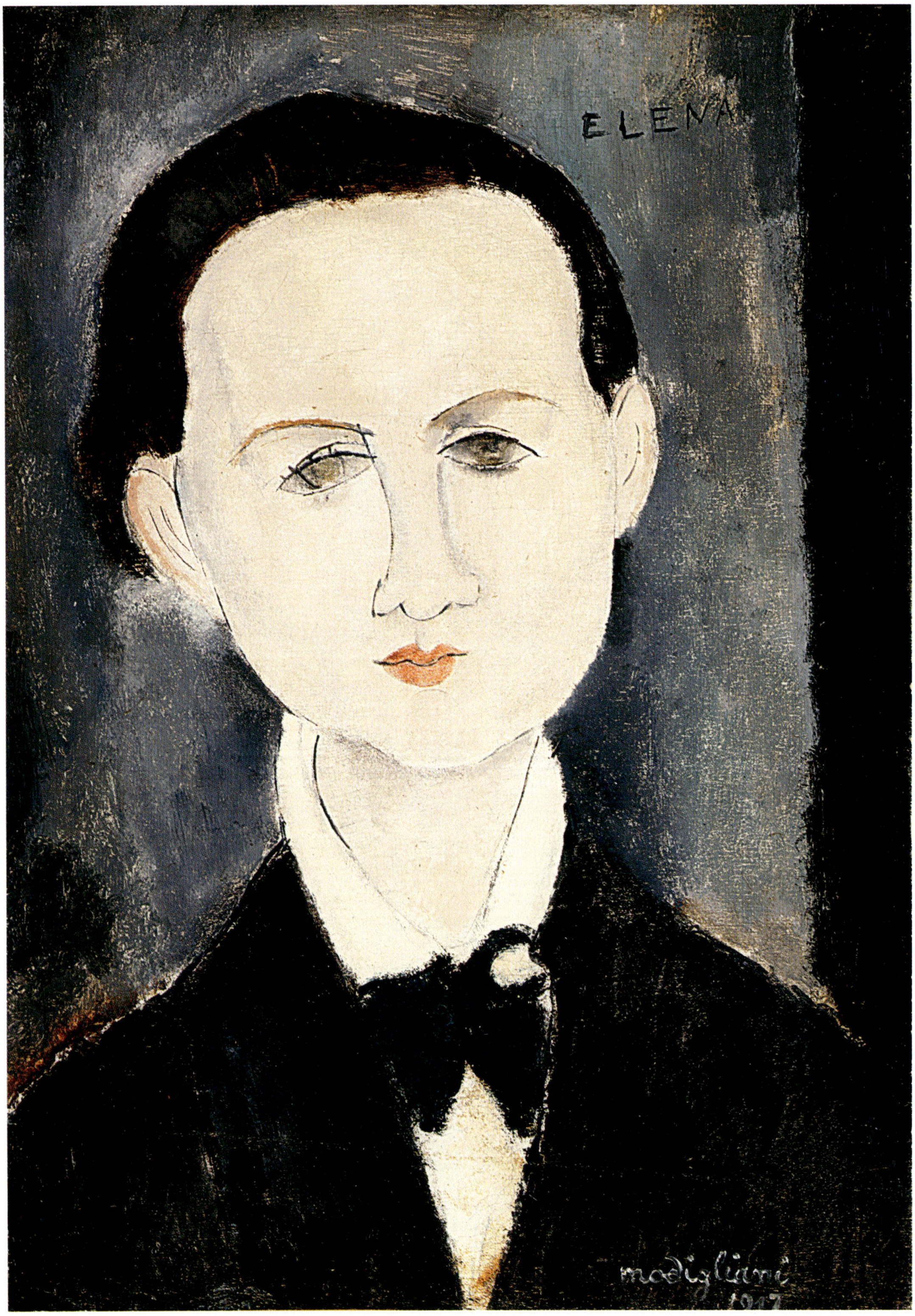

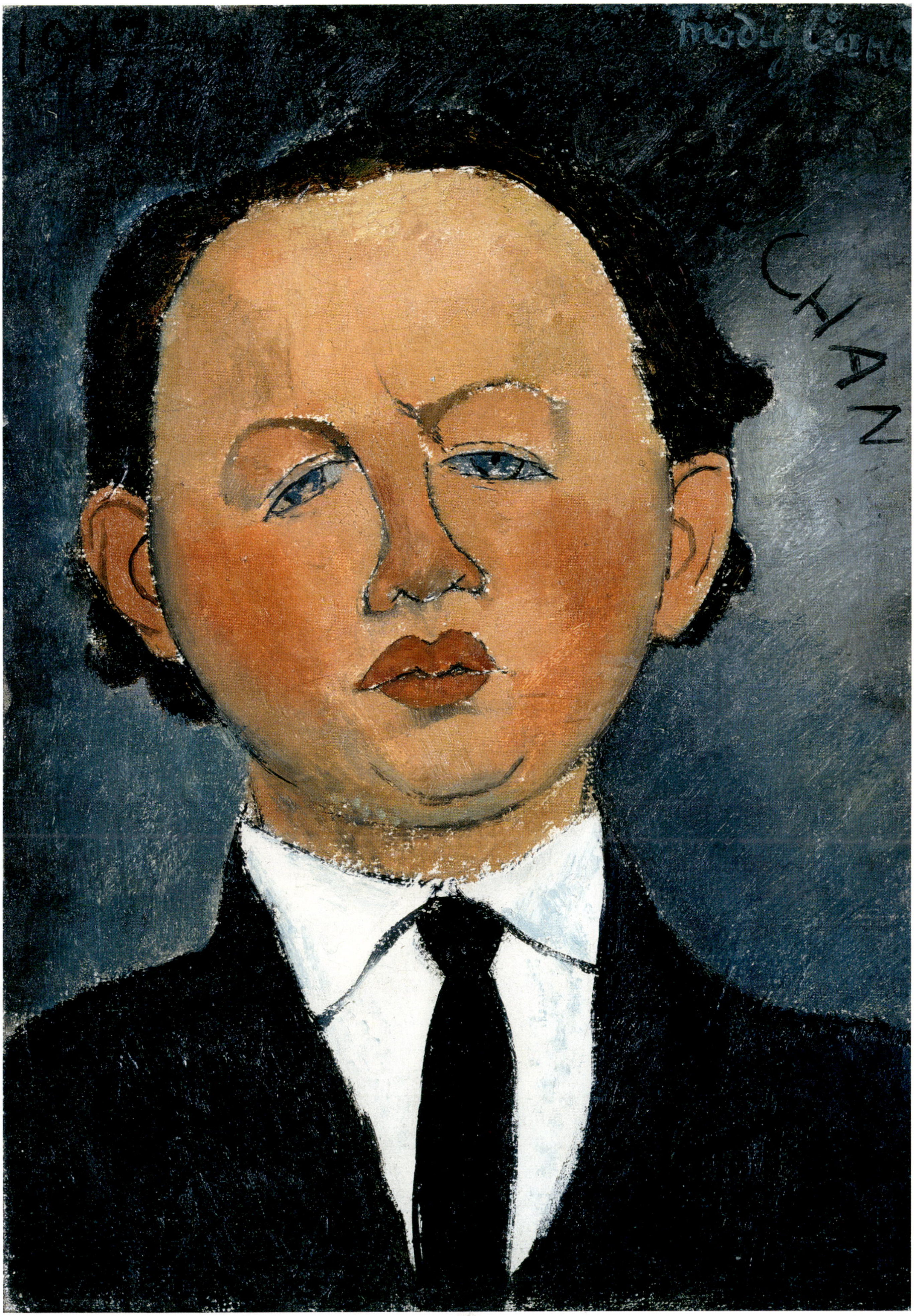
CHAN

21 *Reclining Nude with Outstretched Arms*, 1917
Oil on canvas
60 × 92 cm
Private collection

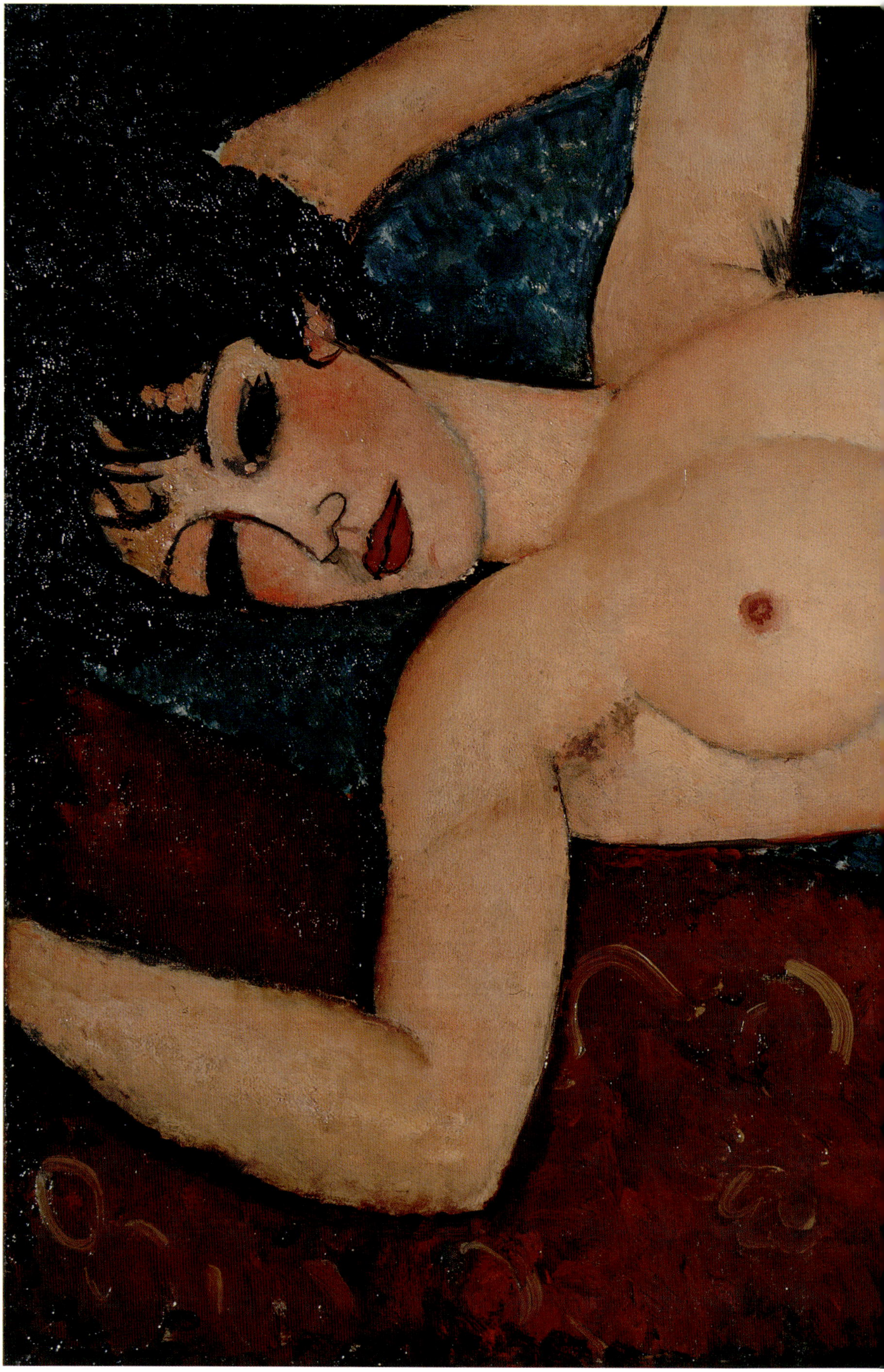

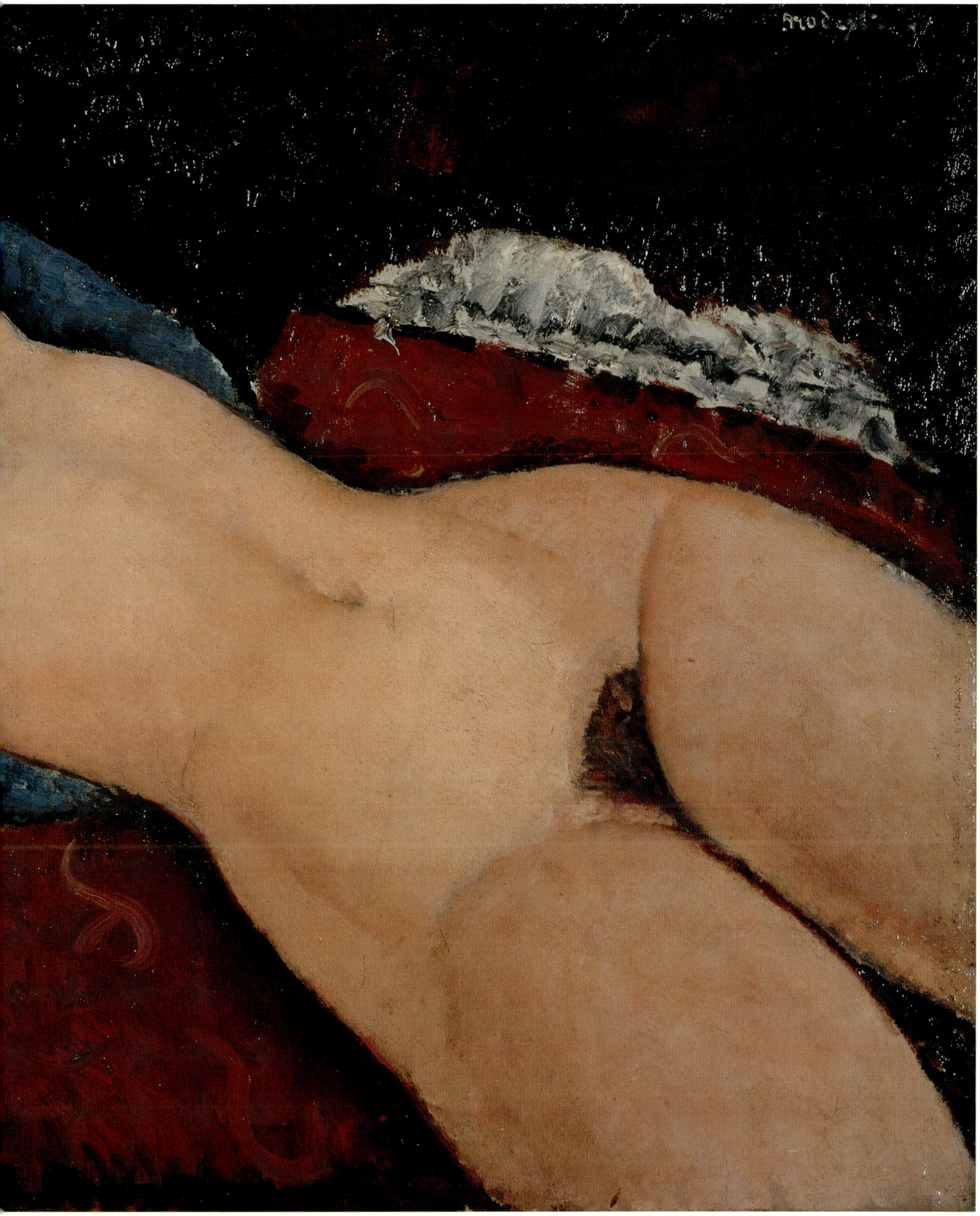

22 *The Italian Woman*, 1917
Oil on canvas
102.6 × 67 cm
Lent by The Metropolitan Museum of Art, New York. Gift of The Chester Dale Collection, 1956 (56.4)

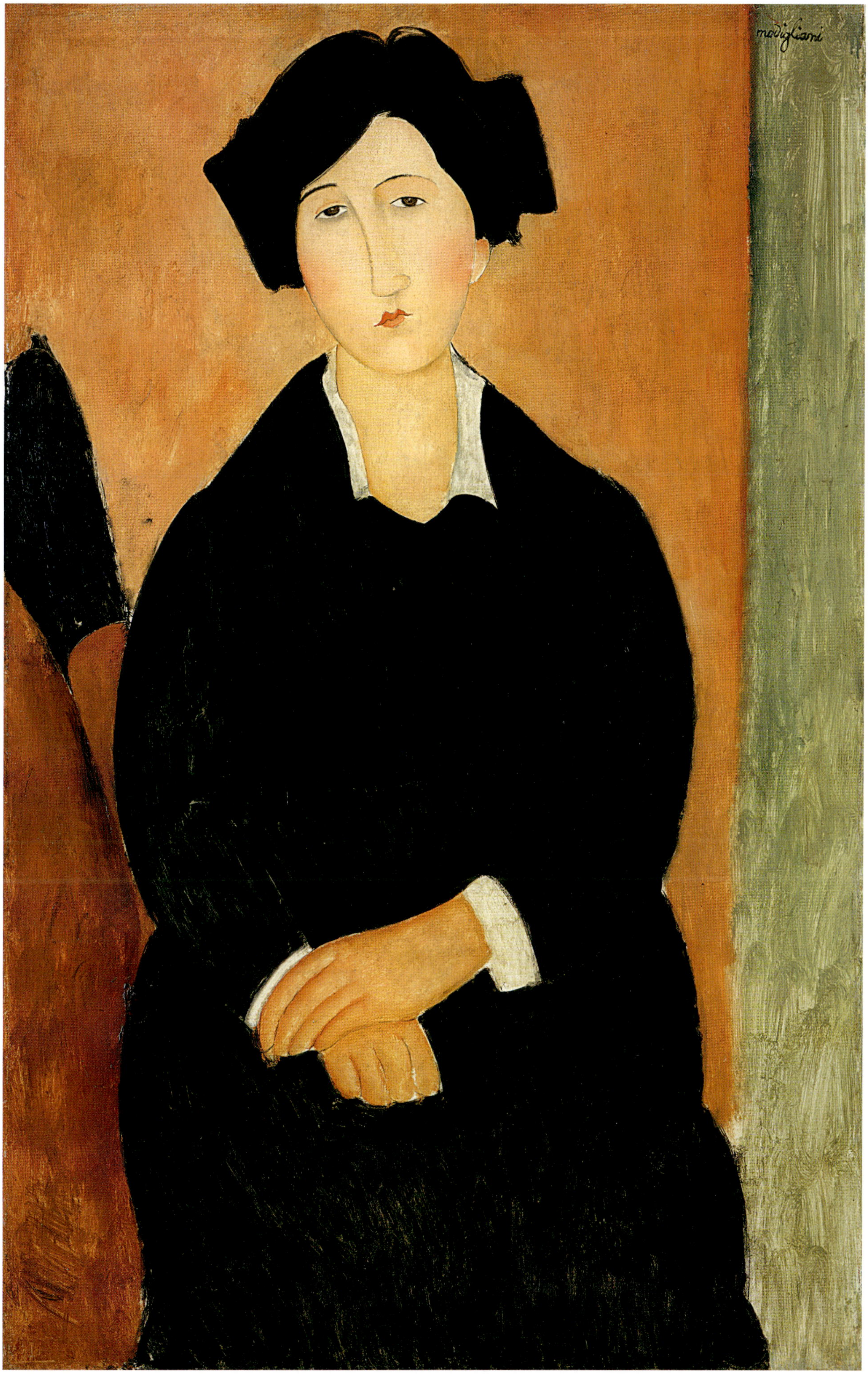
modigliani

23 *Nude*, 1917
Oil on canvas
73 × 116.7 cm
Solomon R.
Guggenheim Museum,
New York.
Gift of Solomon R.
Guggenheim 41.535

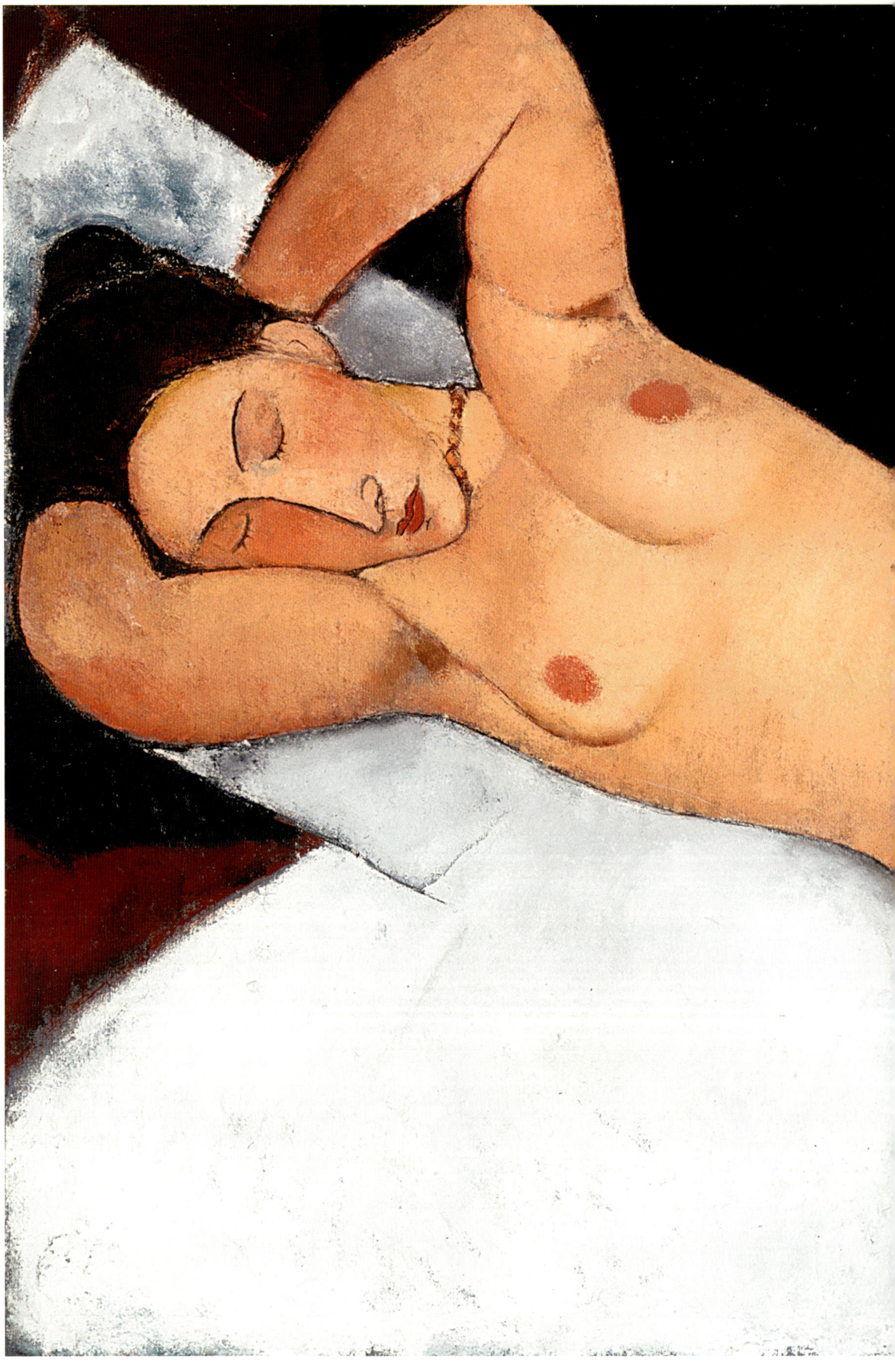

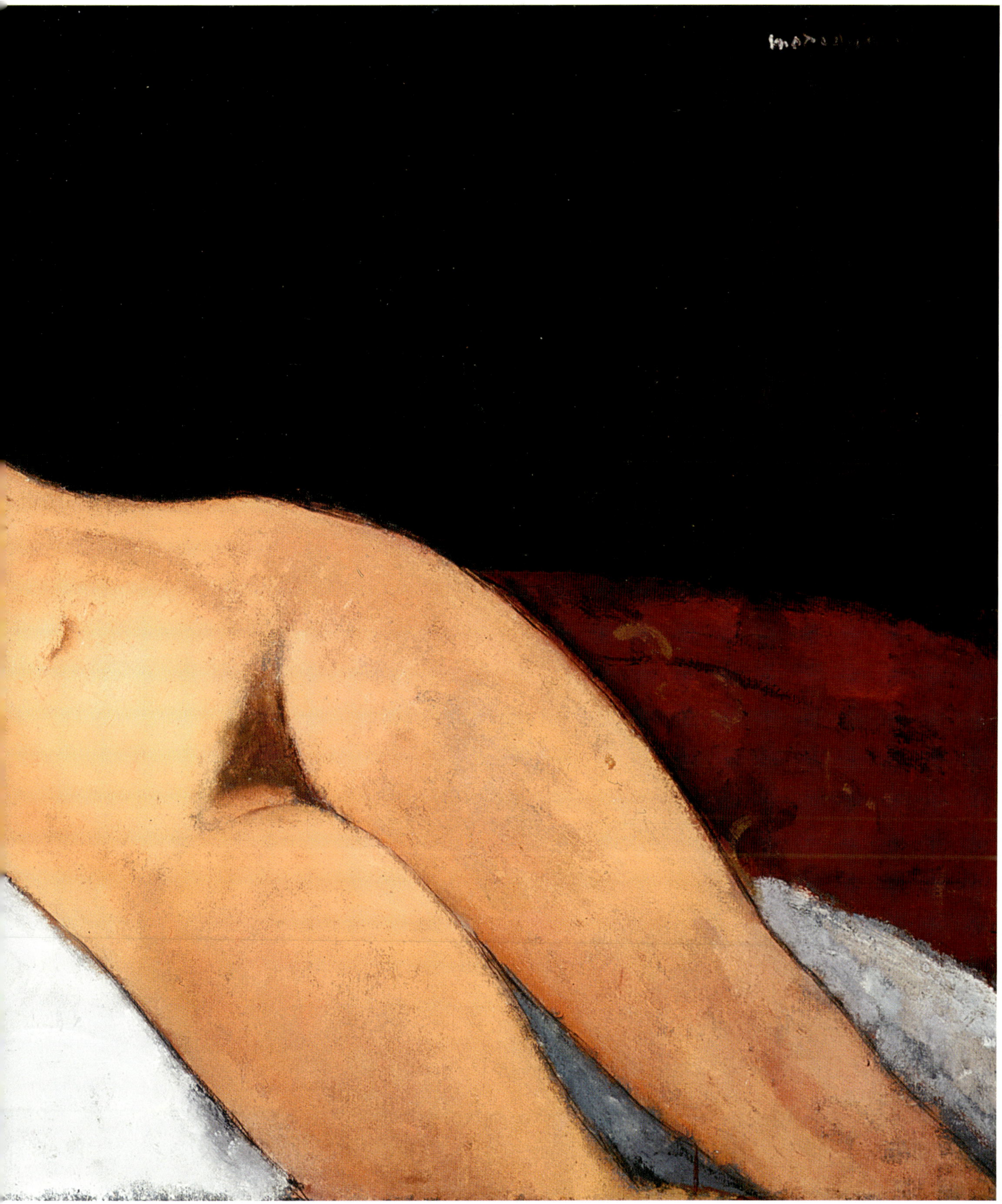

24 *Seated Girl with Brown Hair*, 1918
Oil on canvas
93 × 60 cm
Musée Picasso, Paris

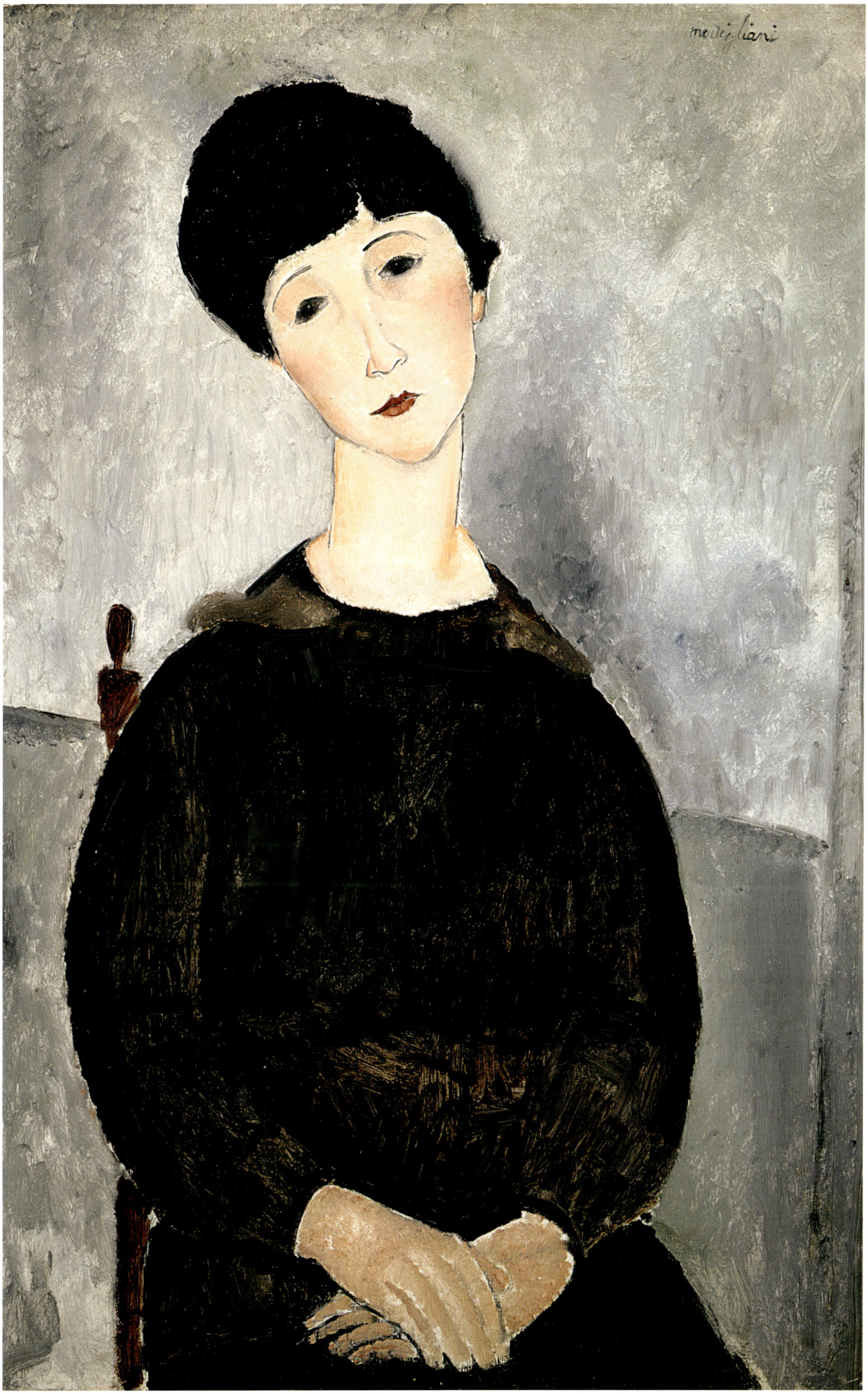
modigliani

25 *Blue Eyes (Portrait of Madame Jeanne Hébuterne)*, 1917
Oil on canvas
54.6 × 42.9 cm
Philadelphia Museum of Art. The Samuel S. White III and Vera White Collection, 1967

26 *Head of Jeanne Hébuterne*, 1917–18
Oil on canvas
44.8 × 27.5 cm
Private collection

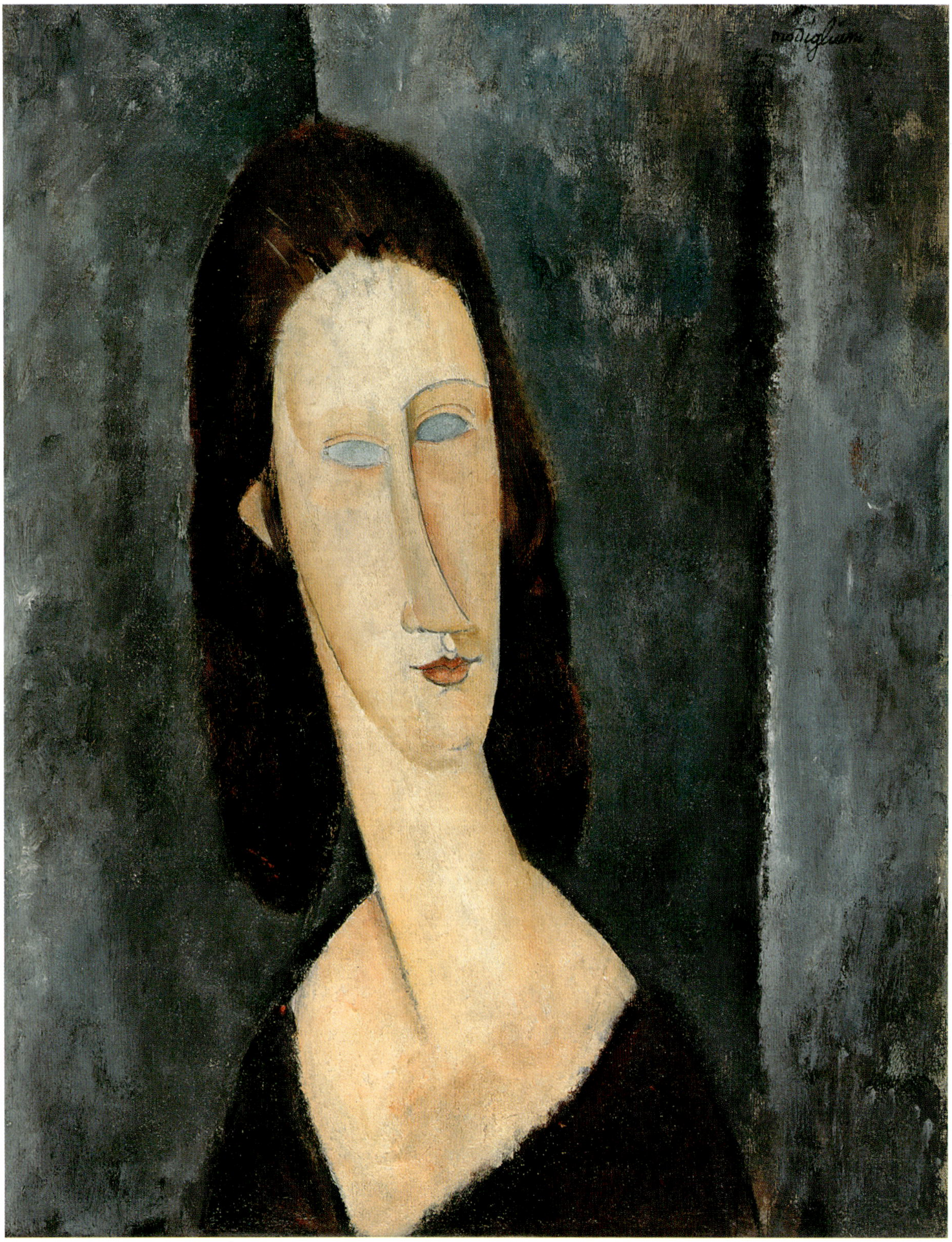

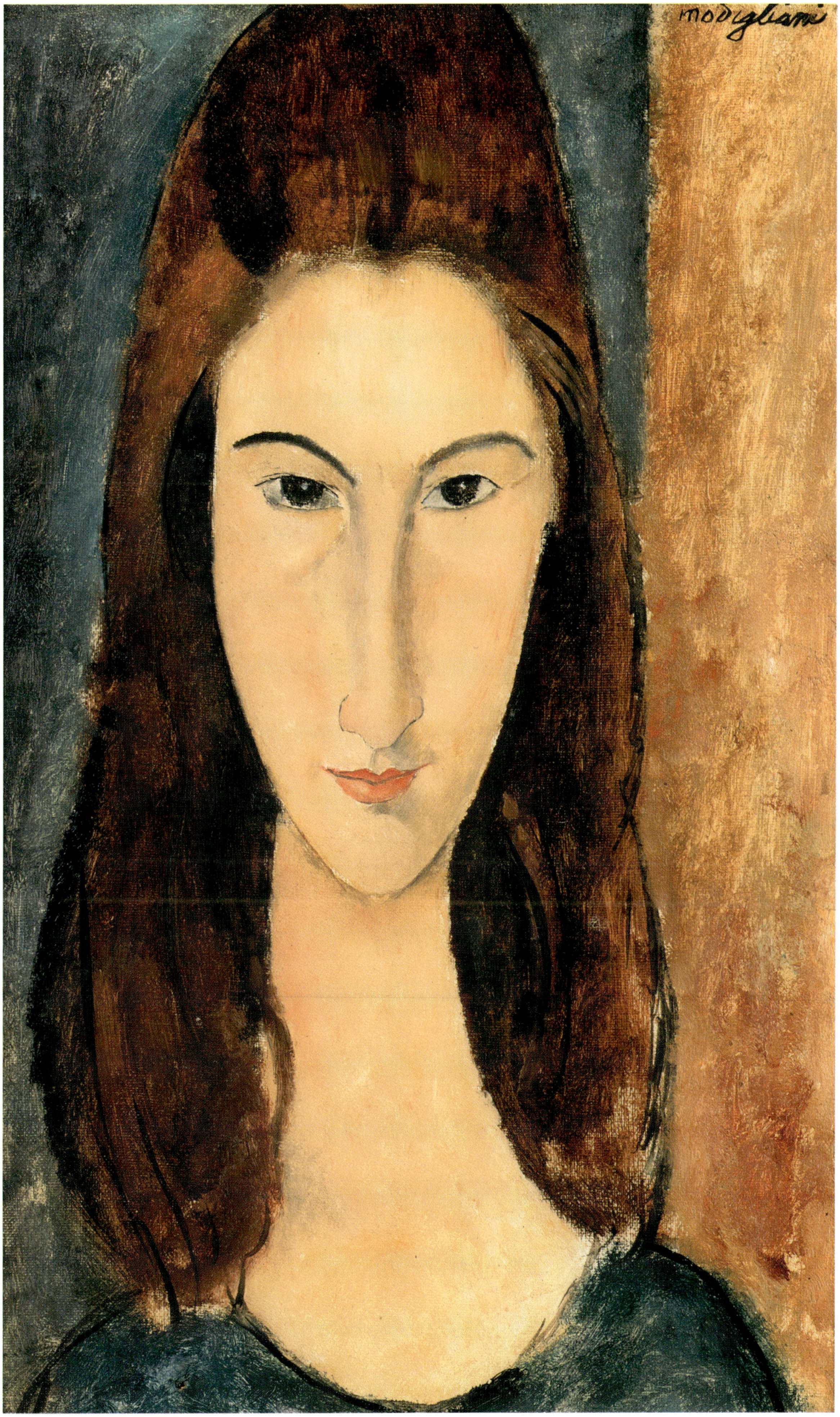
modigliani

27 *Anna Zborowska*, 1917
Oil on canvas
55 × 39 cm
Private collection

28 *Hanka Zborowska*, 1917
Oil on canvas
55 × 38 cm
Galleria Nazionale d'Arte Moderna, Rome

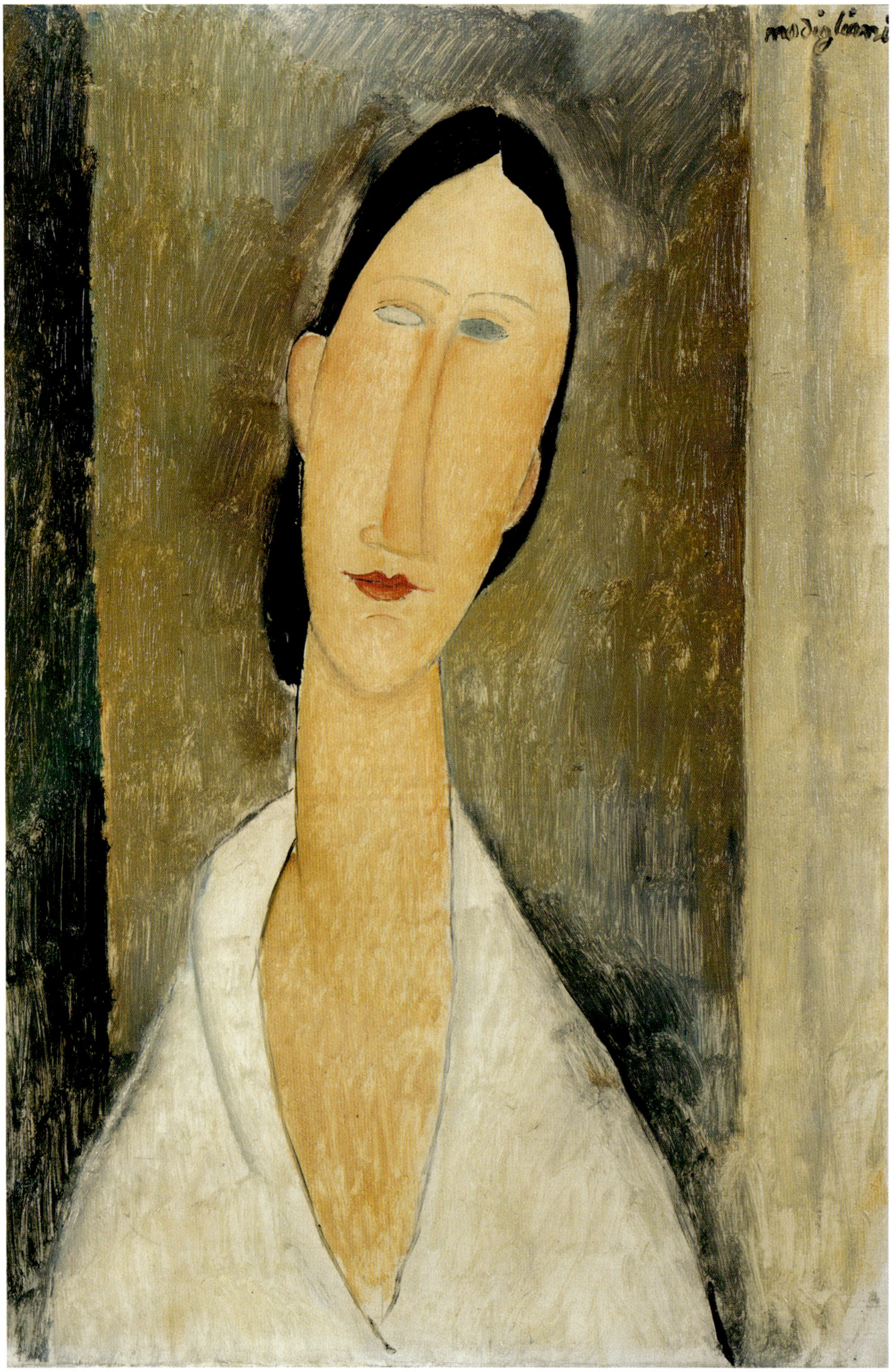

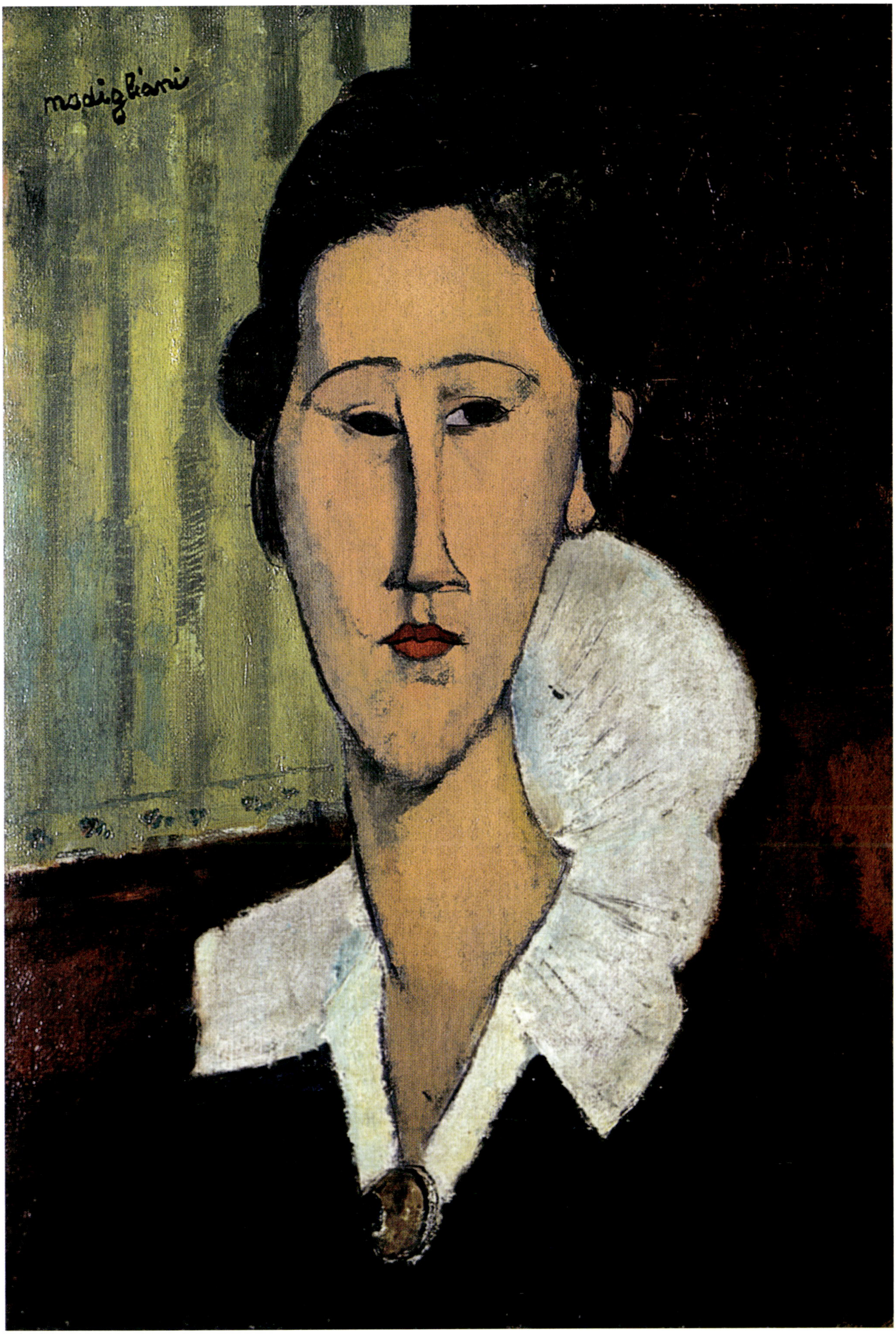
modigliani

29 *Portrait of Léopold Zborowski*, 1917–18
Oil on canvas
73 × 50 cm
Private collection

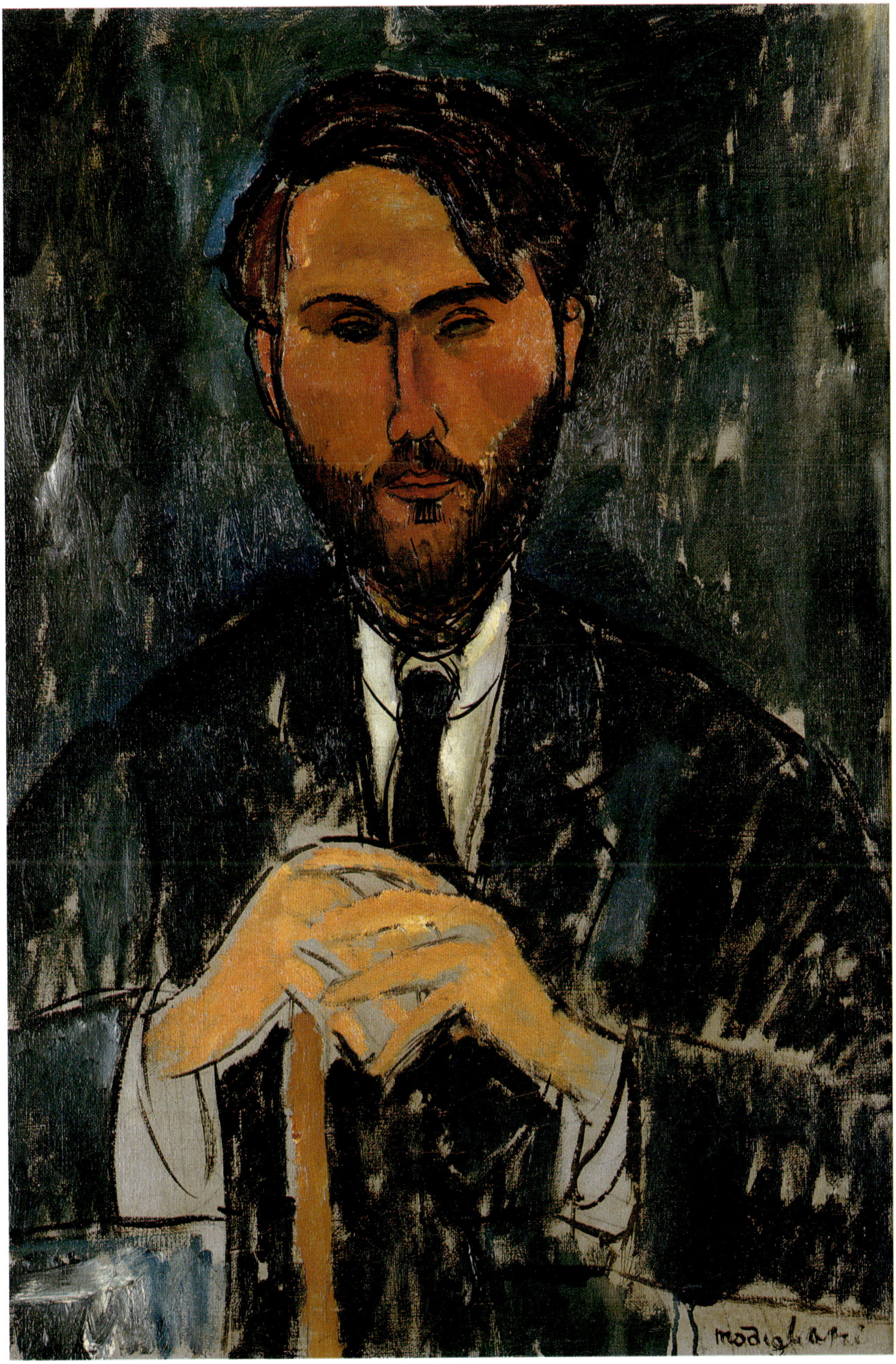

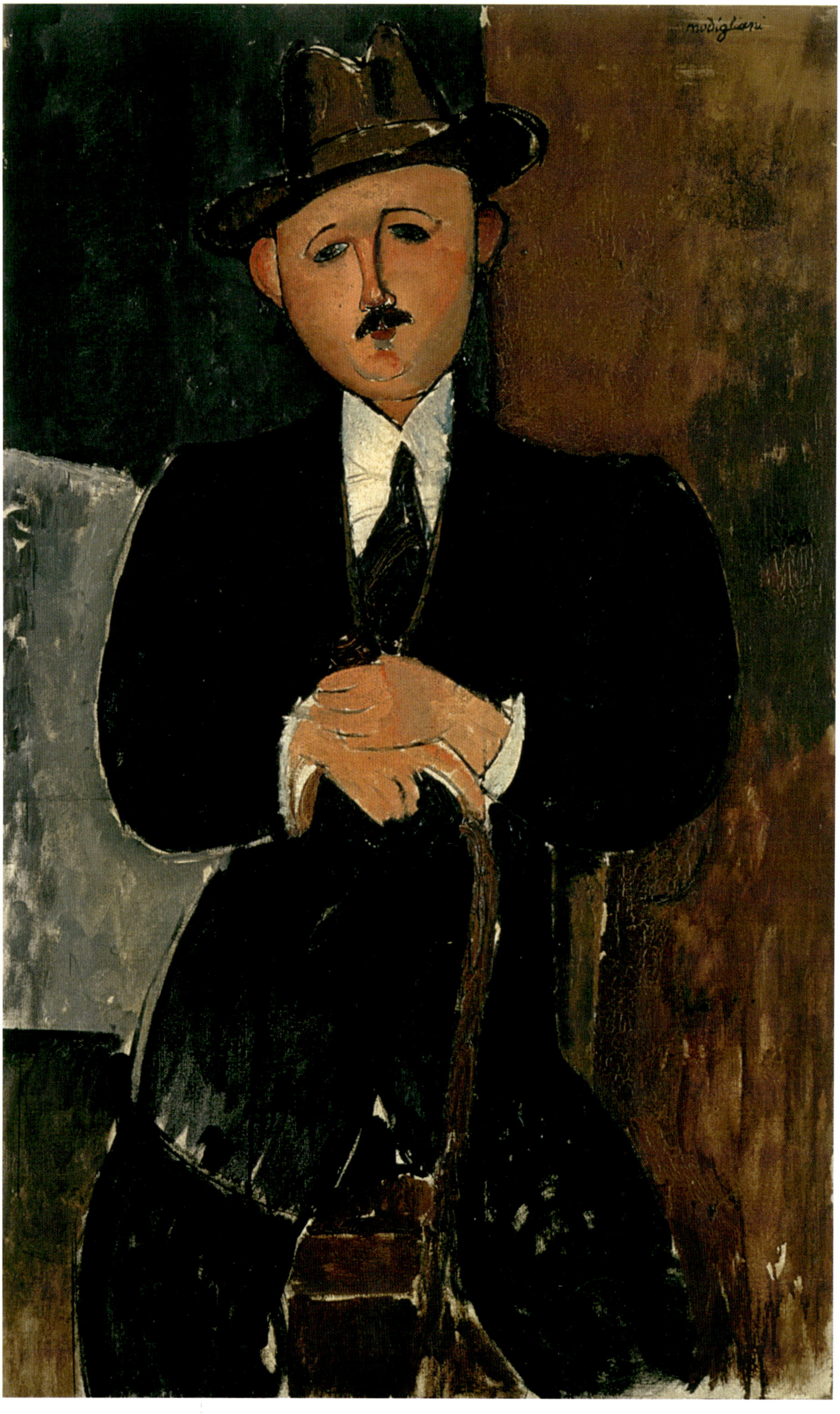
modigliani

30 *Seated Man with a Cane*, 1918
Oil on canvas
126 × 75 cm
Private collection. Courtesy of Helly Nahmad

31 *The Servant Girl*, c. 1918
Oil on canvas
152.4 × 61 cm
Albright-Knox Art Gallery
Buffalo, New York.
Room of Contemporary Art Fund, 1939

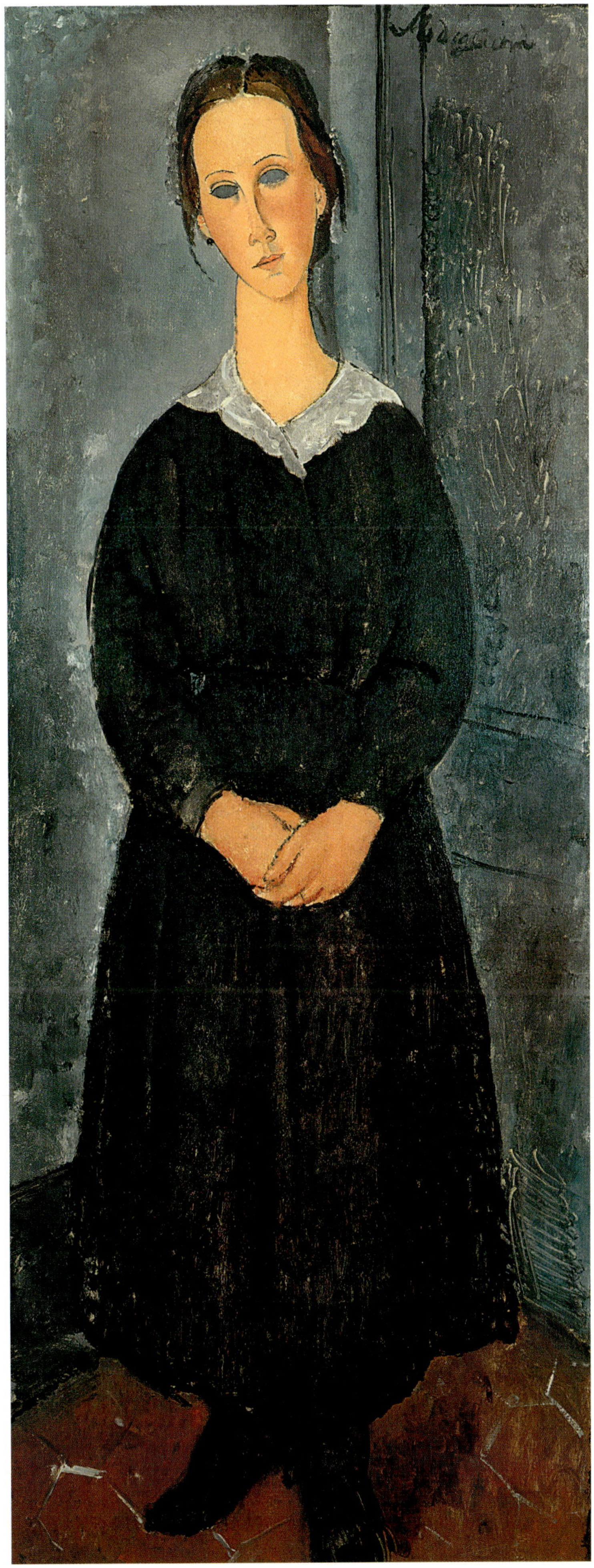

32 *La Belle Epicière*, 1918
Oil on canvas
100 × 65 cm
Private collection.
Courtesy of Helly Nahmad

33 *The Little Peasant*,
c. 1918
Oil on canvas
100 × 64.5 cm
Tate, London.
Presented by Miss Jenny
Blaker in memory of
Hugh Blaker, 1941

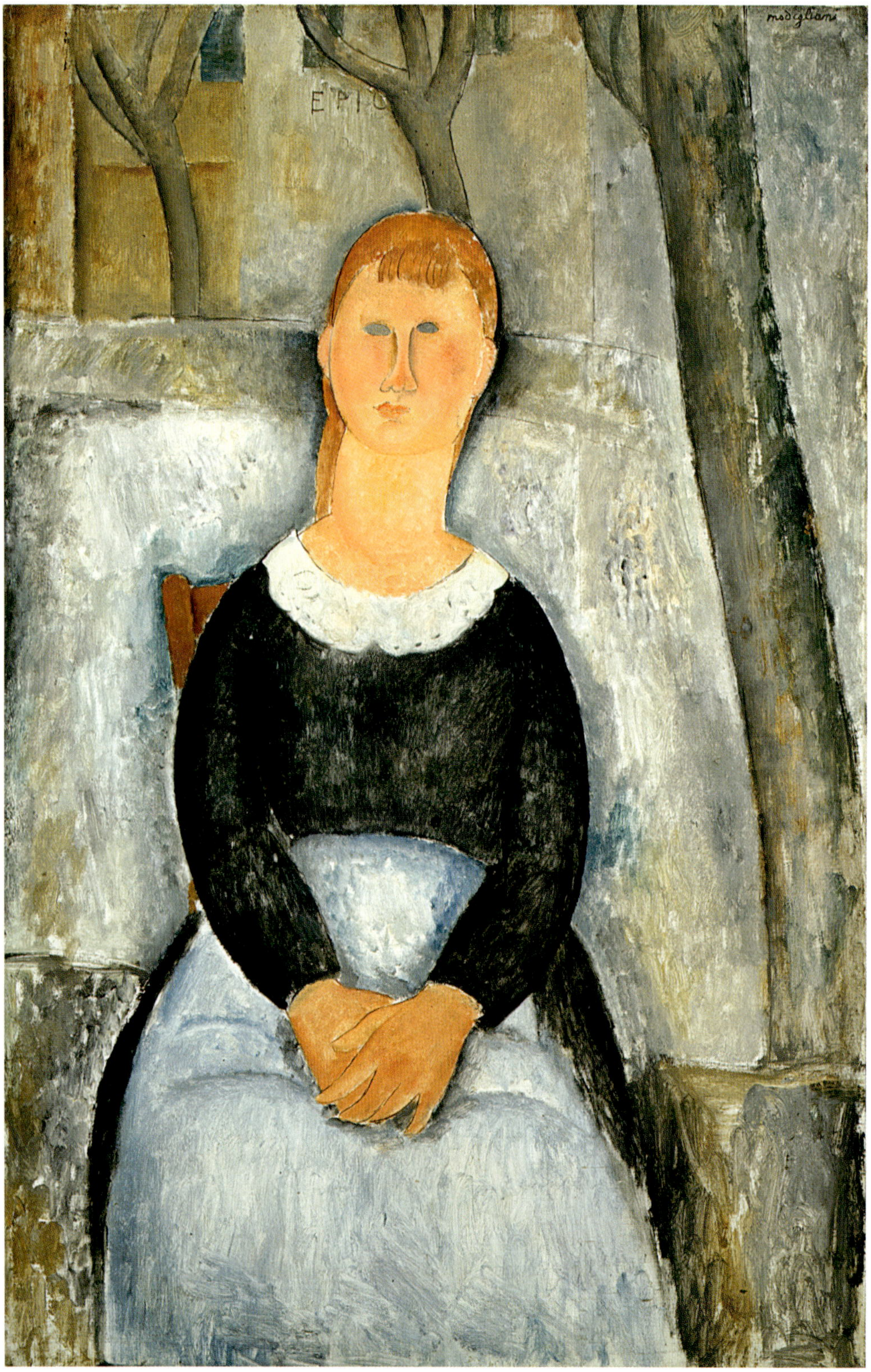

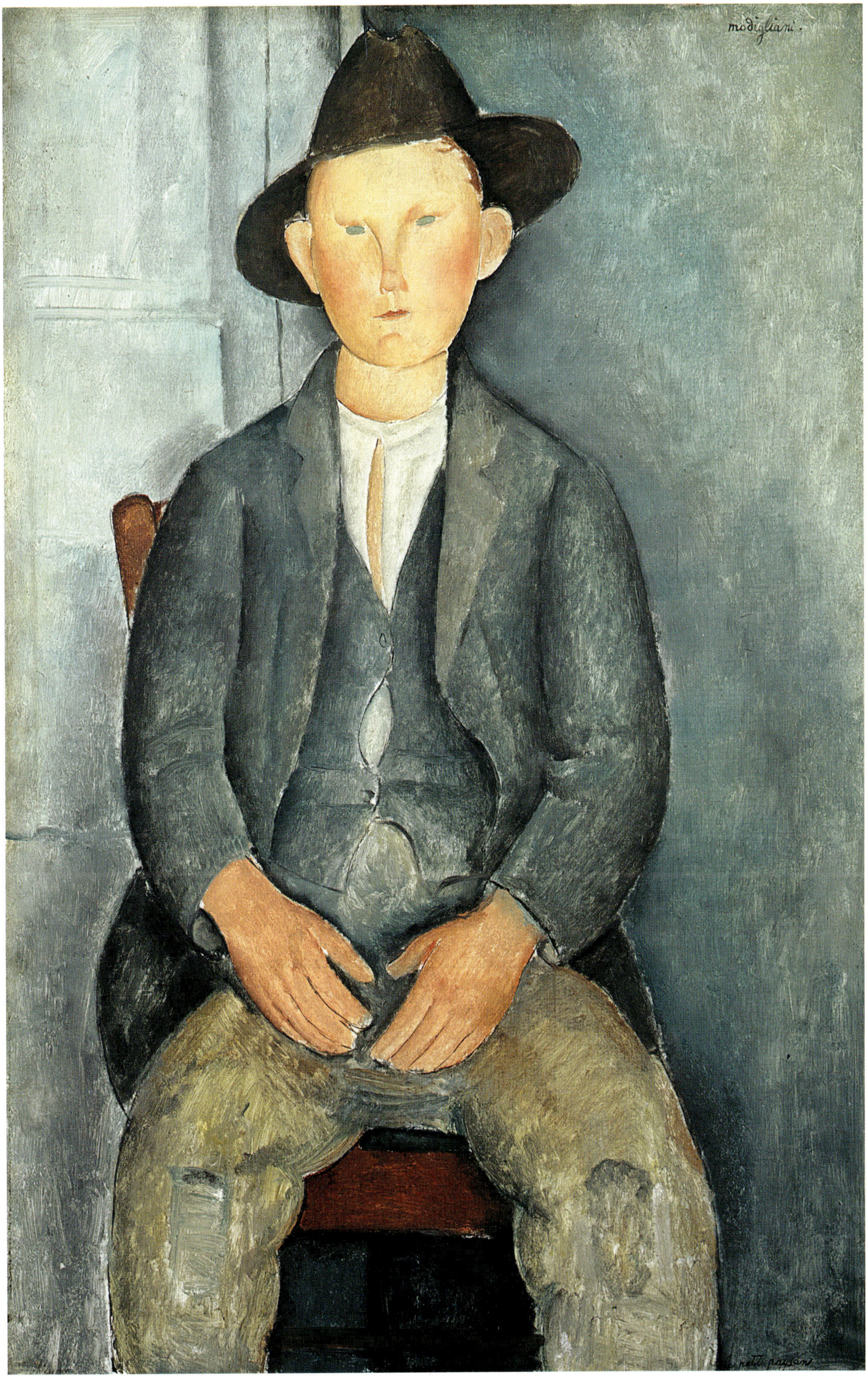

34 *Marie Daughter of the People*, 1918
Oil on canvas
62 × 50.5 cm
Kunstmuseum Basel. Legacy of Dr Walther Hanhart, Riehen, 1975

35 *The Boy (Youth in Blue Jacket)*, 1919
Oil on canvas
92.1 × 60 cm
Indianapolis Museum of Art. Gift of Mrs Julian Bobbs in memory of William Ray Adams, 46.22

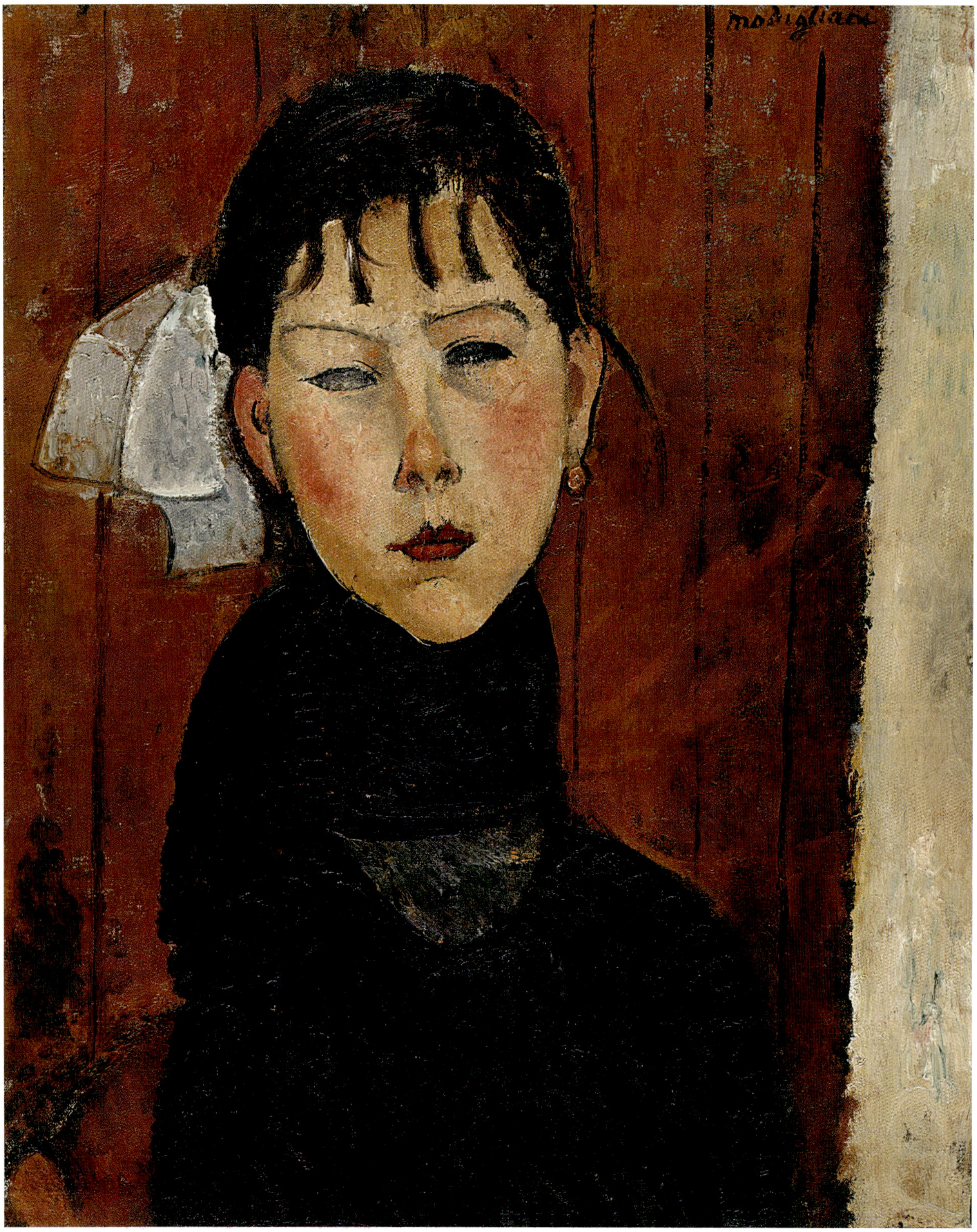

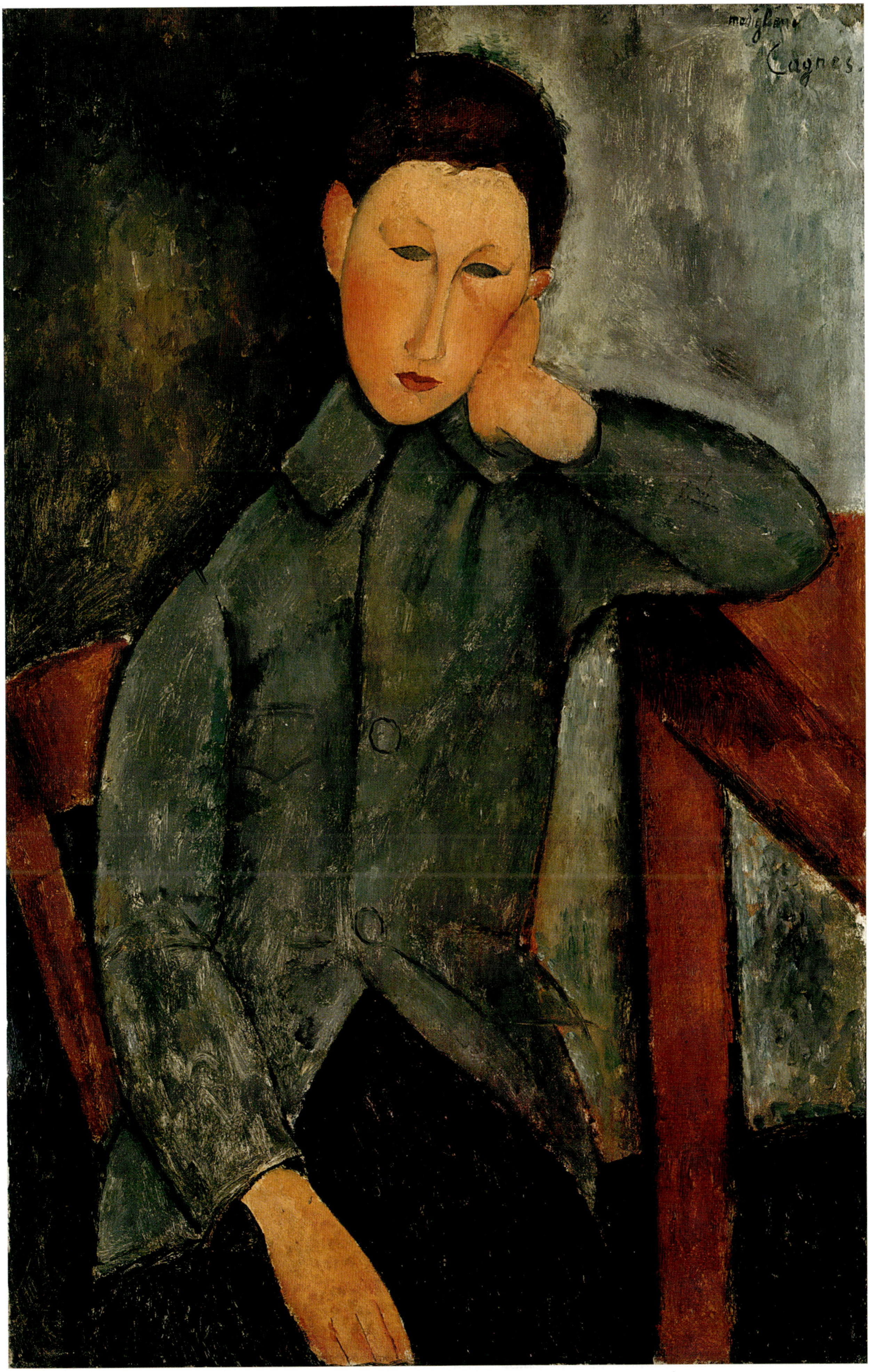
modigliani
Cagnes.

36 *Red-haired Young Woman in a Chemise,*
1918
Oil on canvas
100 × 65 cm
R. & H. Batliner Art Foundation, Vaduz

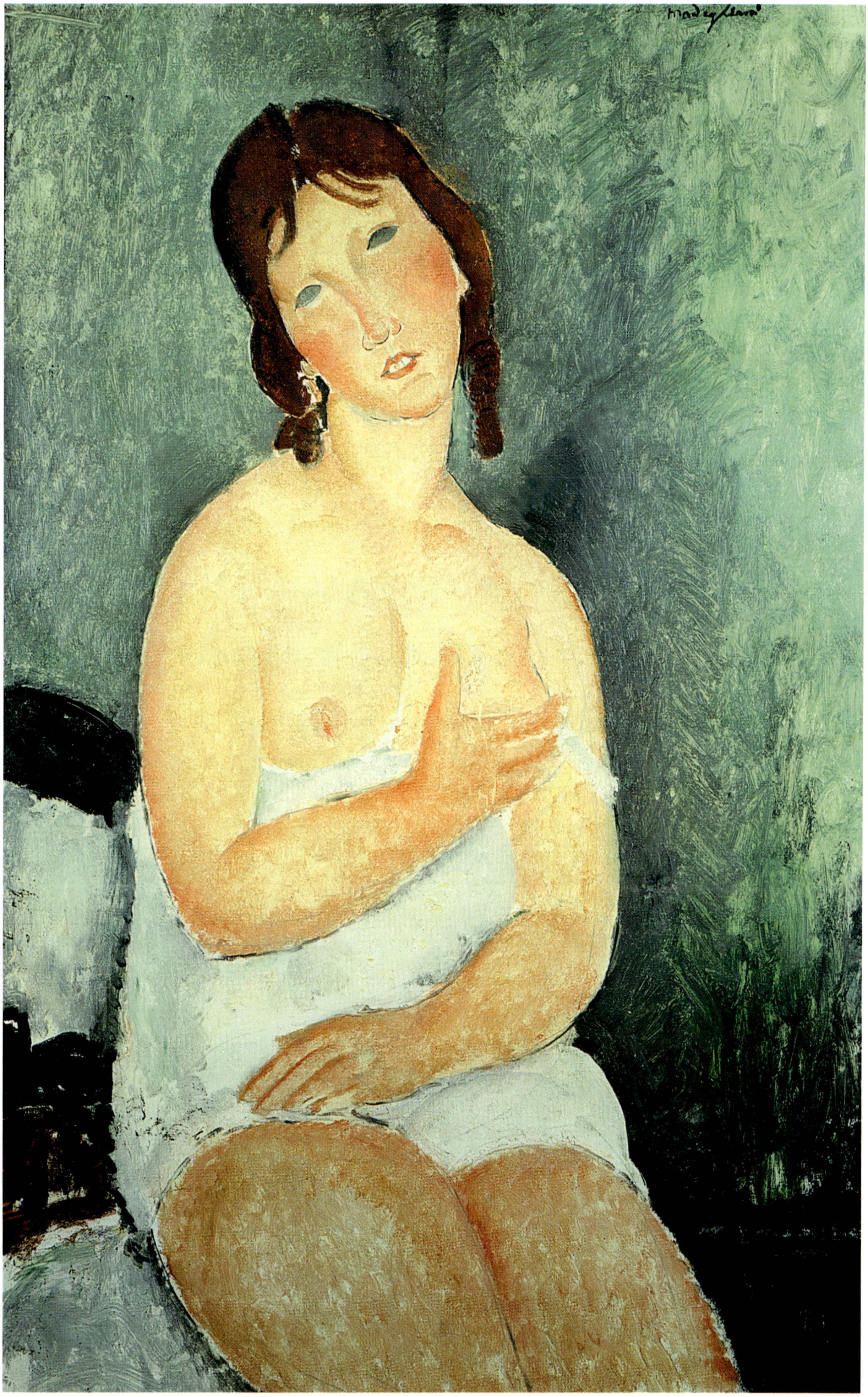
modigliani

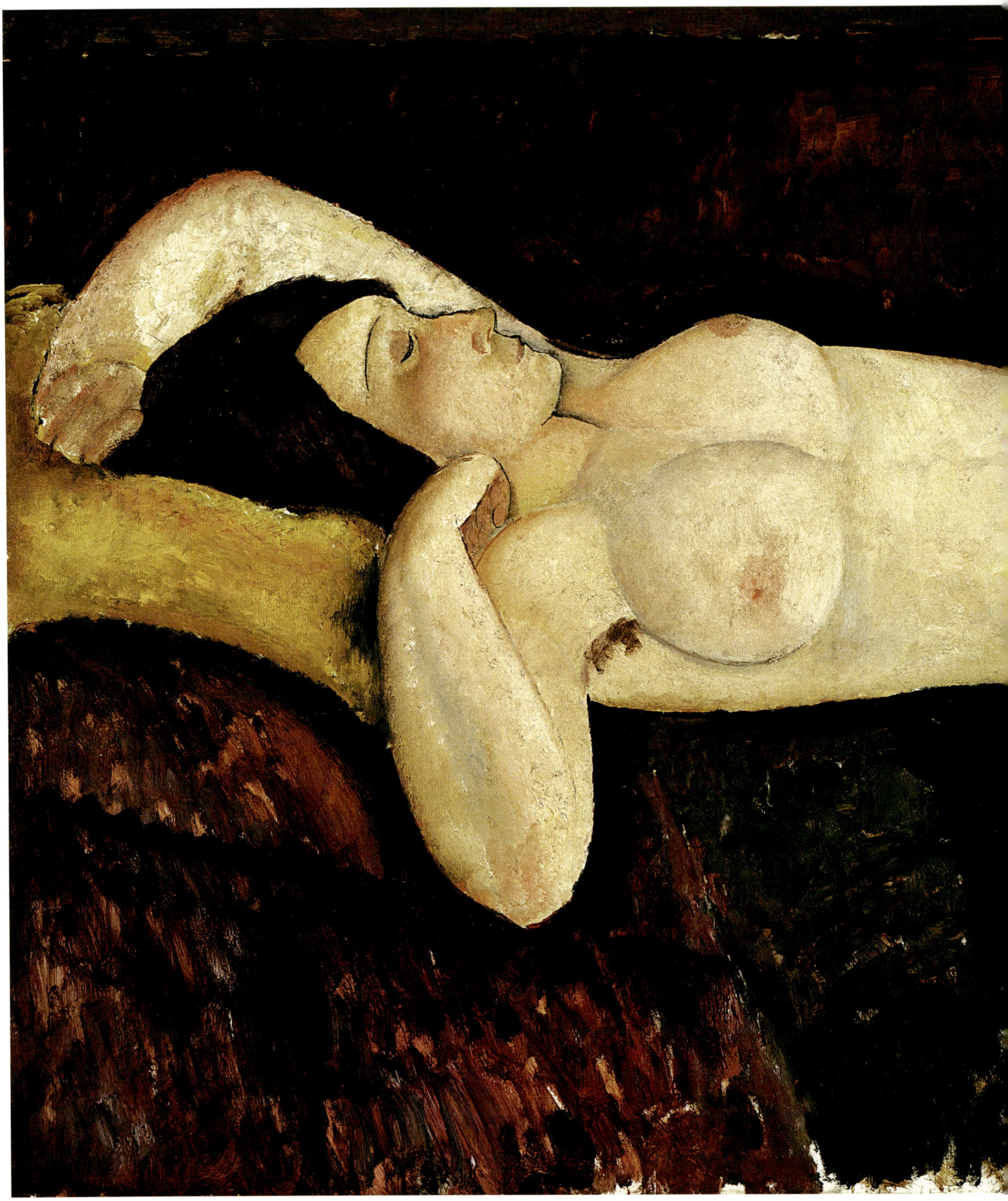

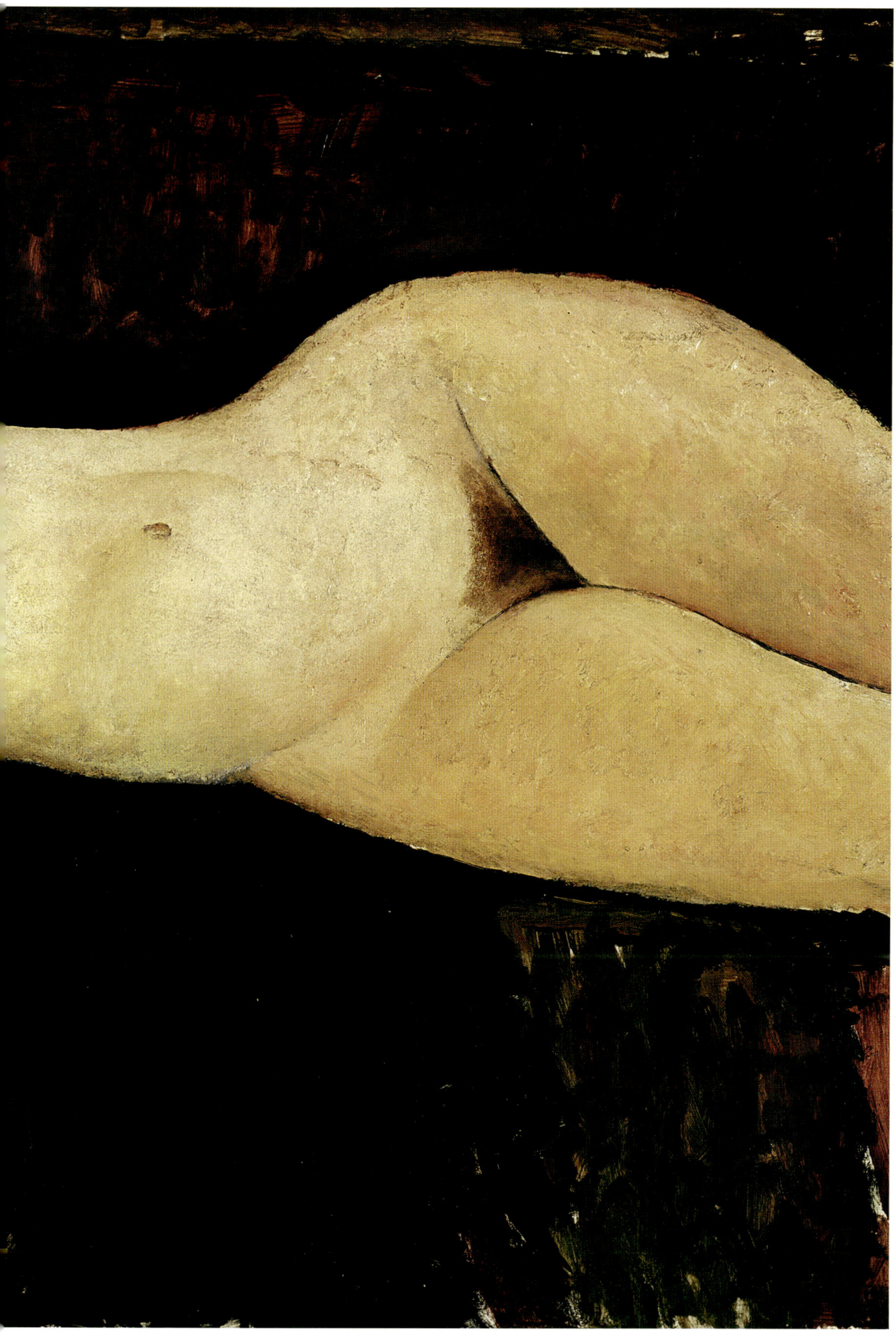

37 *Reclining Nude*, *c.* 1919
Oil on canvas
72.4 × 116.5 cm
The Museum of Modern Art, New York. Mrs Simon Guggenheim Fund, 1950

38 *Jeanne Hébuterne*, 1919
Oil on canvas
91.4 × 73 cm
Lent by The Metropolitan Museum of Art, New York. Gift of Mr and Mrs Nate B. Spingold, 1956 (56.184.2)

39 *Jeanne Hébuterne Sitting*, 1918
Oil on canvas
92 × 60 cm
Private collection, Switzerland

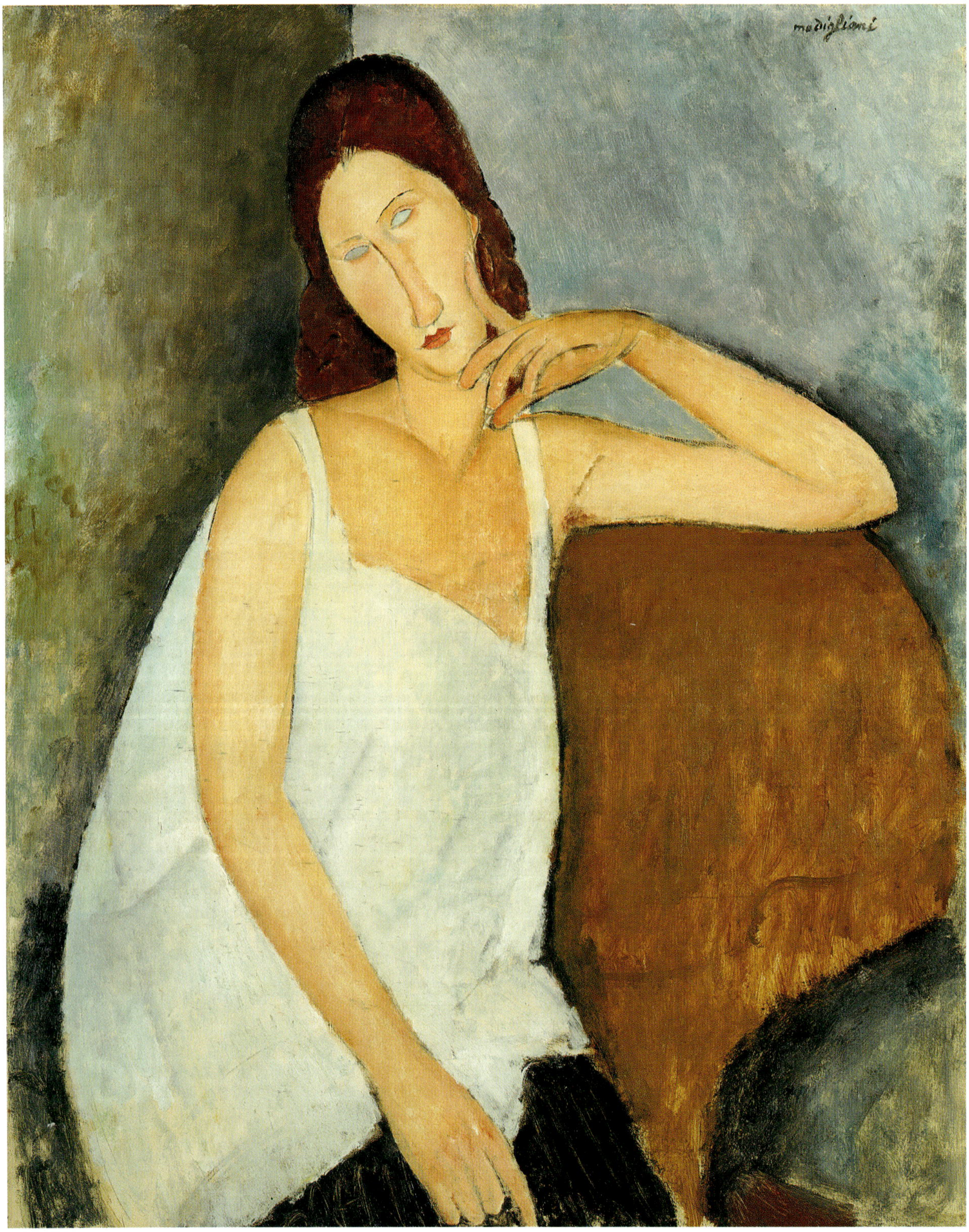

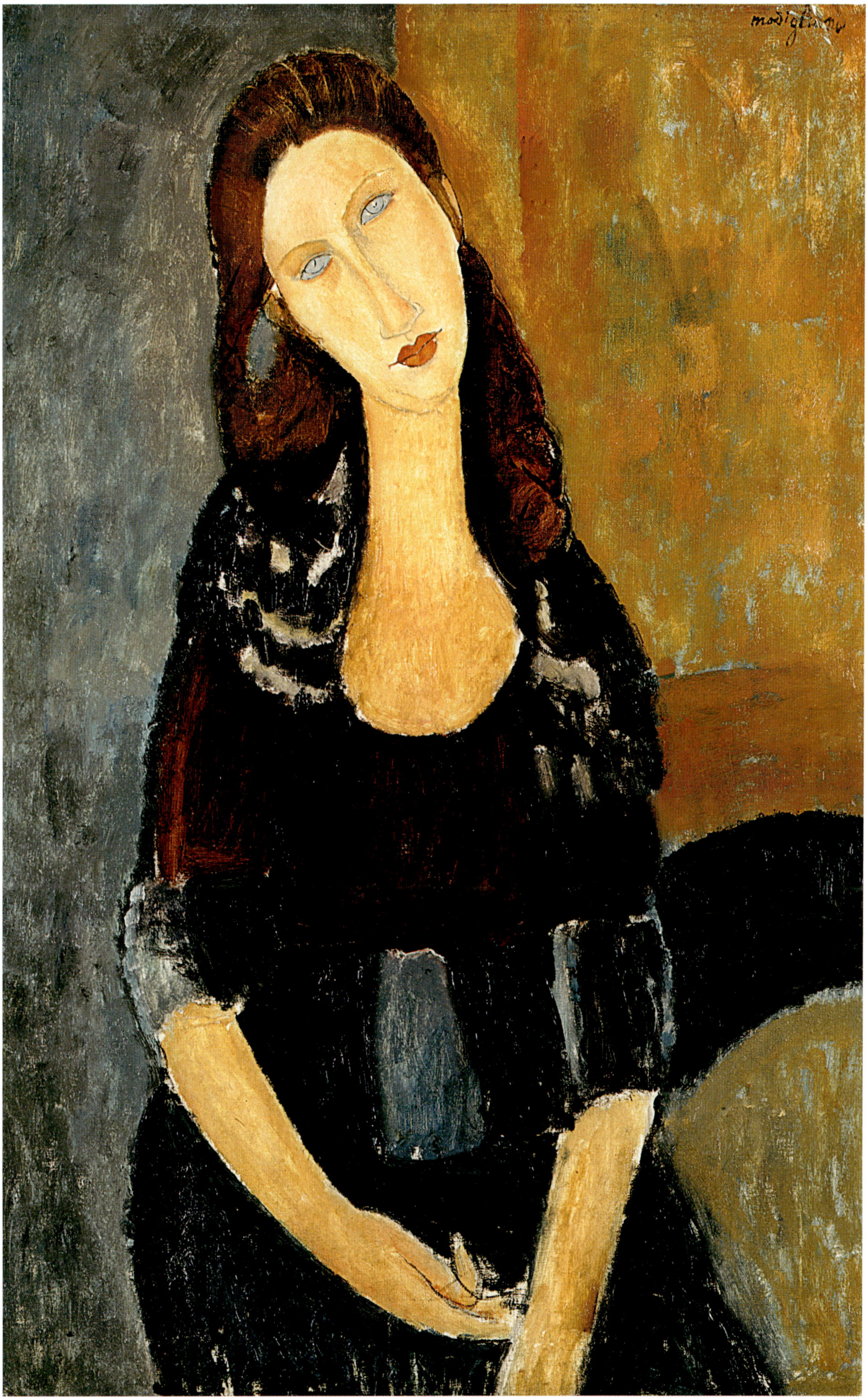
modigliani

40 *Reclining Nude with Her Right Arm under Her Head*, 1919
Oil on canvas
73 × 116 cm
Private collection

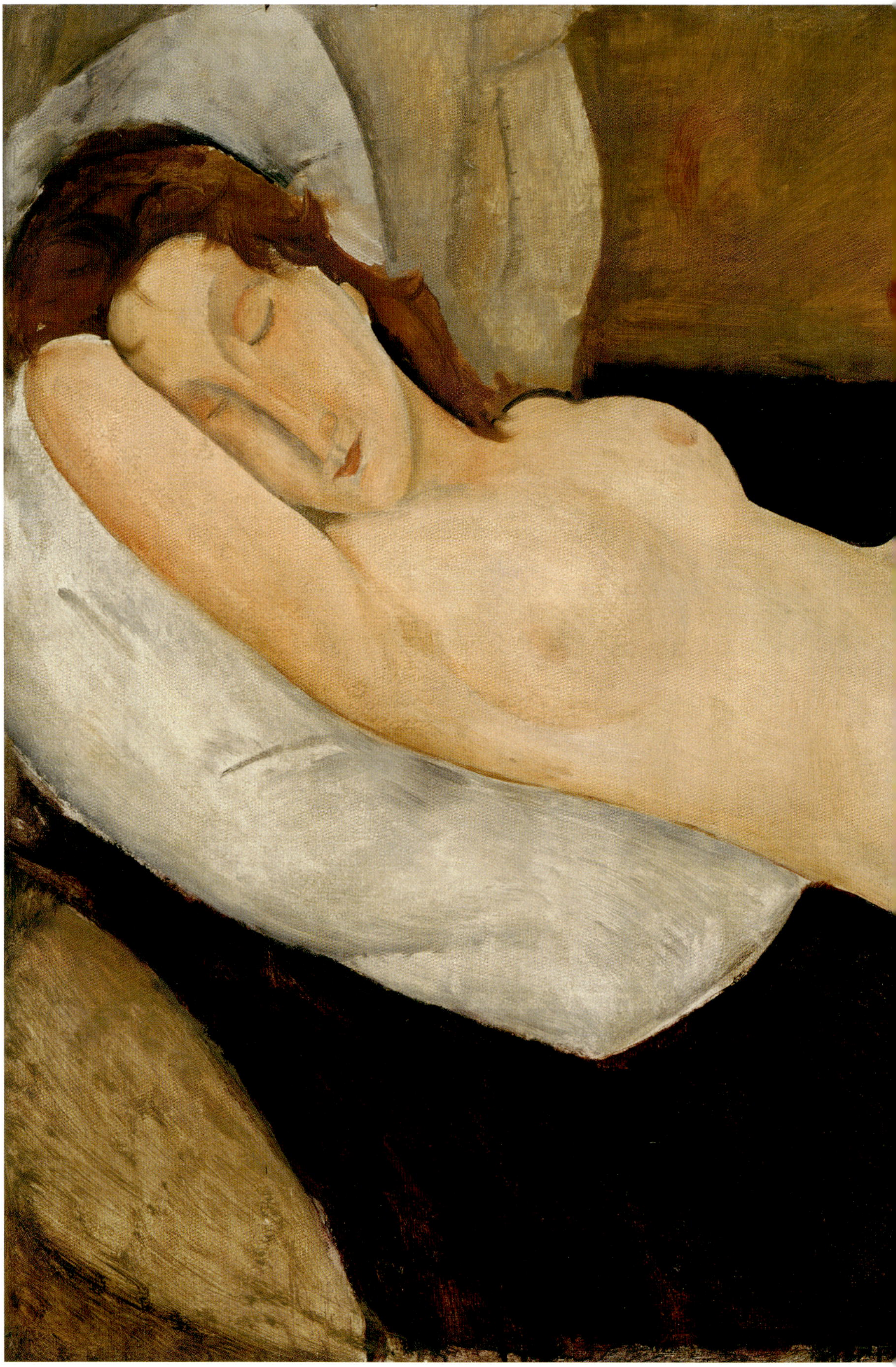

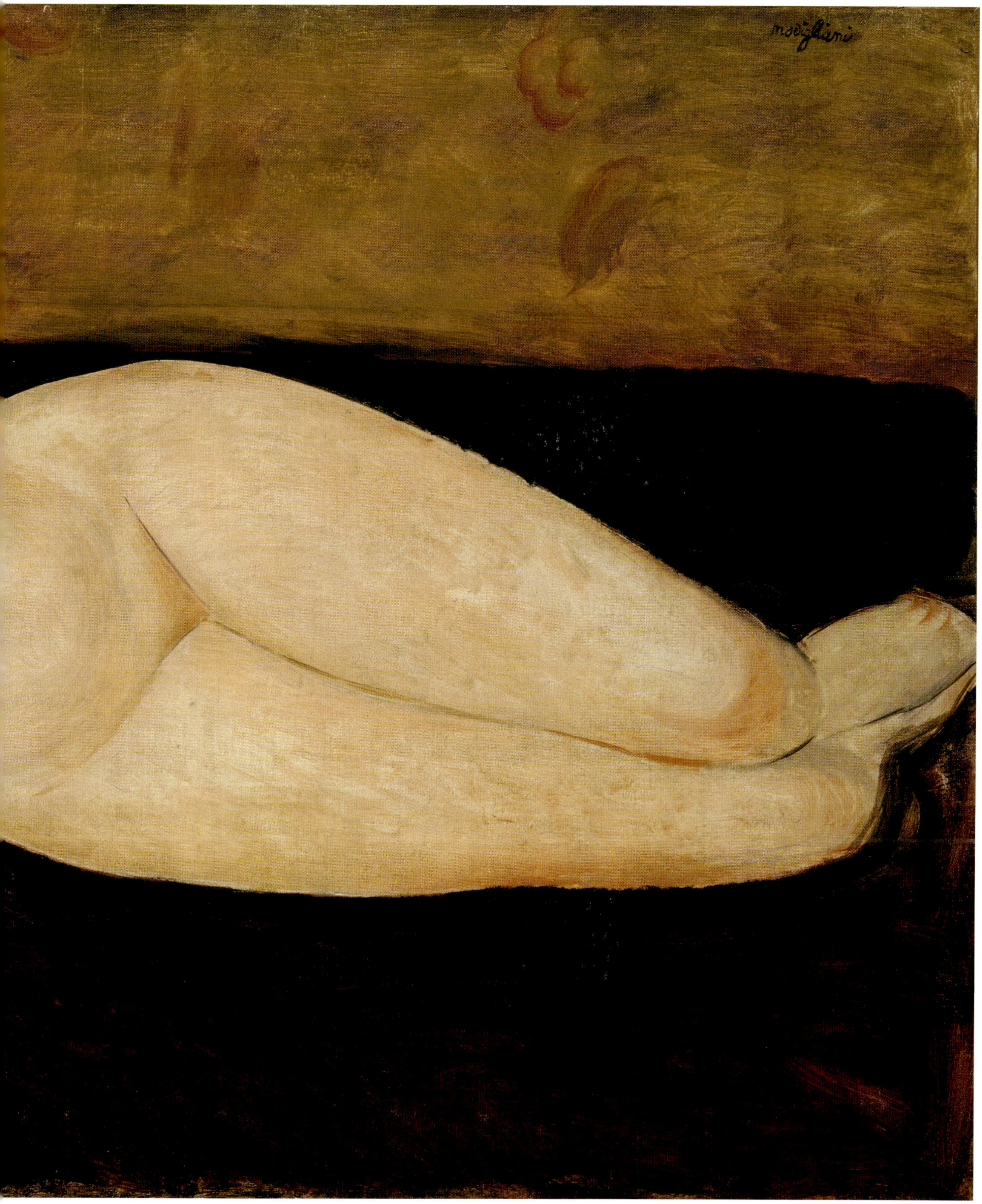

41 *Portrait of Jeanne Hébuterne*, 1919
Oil on canvas
55 × 38 cm
Art & Fragrances S.A., Cham/Switzerland

42 *Portrait of Jeanne Hébuterne*, 1919
Oil on canvas
92.1 × 54 cm
Private collection.
Courtesy of Helly Nahmad

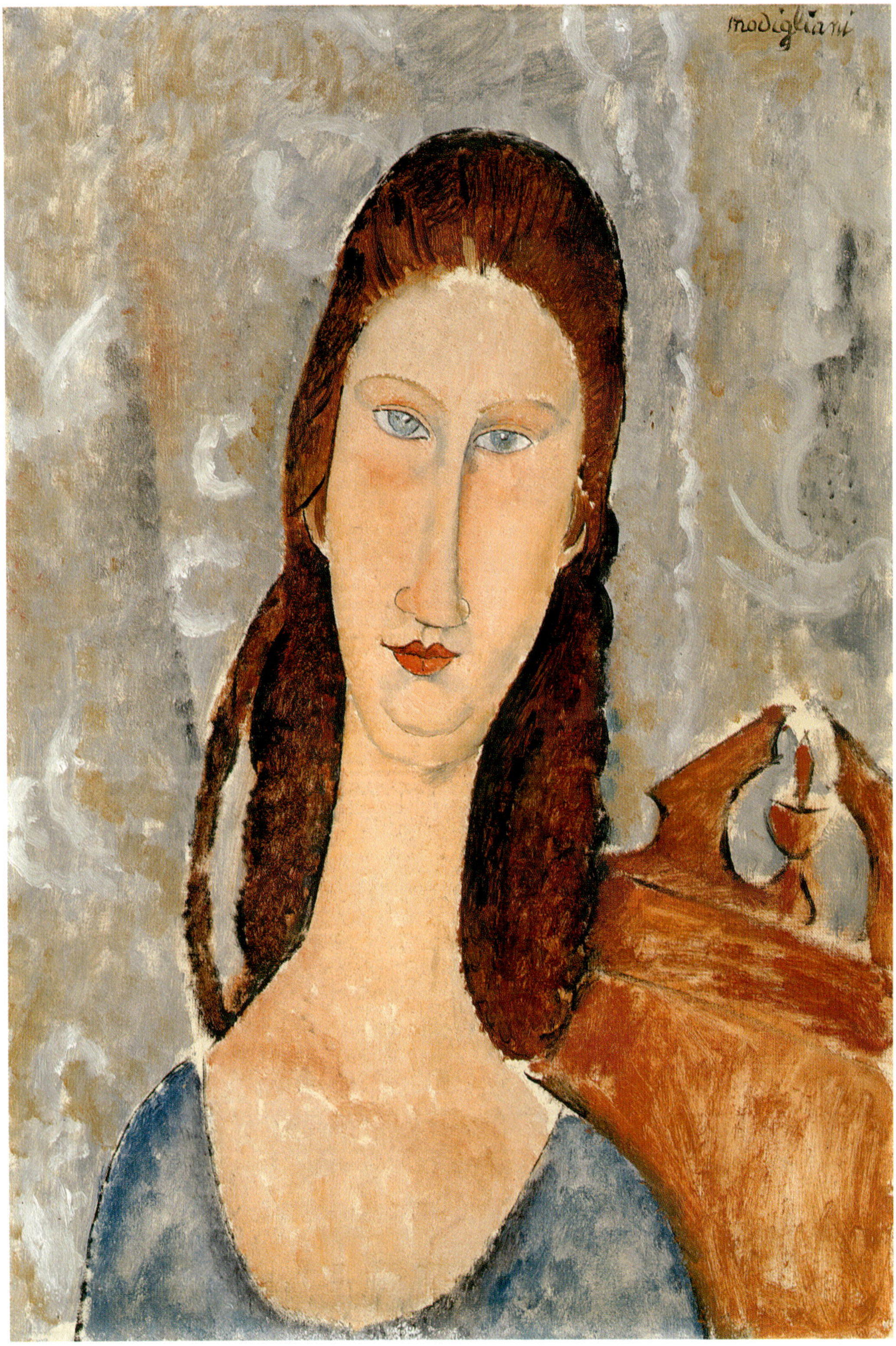

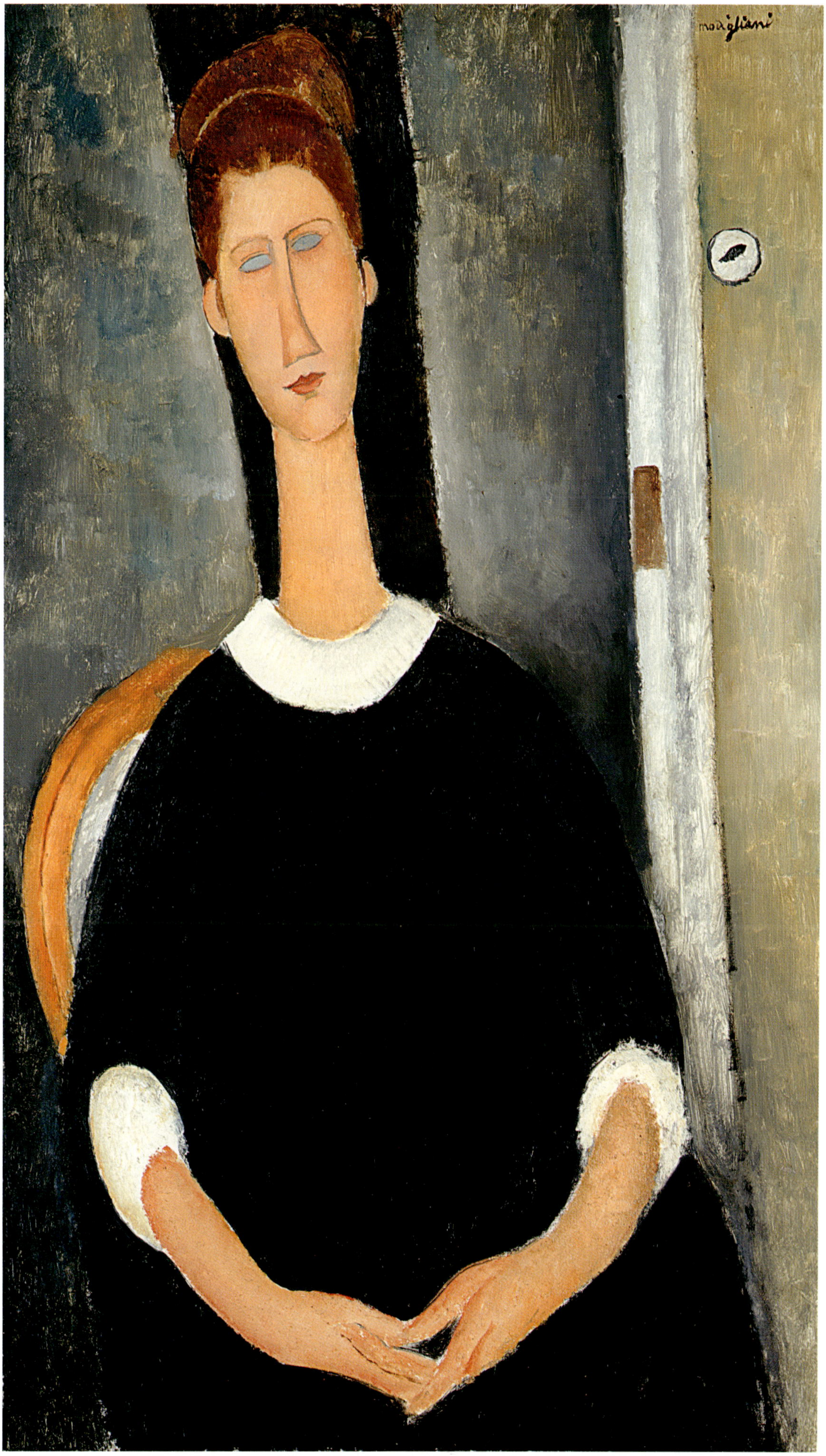
modigliani

43 *Anna Zborowska*, 1917
Oil on canvas
130.2 × 81.3 cm
The Museum of Modern Art, New York. Lillie P. Bliss Collection, 1934

44 *Jeanne Hébuterne, a Door in the Background*, 1919
Oil on canvas
130 × 81 cm
Private collection

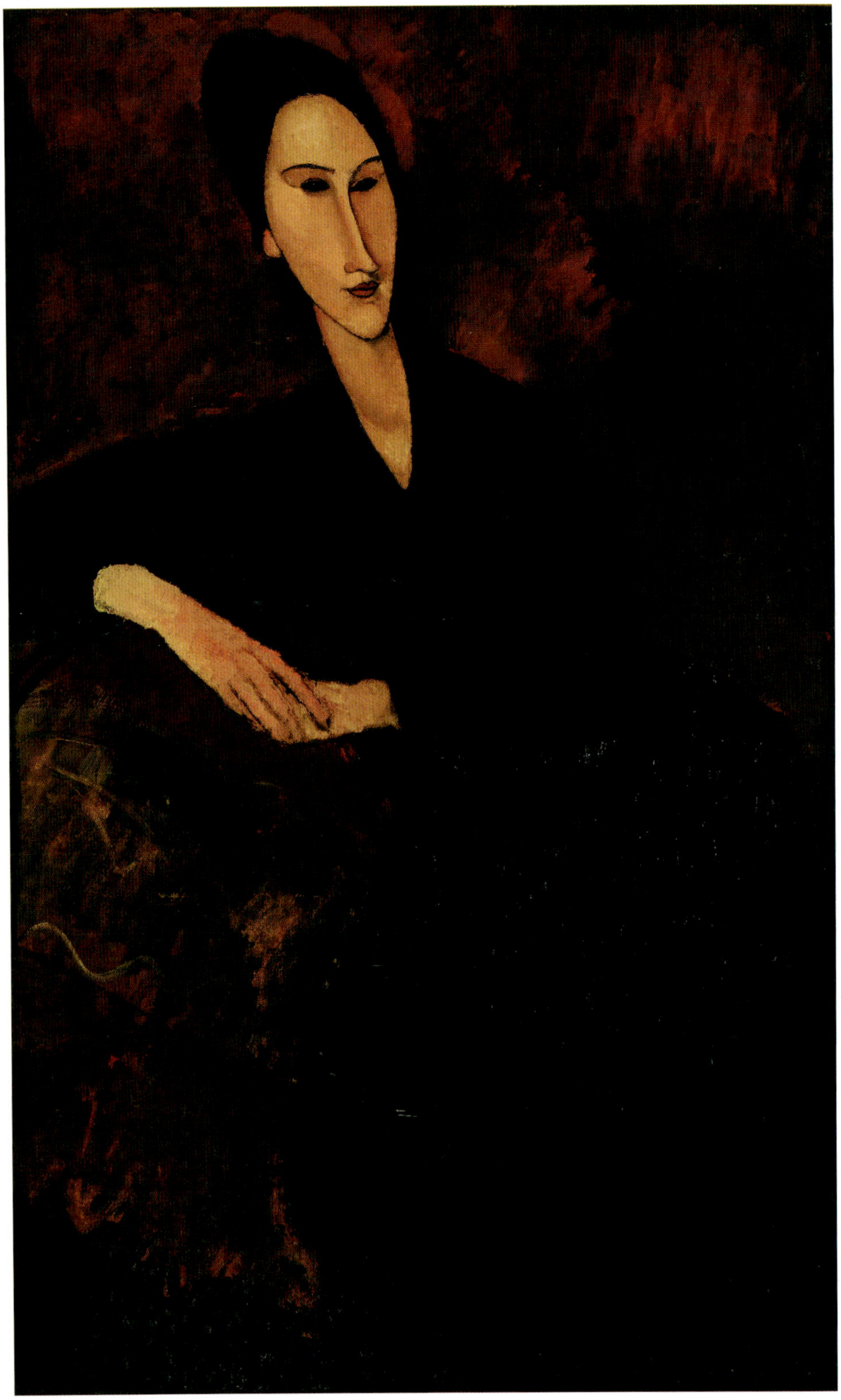

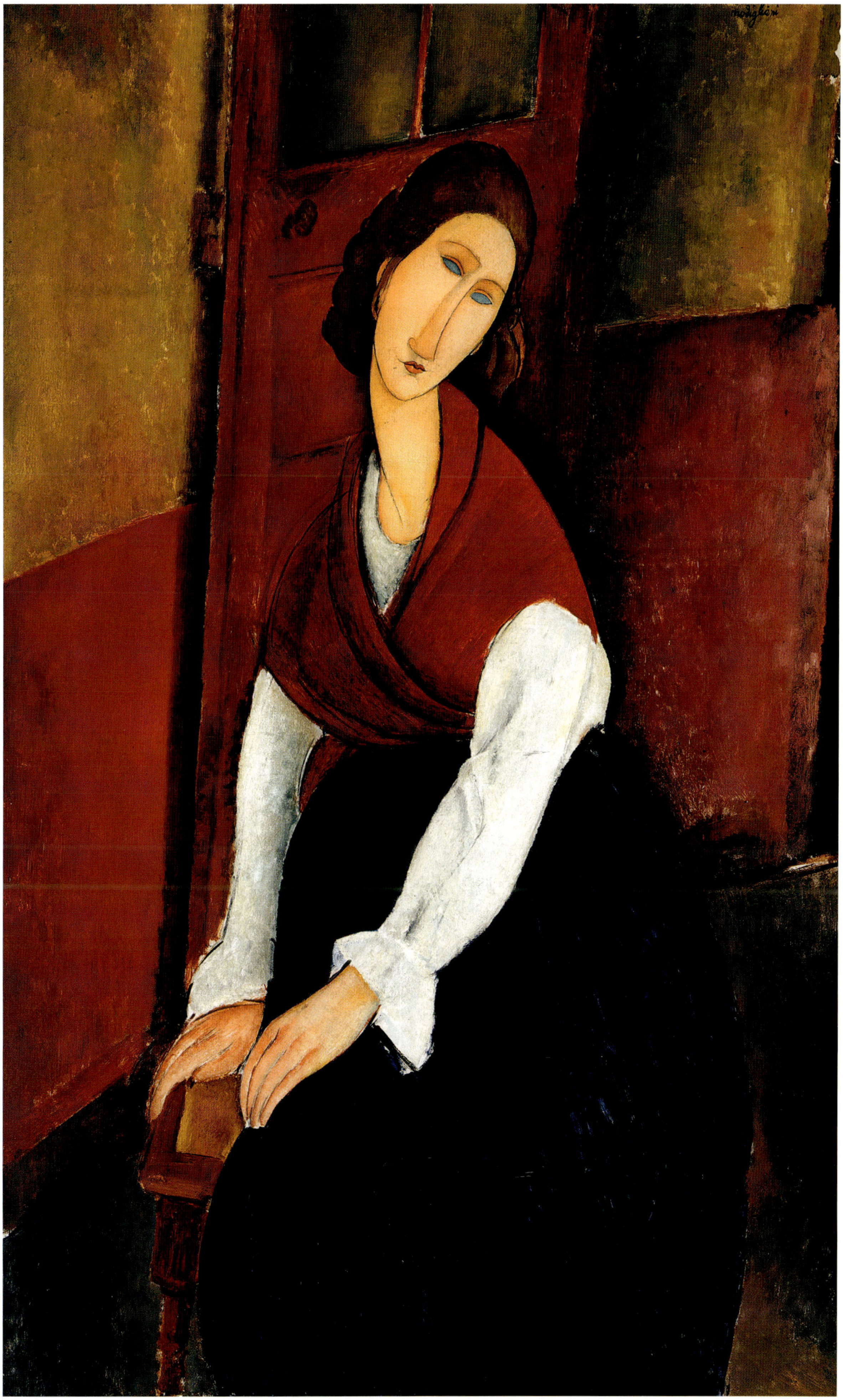

45 *Bust of a Woman with a Necklace*, *c*. 1917–18
Oil on canvas
61.6 × 38.7 cm
Private collection, United States.
Courtesy of Edward Tyler Nahem Fine Art, L.L.C.

46 *Woman with a Red Necklace*, 1918
Oil on canvas
92.8 × 65.8 cm
Private collection.
Courtesy of Nevill Keating Pictures

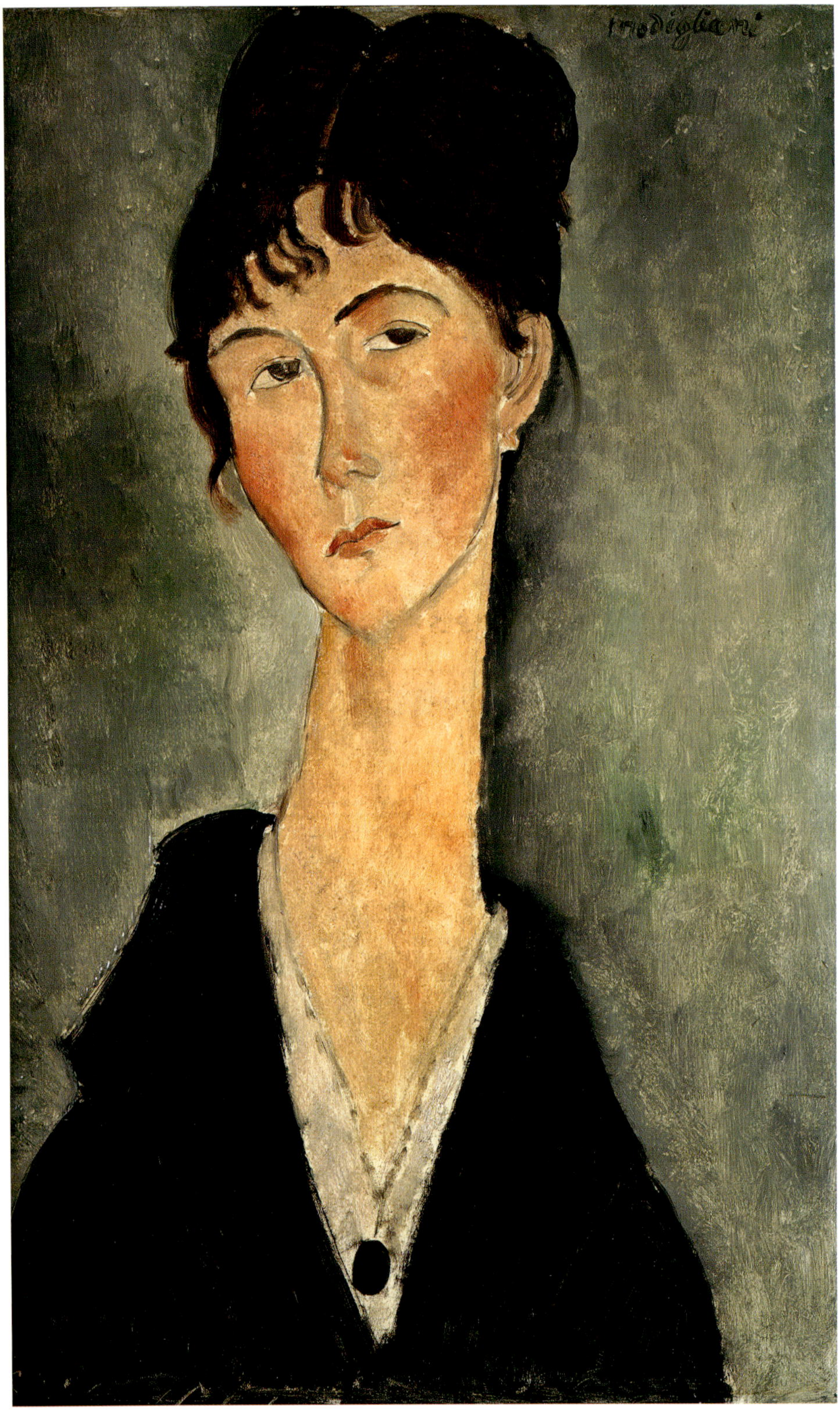

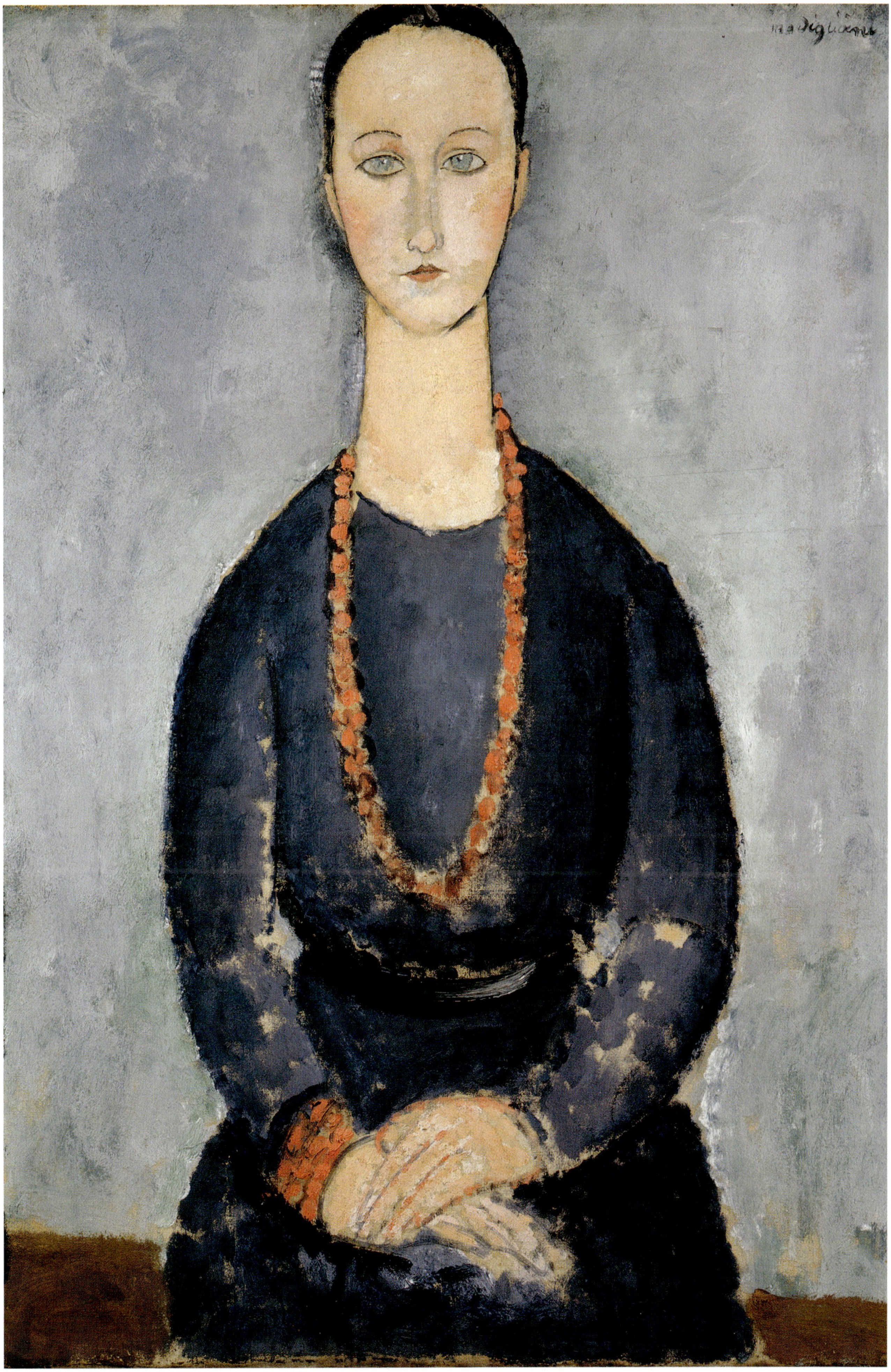
modigliani

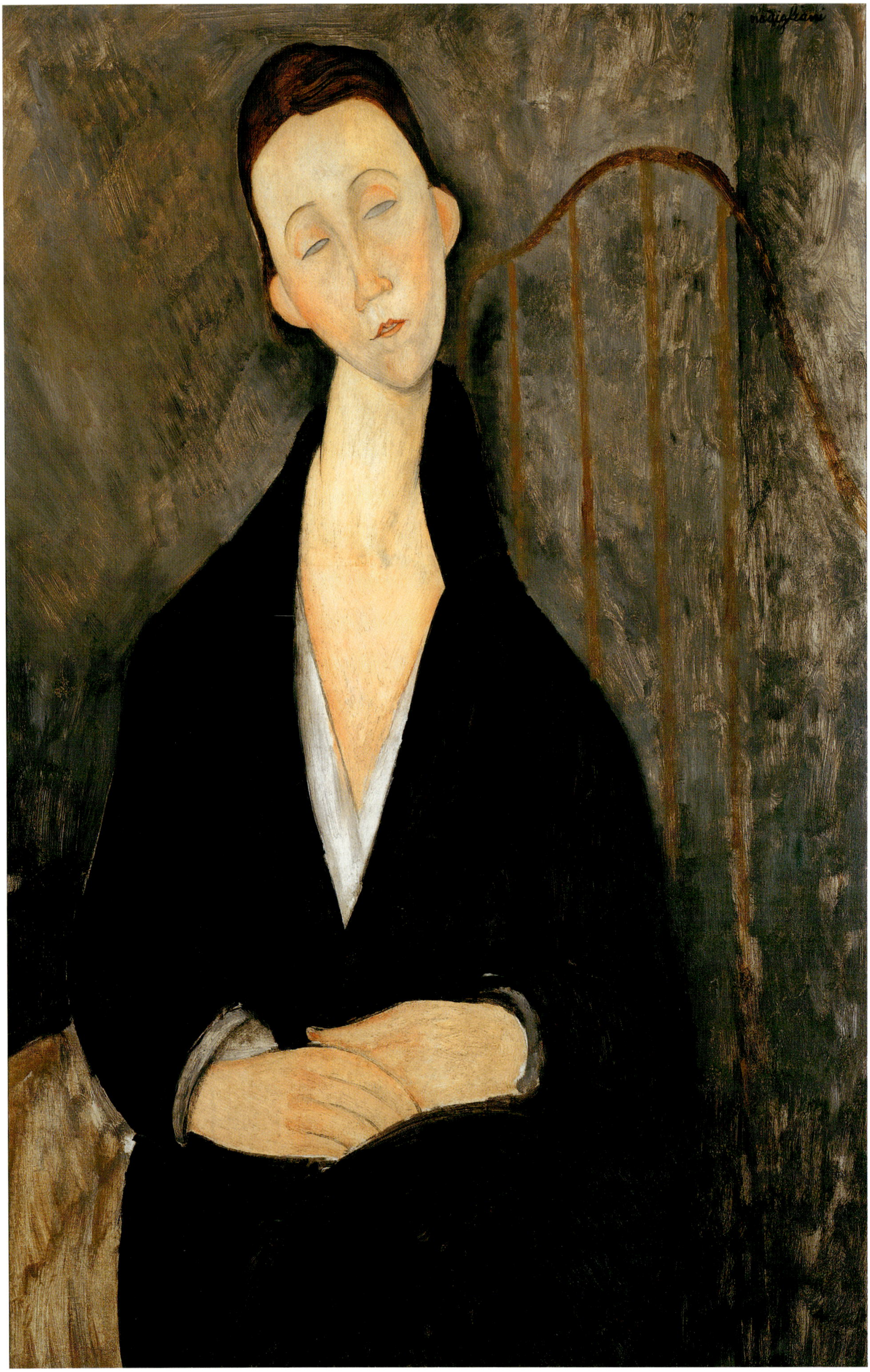

47 *Lunia Czechowska in Black*, 1919
Oil on canvas
92 × 60 cm
Private collection

48 *Portrait of Madame A. Eyraud-Vaillant*, 1919
Oil on canvas
99 × 63.5 cm
Private collection. Courtesy of Richard Nagy Ltd, London

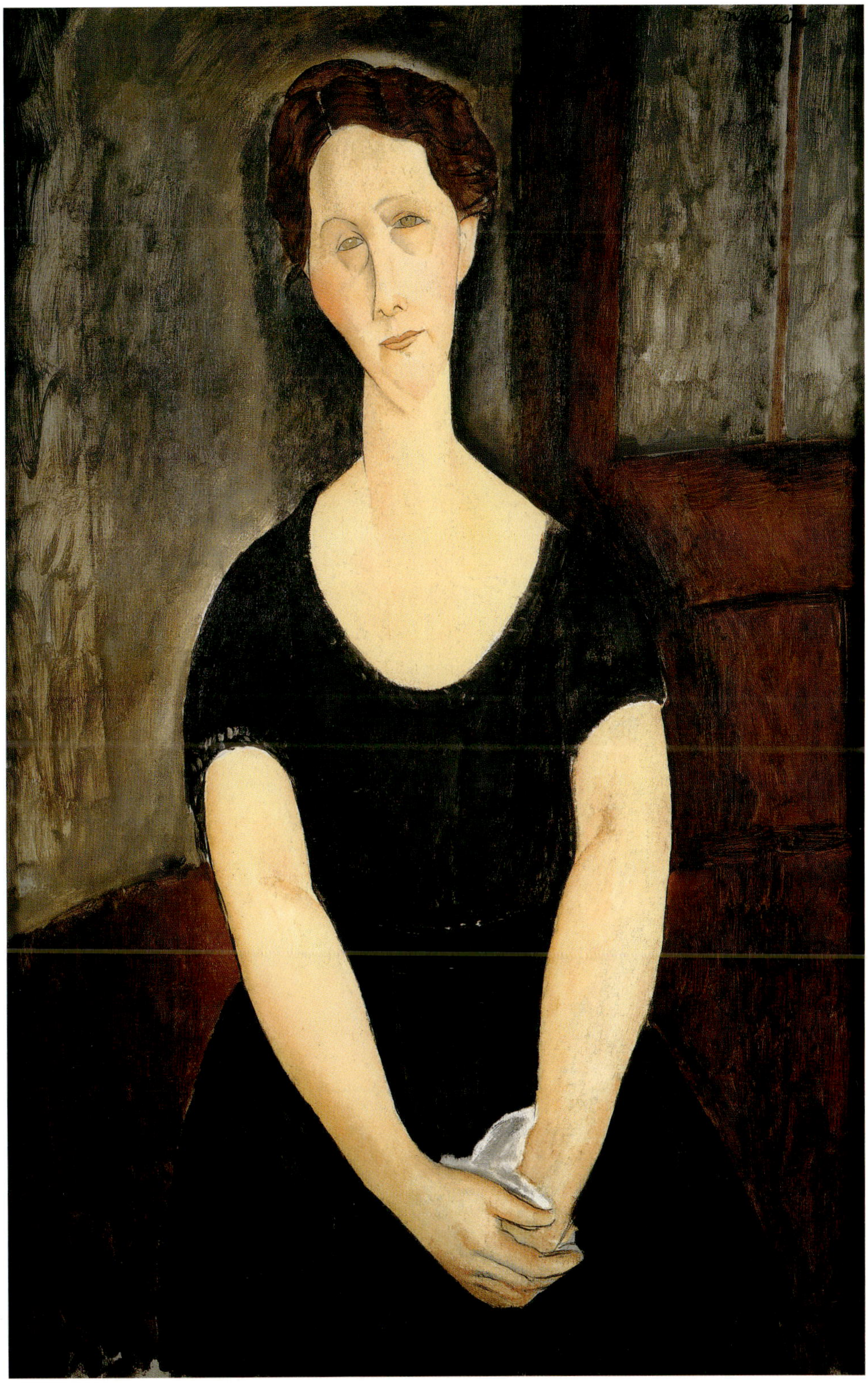

49 *Portrait of Thora Klinckowström*, 1919
Oil on canvas
99.7 × 64.8 cm
Heirs of Evelyn Sharp

50 *Paulette Jourdain*, 1919
Oil on canvas
100 × 65 cm
Collection of A. Alfred Taubman

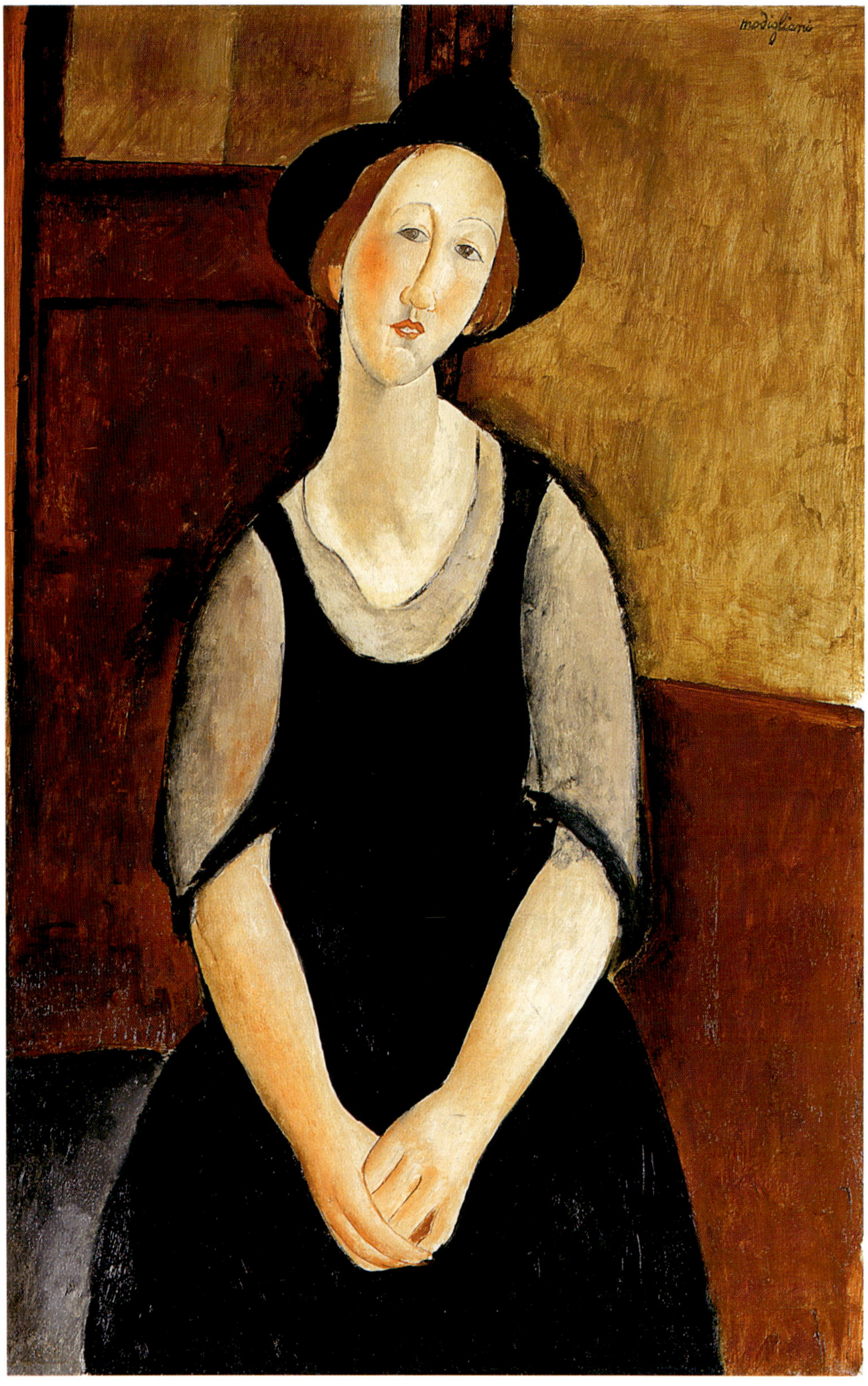

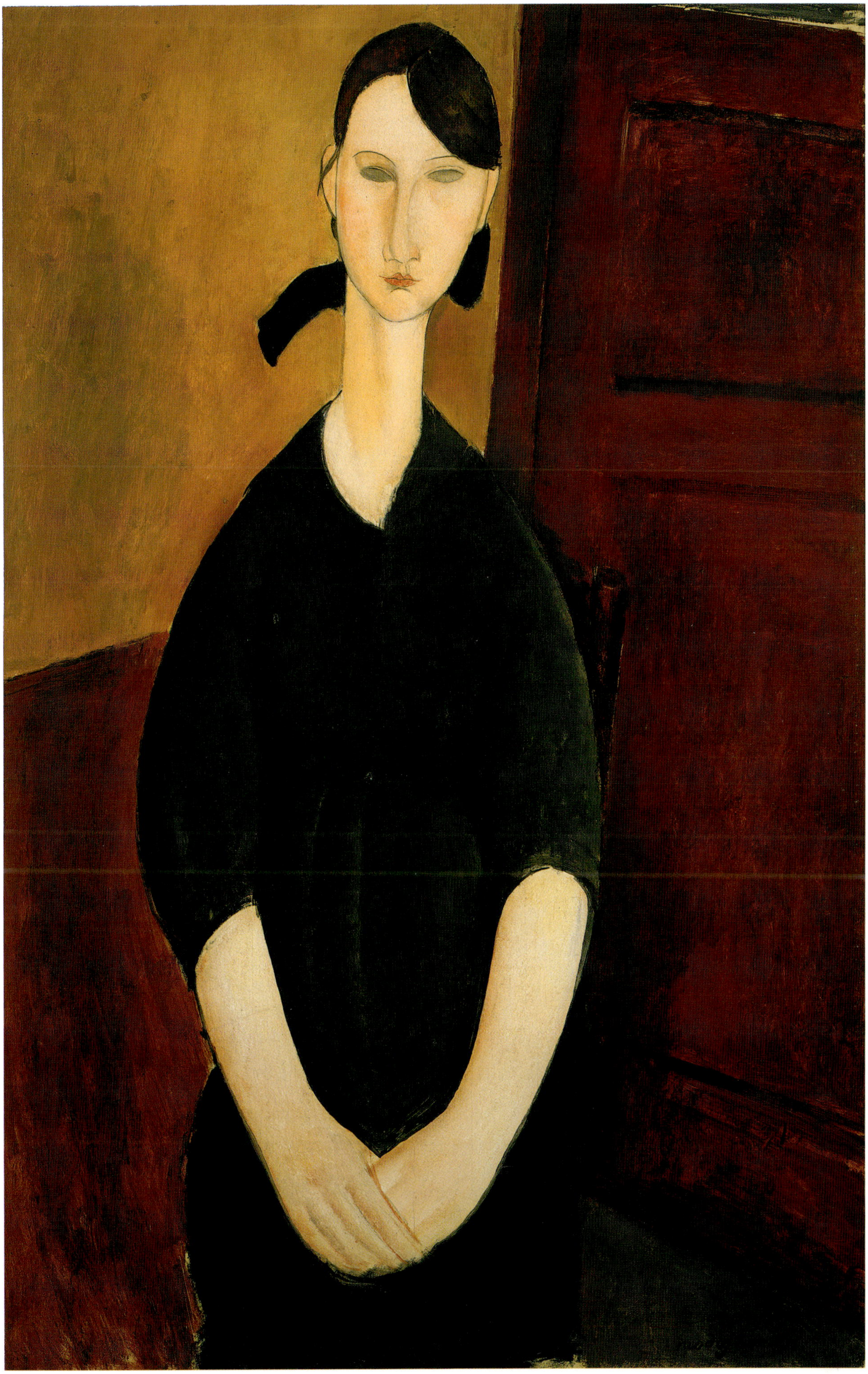

51 *Portrait of Lunia Czechowska*, 1919
Oil on canvas
100 × 65 cm
Musée d'Art Moderne de la Ville de Paris

52 *Self-portrait*, 1919
Oil on panel
100 × 64.5 cm
Museu de Arte Contemporânea da Universidade de São Paulo

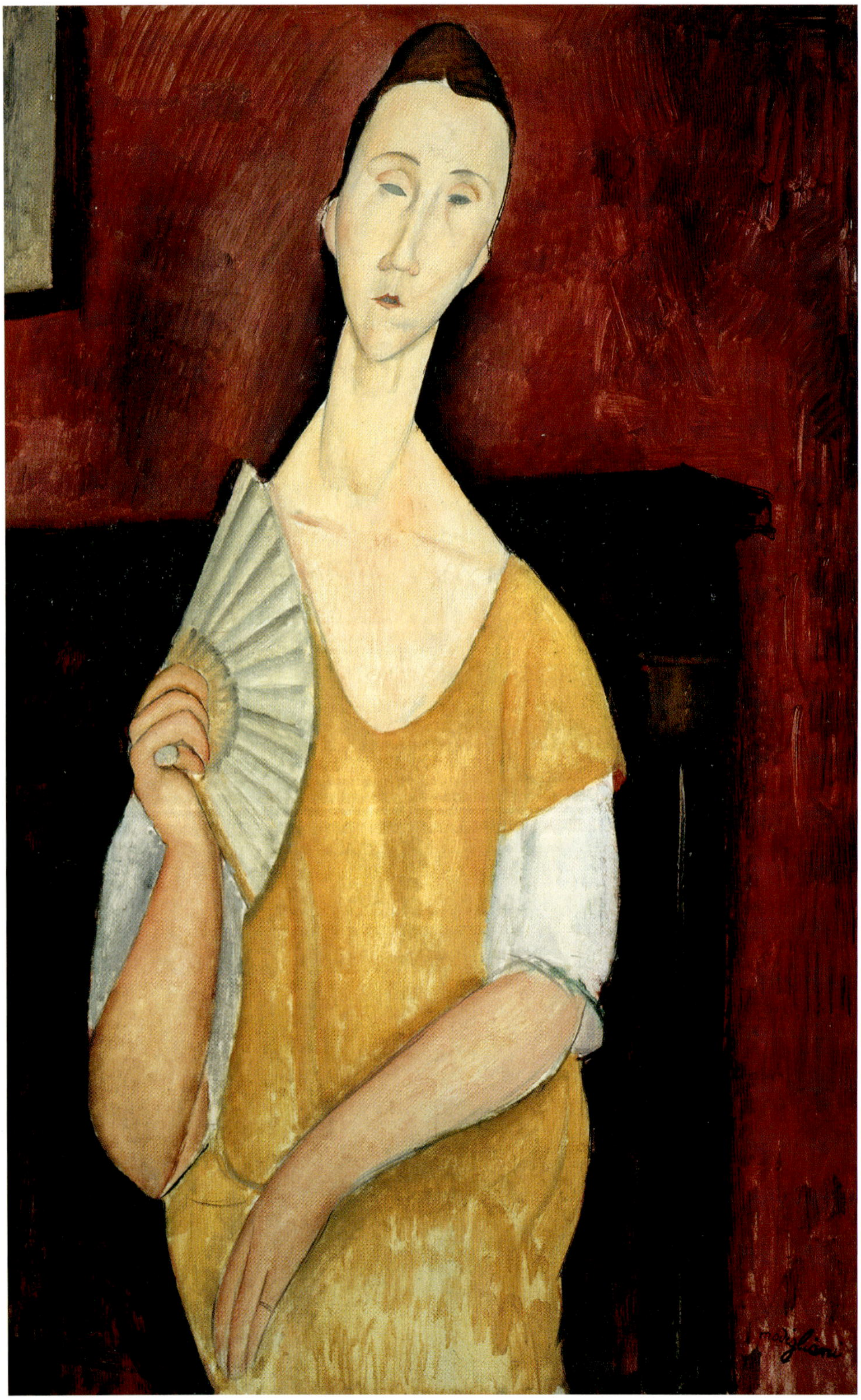

Overleaf
Modigliani (centre right) with Adolphe Basler (right) and unidentified friends at the Dôme, Paris, *c.* 1919
Photograph. Unknown photographer
Archives Roger-Viollet, Paris

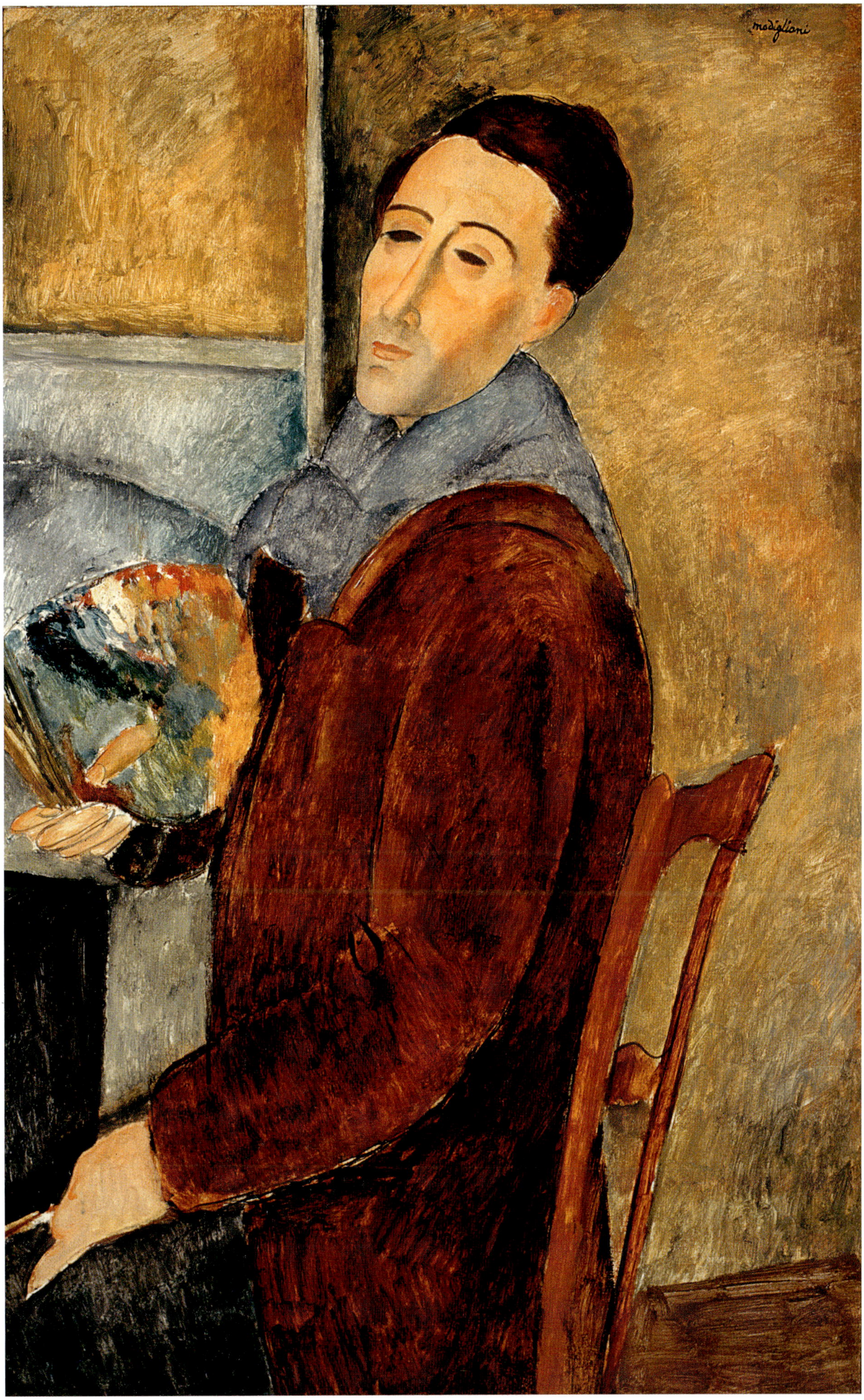
modigliani

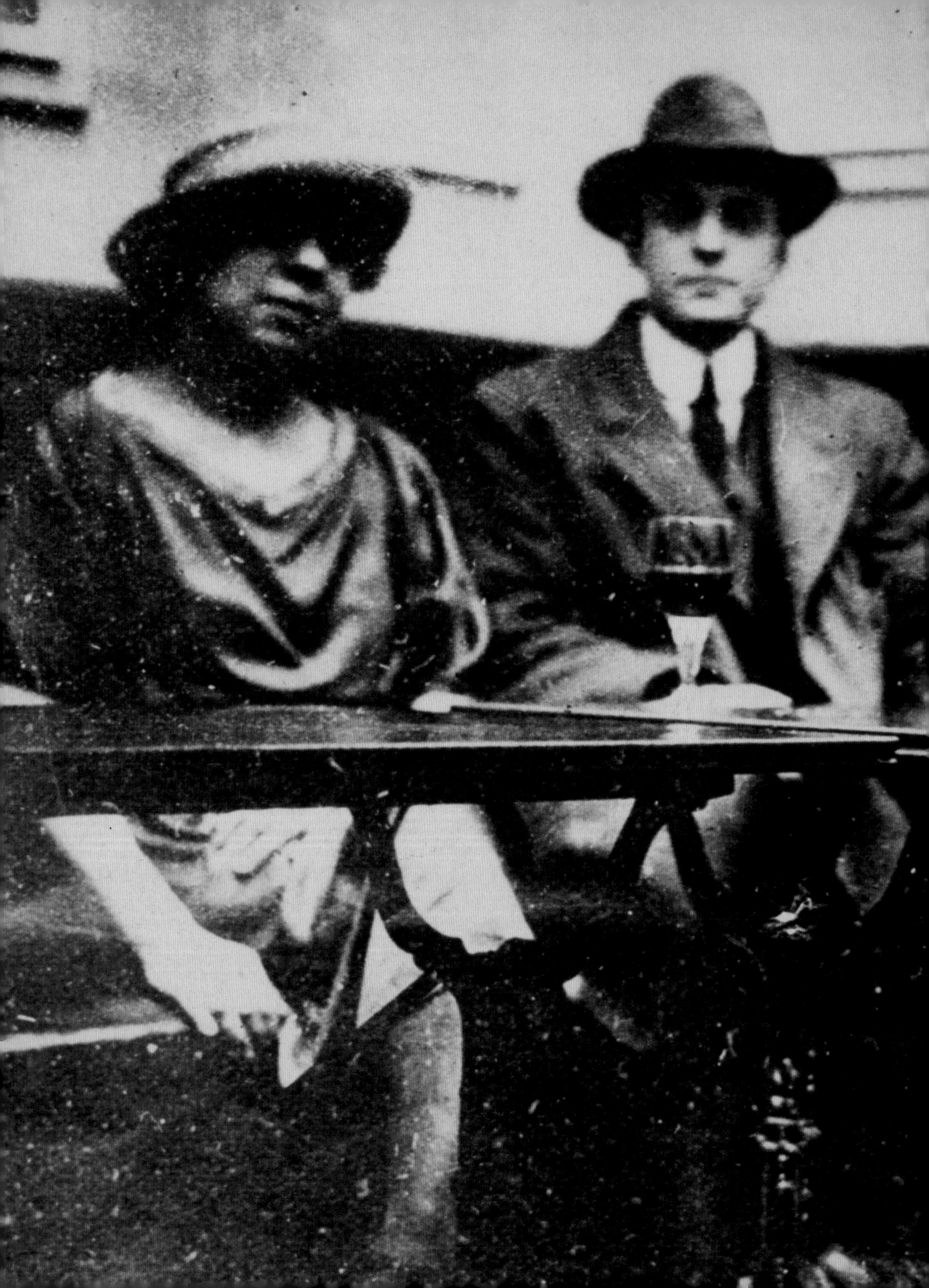

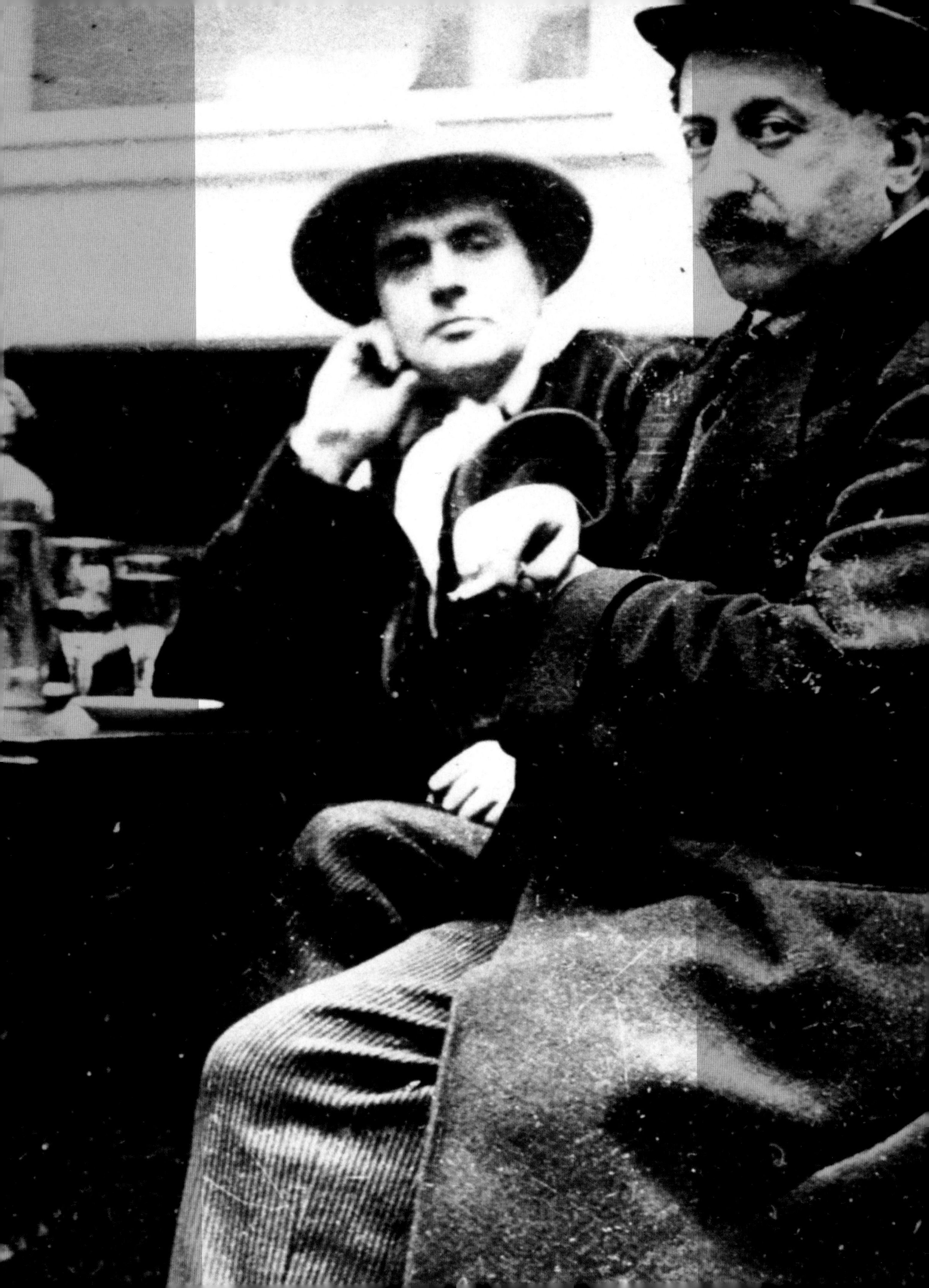

Chronology

Kathleen Brunner

1884

● 12 July: Amedeo Clemente Modigliani (fig. 1) is born in Livorno, near Pisa, the fourth child of Flaminio Modigliani and Eugenia Garsin, both from assimilated families of Jewish descent with liberal views.

● Flaminio Modigliani becomes bankrupt, forcing his extended family to move to a smaller house.

1886–93

● Modigliani's father has little influence on his life. His mother takes charge of the household, providing income from teaching English and French at home, an undertaking that develops into a private school. Modigliani becomes close to his maternal grandfather, Isaac Garsin, who moves in with the family. A highly educated man, he takes 'Dedo' (Modigliani's lifelong nickname) on his first visits to museums.

1894

● The death of his maternal grandfather has a profound effect on Modigliani.

1895

● Modigliani becomes ill with pleurisy, the first of three childhood illnesses that will severely affect his health.

1898

● Modigliani takes up drawing in Livorno with the painter Guglielmo Micheli (1886–1926).

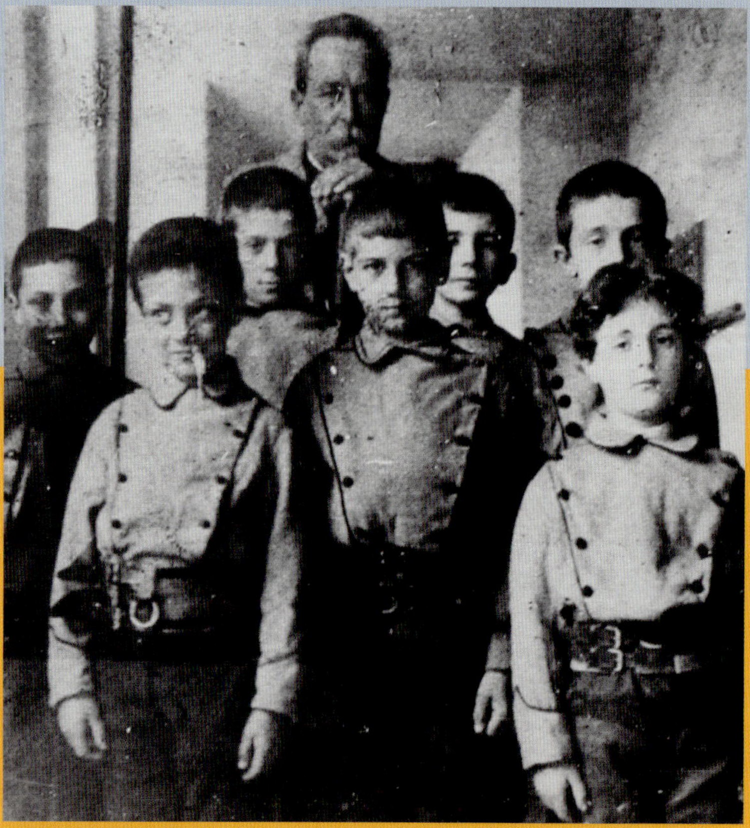

▶ **Modigliani (bottom right) with his class and teacher at his gymnasium in Livorno, *c.* 1889. Photograph. Unknown photographer. Museo Civico Giovanni Fattori, Livorno**

▶ Life drawing at the Académie Colarossi, 1906. Photograph. Unknown photographer. Modigliani Institut, Archives Legales, Paris

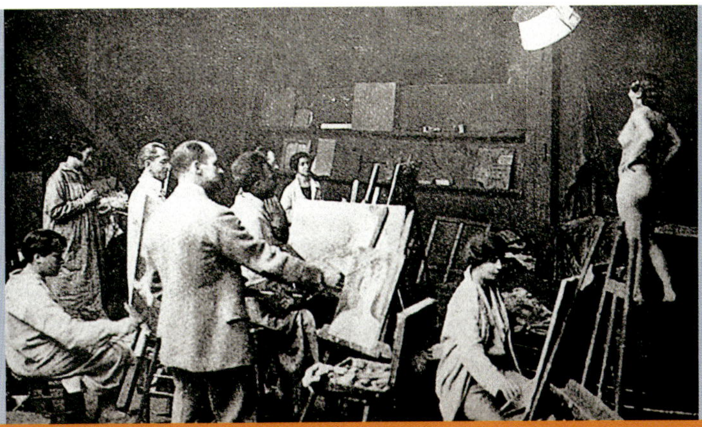

1899

● Modigliani contracts typhoid fever and a long convalescence follows. He continues his art classes on a daily basis, while his mother's sister Laura influences his intellectual development, encouraging him to read widely (Dante, Leopardi, D'Annunzio, Nietzsche and Bergson).

1900–01

● Modigliani becomes very ill with tuberculosis, recuperating on a trip with his mother to Naples, Capri, Amalfi, Florence and Venice, viewing important works of art.

1902

● May: Modigliani begins a course of study at the Scuola Libera di Nudo in Florence.

● Summer: Modigliani experiments with stone carving at Carrara.

1903–05

● Modigliani continues his studies in Venice until the end of 1905.

1906

● Modigliani arrives in Paris, eventually taking an artist's studio, a kind of shed, in Montmartre. He frequents Pablo Picasso's studio in the nearby Bateau-Lavoir, where he sees the artist's new work, inspired by 'primitive' artistic forms. Modigliani develops a close relationship with the poet Max Jacob, one of Picasso's coterie.

● Modigliani enrols at the Académie Colarossi, one of the independent art academies in Montparnasse.

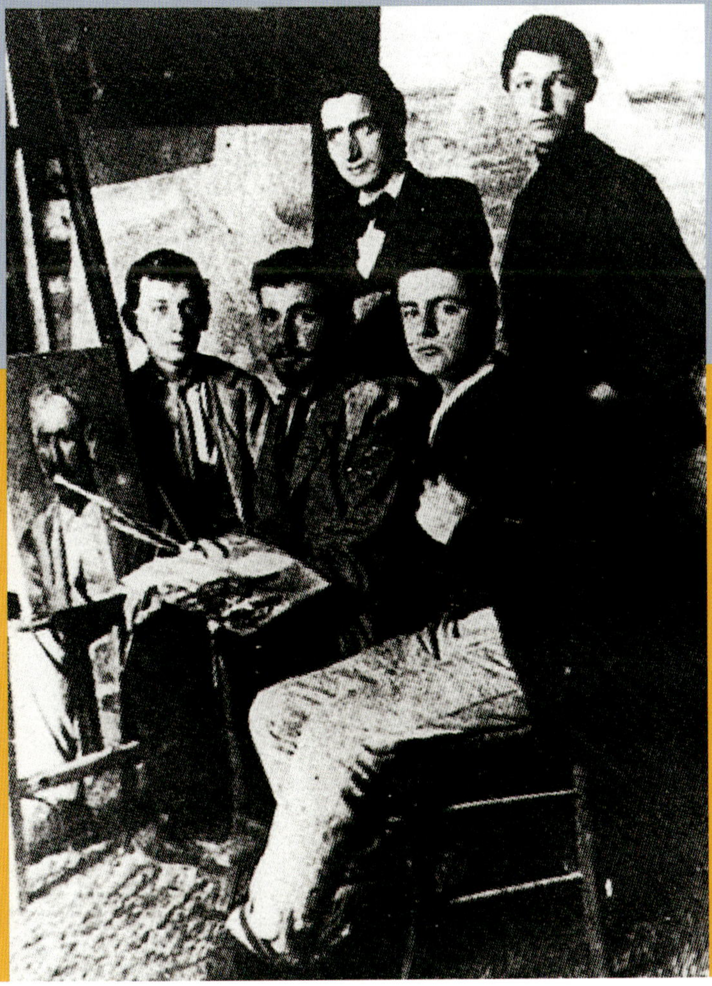

◀ At Romiti's studio, Livorno: (from left) Benvenuto Benvenuti, Gino Romiti, Aristide Sommati, Modigliani (seated, right) and the musician Bartoli, *c.* 1900. Photograph. Unknown photographer. Museo Civico Giovanni Fattori, Livorno

1907

● Modigliani meets his first patron, Dr Paul Alexandre, when he takes a studio at 7 rue du Delta, a condemned building of artists' studios owned by Alexandre. Painter and patron develop a close personal and artistic relationship over the coming seven years. Alexandre creates an important collection of the artist's early work, including some 25 paintings and 450 drawings.

● Modigliani exhibits at the Salon d'Automne, where a Paul Cézanne retrospective is on view. Exhibited for the first time, the late work of Cézanne, who had died the year before, has a tremendous impact on avant-garde artists.

1908

● Modigliani's work shows the influence of Toulouse-Lautrec, Picasso and the Fauves, as he experiments with various avant-garde styles. Cézanne's late portraits prove important for Modigliani's painting. At the instigation of Paul Alexandre, Modigliani exhibits *The Jewess*, along with four other paintings and a drawing, at the Salon des Indépendants, Paris.

1909

● Modigliani moves to a new studio at 14 Cité Falguière in Montparnasse in order to work on sculpture. He meets the Romanian sculptor Constantin Brancusi through Paul Alexandre. Under Brancusi's influence, Modigliani works by carving directly on stone. He begins a period devoted to sculpture, producing a series of stone heads.

● Paul Alexandre commissions three portraits from Modigliani: one of his father, Jean-Baptiste; another of his younger brother Jean; and a third of himself (the first of four portraits of Paul Alexandre).

● Modigliani returns to Livorno for the summer.

1910

● Modigliani exhibits some of his work from Livorno at the Salon des Indépendants, Paris, and receives a mention in reviews by the poet Guillaume Apollinaire and the critic André Salmon. Experiencing increasing financial difficulties, he drinks heavily and takes drugs.

1911

● Modigliani exhibits at the Salon des Indépendants, Paris, and is again mentioned by Apollinaire. He sculpts four heads (see cat. 1) and makes studies for caryatids (see fig. 44), part of a grand sculptural concept called 'Temple to Beauty'.

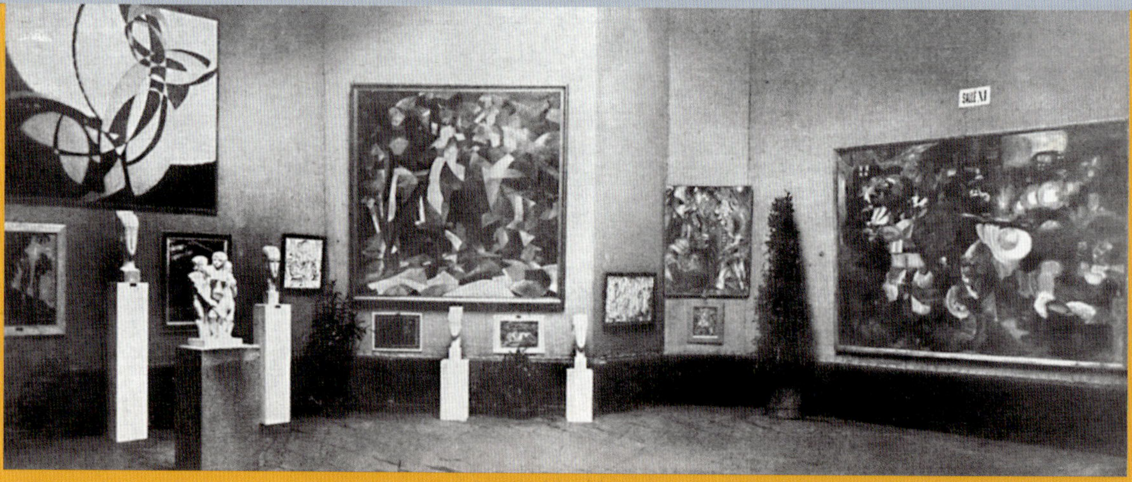

► **A view at the Cubist Room at the Salon d'Automne, 1912, showing four heads by Modigliani among works by Kupka, Le Fauconnier and Metzinger. Photograph. Unknown photographer**

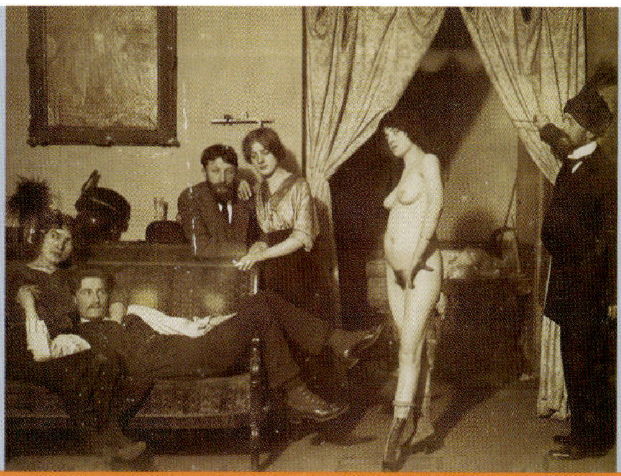

◀ Theatricals at Paul Alexandre's apartment in 7 rue Delta, February 1913. Paul Alexandre (far right) wearing a turban, with, from left, Lucie and Henri Gazan, Henri Doucet and his wife, and Raymonde – the model and mistress of sculptor Maurice Drouard. Photograph. Unknown photographer. Fonds Mercator Albin Michel, Paris

1912

● Modigliani shows seven heads, entitled 'a decorative ensemble' at the Salon d'Automne, Paris, where the Cubists Robert Delaunay, Albert Gleizes, Jean Metzinger and Fernand Léger hold their first group show.

● Modigliani meets the Russian sculptor Jacques Lipchitz through Max Jacob.

● Modigliani becomes friendly with the sculptor Jacob Epstein while Epstein is in Paris for six months.

1913

● Modigliani spends the spring in Livorno, where he concentrates on sculpture.

● Modigliani starts working in oils again.

1914

● During the First World War Modigliani remains in Paris, along with a community of avant-garde artists, such as Picasso, Diego Rivera, Juan Gris, Chaïm Soutine, Moïse Kisling and the poet Max Jacob. They frequent the Café de la Rotonde, the meeting-place of Cubists and revolutionaries.

● Modigliani forms a close friendship with a young émigré artist from Russia (present-day Lithuania), Chaïm Soutine, who moved to Paris the previous year.

● Modigliani begins a relationship with the British-born South African poet and art critic Beatrice Hastings, the subject of fourteen portraits, that lasts until 1916 (cats 8, 9 and 10).

● Paul Guillaume, a young, ambitious specialist in avant-garde and African art, becomes Modigliani's dealer. Due to ill health and the constraints imposed by the war, Modigliani returns almost exclusively to painting. He paints many portraits of his painter-friends, such as Rivera and the American Frank Burty Haviland (cat. 5), drawing on Fauvism, a kind of Pointillism, and Cubism.

● Two works by Modigliani appear in the important exhibition 'Twentieth-Century Art: A Review of Modern Movements' at the Whitechapel Gallery in London, which also includes work by David Bomberg, Vanessa Bell, Jacob Epstein, Roger Fry, Henri Gaudier-Brzeska, Mark Gertler, Duncan Grant, Wyndham Lewis, Paul Nash, Walter Sickert and Stanley Spencer.

● Modigliani exhibits with the Omega Workshops artists.

▶ The removal of Paul Alexandre's belongings from 7 rue de Delta, 5 July 1913. Modigliani's *Head of a Woman* and the 1908 *Study of a Nude* are visible propped up in the foreground. Photograph. Unknown photographer. Modigliani Institut, Archives Legales, Paris

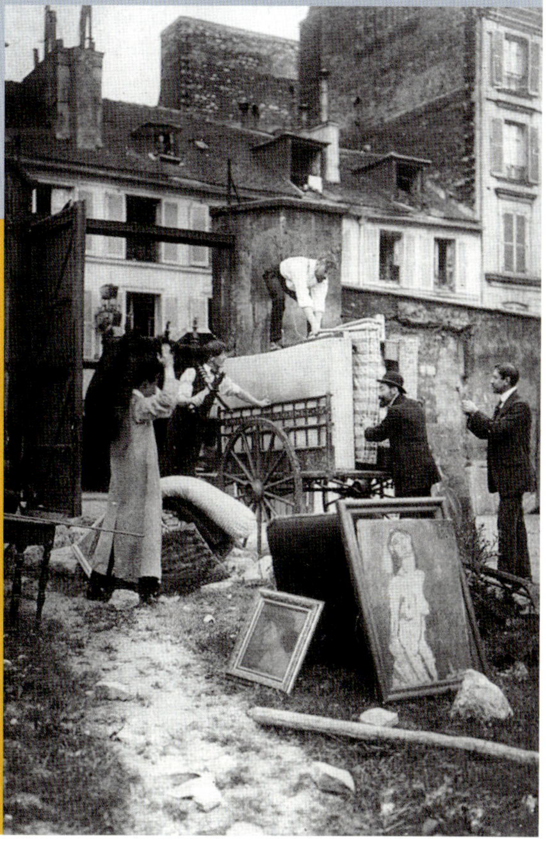

1915

● Modigliani paints portraits of Picasso (cat. 6), Juan Gris (cat. 7) and the Cubist sculptor Henri Laurens.

● Paul Guillaume sends African sculpture and 24 works by Modigliani – mainly drawings, but also a pastel, a painting and two stone sculptures – to Marius de Zayas at the Modern Gallery, Fifth Avenue, New York, for an exhibition.

1916

● Moïse Kisling introduces Modigliani to Léopold Zborowski (fig. 8), who becomes his new dealer. Nevertheless, Modigliani still co-operates unofficially with Paul Guillaume, whom he paints (cat. 13). Modigliani works in a studio at 3 rue Joseph Bara, the apartment building where Zborowski (cat. 16) lives with his companion Hanka, also known as Anna (cat. 15). Kisling also keeps a studio there, where Modigliani paints a number of his most important portraits, such as those of the artist and poet Jean Cocteau (fig. 10), Max Jacob, Soutine and Kisling himself.

● Modigliani starts work on a series of nudes for Zborowski, eventually completing 35 by 1919 (see cat. 14).

● Modigliani exhibits at the Cabaret Voltaire, Zurich, and receives public recognition at the Salon d'Antin and the Lyre et Palette, Paris, where he shows fourteen paintings and many drawings.

● He paints a wedding portrait of Jacques and Berthe Lipchitz (fig. 20).

1917

● Modigliani meets Jeanne Hébuterne (fig. 7), who becomes his companion and his most important model (cat. 26).

● Modigliani paints Lunia Czechowska, a close friend and one of the models who embodies the artist's late, sinuous style.

● This year he also paints his dealer's companion, Hanka Zborowska (cats 27, 28 and 43), and the French artist Elena Povolozky twice (see cat. 19).

● At the end of the year Modigliani has his first and only one-man exhibition at Berthe Weill's gallery, a group of portraits and explicit nudes (cat. 18) that cause a scandal (fig. 6).

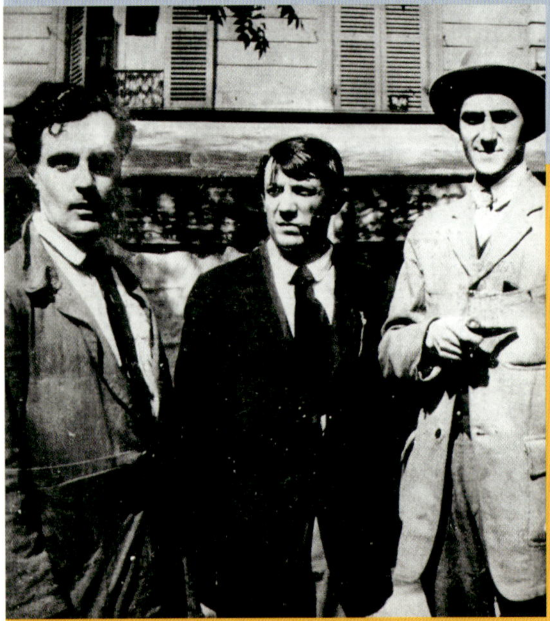

▲ Modigliani, Pablo Picasso and André Salmon, Montparnasse, 12 August 1916. Photograph by Jean Cocteau, from a series interleaved in a book by Max Jacob, *Le Cornet à dés*, 1917. Archives Paul Guillaume, Paris

▼ *Moïse Kisling*, 1916. Oil on canvas, 82 × 47 cm. Musée d'Art Moderne de Villeneuve d'Ascq, Lille

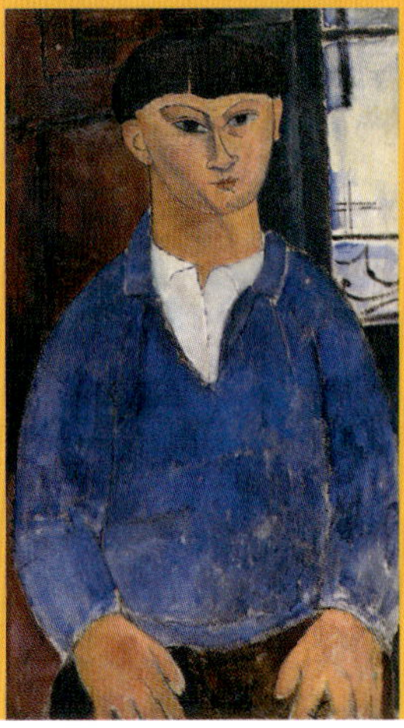

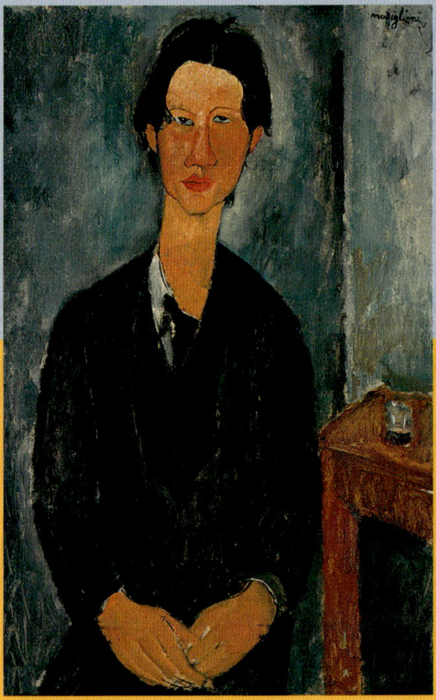

▲ *Chaïm Soutine*, 1917. Oil on canvas, 91.7 × 59.7 cm. National Gallery of Art, Washington DC. Chester Dale Collection NGA 1963.10.47

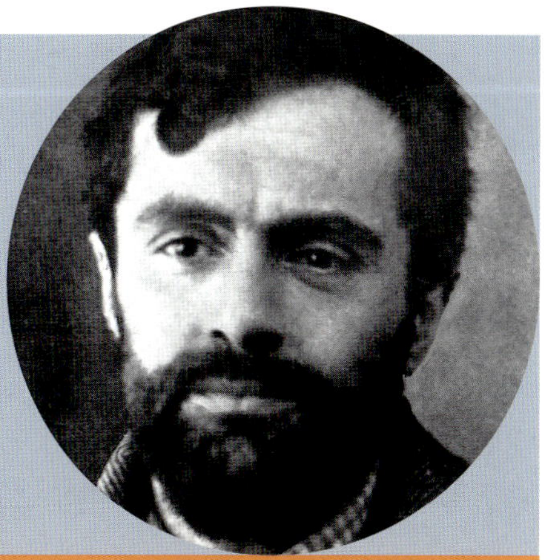

▶ A bearded Modigliani in his last years, *c.* 1919–20. Photograph. Unknown photographer. Modigliani Institut, Archives Legales, Paris

1918

● April: to escape the German shelling of Paris, Modigliani moves to Nice and Cagnes with Jeanne Hébuterne, who is pregnant, and Jeanne's mother. He remains there for over one year and sees a number of friends, including Léopold (cat. 29) and Hanka Zborowska, Léopold Survage, Tsuguharu Foujita, Chaïm Soutine and Blaise Cendrars. In Nice Modigliani paints portraits of a number of local people (cats 32 and 33), as well as many portraits of Jeanne (cat. 39).

● One of Modigliani's most important collectors, the businessman Roger Dutilleul, begins to purchase his work.

● 29 November: Modigliani's daughter Jeanne is born in Nice.

● December: Paul Guillaume includes Modigliani in an important exhibition of modern painters featuring Picasso, Matisse, De Chirico, Derain and Utrillo, among others, at his Faubourg Saint-Honoré gallery.

1919

● February: Roger Fry writes an enthusiastic article about Modigliani's work in *The Burlington Magazine*.

● May: Modigliani returns to Paris to live and work at 8 rue de la Grande-Chaumière, and is later joined by Jeanne Hébuterne.

● August: Zborowski arranges for 9 paintings and 50 drawings by Modigliani to feature in a large exhibition held at Heal's Mansard Gallery, Tottenham Court Road, London.

● Modigliani paints Roger Dutilleul.

● Although Modigliani's health is worsening, he produces a number of portraits, including those of Lunia Czechowska (cats 47 and 51), Jeanne Hébuterne (cats 38, 41, 42 and 44) and Paulette Jourdain (cat. 50) and a self-portrait (cat. 52), probably his last work. He is inspired, too, by chance encounters with his sitters, such as the Swedish art students Thora Klinckowström (cat. 49) and Annie Bjarne.

● Autumn: an exhibition of modern drawings, which includes work by Modigliani, is held in Cambridge.

1920

● Modigliani's health deteriorates.

● 24 January: Modigliani dies of tubercular meningitis.

● 26 January: Jeanne, nine months pregnant with the couple's second child, commits suicide by jumping from a window of her parents' apartment.

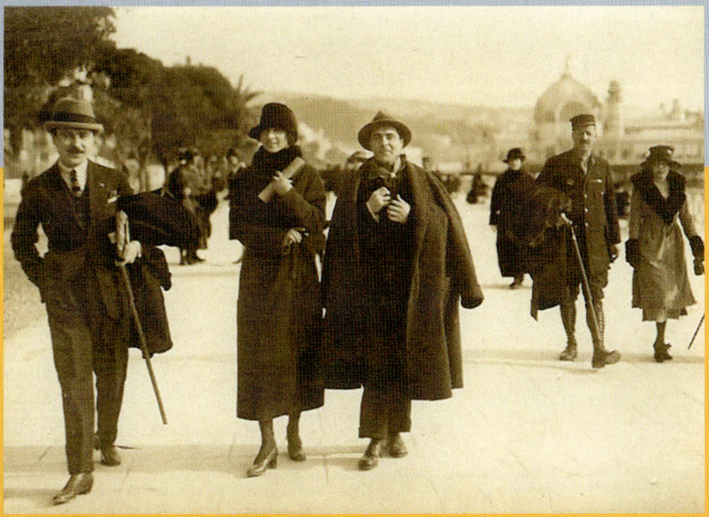

▲ Paul Guillaume, Alexander Archipenko's wife and Modigliani walking on the Promenade des Anglais (where Paul Guillaume had an apartment), Nice, 1918. Photograph. Unknown photographer. Archives Paul Guillaume, Paris

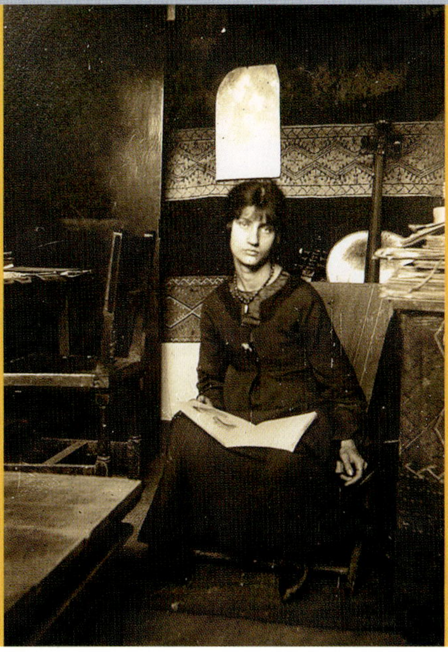

▶ Jeanne Hébuterne in the studio, 1919. Photograph. Unknown photographer. Modigliani Institut, Archives Legales, Paris

Biographies of Modigliani's Models

Kathleen Brunner

Paul Alexandre

(1881–1968)
Paul Alexandre in his apartment in 7 rue Delta, February 1913. Photograph. Unknown photographer. Fonds Mercator Albin Michel, Paris

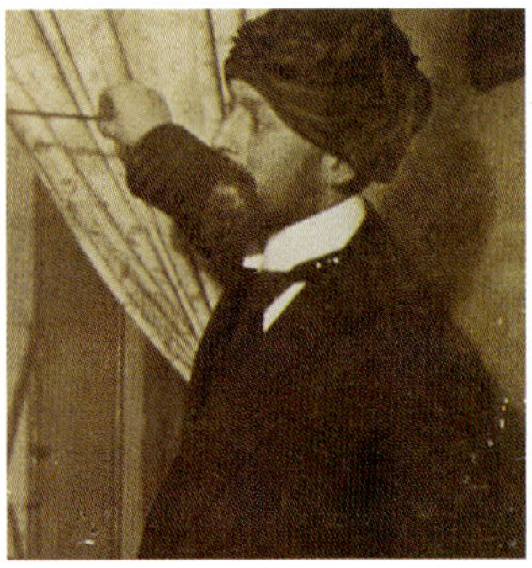

The young Parisian doctor and aesthete Paul Alexandre met Modigliani in 1907 when the artist came to work in some studios that Alexandre owned in a condemned property at 7 rue du Delta in Montparnasse, Paris. A newly qualified dermatologist, Alexandre became Modigliani's first patron, and his collection provides an important record of the artist's early career, documenting his transition from painting to sculpture and the development of his stylised aesthetic between 1908 and 1914. Alexandre's collection, now dispersed, comprised some 25 paintings and 450 drawings that were only made known in a 1993 exhibition ('The Unknown Modigliani: Drawings from the Collection of Paul Alexandre').

It appears that Alexandre, a new type of patron, bought nearly all the artist's early work in exchange for material support, including hashish. He encouraged Modigliani to exhibit at the Salon des Indépendants in 1908, provided him with commissions, including portraits of his brother and father, and introduced Modigliani to Brancusi in 1909. Patron and artist discussed art together, visited the Bernheim-Jeune gallery, where they saw the work of Paul Cézanne and Henri Matisse, the Louvre, the Musée Ethnographique at the Trocadéro, in the heyday of *art nègre*, as well as antique shops.

Their relationship ended when Alexandre went to the Front in 1914. Modigliani and his first patron never saw each other again.

Léon Bakst

(1866–1924)
Léon Bakst in Lausanne, 1915. Photograph by H. Perret (dates unknown). Archives für Kunst und Geschichte, Berlin

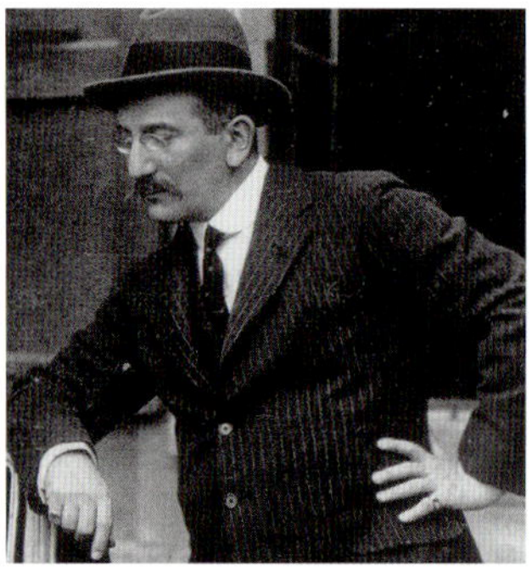

The celebrated Russian painter Léon Bakst designed stage-sets and costumes for Sergei Diaghilev's Ballets Russes (*The Firebird*, 1910; *Afternoon of a Faun*, 1912; and *Daphnis and Chloe*, 1912). Bakst's Art Nouveau designs, which drew on the rich heritage of Russian peasant art, were revolutionary in the early part of the century. He studied and worked between St Petersburg and Paris, where he resided in exile from 1909.

Modigliani was commissioned to paint Bakst's opulent portrait in 1917, just as the Russian artist was beginning to fall out of favour with Diaghilev. He paints Bakst in a vividly coloured, patterned robe, similar to the sitter's designs for the fashion designer Paul Poiret. In *Les Montparnos* (1954) the novelist Michel Georges-Michel gives an undoubtedly embroidered account of one of the sittings, which took place in the Russian's luxurious apartment. Modigliani arrived 'wearing espadrilles and a tight-fitting sweater', with burning eyes and an intense drug-induced gaze (Sichel 1967, pp. 384–5).

Bakst later commented: 'You could not miss his nobleness, though he was shabby. He was a nobleman in frayed cuffs. He strode in – disdained a cup of tea, going straight to work, for it was for that that he had been summoned. He flung the sketch at you, as though to clear his fingers of ordure – witha curious flash of pure pride' (Fifield 1978, p. 129).

Blaise Cendrars

(1887–1961)
Blaise Cendrars pictured shortly before his departure for the Front, 1914. Photograph. Unknown photographer. Centre d'Etudes Blaise Cendrars, Berne

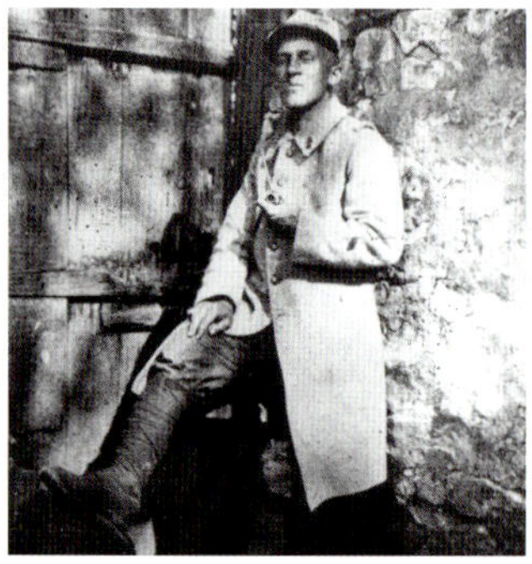

The cosmopolitan Blaise Cendrars (the pseudonym of Frédéric-Louis Sauser) is the author of one of the most famous works of modernist poetry, *La Prose du Transsibérien et de la petite Jeanne de France* (1913), his purported impressions of a railway journey across Europe in 1905. As visual as it is verbal, the poem, with its Cubist illustrations by Sonia Delaunay, captures the effect of speed and technology on mental states and language. Cendrars met Modigliani in 1913, when he frequented the building of artists' studios called La Ruche (The Hive). Cendrars contributed a poem, 'Sur un portrait de Modigliani', to the catalogue of the artist's 'scandalous' 1917 exhibition of nudes at Berthe Weill's gallery. That same year, not long after he returned from the Front as an amputee, Cendrars, who was living in Nice at the same time as Modigliani, commissioned his portrait to help his impoverished friend.

Cendrars embraced Negrophilia in the 1920s in his *poèmes nègres*, inspired by African languages and by the sounds and sensations experienced in the *favelas* of Rio, in Harlem and Guyana. He edited a collection of black poetry, *Anthologie nègre* (1921), and collaborated on a ballet based on West African myths, *La Création du monde* (1923), with Darius Milhaud and Fernand Léger. Throughout his life he remained fascinated by modernity and popular culture, whether as a novelist, a journalist or a filmmaker.

Jean Cocteau

(1889–1963)
Jean Cocteau (at Lausanne?), 1920. Inscribed photograph. Unknown photographer. Archives Alinari, Florence

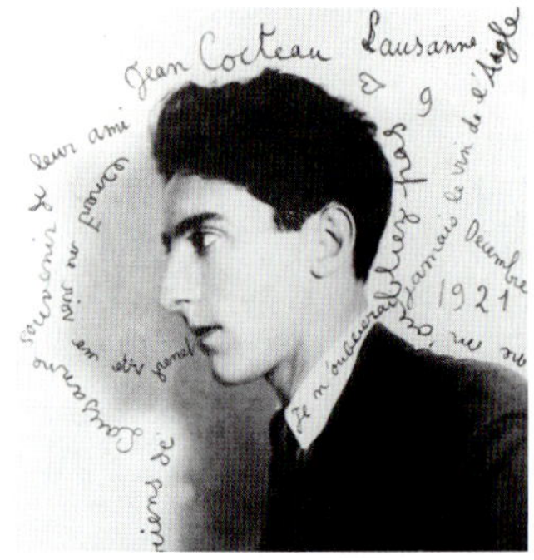

Jean Cocteau, the poet (*The Frivolous Prince*, 1910), draughtsman, designer and filmmaker (*The Blood of a Poet*, 1930; *Beauty and the Beast*, 1946; *Orpheus*, 1950; *Testament of Orpheus*, 1960), remains one of the most influential figures of the period between the wars. Introduced to the Montparnasse avant-garde by Picasso,* whom he began to cultivate in 1915, Cocteau brought together the artistic worlds of Right and Left Bank Paris during the First World War. One of his greatest inspirations was the Cubist ballet *Parade* (1917), an audacious blend of modernism and 'classicism', produced by Sergei Diaghilev, with music by Erik Satie and costumes and sets by Picasso.

Modigliani painted Cocteau's portrait in 1916, at the time of his introduction into Montparnasse life (fig. 10). The sittings took place in Moïse Kisling's studio above the Café de la Rotonde. Years later Cocteau referred to the stylised angular features and pinched mouth of the portrait as 'diabolical', proof that Modigliani 'detested' him. According to the poet Pierre Reverdy, Cocteau called Modigliani 'the only true portraitist of the group, serious and gifted. He flattered no one, including P. R.'. Cocteau spoke with amusement of the portrait's trajectory from Kisling's studio to the restaurant down stairs (in settlement of Kisling's debt to the café owner), to England and finally to America, where it was sold for millions (F. Steegmuller, *Cocteau: A Biography*, New York, 1970, p. 150).

Lunia Czechowska

(1895–post-1970)
Detail of cat. 47
Lunia Czechowska in Black, 1919.
Oil on canvas, 92 × 60 cm. Private collection

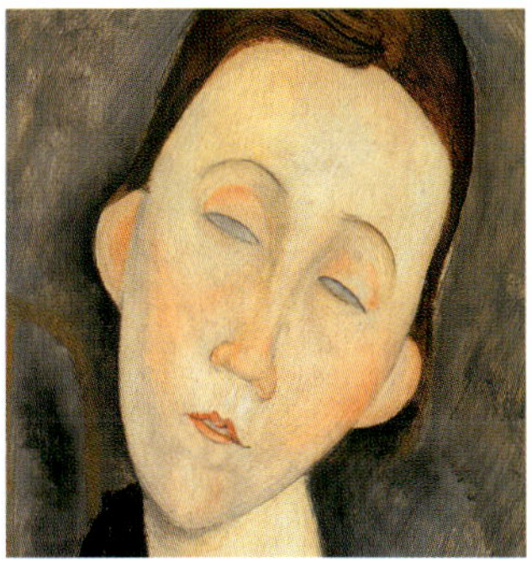

Lunia Czechowska, a Polish émigré, moved in with Modigliani's dealer Léopold Zborowski* and his companion Hanka,* who were living at 3 rue Joseph Bara, in 1916. Czechowska's husband had gone to the Front, entrusting her to the care of Zborowski, his childhood friend. Modigliani painted numerous portraits of the elegant young woman in the graceful feminine style of his final years (cats 47 and 51; both 1919), as his health continued to deteriorate. The first group of three portraits was particularly sombre: the sitter wears black against a charcoal-grey background.

During the war, Czechowska and Modigliani became extremely close, although it seems that their relationship remained platonic. Czechowska wrote a memoir of her friendship with Modigliani in 1953, in which she tells of the deep bond between them from their first meeting, when he proposed painting her (see Ceroni 1958). She describes the strong emotions of the painter and his model: 'Before his model, Modigliani became completely different; he obsessively tried to capture her character in his work. As for the model, she felt as though she had bared her soul, and she found it strangely impossible to hide her feelings.' (Ceroni 1958, pp. 19–34.)

Modigliani and Czechowska separated because of her poor state of health and because of the artist's involvement with Jeanne Hébuterne,* his companion, and the birth of his baby daughter.

Roger Dutilleul

(1874–1957)
Roger Dutilleul standing in the middle of his paintings. Photograph. Unknown photographer

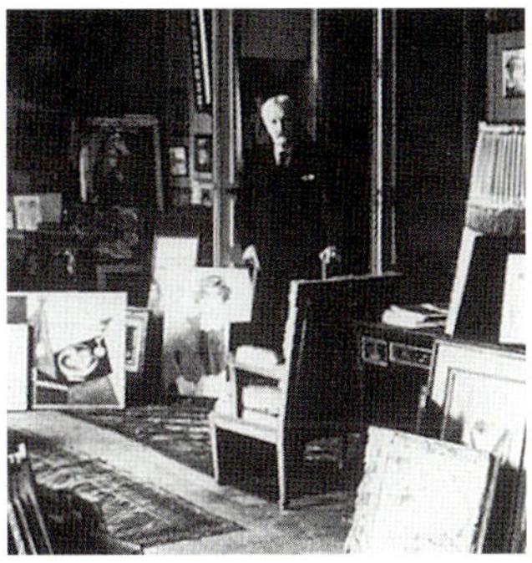

One of Modigliani's most important collectors, the businessman Roger Dutilleul owned about a tenth of the artist's production (which he purchased from 1918 to 1925), including the 1919 portrait of himself. As a student of modest means, Dutilleul began collecting avant-garde art in 1905. He purchased the Fauves from Daniel-Henry Kahnweiler, soon exchanging them for works by Pablo Picasso* and Georges Braque, still unknown at the time. Other works were bought from the dealers Ambroise Vollard and Léonce Rosenberg. Dutilleul's collection of early twentieth-century modernists, including André Derain, Kees van Dongen, Henri Laurens, Vassily Kandinsky, Fernand Léger, Joan Miró and André Masson, was formed by instinct. He was particularly drawn to artists who favoured the representation of the human figure. Collectors such as Dutilleul conferred legitimacy on avant-garde artists working outside the conventional Salon and state systems, as the art market was expanding, along with consumer society.

When Dutilleul died, his nephew Jean Masurel, an industrialist, inherited the collection, which he donated in 1979 to the Musée d'Art Moderne de Lille in Villeneuve d'Ascq (opened 1983). This collection remains an important archive of the pioneers of modernism.

Juan Gris

(1887–1927)
Juan Gris in Paris, 1922. Photograph by Man Ray (Emmanuel Radnitsky; 1890–1976). Collection Man Ray Archive, Paris

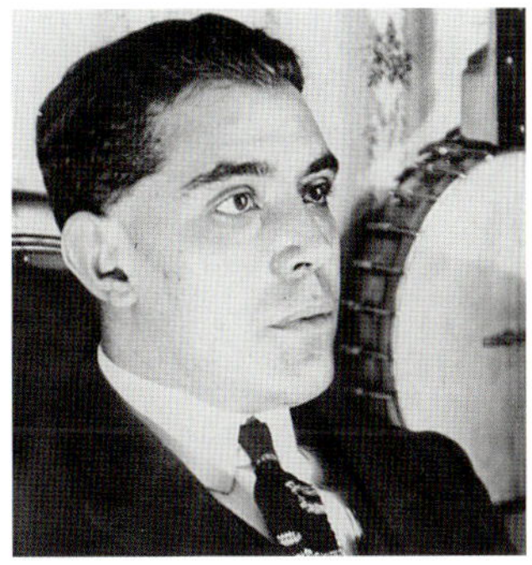

Juan Gris (pseudonym of José Victoriano González-Pérez) is one of the artists most closely associated with the early development of Cubism, after Picasso* and Braque. Before his arrival in Paris in 1906, the Spanish painter Gris had studied mathematics, physics and engineering, as well as academic painting. Taking a studio in the Bateau-Lavoir, he became an illustrator for popular publications, such as *L'Assiette au beurre*. In his paintings, Gris closely followed the development of Picasso, his mentor, while working in a more structured manner, using mathematical calculations. In 1912 he exhibited in the Salon des Indépendants and the Cubist show 'Section d'Or'. Works such as *Still-life with Bottle and Watch* (1912) confirm his original contribution to Cubism. In his Synthetic Cubism, Gris superimposes a framework of squares, triangles and cylinders on the subject, which the viewer must reintegrate, or synthesise.

When Modigliani painted Gris's portrait in 1915 (cat. 7), both artists were working in the Bateau-Lavoir. The two must have become close, particularly as Modigliani was incorporating Cubist elements into his paintings. There is some dislocation in the features and neck of the portrait, although the work bears none of the more overtly Cubist characteristics of Modigliani's portrait of Max Jacob,* painted the following year.

Paul Guillaume

(1891–1934)
Paul Guillaume in his apartment in Paris, 1916. Photograph. Unknown photographer. Modigliani Institut, Archives Legales, Paris

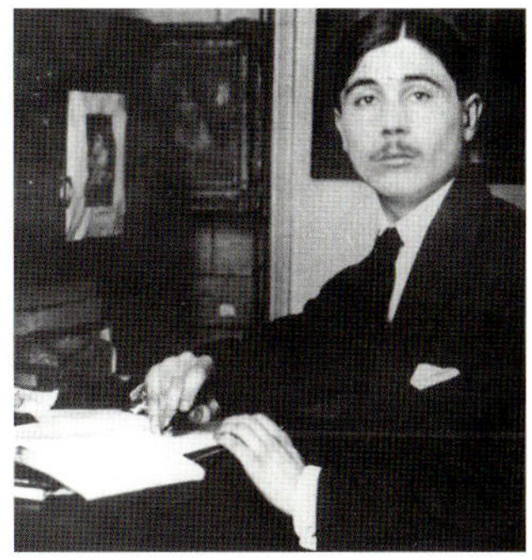

Paul Guillaume was the quintessential avant-garde dealer in Paris during the First World War. Guillaume started dealing in African art while he was employed in a garage, at which time, through his associations with rubber entrepreneurs, he purchased his first African statue and became an important authority on the subject. Very ambitious and completely self-taught, Guillaume acted as a tastemaker and creator of artistic reputations through his catalogues, his review *Les Arts à Paris* (1918), and Dada-type artistic events. Max Jacob* introduced Guillaume to Modigliani in 1914 and Guillaume became Modigliani's exclusive dealer until Léopold Zborowski* took over in 1916. One of the portraits of Guillaume entitled '*Novo Pilota*' (*The New Helmsman*) (1915) commemorates their contract, Guillaume encouraging him to return to painting exclusively. Other portraits of Guillaume depict the urbane dealer in his milieu, sitting at his ease and dressed either informally in a pale green jacket (cat. 12) or in his more usual dark suit and tie (cat. 13). In the latter, one of his eyes is blanked out, symbolic of the inner vision usually reserved for poets.

Guillaume absorbed a great deal of knowledge from the artistic milieu of Montmartre and was closely associated with poets and critics such as his mentor Guillaume Apollinaire, André Salmon, Blaise Cendrars,* Pierre Reverdy, Jean Cocteau* and André Breton (Colette Giraudon, *Paul Guillaume et les peintres du XXeme siècle: de l'art nègre à l'avant-garde*, Paris, 1993, pp. 17–18). André Derain was the first important artist he represented, and he served as the representative of the American collector and industrialist Albert C. Barnes from 1927. Guillaume formed a private collection of museum quality, which his wife Dominica bequeathed to the Musée de l'Orangerie in Paris.

Beatrice Hastings

(1879–1943)

Beatrice Hastings in Paris, 1918. (Inscribed in her own hand 'very ill'.) Photograph. Unknown photographer. HPB Library, Toronto

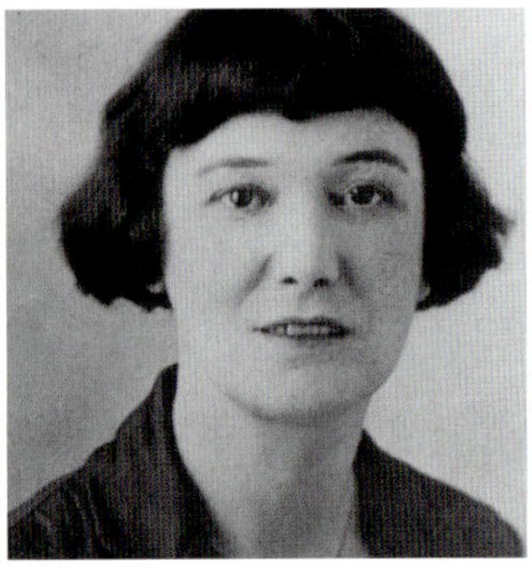

Beatrice Hastings (the pseudonym of Emily Alice Haigh), an English poet, journalist and critic, was Modigliani's companion from 1914 to 1916, and one of his most important models. Modigliani lived with Beatrice, an intellectual who was perceptive about modern art, during his transition from sculpture to painting. Their relationship, fuelled by hashish and alcohol, was tempestuous. An inveterate fabricator of her life in writing, Beatrice romanticised her relationship with Modigliani in 'Minnie Pinnikin', a Surrealist novella, and in her diary-like articles on the Paris avant-garde, 'Impressions de Paris', which appeared in the London journal, *The New Age* (see Appendix, 'Excerpts from "Minnie Pinnikin" by Beatrice Hastings' in Buffalo 2002, pp. 204–11). More realistically, Beatrice allegedly characterised Modigliani thus: 'A complex character. A pig and a pearl.' (Sichel 1967, p. 270, reproduced from Lipchitz 1952.)

Yet this self-obsessed, opinionated rebel from an affluent, middle-class family, resident in South Africa, conveys, with her varied moods and eccentric hats, the image that Modigliani sought while exploring the medium of painting. Modigliani painted fourteen portraits or nudes of her, using a variety of techniques (cats 8, 9 and 10). Initially, in 1914, he employed a dark, Expressionist brushstroke combined with 'Pointillism', followed by a more structured, linear treatment derived from Cubism. The model's stylised, sculptural head and features, as well as her colouring and demeanour, diverged wildly from her actual appearance. She is by turns elegant and comical, sombre, bright and fresh-faced, vulnerable and hard. Beatrice, a disturbing, mercurial character, ended her life by apparent suicide in 1943.

Frank Burty Haviland

(1886–1971)

Frank Burty Haviland in the studio at 11 boulevard de Clichy, Paris, autumn–winter 1910. Photograph by Pablo Picasso. Musée Picasso, Paris

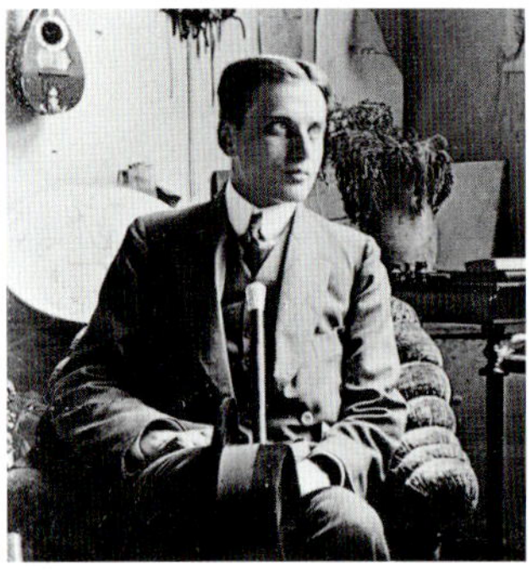

Frank Burty Haviland, a wealthy American, went to Paris to paint at the age of eighteen. His grandfather founded the French porcelain company, Haviland & Compagnie, and he had artistic connections through his mother, who was the daughter of Philippe Burty, a well-known art critic and friend of Eugène Delacroix, Pierre-Auguste Renoir, Edgar Degas and Edouard Manet. Haviland became Picasso's disciple in 1909, and took a studio next door to the artist in the rue Schoelcher in Montparnasse. Haviland introduced Picasso to the French Catalan town of Céret, inviting him to his chateau in the summer of 1911, an important period in the development of Cubism. The artists Georges Braque, André Derain, Juan Gris,* Chaïm Soutine* and others also painted at Céret. Haviland, unsuccessful as a painter, later became the curator of a small museum in the town.

Haviland gave grand dinners for his artist friends at his home in Paris. Modigliani, who used to visit him there with his companion Beatrice Hastings* (from 1914 to 1916), was fascinated by Haviland's collection of African sculpture. It inspired the artist's new direction in painting. Modigliani painted Haviland's portrait in 1914 (cat. 5) in a style derived from Pointillism that was popular with Picasso and other artists at the time. He depicts Haviland in profile, capturing his formal demeanour and distinctive bouffant hairstyle, parted in the middle.

Jeanne Hébuterne

(1898–1920)

Jeanne Hébuterne, *c.* 1919. Photograph. Unknown photographer. Archives Roger-Viollet, Paris.

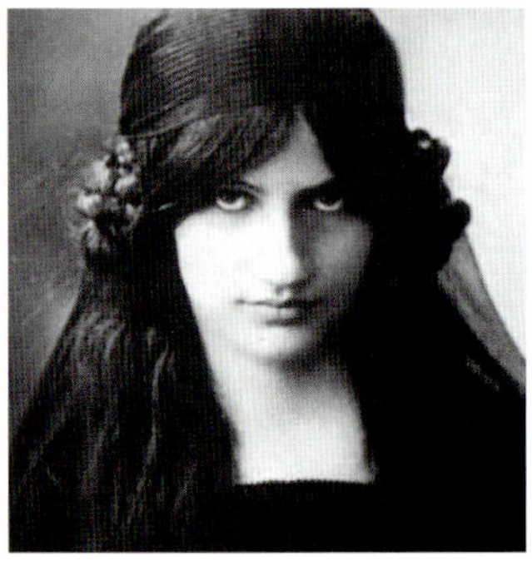

Jeanne Hébuterne met Modigliani in 1917, while she was a young art student at the Académie Colarossi. The following year she became his companion and the model who embodied the graceful, Italianate aesthetic of his late work. Hébuterne's look – her enigmatic expression and her long chestnut-coloured hair with auburn highlights – inspired some 25 of Modigliani's portraits (see cats 26, 38, 39, 41, 42 and 44). Her own artistic talent came to light in 2000, when about sixty of her drawings and six paintings were included in a Modigliani exhibition at the Fondazione Giorgio Cini in Venice.

Hébuterne was devoted to Modigliani, as he was to her, even pledging in writing to marry her. She was introspective and compliant, although she may have had a stronger character than is commonly acknowledged and possibly had other liaisons before Modigliani. Hébuterne's family disapproved of the match, to the point of disowning her. The relationship seemed to revolve around Modigliani's drinking, and Hébuterne's searching for him when he failed to return home. During their year in Nice – where their baby Jeanne (also known as Giovanna) was born on 29 November 1918, and where they had gone to escape German shelling – their situation only worsened, although it was there that Modigliani developed his attenuated, Renaissance-revival style. In their final months, in Paris, Modigliani painted some of his most poignant, Madonna-like portraits of Hébuterne, pregnant for the second time. When Modigliani died on 24 January 1920, Hébuterne was distraught and, two days later, committed suicide by leaping from an upstairs window. Her unborn child was also killed.

Max Jacob

(1876–1944)

Max Jacob at the Café de la Rotonde, Montparnasse, 12 August 1916. Photograph by Jean Cocteau from a series interleaved in a book by Max Jacob, *Le Cornet à dés*, 1917. Musée Picasso, Paris, MP2003-15; fol.74

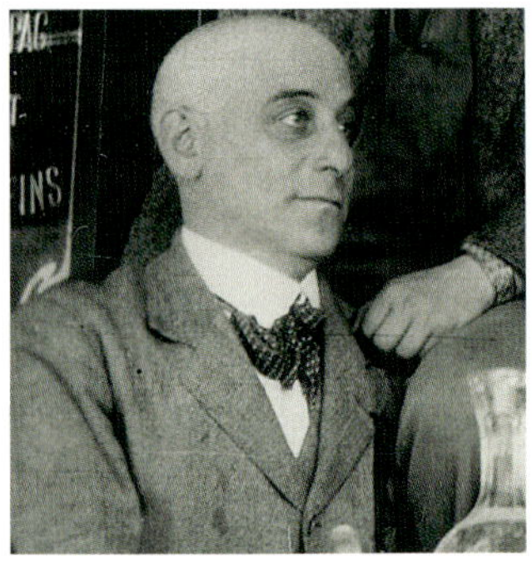

The poet Max Jacob was a key member of Picasso's circle in 1906, and perhaps the only member of the group to recognise Modigliani's talent when he frequented their studios in the Bateau-Lavoir. A convert to Catholicism in 1914, Jacob was very religious, with a predilection for mysticism. He is credited with introducing Modigliani to the occult. As for his aesthetic leanings, Jacob was a dedicated modernist who eschewed the subject. The poems of Jacob's 1917 collection *Le Cornet à dés* (*The Dice Cup*) are composed by chance and arranged haphazardly on the page, a reference, of course, to Stéphane Mallarmé's poem *Un Coup de dés* (*A Dice-Throw*) of 1897. Modigliani, for his part, sought to create a modern style that respected the Old Master tradition.

One of Modigliani's portraits of Jacob, which was in a Cubist style, shows the poet in the typical attire of his father's suit, stiff shirt, tie and top hat (1916). One of his eyes is blanked out with hatching marks, a reference, Modigliani said, to the poet's inner vision. The portrait's sculptural quality recalls Modigliani's transition from sculpture to painting, which Jacob claimed to have influenced. In 1921 he retreated to the monastery of St-Benoît-sur-Loire to atone for his homosexuality, drinking and drug addiction. He died in 1944 in the Nazi deportation camp at Drancy, north of Paris.

Paulette Jourdain

(1904–97)

Paulette Jourdain with Chaïm Soutine and 'Riquette' (their housemaid Amélie's dog), outside Soutine's studio in their rented farmhouse at Le Blanc, 1925. Photograph. Unknown photographer. Private collection

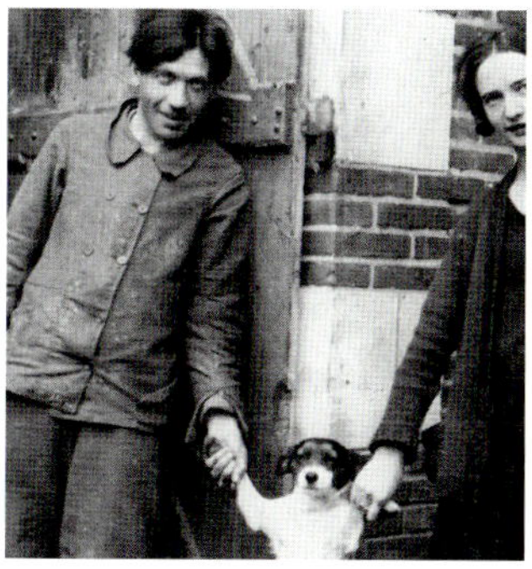

Paulette Jourdain first met Modigliani at the Académie Ranson at 7 rue Joseph Bara, where she worked as a model. She also encountered him at the home of his dealer Léopold Zborowski,* at 3 rue Joseph Bara. Jourdain was only fifteen when Modigliani painted her in 1919 (cat. 50). She must have been his last sitter, as he died of tubercular meningitis a few weeks later. A sober Jourdain is shown in three-quarter length, seated in a chair in front of a partly open door. The wall behind, ochre above and brown below, serves as a backdrop. Jourdain wears a simple black dress that contrasts with the luminous whiteness of her arms, face and long swan-like neck. In the middle of the sitting, Modigliani sent her out for alcohol. According to Jourdain, he would drink one small glass after another, finish drunk and go straight to the Café de la Rotonde (Fifield 1978, pp. 131–2).

Jourdain went on to model for Chaïm Soutine in 1925, and claimed to have brought him blood from the slaughterhouse at La Villette to refresh his animal carcasses. She eventually became Zborowski's companion and had a daughter by him. Paulette Jourdain ran the Galerie Zborowski at 26 rue de Seine from its opening in 1927 to 1942, when it closed because of the German Occupation.

Moïse Kisling

(1891–1953)

Moïse Kisling standing in front of his painting of Paulette Jourdain, 1920. Photograph. Unknown photographer. Archives Roger-Viollet, Paris

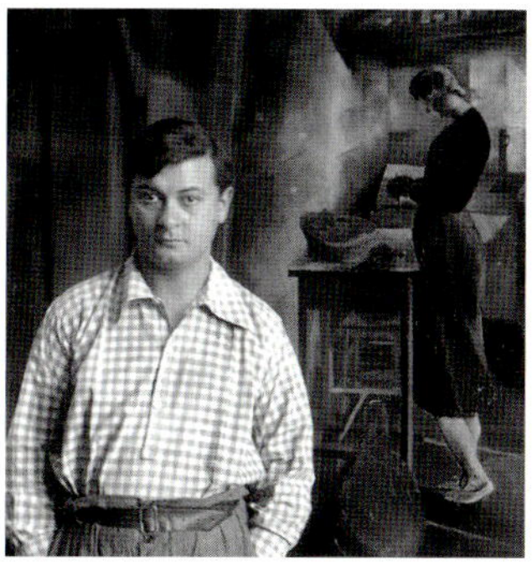

Moïse Kisling arrived in Paris from Poland in 1910 and became assimilated into the group of émigré artists in Montparnasse. He knew Picasso* and his coterie, including the poet Max Jacob* and the critic André Salmon, who introduced him to Modigliani. Kisling joined the Foreign Legion in 1914, but was invalided out the next year. He took a studio at 3 rue Joseph Bara, which he subsequently shared with Modigliani, providing him with canvases and models. In 1916 Modigliani's new dealer Léopold Zborowski* took an apartment there. Modigliani produced many drawings and painted three portraits of Kisling, notably one of 1916 in which he wears his preferred mechanic's boiler suit. Upon Modigliani's death, Kisling made a mask of the artist for the sculptor Jacques Lipchitz* to cast in bronze.

In the 1920s Kisling became one of the leaders of the school of modern 'eclectic' painters – drawing on the great 'classical' styles – and had tremendous success with the dealers Paul Guillaume* and Paul Rosenberg. In the era when modern painters returned to the French tradition, Kisling painted nudes, landscapes and children. He was seen at the time as one of the most important artists to develop independently of Picasso and the Cubists.

Thora Klinckowström

(1899–1995)

Detail of cat. 49
Portrait of Thora Klinckowström, 1919. Oil on canvas, 99.7 × 64.8 cm. Heirs of Evelyn Sharp

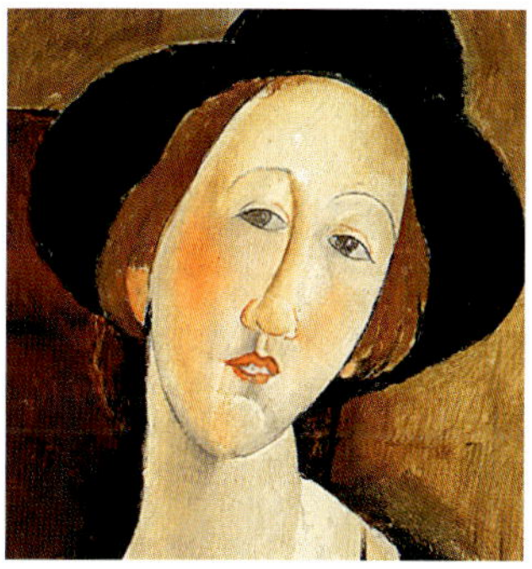

Thora Klinckowström was a twenty-year-old Swedish art student when she met Modigliani at the Café de la Rotonde in October 1919. She described the once-handsome Modigliani as drunk and debauched. Modigliani sketched her portrait at the café table and invited her to pose for a portrait (cat. 49) in his studio at 8 rue de la Grande Chaumière, where he lived with his companion Jeanne Hébuterne.* Klinckowström recounts that she accepted the offer and went to the studio on 8 November, accompanied by a friend, Annie Bjarne, whom the artist also painted. Modigliani worked quickly and intensely, while drinking rum, finishing her portrait in two sittings. He was coughing up blood, but she thought this was due to the coal dust on the floor. Not realising that Modigliani was so ill, Klinckowström was astonished to hear of his death and that of Jeanne, so soon after she had met them.

Klinckowström married her fiancé, the Swedish painter Nils Dardel, whom she had accompanied to Paris, and they lived in the French capital for thirteen years. She next heard of Modigliani's portrait of her in 1965. Six years later the work was sold at Christie's in London for a world-record price of £120,250. (The portrait belongs to the Heirs of Evelyn Sharp and is on long-term loan to the Moderna Museet in Stockholm.)

Henri Laurens

(1885–1954)

Henri Laurens, c. 1930s. Photograph. Unknown photographer

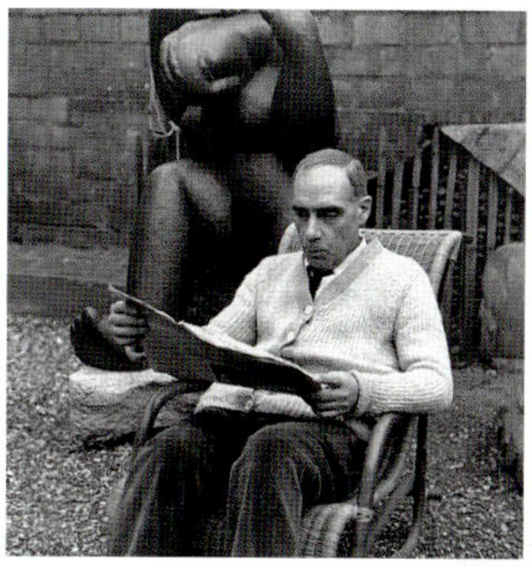

The French sculptor Henri Laurens was one of the first artists to recognise the possibilities of Cubist space for three-dimensional works. Laurens was completely self-taught, having begun sculpting as an assistant to an ornamental stonemason. His interaction from 1909 with avant-garde artists, such as Jacques Lipchitz* and Fernand Léger, at La Ruche (The Hive, a building of artist's studios) in Montparnasse, marked a change of direction. He became close to Georges Braque in 1911 and was very responsive to the work of Picasso,* especially his constructions, such as *Guitar* (1912), a crude-looking object made of sheet metal and wire. During the First World War, Laurens, one of the few French artists remaining in Paris – his leg had been amputated in 1909 – developed his series of *Constructions* (1914–15) in wood or polychrome plaster, and sculptures such as *Clown* (1915), *Figure* (*Woman*) (1917) and *Guitar* (1917–18).

When Modigliani painted his portrait of Laurens in 1915, both artists belonged to the Cubist circle. Laurens, in shirt and tie, sits at a table on which he has placed his pipe and tobacco pouch, his left leg obviously missing. One of the sculptor's eyes seems to be closed. Behind Laurens's head appears one of his painted metal sculptures. The portrait conveys the world of the Cubists, as well as their higher poetic calling, denoted by the sculptor's 'blindness'.

Jacques Lipchitz

(1891–1973)

Jacques Lipchitz, 1920. Photograph. Unknown photographer. Archives Roger-Viollet, Paris

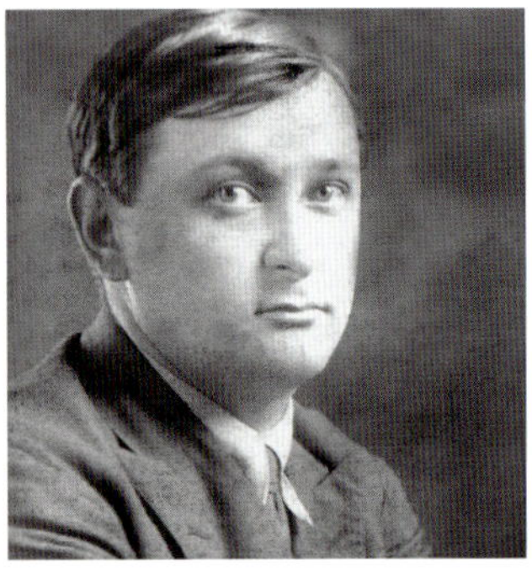

Jacques Lipchitz was among the first to translate the innovations of Cubist space into three dimensions. A student at the conservative Ecole des Beaux-Arts and the Académie Julian in Paris from 1909, Lipchitz only became involved with the avant-garde in 1912, after a return to Lithuania. He was acquainted with Modigliani, Chaïm Soutine,* Alexander Archipenko and Max Jacob.* Modigliani invited Lipchitz to his studio in the Cité Falguière, where Lipchitz saw his group of carved stone heads (1912). Lipchitz recalled Modigliani's intense discussion of direct stone carving and the importance of feeling as the way forward for sculpture after Rodin (Lipchitz 1952, unpaginated). However, more important artistically for Lipchitz was the influence of Picasso, whom he met in 1913, after which he began to develop an abstract, Cubist style. Lipchitz's most important early work, *Man with a Guitar* (1915), a tall, architectural limestone sculpture, marks the beginning of his most inventive period. From 1916, Lipchitz became close to the Cubist painter Juan Gris* through their mutual philosophical and theoretical approach to Cubism.

The year 1916 proved to be a turning-point for Lipchitz, who was now represented by Léonce Rosenberg, the most important Cubist dealer in Paris. Lipchitz also married that year and commissioned Modigliani to paint a portrait of himself with his wife Berthe (fig. 20). During the first sitting Modigliani drew furiously and rapidly, establishing the pose inspired by the couple's wedding photograph (fig. 19), and virtually completed it the following day. The sittings continued for a further two weeks, so that Lipchitz could pay the impecunious Modigliani the fee of ten francs per sitting plus alcohol (Lipchitz 1952).

Oscar Miestchaninoff

(1886–1956)

Oscar Miestchaninoff at a costume party in Paris, dressed as a gypsy, date unknown (probably *c.* 1914). Photograph. Unknown photographer. Instituto Nacional de Bellas Artes, Mexico City

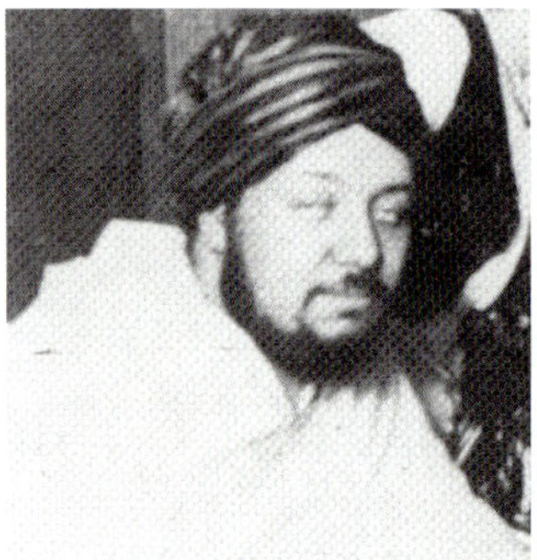

The Russian sculptor Oscar Miestchaninoff arrived in Paris in 1909, having studied at the School of Fine Art in Odessa. He took a studio in the Cité Falguière, a building of sculptors' studios, where he met Modigliani, who worked there from 1909 to 1913 or 1914. Along with other Russian artists, such as Alexander Archipenko, Jacques Lipchitz* and Ossip Zadkine, Miestchaninoff was enrolled at the Académie Russe in Montparnasse, which was founded in 1910 and where students worked from a live model. Modigliani also sketched there.

Miestchaninoff was one of the few non-Cubist artists painted by Modigliani. In 1917 he portrayed the round-faced sculptor wearing a black suit and tie and a white shirt against a mottled green background (cat. 20). He inscribed the word 'Mechan', short for 'Mechano', the nickname of the young modern artists, especially the Cubists, who wore mechanics' suits, as did Miestchaninoff himself in a 1916 portrait by Modigliani. In the 1920s Miestchaninoff produced sculpture that was classical in style, such as the bronzes *Head of a Young Bulgarian* (1920) and *Young Girl with Bouquet* (1924), often exhibiting with other Jewish artists. The sculptor moved to the United States during the Second World War and remained there for the rest of his life, taking up American citizenship.

Pablo Picasso

(1881–1973)

Self-portrait by Picasso in front of *Homme assis au verre* (in progress) in his studio in the rue Schoelcher, c. 1915–16. Photograph by Pablo Picasso. Musée Picasso, Paris

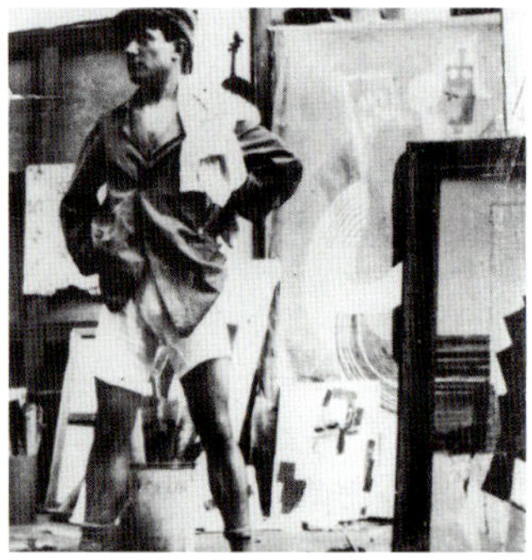

Modigliani met Picasso in 1906, when he arrived in Paris and took up a studio in Montmartre, not far from Picasso's in the Bateau-Lavoir. That year Picasso was one of a group of avant-garde artists, among them Derain, Maurice de Vlaminck and Matisse, who began to explore non-Western aesthetic forms, particularly those of 'les Nègres'. On visits to Picasso's studio, Modigliani would have seen the audacious work that preceded the iconic modernist painting *Les Demoiselles d'Avignon* (1907). The depersonalised, masklike faces of Picasso's 'primitivist' paintings and the simplified, volumetric forms, derived from African sculpture, influenced Modigliani's modernist approach to portraiture.

During the First World War Picasso became reacquainted with Modigliani when they both lived among the foreign artists remaining in Montparnasse. Picasso's return to portraiture in 1914, after the years of Cubist experimentation, at around the same time that Modigliani was searching for a new style of painting in his transition from sculpture, drew the two artists closer (see Pierre Daix, 'Picasso and Modigliani' in Paris 2002, pp. 66–8). The polemic around Cubism was raging and even Picasso was thought, erroneously, to have desisted from his modernist experiments. Modigliani's portrait of Picasso (1915; cat. 6), with its rough brushstrokes and unfinished look, as well as the possibly ironic inscription 'SAVOIR' (knowledge, or enquiry ['savoir' also means to find out]) may refer to that polemic. For Picasso's new direction was questioned, if not derided, among artists and critics at the time. Picasso's respect for Modigliani is evident from the inclusion of Modigliani's *Seated Girl with Brown Hair* (1918; cat. 24) in his personal art collection.

Elena Povolozky

(dates unknown)

Detail of cat. 19

Elena Povolozky, 1917. Oil on canvas, 45.8 × 33.1 cm. Private collection. Courtesy of Helly Nahmad

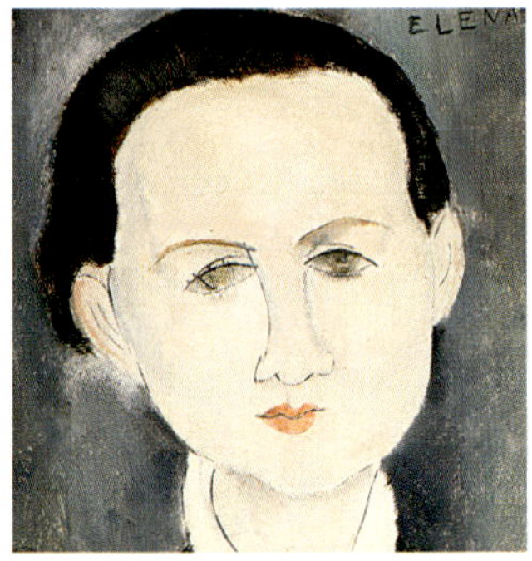

The French artist Elena Povolozky was the wife of the émigré dealer-publisher Jacques Povolozky, who owned the Galerie Povolozky, also known as Galerie La Cible, in the rue Bonaparte. He was one of the most prominent dealers in avant-garde art in the Latin Quarter and Montparnasse between the two world wars. The Galerie Povolozky represented some of the lesser-known Cubists, such as Albert Gleizes, Jacques Villon, Jean Lurçat and Léopold Survage,* and artists associated with the movement. It gave the Czech abstractionist Frantisek Kupka his first one-man exhibition in Paris, and it showed the work of Picabia and other Dadaists. Jacques Povolozky also published artists' theoretical writings, such as Gleizes's *La Peinture et ses lois* (*Painting and Its Laws*) of 1924. The dealer's interest in his artists, as much intellectual as commercial, was matched by material assistance provided by his wife.

Elena Povolozky was a friend to Modigliani and Soutine,* giving them food and money. In exchange for her support, Modigliani painted her twice in 1917 (see cat. 19). Elena is shown dressed in a fashionable fur-collared coat and white blouse with blue tie, within a dark interior. Her black hair is scraped back from a round white face with Slavic features (represented naturalistically), which stands out against the dark ground. Her style is severe, almost masculine, as Modigliani depicts her.

Diego Rivera

(1886–1957)

Diego Rivera sitting on a bank in Paris, 1919. Photograph. Unknown photographer. Modigliani Institut, Archives Legales Modigliani, Paris

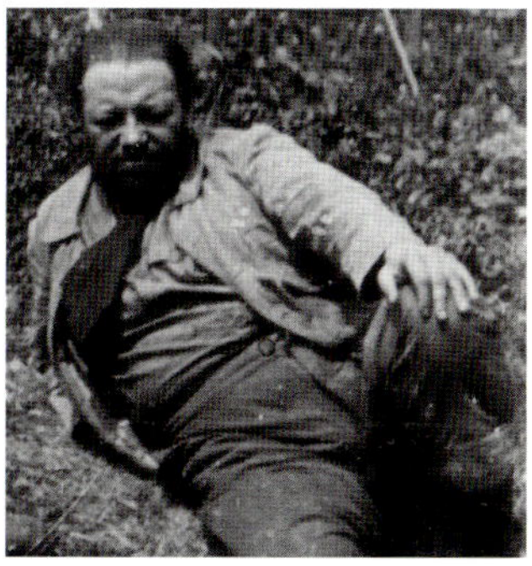

The Mexican painter Diego Rivera studied painting in Mexico City and Madrid before settling in Paris in 1911, where he remained until 1920. Rivera was for several years one of the leading Cubists, part of the group around Picasso* and Juan Gris,* whom he met early in 1914. He painted figures, still-lifes – *Still-life with Fruit Bowl* (1915) – and portraits – *Jacques Lipchitz* (*Portrait of a Young Man*) (1914) – in a Cubist style until 1915 or 1916, turning to a form of classicism at the end of the First World War. In 1921 Rivera returned to Mexico, where he became the leader of the revolutionary art movement and a member of the Communist Party. He was the most renowned of the great muralists, imbued with the social and political purpose of art.

Rivera was an extremely large man with an ebullient personality, a popular figure at the Café de la Rotonde, a meeting-place for Cubists and revolutionaries: Lenin and Trotsky were often seen there. Modigliani's 1914 portraits of Rivera illuminate the character of his subject, his energy and his 'savage' look, through the use of a wild, Expressionist brushstroke and a kind of Pointillism, in blue and black against an ochre background (fig. 11). Rivera's large round head with dark curly hair sits on top of his huge rounded shoulders. To achieve the work's unusual perspective, Modigliani apparently sat on the floor while he painted with his subject towering over him (Sichel 1967, pp. 253–4).

Chaïm Soutine

(1893–1943)

Chaïm Soutine, 1913. Photograph. Unknown photographer. Archives Roger-Viollet, Paris

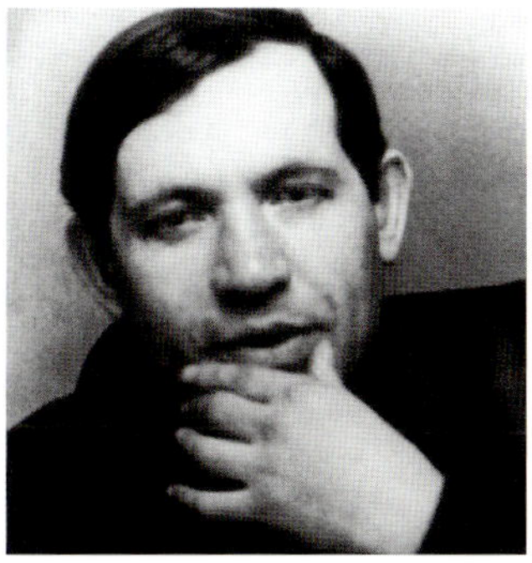

When the twenty-year-old artist Chaïm Soutine moved to Paris in 1913, he was introduced to Modigliani by Jacques Lipchitz* and became a close friend. Born into a poor family of Orthodox Jews, Soutine nevertheless studied drawing in Minsk and Vilnius. One of Modigliani's four portraits of Soutine, which displays his rough, peasant-like appearance, was painted on a door in Zborowski's apartment (1917). 'It was Modigliani who gave me confidence in myself,' he said. Soutine was known for his difficult character, but was protected by Modigliani, whose dealer Léopold Zborowski,* it seems, took on Soutine against his will. Zborowski and Soutine did not get on, although Soutine admitted that he could never have realised his work without him. Soutine found patronage from 1923, when Zborowski sold about a hundred of his paintings to Alfred C. Barnes.

Soutine painted portraits, landscapes and still-lifes, such as his famous *Carcass of Beef* (1925), in an expressionist style influenced by Rembrandt and other Old Masters. Such works also gained intensity from Soutine's practice of painting from animal carcasses in his studio. A strong representative of the French tradition, Soutine became one of the most successful of the Ecole de Paris artists.

Léopold Survage

(1879–1968)

Germaine Survage

(dates unknown)

Léopold Survage, undated. Photograph. Unknown photographer. Archives Roger-Viollet, Paris

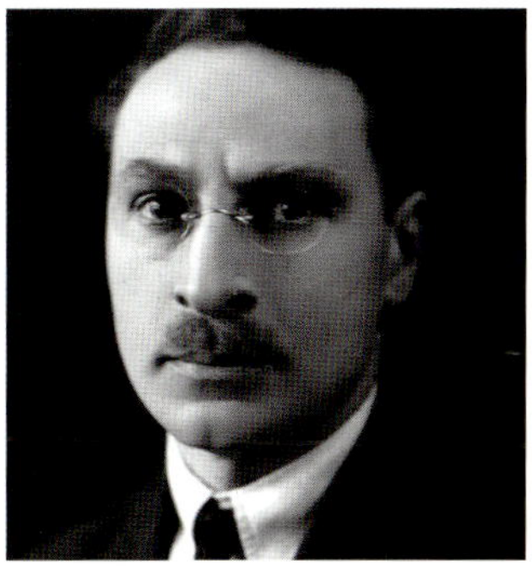

The pianist Germaine Survage was the wife of the Finnish-born Russian painter and set designer Léopold Survage. In 1908 Survage settled in Paris to study painting under Matisse. However, he was more attracted by the experiments of the Cubists and exhibited with them at the 1911 Salon des Indépendants. Preferring landscapes to still-lifes, he became a minor but individual figure within the movement. By 1920 he had abandoned Cubism in favour of a serene form of Surrealism.

Survage was a friend of Modigliani and the two were close from 1918 to 1919, when they were both living in Nice. Survage had yet to meet his future wife, Germaine Meyer, who was in Nice that same year visiting her sister and brother-in-law, Marcelle and Pierre Bertin. (Marcelle, a concert pianist, was associated with Jean Cocteau and the group of French composers, among them Darius Milhaud and Francis Poulenc, who were known as 'Les Six'.)

On a visit to his friend Pierre Bertin, Modigliani saw Germaine in a sky-blue blouse and asked if he might paint her. According to Germaine, 'He had me play the piano – and suddenly after ten minutes he said: "That's fine. Let's begin."' (Fifield 1978, pp. 257–8.) Modigliani painted three portraits of Germaine, her graceful face, neck and shoulders left bare. 'I was a veritable ageing virgin, twenty-nine, having thought to devote my life to music,' she said (Fifield 1978, pp. 257–8). Survage met Germaine in 1921 while visiting her sister to discuss a musical matter, and happened to mention Modigliani. Germaine produced his portrait of her, which drew them together. Six months later, the couple married.

Léopold Zborowski

(1889–1932)

Hanka Zborowska

(dates unknown)

Hanka and Léopold Zborowski, 1919. Photograph by Pierre Choumoff (1872–1936). Archives Roger-Viollet, Paris

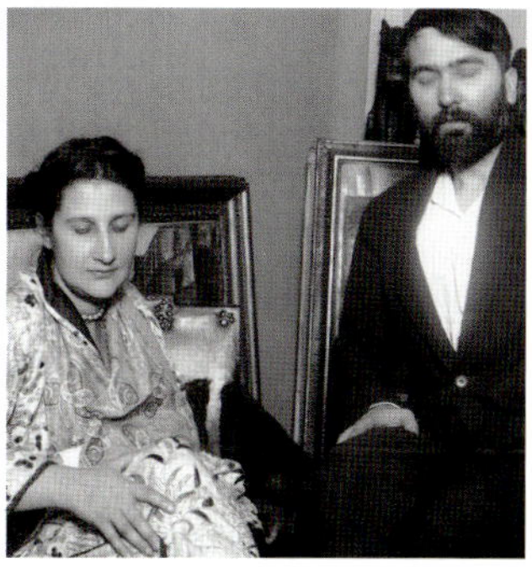

The Polish poet and art dealer Léopold Zborowski represented Modigliani from 1916, providing him with financial support, art materials and accommodation in exchange for his entire output. He was one of the first of a new type of art dealer to emerge during the First World War, who represented unknown avant-garde artists from premises in their own domestic apartments, rather than from established galleries. Zborowski was very struck by Modigliani's painting, which he first saw at an exhibition organised by the dealer Paul Guillaume* in the summer of 1915. The following March Guillaume passed Modigliani on to Zborowski, although the two dealers appeared to continue working together.

A student émigré from Zaleszczyki near Lvov in Galicia, Zborowski came to Paris around 1910 or 1914 (accounts vary) to study French literature and art. He tried to earn a living selling antiquarian books and engravings. On the fringes of the avant-garde, and following only his instincts, he determined to make Modigliani's reputation, along with that of a few other young unknowns, such as Maurice Utrillo and Chaïm Soutine.* In 1916 he took an apartment with his companion Hanka (their marital status was never clear) at 3 rue Joseph Bara, a block of artist's studios. Hanka (or Anna), a Polish aristocrat from a wealthy family, had been studying to become a teacher in Paris when she met Zborowski. Her distinctive, dark beauty and elegance inspired a number of Modigliani's most important 'classical' portraits (cats 15 and 43), in which his line becomes more sinuous. Zborowski himself was one of Modigliani's subjects: six portraits of him exist in various guises, as a distinguished and worldly art dealer in suit and tie (1916; cat. 16 and 1917–18; cat. 29) and as the idealised poet in a Byronic shirt (1918).

Success came to Zborowski, and Modigliani, after Modigliani's death, as the artist's reputation and the prices of his work rose. The financial crash of 1929, as well as his poor health and the effects of high living, led to his death in 1932.

Select Bibliography

Alexandre 1993
Noël Alexandre, *The Unknown Modigliani: Drawings from the Collection of Paul Alexandre*, New York, 1993; London, 1994

Basler 1931
Adolphe Basler, *Modigliani*, Paris, 1931

Bernhardt 1999
Sarah Bernhardt, *My Double Life: The Memoirs of Sarah Bernhardt*, trans. by Victoria Tietze Larson, Albany, 1999

Buffalo 2002
Modigliani and the Artists of Montparnasse, Kenneth Wayne, exh. cat., Albright-Knox Art Gallery, Buffalo, Kimbell Art Museum, Fort Worth, Texas; Los Angeles County Museum of Art, Los Angeles, 2002

Butler 1994
Stephen Butler, *Modigliani*, London, 1994

Carco 1919
Francis Carco, 'Modigliani', *L'Eventail* II, no. 7 (15 August 1919)

Ceroni 1958
Ambrogio Ceroni, *Amedeo Modigliani: Peintre: suivi des 'souvenirs' de Lunia Czechowska*, Milan, 1958

Ceroni 1965
Ambrogio Ceroni, *Amedeo Modigliani: Dessins et Sculptures*, Milan, 1965

Ceroni 1970
Ambrogio Ceroni, *I dipinti di Modigliani*, Introduction by Leone Piccioni, Milan, 1970 (French edition: *Tout l'Oeuvre peint de Modigliani*, 1972)

Chaplin 1990
Patrice Chaplin, *Into the Darkness Laughing: The Story of Modigliani's Last Mistress, Jeanne Hébuterne*, London, 1990

Cocteau 1950
Jean Cocteau, *Modigliani*, London and Paris, 1950

Douglas 1941
Charles Douglas, *Artist Quarter: Reminiscences of Montmartre and Montparnasse in the First Two Decades of the Twentieth Century*, London, 1941

Düsseldorf 1990
Amedeo Modigliani: Paintings, Sculptures and Drawings, Werner Schmalenbach, exh. cat., Kunstsammlung Nordrhein-Westfalen, Düsseldorf; Kunsthaus Zurich, 1990 (rev. ed., 2005)

Edinburgh 1963
Modigliani, John Russell, exh. cat., Royal Scottish Academy, Edinburgh; Tate Gallery, London, 1963

Fifield 1976
William Fifield, *Modigliani*, New York, 1976; London, 1978

Gray 2004
Stephen Gray, *Beatrice Hastings: A Literary Life*, London, 2004

Hall 1979
Douglas Hall, *Modigliani*, London, 1979 (2nd edition, 1984; rev. ed., 1998)

Hamnett 1932
Nina Hamnett, *Laughing Torso*, London, 1932

Harrison 2000
Sara Harrison, 'Amedeo Modigliani: Portraiture and the Language of Caricature', MA thesis, Courtauld Institute of Art, London, June 2000

Klüver and Martin 1989
Billy Klüver and Julie Martin, *Kiki's Paris, Artists and Lovers 1900–1930*, New York, 1989

Kruszynski 1996
Anette Kruszynski, *Amedeo Modigliani: Portraits and Nudes*, London, Munich and New York, 1996

Krystof 2000
Doris Krystof, *Modigliani, 1884–1920: The Poetry of Seeing*, London and Cologne, 2000

Lanthemann 1970
Joseph Lanthemann, *Modigliani 1884–1920: Catalogue raisonné*, Barcelona, 1970

Lipchitz 1952
Jacques Lipchitz, *Amedeo Modigliani*, New York, 1952

Lugano 1999
Amedeo Modigliani, Rudy Chiappini (ed.), exh. cat., Museo d'Arte Moderna della Città di Lugano, 1999

Maiolino 1981
Enzo Maiolino, *Modigliani vivo. Testimonianze inedite e rare*, Turin, 1981

Mann 1980
Carol Mann, *Modigliani*, London, 1980

Meyers 2006
Jeffrey Meyers, *Modigliani: A Life*, New York, 2006; London, forthcoming

Modigliani 1958
Jeanne Modigliani, *Modigliani: Man and Myth*, New York, 1958; London, 1959 (French edition: *Modigliani sans légende*, 1961)

New York 1985
The Circle of Montparnasse: Jewish Artists in Paris, 1905–1945, Kenneth E. Silver and Romy Golan (eds), exh. cat., The Jewish Museum, New York, 1985

New York 1989
Gardens and Ghettos: The Art of Jewish Life in Italy, Vivian B. Mann (ed.), exh. cat., The Jewish Museum, New York, 1989

New York 2004
Modigliani: Beyond the Myth, Mason Klein (ed.), exh. cat., The Jewish Museum, New York; Art Gallery of Ontario; Phillips Collection, Washington DC, 2004

Paris 1981
Amedeo Modigliani, 1884–1920, Daniel Marchesseau (ed.), exh. cat., Musée d'Art Moderne de la Ville de Paris, 1981

Paris 2000
L'Ecole de Paris, 1904–1929, La part de l'Autre, Jean-Louis Andral and Sophie Krebs (eds), exh. cat., Musée d'Art Moderne de la Ville de Paris, 2000

Paris 2002
Modigliani: L'Ange au visage grave, Marc Restellini (ed.), exh. cat., Musée du Luxembourg, Paris; Palazzo Reale, Milan, 2002 (English edition: *Modigliani: The Melancholy Angel*, 2002)

Parisot 1990
Christian Parisot, *Modigliani: Catalogue raisonné*, Livorno, 2 vols, 1990

Patani 1991–4
Osvaldo Patani, *Amedeo Modigliani, Catalogue Generale*, Milan, 3 vols, 1991–4

Pfannstiel 1929
Arthur Pfannstiel, *Modigliani*, Paris, 1929

Rose 1990
June Rose, *Modigliani: The Pure Bohemian*, London and New York, 1990

Roy 1958
Claude Roy, *Modigliani*, Lausanne, 1958

Salmon 1926
André Salmon, *Modigliani: Sa Vie et son oeuvre*, Paris, 1926

Salmon 1957
André Salmon, *La Vie passionnée de Modigliani*, Poitiers 1957 (English edition: *Modigliani: A Memoir*, 1961)

Scheiwiller 1927
Giovanni Scheiwiller, *Amedeo Modigliani*, Milan, 1927

Sichel 1967
Pierre Sichel, *Modigliani: A Biography of Amedeo Modigliani*, London and New York, 1967

Venice 2000
Modigliani e i suoi: Jeanne Hébuterne, Amedeo Modigliani, André Hébuterne, Georges Dorignac, Max Jacob, Pablo Picasso, Georges Rouault, Maurice de Vlaminck, Suzanne Valadon, Christian Parisot (ed.), exh. cat., Fondazione Giorgio Cini, Venice, 2000

Verona 1988
Modigliani a Montparnasse, 1909–1920, exh. cat., Palazzo Forti, Verona, 1988

Vlaminck 1925
Maurice de Vlaminck, 'Souvenir de Modigliani', *L'Art Vivant* (1 November 1925)

Weill 1933
Berthe Weill, *Pan! Dans l'Oeil! Ou trente ans dans les coulisses de la peinture contemporaine 1900–1930*, Paris, 1933

Werner 1962
Alfred Werner, *Modigliani the Sculptor*, London and New York, 1962

Werner 1966
Alfred Werner, *Amedeo Modigliani*, New York, 1966; London, 1990

Wight 1957
Frederick Wight, *Verge of Glory*, London, 1957

List of Works

1 *Head, c.* 1911–12. Limestone, 89.2 × 14 × 35.2 cm (including stand). Tate, London. Transferred from the Victoria and Albert Museum, London, 1983
2 *Caryatid,* 1913. Oil on canvas, 81 × 45 cm. Private collection
3 *Large Red Bust,* 1913. Oil on cardboard, 81.5 × 51 cm. Courtesy of Gallery Cazeau-Béraudière, Paris
4 *Young Gypsy,* 1909. Oil on canvas, 81 × 54 cm. Private collection
5 *Portrait of Frank Burty Haviland,* 1914. Oil on cardboard, 73 × 60 cm. Gianni Mattioli Collection. On long-term loan to the Peggy Guggenheim Collection, Venice
6 *Portrait of Picasso,* 1915. Oil on board, 34.2 × 26.3 cm. Private collection, Moscow
7 *Juan Gris,* 1915. Oil on canvas, 54.9 × 38.1 cm. Lent by The Metropolitan Museum of Art, New York. Bequest of Miss Adelaide Milton de Groot (1876–1967), 1967 (67.187.85)
8 *Woman Seated in front of a Fireplace (Beatrice Hastings),* 1915. Oil on canvas, 81 × 65 cm. Private collection. Courtesy of Helly Nahmad
9 *Beatrice Hastings in front of a Door,* 1915. Oil on canvas, 81.3 × 46.4 cm. Private collection. Courtesy of Ivor Braka Ltd
10 *Beatrice Hastings in Checkered Shirt,* 1916. Oil on canvas, 65 × 46 cm. John C. Whitehead. Courtesy of Achim Moeller, New York
11 *Young Woman In a Striped Blouse,* 1917. Oil on canvas, 92 × 60 cm. Private collection. Courtesy of Helly Nahmad
12 *Paul Guillaume,* 1915. Oil on board, 74.9 × 52.1 cm. Lent by The Toledo Museum of Art. Gift of Mrs C. Lockhart McKelvy
13 *Paul Guillaume Seated,* 1916. Oil on canvas, 81 × 54 cm. Civico Museo d'Arte Contemporanea, Milan
14 *Female Nude, c.* 1916. Oil on canvas, 92.4 × 59.8 cm. The Samuel Courtauld Trust, Courtauld Institute of Art Gallery, London
15 *Anna Zborowska,* 1916. Oil on canvas, 76.2 × 45.1 cm. Courtesy of The Metropolitan Museum of Art, New York. Lent by The Alex Hillman Family Foundation (L.1991.19.24)
16 *Léopold Zborowski,* 1916. Oil on canvas, 65 × 43 cm. Collection of The Israel Museum, Jerusalem
17 *Draped Nude,* 1917. Oil on canvas, 114 × 74 cm. Koninklijk Museum voor Schone Kunsten, Antwerp
18 *Reclining Nude on Red Couch,* 1917. Oil on canvas, 60 × 92 cm. Staatsgalerie Stuttgart
19 *Elena Povolozky,* 1917. Oil on canvas, 45.8 × 33.1 cm. Private collection. Courtesy of Helly Nahmad
20 *Oscar Miestchaninoff,* 1917. Oil on canvas, 46 × 33 cm. Private collection. Courtesy of Helly Nahmad
21 *Reclining Nude with Outstretched Arms,* 1917. Oil on canvas, 60 × 92 cm. Private collection
22 *The Italian Woman,* 1917. Oil on canvas, 102.6 × 67 cm. Lent by The Metropolitan Museum of Art, New York. Gift of The Chester Dale Collection, 1956 (56.4)
23 *Nude,* 1917. Oil on canvas, 73 × 116.7 cm. Solomon R. Guggenheim Museum, New York. Gift of Solomon R. Guggenheim 41.535
24 *Seated Girl with Brown Hair,* 1918. Oil on canvas, 93 × 60 cm. Musée Picasso, Paris
25 *Blue Eyes (Portrait of Madame Jeanne Hébuterne),* 1917. Oil on canvas, 54.6 × 42.9 cm. Philadelphia Museum of Art. The Samuel S. White III and Vera White Collection, 1967
26 *Head of Jeanne Hébuterne,* 1917–18. Oil on canvas, 44.8 × 27.5 cm. Private collection
27 *Anna Zborowska,* 1917. Oil on canvas, 55 × 39 cm. Private collection
28 *Hanka Zborowska,* 1917. Oil on canvas, 55 × 38 cm. Galleria Nazionale d'Arte Moderna, Rome
29 *Portrait of Léopold Zborowski,* 1917–18. Oil on canvas, 73 × 50 cm. Private collection
30 *Seated Man with a Cane,* 1918. Oil on canvas, 126 × 75 cm. Private collection. Courtesy of Helly Nahmad
31 *The Servant Girl, c.* 1918. Oil on canvas, 152.4 × 61 cm. Albright-Knox Art Gallery, Buffalo, New York. Room of Contemporary Art Fund, 1939
32 *La Belle Epicière,* 1918. Oil on canvas, 100 × 65 cm. Private collection. Courtesy of Helly Nahmad
33 *The Little Peasant, c.* 1918. Oil on canvas, 100 × 64.5 cm. Tate, London. Presented by Miss Jenny Blaker in memory of Hugh Blaker, 1941
34 *Marie Daughter of the People,* 1918. Oil on canvas, 62 × 50.5 cm. Kunstmuseum Basel. Legacy of Dr Walther Hanhart, Riehen, 1975
35 *The Boy (Youth in Blue Jacket),* 1919. Oil on canvas, 92.1 × 60 cm. Indianapolis Museum of Art. Gift of Mrs Julian Bobbs in memory of William Ray Adams, 46.22
36 *Red-haired Young Woman in a Chemise,* 1918. Oil on canvas, 100 × 65 cm. R. & H. Batliner Art Foundation, Vaduz
37 *Reclining Nude, c.* 1919. Oil on canvas, 72.4 × 116.5 cm. The Museum of Modern Art, New York. Mrs Simon Guggenheim Fund, 1950
38 *Jeanne Hébuterne,* 1919. Oil on canvas, 91.4 × 73 cm. Lent by The Metropolitan Museum of Art, New York. Gift of Mr and Mrs Nate B. Spingold, 1956 (56.184.2)
39 *Jeanne Hébuterne Sitting,* 1918. Oil on canvas, 92 × 60 cm. Private collection, Switzerland
40 *Reclining Nude with Her Right Arm under Her Head,* 1919. Oil on canvas, 73 × 116 cm. Private collection
41 *Portrait of Jeanne Hébuterne,* 1919. Oil on canvas, 55 × 38 cm. Art & Fragrances S.A., Cham/Switzerland
42 *Portrait of Jeanne Hébuterne,* 1919. Oil on canvas, 92.1 × 54 cm. Private collection. Courtesy of Helly Nahmad
43 *Anna Zborowska,* 1917. Oil on canvas, 130.2 × 81.3 cm. The Museum of Modern Art, New York. Lillie P. Bliss Collection, 1934
44 *Jeanne Hébuterne, a Door in the Background,* 1919. Oil on canvas, 130 × 81 cm. Private collection
45 *Bust of a Woman with a Necklace, c.* 1917–18. Oil on canvas, 61.6 × 38.7 cm. Private collection, United States. Courtesy of Edward Tyler Nahem Fine Art, L.L.C.
46 *Woman with a Red Necklace,* 1918. Oil on canvas, 92.8 × 65.8 cm. Private collection. Courtesy of Nevill Keating Pictures
47 *Lunia Czechowska in Black,* 1919. Oil on canvas, 92 × 60 cm. Private collection
48 *Portrait of Madame A. Eyraud-Vaillant,* 1919. Oil on canvas, 99 × 63.5 cm. Private collection. Courtesy of Richard Nagy Ltd, London
49 *Portrait of Thora Klinckowström,* 1919. Oil on canvas, 99.7 × 64.8 cm. Heirs of Evelyn Sharp
50 *Paulette Jourdain,* 1919. Oil on canvas, 100 × 65 cm. Collection of A. Alfred Taubman
51 *Portrait of Lunia Czechowska,* 1919. Oil on canvas, 100 × 65 cm. Musée d'Art Moderne de la Ville de Paris
52 *Self-portrait,* 1919. Oil on panel, 100 × 64.5 cm. Museu de Arte Contemporânea da Universidade de São Paulo

List of Lenders

Antwerp, Koninklijk Museum voor Schone Kunsten
Art & Fragrances S.A., Cham/Switzerland
Kunstmuseum Basel
R. & H. Batliner Art Foundation, Vaduz
Buffalo, New York, Albright-Knox Art Gallery
Indianapolis Museum of Art
Jerusalem, The Israel Museum
London, The Samuel Courtauld Trust, Courtauld Institute of Art Gallery
London, Tate
Milan, Civico Museo d'Arte Contemporanea
New York, The Alex Hillman Family Foundation, Courtesy of The Metropolitan Museum of Art
New York, The Metropolitan Museum of Art
New York, The Museum of Modern Art
New York, Solomon R. Guggenheim Museum
Paris, Gallery Cazeau-Béraudière
Paris, Musée d'Art Moderne de la Ville de Paris
Paris, Musée Picasso
Philadelphia Museum of Art
Private collection. Courtesy of Ivor Braka Ltd
Private collection. Courtesy of Helly Nahmad
Private collection. Courtesy of Nevill Keating Pictures
Private collection. Courtesy of Richard Nagy Ltd, London
Private collection, Moscow
Private collection, Switzerland
Private collection, United States.
Courtesy of Edward Tyler Nahem Fine Art, L.L.C.
Rome, Galleria Nazionale d'Arte Moderna
Heirs of Evelyn Sharp
Museu de Arte Contemporânea da Universidade de São Paulo
Stuttgart, Staatsgalerie
A. Alfred Taubman
Toledo, Museum of Art
Venice, Gianni Mattioli Collection, on long-term loan to the Peggy Guggenheim Collection
John C. Whitehead. Courtesy of Achim Moeller, New York
and others who wish to remain anonymous

Photographic Acknowledgements

All works of art are reproduced by kind permission of the owners.

Specific acknowledgements are as follows:

Basel, Kunstmuseum/Martin Bühler, cat. 34
Baltimore, Museum of Art/ © Succession H Matisse/ DACS 2006, fig. 32
Chicago, © The Art Institute of Chicago, fig. 20
Florence, © 2006 The Museum of Modern Art/Scala, cats 37, 43, fig. 34
Fonds Mercator Albin Michel (original copyright unknown), fig. 14, pp. 145 (top) and 148 (far left)
Roy Fox, cat. 2
Patrick Goetelen, cat. 29
Antonio Idini, cat. 28
Jerusalem, © The Israel Museum, Jerusalem/Meidad Suchowalski, cat. 16
Nelson Kon, cat. 52
London, © AKG Images, fig. 21; (Jewish Chronicle/Ullstein Bilderdienst) fig. 4; (Erich Lessing) figs 11, 28, 29, p. 148 (second from left)
London, Bridgeman Art Library, fig. 30
London, © The British Library, figs. 26, 27
London, © Christie's Images Ltd, 2002, cats 9, 41
London, The Samuel Courtauld Trust, Courtauld Institute of Art Gallery, cat. 14
London, © Getty Images, p. 153 (far right)
London, © Rex Features, figs 7, 8, pp. 140–41, 148 (far right), p. 150 (second from right), p. 151 (second from left), p. 152 (far left), p. 153 (second from left), p. 153 (second from right)
London, © Tate 2006, cats 1, 33; figs 37, 42, (© Estate of J. Epstein) fig. 45
London, © V&A Images, figs 38, 43
Milan, Saporetti Immagini d'Arte Snc, cat. 13
New York, courtesy of David Zwirner/© the artist, fig. 25
New York, © The Metropolitan Museum of Art, cats 7, 15, 22, 39
New York, courtesy of Phillips de Pury and Co./© Estate of Paul Outerbridge, fig. 23
Paris, Alain Bouret, figs 1, 16, 17, 18, pp. 74–5, 146 (far left), 147 (bottom left)
Paris, © Man Ray Trust/ADAGP-DACS/Telimage 2006, p. 149 (second from right)
Paris, Modigliani Institut, Archives Legales, figs 2, 6, pp. 143 (top), 145 (bottom), 147 (top right), 147 (bottom right), 149 (far right), 153 (far left)
Paris, © Photos12, p. 151 (far right)
Paris, © PMVP/Joffre, cat. 51
Paris, © RMN/Daniel Arnaudet, fig. 12
Paris, © RMN/© droits réservés/ © Succession Picasso ADAGP-DACS, 2006, pp. 150 (second from left), 152 (second from right)
Paris, © RMN/© René-Gabriel Ojèda, cat. 24
Paris, © RMN /© Thierry Le Mage/© ADAGP, Paris and DACS, London 2006, frontispiece, fig. 5, p. 150 (far right)
Pennsylvania, Philadelphia Museum of Art/© Succession Marcel Duchamp/ADAGP, Paris and DACS, London 2006, fig. 35
Princeton © Bruce M. White, fig. 10
Rouen, Didier Tragin/Catherine Lancien, fig. 15
San Francisco, courtesy of Fraenkel Gallery and Lee Friedlander © Lee Friedlander, fig. 24
Stockholm, Moderna Museet, cat. 49, p. 151 (second from right)
Washington DC, Hirshhorn Museum and Sculpture Garden, Smithsonian Institution © Lucian Freud, fig. 33

Index

All references are to page numbers; those in **bold** type indicate catalogue plates and those in *italic* type indicate other illustrations

N

O

P

R

S

T

U

V

W

Y

Z